In Dvořák's Footsteps

Antonín Dvořák (1841–1904)

In Dvořák's Footsteps

Musical Journeys in the New World

Miroslav Ivanov

Translated by Stania Slahor
Edited by Leon Karel

THE THOMAS JEFFERSON UNIVERSITY PRESS
KIRKSVILLE, MISSOURI - USA
1995

Copyright ©1995 The Thomas Jefferson University Press
at Northeast Missouri State University
Kirksville, MO 63501-4211 USA

Originally published as *Novosvetska*, by Miroslav Ivanov.
Copyright ©1984 Miroslav Ivanov
Photographs © 1994 Vaclav Novak
All rights reserved.

Printed in the United States of America.

British Cataloging in Publication information available.

Distributed by arrangement with
University Publishing Associates,^SM Inc.
4720 Boston Way
Lanham, MD 20706

3 Henrietta Street
London WC2E 8LU England

Library of Congress Cataloging-in-Publication Data
Ivanov, Miroslav.
    [Novosvetska. English]
    In Dvorak's footsteps : musical journeys in the New World / by Miroslav Ivanov ; translated by Stania Slahor ; edited by Leon Karel.
        p. cm.
    Includes bibliographical references (p.) and index.
    ISBN 0–943549–25-6 (cloth, alk. paper)
    1. Dvorak, Antonin, 1841–1904—Journeys—United States.   2. United States—Description and travel—1865–1900.   3. Composers—United States—Biography.   I. Slahor, Stania. II. Title.
ML410.D99 I913   1994
780'.92—dc20
[B]   94-11011
                                                    CIP
                                                      MN

Handwritten: ML 410 D99 1913 1994

∞The paper used in this publication meets the minimum requirements of the American National Standard for Permanence of Paper for Printed Library Materials ANSI Z39.48, 1984.

To my grandsons, Filip and Tomas,
and to all lovers and admirers of Dvořák's music
around the world.

. . . amicus Plato, amicus Aristoteles, sed magis amica
veritas. . . .

(. . . Plato is my friend, Aristotle is my friend, but my
best friend is Truth. . . .)

Old Latin proverb – Ivanov's creed

I have just finished the second movement of my new symphony, and as usual, I feel happy and contented while I am composing. God bless my good fortune; I hope to have the same emotions in doing all my future compositions. This is, and always will be my motto: "God—Love—Homeland!" That and only that can bring me to my goal!

from Dvořák's letter to Alois Gobl,
New Year's Eve 1884

Contents

Illustrations

Foreword

WITH MY SINCERE BLESSING, I send this pioneering book by Miroslav Ivanov on its international journey. I am not worried about its fate and acceptance by American readers. Its major theme comes from the most popular and valuable treasure of Czech culture, Dvořák's music. Above all, it relates to the origin of the composer's best-known work, the celebrated *From the New World* (*Novosvetska*) Symphony, written during his sojourn in the United States of America.

Each time I listen to the perfect sounds of his symphony I feel great astonishment and fascination. As I hear it in my heart and soul I perpetually wonder how Dvořák composed his work, how flawlessly he developed the amazing diversity of each movement and the colorful vibrancy of its moods. The perfection of the entire symphony is in the richness of musical ideas expressed by the ravishing orchestral sound.

Dvořák's *From the New World* Symphony has been the most frequently performed work in my repertoire. I have conducted it everywhere fate has brought me. This music stays always young, and undoubtedly its demanding complexity gives an interpreter a constant challenge by calling for absolute concentration, and it repeatedly provokes great tension. It is indeed the most splendid symphony ever written by a Czech composer.

Miroslav Ivanov's book is not just another work of musicology with old and newly discovered facts. Ivanov's book about Dvořák and his sojourn in America is an interesting narrative, exceptionally communicative and informative. I sincerely repeat that I am not worried about its acceptance by Americans and other English-speaking readers.

Bless you, *Novosvetska*!

VACLAV NEUMANN
Director and Principal Conductor
of the Czech Philharmonic

Foreword

I N MY LIFETIME I HAVE READ several books about Antonín Dvořák, written in both Czech and English. However, Miroslav Ivanov's Czech version of *Novosvetska* greatly aroused my interest and attention. I have been captured by this author's desire to discover the real emotions that Dvořák must have felt when he composed the famous *From the New World* Symphony and other works which originated during his sojourn in America, one hundred years ago. The author's style shows the celebrated composer, his career, and his achievements from a different angle than ever before. Ivanov does not simply summon the existing facts—which are well known, described, and compared by many writers, musical historians, and scholars; rather, he seeks to open new passages into the very soul of the great genius and to search within for a true account of his creative workmanship. Here, Ivanov's mastery succeeds fully in attaining his noble aim. Therefore, I treasure his book as the best work ever written about Dvořák.

As a concert cellist I had the opportunity to play Dvořák's Cello Concerto in B Minor throughout Europe, North Korea, China, and America. When I decided to finish my career as the soloist because of progressive arthritis in my left hand, I chose this musical jewel of the cello literature to perform for my farewell. However, when I played it for the last time, knowing that never, never in my life would I perform that magnificent work again, several times I had to hold back my tears. Still, at the end of the last movement I was unable to restrain myself from crying. At that moment, I suppose, I was very close to Dvořák himself.

The translator and the editors of Ivanov's book have each earned a special merit for their sensitive comprehension of this exceptional work and their task of bringing it to English-speaking readers.

FRANTISEK SMETANA

Editors' Preface

STANIA SLAHOR, A NATIVE of the Czech Republic, fled her native country in 1968 when the Russians took over. In 1988, she first read Miroslav Ivanov's *Novosvetska* in the Czech edition of 1984, and she felt it should be of interest to American readers.

She enlisted the aid of Nan and Leon Karel of Florida. Both were musicians and students of languages, and they collaborated in preparing the translation in idiomatic English. A number of problems arose, however:

First, Ivanov's style was more nonsequential than American readers are used to; the book was a mixture of biography, autobiography, history, and musicology, together with impressions, moods, travelogue details, and more. In the book, Dvořák and Ivanov together experience America a century apart, moving through cities and towns, drinking in the newness and vastness of this land.

A second problem arose from the translation's having begun while the Communist regime still held power in former Czechoslovakia. Our letters to Ivanov had to be couched in guarded terms, and his replies were noncommittal. As the "Velvet Revolution" of 1989 approached, however, we were able to write and receive more open letters, and today Dr. Ivanov has visited America, and the Slahors have been able to visit the Czech Republic, Vysoka, and Prague. Many translation difficulties were solved by this new freedom.

Third, we felt that it was the translator's responsibility to reflect the ideas of the author as clearly as possible. Occasionally, Ivanov's opinions concerning various aspects of Dvořák's life and music differ from those of other authorities. We have tried to translate these as accurately as we can, and do not feel that we have the right to dispute Ivanov in this respect.

A fourth problem arose from the original translation of American newspaper and magazine articles into Czech. Our translation of these articles back into English (from the book) could never recreate the original text, so we had to return to the original files from the 1890s, and now have these, word for word, as they appeared in Dvořák's day.

Fifth, other documents which Ivanov had found in research for his book were turned over by him to the Museum of Czech Music in Prague after he finished his manuscript. These have been largely lost or misplaced, and we have had to conduct our own search for these, with only limited success.

Sixth, Ivanov wrote his book under Communist rule. He had to get permission to make the trip to America. He took with him an officially approved companion/photographer, stayed at the Czech Consulate, and so on. His original manuscript was written with one eye on the censor, and even after it was finished, it was criticized as being "too apolitical." Publication came only after a second critique by the eminent music historian, Vaclav Holzknecht, who approved. (The charge of "apolitical" was perhaps not surprising because Ivanov had never joined the Communist Party and thus could not follow the Party Line. His refusal to join, however, caused him to suffer professionally, and he became a freelance writer.) We have consulted with Dr. Ivanov in revising some of the censor-inspired passages, bringing them more into line with the author's ideas.

Seventh, Ivanov wrote his book for Czechs whose travel was severely restricted under the Communists. In it he included details of America which he knew his countrymen would enjoy: items in store windows, prices of food, sights and sounds, the freedom with which a Xerox copier could be used, what one could find in a public library, the details of train and plane travel, and the like. We have omitted or curtailed many of these as being commonplace for American readers.

And finally, there is the problem of the Czech language itself. There are no definite or indefinite articles in Czech, no "the," "a," or "an". Thus, we had to decide from the context whether Dvořák would have said, "I see *a* book" or "I see *the* book." A similar problem is the use of diacritical marks, which are found above certain Czech letters. Rather than use these on all the Czech names of people, towns, villages, and provinces, we used them only for Antonín Dvořák's own name, which—as he vehemently insisted—should be spelled correctly no matter what language it was printed in. Another difficulty is the use of feminine endings for women's names. In Czech, Mrs. Dvořák's name would have been "Dvořáková," and Miss Cermak would be addressed as "Cermakova." In the matter of the titles of Dvořák's compositions, however, Anglicization becomes more complicated. Some titles are given in Czech first (those well known by their original titles, such as *Rusalka*), followed by the translated title (*Water-Nymph*). For works well known in America by their English titles, we used that title first and added the Czech title if necessary. Some works do not need translation at all. The Czech title of the *From the New World* Symphony is *Novosvetska*. There are no capital letters used in Czech titles, except at the beginning or for proper names, for example *Moravske dvojzpevy* (*Moravian Duets*), or *Golden Spinning-Wheel* (*Zlaty kolovrat*).

It was a great pleasure for us to translate Ivanov's book and do our additional research and study of the documents. Our work went through several metamorphoses, and this enchanting process captivated us completely.

We also enjoyed being in personal contact with the author, and exchanged many letters about the work. The timing for the communication could not have been better, because the political situation in former Czechoslovakia began finally to change. The earlier destruction of the Berlin Wall was a signal for the fall of the Communist regime, and the occupation of the Eastern Block countries and the cold war had suddenly come to an end. We received numerous letters expressing the author's frustration and tremendous joy, welcoming the new freedom and open roads to the rest of the world. Now, Dvořák's symphony *From the New World* sounds even more powerful throughout the world.

We especially thank all our friends and the members of our families for their encouragement and belief in the mission and importance of our work.

STANIA SLAHOR
LEON KAREL

Acknowledgments

A N ENGLISH TRANSLATION OF MY BOOK on Dvořák's 's sojourn in the United States has been published, thanks to the efforts of the painter, poet, and translator, Stania Slahor. Her enthusiasm for and devotion to Dvořák's work, and her love for his music helped her overcome many difficulties and obstacles. For that I sincerely thank her.

I also express my gratitude for the professional expertise and careful attention of the editors, Leon and Nan Karel, who helped to complete the work. I hope that my book will touch the hearts of many Americans with love for music and for life itself.

There was one disappointment that we could not prevent. Dvořák'shouse on East 17th Street in New York City could not be saved from recent demolition. In spite of urgent intervention and appeals to the public, this memorable house was pulled down. It was there that Antonín Dvořák stayed during his residence in New York City, and there that his music, including *From the New World* Symphony, was written. The author and the translator of this book sent letters to many organizations to stop the impending cultural disaster, but to no avail. We hope this book will be a memorial to the composer and his music.

I am grateful to the Pierpont Morgan Library, the New York Public Library, Columbia University Libraries, the Newberry Library, the Czechoslovak Society of Chicago, the University of Chicago, the State Historical Memorial and Art Building of Des Moines, Iowa, and the Iowa State University Library for their support and for providing valuable documents for my research.

I am grateful to Antonín Dvořák's grandson Josef Suk, who loaned me precious materials, and to the composer's granddaughter Vera Johnova for her information and encouragement. I appreciate the help of many Americans, especially Lilly Picha, Marie Hosek, Roger Dvořák, Draga Shillinglaw, and the citizens of Spillville: the Kalas brothers, J. Balik, K. Sobolik, and many others.

I feel indebted to the musicologists, most of all to Dr. J. Maly, director of the Museum of Czech Music; Dr. Ludmila Bradova, director of the Antonín Dvořák Museum in Prague; and Jan Einhorn, the photographer who had accompanied me to America. I received aid and support from researchers K. Nejdl of Karlovy Vary and Michal Bulir of Prague as well as from G. Cherkaskij of New York. I thank Vaclav Novak, photographer, and Jiri Skopek, academic painter, for their help. The encouragement of all these people helped me finish my work in the Czech language and discover several new documents not previously known and published in Dvořák literature. They should be credited with contributions to musicology. Finally I must thank Ludo Slahor and Jiri Pokorny for their aid in transferring the manuscript of the English translation to computer disks.

In conclusion, I want to express my gratitude to the publisher of the American version, to Dr. Robert V. Schnucker, director, and Tim Rolands, typographer, of the Thomas Jefferson University Press at Northeast Missouri State University for their exceptional interest in publishing this book on the occasion of the one-hundredth anniversary of Dvořák's 's *From the New World* Symphony, which was first performed in New York City in 1893.

MIROSLAV IVANOV

Translator's Notes

1. In the alternating "A" and "B" chapters the author switches from Dvořák's historically documented trip to the United States to his own travels in search of the Dvořák story. Thus, each pair of chapters gives the reader a sense of comparison and contrast as well as insight into the difficulties faced by an author-researcher coming from a Communist-controlled society to a free one.

2. Dvořák's House in New York City, at 327 East 17th Street is no more. It was purchased by the Beth-Israel Medical Center for use as an AIDS treatment center despite the fact that it was too small to meet New York State requirements for such use.

This house, where Antonín Dvořák had lived for almost three years and where he had written *From the New World* Symphony, was designated a landmark and honored by Mayor LaGuardia in 1941 with a commemorative plaque and a ceremony on the one-hundredth anniversary of the composer's birth.

In 1991, Mayor Dinkins refused to veto the city council's decision to reverse the judgment of the Landmarks Preservation Commission, and allowed the house to be razed in August 1991. Its destruction was supported by a *New York Times* editorial on March 7 of that year, according to the *New York Press,* vol. 4, no. 45.

Thus, a century after the city's press and public welcomed Dvořák to our shores, the city's press and public allowed this landmark of his sojourn to be obliterated despite protest from many historians, musicians, and music lovers. The fireplace from the Dvořák House was given to the Bohemian Benevolent and Literary Association at 321 East 73rd Street, where a Dvořák museum is planned.

On November 28, 1991, New York's Mayor Dinkins signed into law the establishment of a "Dvořák Place," an area following 17th Street between First and Second Avenue.

Dvořák dedicated his *From the New World* Symphony to the New York Philharmonic Orchestra, and this fact could be a key to a happier Dvořák outcome. On the roof of the Lincoln Center's Avery Fisher Hall, the orchestra's home, there is a life-size bronze statue of Dvořák by the American sculptor Ivan Mestrovic. The Philharmonic gave the statue to the Dvořák American Heritage Association, a New York–based organization that will place the monument in the same Stuyvesant Park through which the composer strolled every day of his life in New York. It is a generous gift from America's oldest orchestra, which premiered the Symphony *From the New World* with Dvořák in the audience, and has performed it proudly time and again since 1893.

On March 15, 1993, the Oratorio Society of New York performed at Carnegie Hall Antonín Dvořák's *Saint Ludmila* Oratorio. The performance was to benefit the Statue Fund of the Dvořák's Heritage Association in collaboration with the Stuyvesant Park Neighborhood Association.

STANIA SLAHOR
LEON KAREL

Prologue

"THIS IS MY GRANDFATHER'S PASSPORT. He needed it for his journey to America in 1892."

My companion, a gray-haired woman, talked to me with a gentle smile on her face. When opening that little booklet, her movements showed deep concern and respect. The title page was decorated with an emblem of the Austrian Empire, used at the end of the last century. She read quietly to me, "Passport number 56,031/927. Im Namen Seiner Majestat...."

In the name of His Majesty Franz Joseph I, Emperor of Austria, King of Bohemia,... It was the year 1892 and Bohemia was a part of the Austro-Hungarian Empire. The official language in Bohemia was German, and the passport stated that the travel document was issued to Mr. Anton Dvořák, occupation "composer," of Nelahozeves, county Slany, "Kronland Bohmen."

The composer's granddaughter put the tiny sixteen-page booklet aside, and suddenly I felt a little embarrassed at the extraordinary circumstances of my mission. However, I took up the passport, turned a leaf, and read: "Personal description of the passport holder: year of birth—1841; stature—medium; face—oval; hair—dark brown (slightly gray); eyes—brown; mouth—symmetrical; nose—dull; special marks—none."

At the bottom was a signature, in energetic handwriting—especially the *D* and *k* of the name Antonín Dvořák. He was most definite in marking the letters, which when surrounded by the German type, looked quite obstinate. Antonín Dvořák never adapted his name to a foreign language. Six years

1

before this travel document was issued to him in 1886, he wrote in one of his letters:

> Dear Sir:
> I have to let you know that your letter stunned me by the expression of your overwhelming devotion and humility, and especially by your speaking to me as if I were almost a god. I have never have felt like being one, and never will. I am only a simple Bohemian musician who dislikes submissive behavior, and despite my frequent travels around the musical world, I will always be as I always was before—the simple, Bohemian musician.

The last three words showed a modesty which could not be changed by any ovations received on the podiums of London, Moscow, or New York City.

However, the New York concert halls still awaited him when this document, with its one-zlaty stamp, was issued as a permit to travel over the "European states and America" for three years. The date of issue from Prague was August 31, 1892. The illegible names of the Ceska Kamenice vice-consul and the chief of the police board of directors suggest that the great overseas journey of that simple Czech musician, already renowned in Europe, would become a reality in two weeks. The next page of the passport shows that he would be accompanied by his wife, Mrs. Anna Dvořáková, 39, his daughter Otilie Dvořáková, 14, and his son Antonín Dvořák, 9.*

The last days before Dvořák's trip in September 1892 were probably similar to the late summertime of my own visit. The trees in the garden outside the open window were a little tired of their heavy abundance of fruit; the fragrance of roses penetrated the room. Only the pigeons bred by Dvořák a century ago were missing.

The rest of the passport was blank, without further stamps or notes. Dvořák's granddaughter added, "We have no other passport that grandpa used, although he visited Germany and England several times in 1892. He kept this one as a souvenir of his longest journey abroad."

"And that is all?" I wondered.

"Not at all, I have much more to show you. Do you want to see it all?"

That afternoon I had gone to Dvořák's Vysoka, his summer estate at Pribram. The little village was scattered on a high, gently sloping plateau, with

---

*For information about Antonín Dvořák's family, see "Appendix C Antonin Dvorak's Family" on page 405. –Eds.

Vysoka at Pribram, Dvořák's summer estate

pleasant meadows surrounded by hills, and forest resounding with birds. This was the country long associated with the composer. A castle in the forest which had belonged to the composer's brother in law, Count Václav Kounic, was now a Dvořák museum. Dvořák had bought a part of this estate, called *Spejchar* (the Granary), in 1884. The two-story building, which folks called *Ovcinec* (the Sheepfold) was decorated with art nouveau reliefs, and was surrounded by a large garden divided into two sections, one for ornamental trees and the other for an orchard. The privacy of the estate was preserved by a stone wall.

Dvořák's granddaughter, Vera Johnova, remembered the days she and the other children played hide-and-seek under the majestic elms, fragrant linden trees, red beeches, ashes, and hawthorns. How they ran between large bushes of lilacs and jasmines! Her face still beamed with joy at the memory.

She took me for a walk, and another delightful recollection made her smile: "My mother always said that these junipers, grandpa's opera *Jacobin,* and she herself are the same age. Now the junipers are bent, she died a long time ago, and only the music is still alive."

We went back inside the ochre building. As I stood at the piano which had served Dvořák for twenty years, I thought about the story that I had just heard. The keyboard of this instrument was touched by the composer's fingers, playing his cheerful or melancholy melodies, depending on his mood and circumstances. The narrow, cold, stony stairs were just a few steps from the piano; how could they...? But Dvořák's granddaughter explained before I could finish.

"Grandpa wanted his piano here, but the stairs were too narrow to carry it up. So they made a hole in the front wall, and when they got the instrument in, they repaired the wall and put a window there."

A slender elm facing the window had grown tall, and on the right side, at the edge of the orchard, an American nut tree flourished. In the study under the window was a display cabinet with a large collection of letters from various people; a yellowed page dated Spillville, June 10, 1895, was signed by Joseph J. Kovarik, who sent it to Dvořák: "My delayed wishes are better than nothing...."

"Here is a photograph of Kovarik."

My companion showed me a picture of Dvořák's general assistant, secretary, and English teacher with whom he went to America.

I looked carefully at the picture of a young man with a narrow face and short whiskers, spectacles, short hair, and a flower in his lapel. His apparent self-confidence was balanced well by his correctness. On the back side of the photo was an address of the photographer, and beside it an interesting note written in ink: "Joseph J. Kovarik, Prague, Boh. 18 26/6 92." This was just two-and-a-half months before he went with Dvořák to New York. Was it a passport picture? Nonsense, there is no photo in Dvořák's passport.

"This is a photo of a bouquet which my grandpa received as they welcomed him in New York. There is a note about it on the back."

The bouquet, probably orchids, was richly decorated with ribbons. The note said that the photo was made by "W. M. Spiess, 54 2nd Ave. Corner 3rd St., N.Y."

The brownish photo suggested dozens of interesting questions, and it awakened my curiosity. The time spent in America must have been a great and important intermezzo for Dvořák. The question was, had it been only an intermezzo? Europe had known his music, and now a country beyond the immense ocean was inviting him, offering him a great opportunity, and begging him to stay. How did he feel about this? What ideas came to him during the premiere of his Symphony *From the New World*?

I was holding a gray receipt which affirmed that on March 16, 1894, Antonín Dvořák had paid one hundred fifty dollars for cabins 99 and 103 on the ship *Aller*. The owner of the P. V. Rovnianek and Company travel agency in New York City was probably Polish. Dvořák had used the services offered by his office, which was located on 25th Street.

The *Aller* was a huge and comfortable vessel; its passenger list was long—almost two hundred names, including the children. The captain was H. Christoffers, and the list showed the names of the ship's engineer, treasurer, doctor, chief steward, and others.

Even the names of the passengers who were to travel with the ship back to Europe were there. The Dvořák family was listed completely: "Dr. and Mrs. Antonín Dvořák, Miss Otilie Dvořák, Miss Annie Dvořák, Miss Marie Dvořák, Miss Zichy Dvořák, Master Anton Dvořák, Master Otto Dvořák."

So, Dr. Antonín Dvořák, with a wife, four daughters, and two sons, was ready to cross the ocean. The passenger list of the imperial German and U. S. Mail steamship *Aller* was correct, but the date indicated that the ticket was not purchased for his last trip. I asked my hostess about this.

She explained the details of Dvořák's trips:

"It helps to consider the number of children. Originally—as you can see in the passport—in September 1892, only my grandpa and grandma, with daughter Otilka and son Tonik [Antonín], made the trip to New York City. In the summer of 1893 they did not go to Bohemia for a holiday, but accepted the invitation of Kovarik to spend their vacation in Spillville. Kovarik's father was still a teacher in this village of Czech immigrants. Therefore, my grandfather had the rest of the children—Anicka, Magda (nicknamed Marie), Zichy, and Otakar—come to New York City, and together they traveled to the American Midwest.

"After they returned to New York in September 1893, the children stayed with their parents until the spring of 1894. On May 19 the whole Dvořák family returned on the *Aller* to Bohemia. However, grandpa—still bound by his contract—had to return to New York City in the fall of 1894. He continued his work there as director of the Conservatory."

While my hostess prepared coffee, I investigated Dvořák's desk: ink pot, spectacles, lots of souvenirs of his great life and work. When did he reach the peak of his career? I could touch the books on the shelf of his antique desk. Dvořák signed each of them on the first page to indicate that he had read or studied it.

One of them had a bright red, ornamented cover, and was titled *Ceske osady v Americe. Rocnik*, IV. 1888/90 (*The Bohemian Settlements in America*, 4th edition 1888/90). The editor was Josef Pastor from Hamburg. This guide for immigrants contained brief information about "the promised land," along with the basics of English grammar and idioms. Here, too, were Dvořák's notes. Might he have studied the guide before he traveled to America for the first time, and kept it at hand for further reference, especially when he was forced to decide whether he should go or not?

We had coffee downstairs at the spacious table with wicker-back chairs. In a corner was a chest of drawers from the last century, and between the windows stood an old sofa, covered with gray flowered fabric. Above it all hung a mirror and a picture of Anna Dvořák.

"This is the sofa where my grandma died," my hostess informed me sadly.

Everywhere on the walls were photos and glass-framed letters. In the opposite corner was a bed. "Also, the china cabinet behind you contains some souvenirs of my grandpa."

There was something green hanging from the cabinet, perhaps a wreath made of parrot feathers which they brought from America. The feathers were faded, and it had been a long time since the bird had flown in some exotic part of the world, before being placed here at Vysoka, in the Czech village with geese and hens. There is a story about Dvořák's attraction for some little red bird in America.

Dvořák's granddaughter had her instant explanation: "It was in Spillville; grandpa had seen the bird on his walk along the Turkey River."

"Do you have any pictures from that period?"

"Oh yes. My grandpa brought a few photos from his vacation in Spillville in 1893. Look."

She handed me three dog-eared, yellowish pictures on hard paper. Each was of same subject: Indians. The note on the bottom said that the photos were taken in Yankton, South Dakota. The firm's name was covered by tape, where the names of the people in the picture were typed.

"Did your grandpa label them?"

"Probably his son Otakar, my uncle, did it. He spent the summer of 1893 in Spillville and knew well the story about how the photos were obtained."

The first picture showed an old Indian decorated with ornaments, sitting in front of his tepee. His skin was deeply wrinkled, and he had two feathers thrust into his hair, which had long braids down his chest. On his lap was a headpiece made of feathers, and he held a long pipe. His face was interesting and proud, his look firm. The typed information recorded "Big Moon, Spillville, Iowa, USA." Somewhere I had read that during Dvořák's vacation in Spillville, a group of Indians came to the village. They played and sang their songs, and also sold herbs. Such an activity was indeed a strange ending for Big Moon's life.

The second picture was a portrait of an Indian woman in her middle years. Her raven black hair was parted in the middle, and some sort of white ornaments were draped on her shoulders. Her face was extraordinary; her lips looked thin, and the eyes despondent. The inscription read: "Old squaw Large Had, Spillville, Iowa." Otakar probably made an error in the name, meaning to write Large Head.

The third picture represented a half-dressed Indian. He wore a short skirt with fringe-trimmed leather trousers beneath; on his feet were moccasins, and he had a quilt draped over the shoulders. His black hair was also decorated with two feathers, and a white necklace hung around his neck. He held a long gun and had a cartridge box at the waist. His features were grave, with a warlike look, but there seemed to be an air of sadness about him. Thus did "John Fox, Spillville, Iowa, USA," portray those proud but bitter people.

Meeting with Indians was quite an experience for Dvořák. His feelings for them were probably reflected in his new works. There were rumors that his Symphony *From the New World* featured Negro and Indian motifs.

"So much has already been said about it," remarked my hostess. "They even suggest that my grandpa wrote the Symphony during his vacation in Spillville."

That was also my question. How had it originated? Where and when? What was its significance in the context of his life?

I remained silent, however, because further questions would interfere with the magical moments of this visit. I took one more look from the window of the ochre house at Vysoka, skillfully changed from the Granary to this comfortable home which became Dvořák's residence for nineteen years.

The fragrance of roses and the pleasant scent of grass made me wonder: What did summer on 17th Street in New York City or in distant Spillville smell like?

A simple idea struck me with sudden clarity: I must go to America and see for myself.

Dvořák's gray-haired granddaughter understood, and nodded her assent to me with her encouraging smile.

Adagio

Antonín Dvořák first made contact with the New World on September 27, 1892. Already known and recognized worldwide as an outstanding musician and composer, he received a royal welcome when he landed in New York City. What were the events that led up to this great moment? Let us start at the beginning.

Antonín Dvořák was born in Bohemia on September 8, 1841. At that time, Bohemia was a part of the Austro-Hungarian Empire, and was a land where musical traditions were deeply rooted in society. Music was often a family affair. Many good Czech musicians developed in this cultural atmosphere and spread out over Europe. Frantisek Benda and Jiri Antonin Benda were known in Germany, as were Johann Stamitz and his son Carl. Francis Mica was prominent in Bohemia, along with Francis Xaver Brixi. Josef Myslivecek, who worked in Italy, was admired by Mozart. Beethoven's friend Antonin Rejcha was influential in France, and his name is written in the history of European music. In 1792, Charles Burney, in his famous book on musical travels, *A Musical Journey across Lower Austria and Germany to Vienna, Prague, and through Hamburg to Holland*, emphasized the role of Czech musical artistry in European culture during the eighteenth century.

The foundation for modern Czech music had been laid by Bedrich Smetana, the son of a brewer. Antonín Dvořák was destined to carry on Smetana's work, but the task would not be an easy one. To begin with, according to family tradition, Antonín was to take over his father's trade of butcher and

8

Dvořák's father, Frantisek, 1892

Antonín Dvořák's birthplace, the family house in Nelahozeves, Bohemia

innkeeper, but he had an inborn love of music, which grew as he participated in family music sessions. Self-taught, the Dvořáks played with the same enthusiasm as the teacher-families all over Bohemia. Antonín's father could play violin and zither, and his brothers were good musicians as well. They played in every nearby town band and for pilgrimages or wakes far and wide. As an eight-year-old, Antonín attended a one-room elementary school in Nelahozeves. Luckily for him, his teacher was Joseph Spitz, an organist who "could play all the musical instruments." Spitz recognized Antonín's musical talent, and he taught the boy violin in addition to the alphabet. Soon Antonín was giving his own concerts in his father's inn, amazing the guests. It did not occur to them, however, that Antonín Dvořák would one day become world-famous. Perhaps no other Czech composer would ever receive such high praise.

In 1853 (some scholars say 1854) his father sent Antonín to an uncle to learn the German language. His uncle's small town, Zlonice, with its baroque hospital and church, turned out to be a lucky place for the boy because his teacher at the German school was an organist, composer, and bandmaster. Antonin Liehmann wrote many waltzes, polkas, mazurkas, and galops, all in the traditional Czech spirit.

The twelve-year-old youngster could not have been in better hands. Liehmann realized Antonín's talents, and besides teaching him German, gave him the basics of musical composition. This was Dvořák's first instruction in musical theory. During this time Antonín perfected his violin playing skills, and he learned to play the organ, piano, and viola. Antonín's father saw that the youth was spending too much time in these studies, and so had him transferred to another town, Ceska Kamenice, where he resumed the study of German, a much-needed language for a future butcher and innkeeper. Again, however, his teacher was a musician and church choir director, and young Dvořák repeated his experiences in Zlonice. He even occasionally substituted for his teacher at the local church. Returning home in 1855, the fourteen-year-old made a definite decision to become a musician.

Man can lay his plans, but destiny often changes them. Dvořák's father, faced with a growing family and declining income, had to move to Zlonice. Now young Antonín could not be sent to Prague for music study—he would have to stay at home and take over the butcher's trade. For the next two years, the boy had to work in his father's shop. Only on Sundays could he escape to his church choir and the organ. Occasionally, young Dvořák got to play with a band at the castle, or for weddings and wakes. He butchered on weekdays; made music on weekends.

Both the teacher and Antonín's uncle tried to persuade Frantisek Dvořák to allow the boy to study music, and begged him not to spoil the lad's future happiness. Only when the uncle offered financial help did the situation change. Now young Dvořák, sixteen years of age, could prepare for his journey to Prague, and by the fall of 1857 he was registered at the organ school there.

He worked at music theory, performance, and singing—a course of study for the all-around musician. He played viola once a week, becoming familiar with the German romantics and neoromantics through the Saint Cecilia Union. He had never heard the music of Schumann and Wagner before. Now he could live with it, forgetting long days at the butcher's block, as he studied the scores of the masters. He also became a friend of Karel Bendl, an older organ student and future composer.

Bendl's life had been much easier than Dvořák's. His father owned the Prague Konvikt, an inn with a large hall where music was played. Thanks to this situation, Bendl was able to play music whenever he wished. There was also an extensive musical library at the Bendl home. All of this was convenient for young Dvořák's needs, and he used thoroughly the Bendl facilities. Dvořák's knowledge of musical literature and culture, recognized in later life, actually started in the Bendl library. It was here that Dvořák dedicated himself to a musical career.

Antonín's support from home now ceased; his father's business had failed completely. The young Dvořák got some help from his uncle, but he supported himself mainly by giving lessons to younger and less advanced classmates. He was living with poor relatives on Charles Square. An uncle, Vaclav Dusek, was a railway employee, and in his home Dvořák had one daily certainty: breakfast. Funds for other necessities had to come from other sources; he was barely able to earn enough for dinner and supper. This experience taught Dvořák the value of his daily bread, the value of music, and the price one pays to achieve worthy goals in life.

Two years passed quickly at the organ school. Dvořák finished his study at the beginning of 1859, second in his graduating class of twelve. He had good marks and was evaluated as having "an excellent but more practical talent. Practical knowledge and accomplishment seem to be his aim. In theory he is somewhat weaker."

This evaluation of the eighteen-year-old Dvořák probably describes accurately his musical education, and seems to have predestined him for a career as a performing musician. This actually happened, for to sustain himself, Dvořák took a playing job in the Karel Komzak orchestra, a group that appeared in Prague restaurants. It was his first wage-earning position. During his free time, however, he worked on his compositions. These showed some traces of Haydn and Mozart in their simple, happy character—uncomplicated and naive. Later on, Marie Cervinkova-Riegrova, Dvořák's librettist, wrote about him after he became famous in Europe:

> He is enormously good-natured and natural. He might, in a group of people, begin to whistle at any time, or start on a train of thought, breaking off a conversation. He is passionately in love with music and convinced that it is the best career in the world. The line dividing his forehead is at its deepest while he analyzes music. Dvořák is not conceited though. His world-wide fame has not changed him; he has stayed as natural as before.

The librettist extends this characterization further in a letter written to her father: "Dvořák is a special man, apparently a good fellow and *Natur-Mensch* at the same time. Social conventions cannot restrain him...his manners are quite natural, he does not show any conceit, and expresses his opinions absolutely openly." The word *natural* appears in her statement three times. It is not just an accident that Dvořák's colleague emphasizes precisely this feature. He was natural, and so is his music.

The road to Dvořák's success was not easy. His biographer, Otakar Sourek, speaks of two composers who "influenced Dvořák artistically and were decisive in directing his life toward specific goals"—Beethoven and Schubert. Beethoven's music showed Dvořák how to build a complete musical structure from motifs growing out of long, expressive, breathing themes while using a wealth of melodic and rhythmic modifications. As a direct heir of Beethoven's bold, powerful spirit, Dvořák based his compositions on the master's majesty of style and clarity of form.

> Dvořák was bound to Schubert by more intimate ties—artistic and creative congeniality, their spontaneity, and their heaven-sent inspiration. Their talents seem free of agonizing creative struggle; their output is virile, direct, and sound. There are no sickly exaggerated sensitivities and sentimental moods. Dvořák learned from Beethoven, but with Schubert he shared common qualities which cannot be learned, but are the property of genius.

This quotation rings true, even when expressed in the 1916 literary style of Sourek. It captures Dvořák's creative joy, the matter-of-factness without sentimentality which sounds in his music. Dvořák speaks about his relationship with Beethoven's music several times in letters to friends. He refers to him as "Papa Beethoven, whose picture hangs above my writing desk," and adds, "During my composing, I often look up, asking him to intercede for me in heaven." Beethoven was his god; Schubert, a kind and beloved friend. With them by his side, he was creating his own world of music.

Dvořák's first work was finished on June 6, 1861. It was a quintet for two violins, two violas, and a cello, written in A minor and bearing the autograph "Antonín Leop. Dvořák." He used the middle name Leopold (probably given him at confirmation) several times at the beginning of his career.

His early years as a musician were not easy. He was unknown, and had only himself to depend on. Music writing was his sole means of advancement. At night he played in Komzak's group, for which he wrote a polka and a galop. Komzak's orchestra was well known in Prague, and played in many restaurants, although the musicians' salaries did not reflect the group's success. Dvořák added to his meager income by giving private music lessons. Even in 1862, when Komzak's orchestra was hired to play in the Czech Provisional Theatre, the wages showed no improvement. The monthly salary was eighteen zlatys. Remember this sum, and compare it with what he was later offered to come to America. Suffice it to say that eighteen zlatys afforded only misery and hunger. His evenings were spent in rehearsals, theatre performances, and playing in restaurants with Komzak's band. Although the group later became employed full-time in the Czech Provisional Theatre, Dvořák's financial situation improved little. Still, he kept on writing music, and continued to have little success with it.

His next work was the String Quartet in A Major, signed "Ant. Leop. Dvořák—Thanks be to God." Other compositions followed, among them his first symphonic work, subtitled *Zlonicke zvony* (*The Bells of Zlonice*) no. 1. Melodies and ideas flowed from his pen; he lived for his music, but still no recognition came. In fact, during this stage of Dvořák's development his work received some adverse criticism about the formal doctrine of his musical structure. His answer was the Symphony no. 2 in B-flat Major, followed by a cycle of eighteen songs based on poems of Gustav Pfleger-Moravsky, entitled *Cyprise* (*Cypresses*).

These lyrical love poems of Pfleger-Moravsky appeared in 1861, about the time that Dvořák fell in love with one of his students. Dvořák was living in a rooming house that had a piano which he was allowed to use. Always in need of money, he accepted two piano students: the Cermak sisters, Josefa (nicknamed Josefina) and Anna.

The Cermakova sisters Josefina, *l.*, who was Dvořák's first love, and Anna, *r.*, his wife

Now, at age twenty-four, he was inspired to set the poems to music and to express his feelings for the beautiful sixteen-year-old Josefina through those poems. Evidently Josefina was not romantically attracted to him; she later became a famous actress in the Prague Czech Theatre and married Count Vaclav Kounic. She also became Dvořák's sister-in-law when he married her younger sister Anna in 1873.

Dvořák returned to composition with a greater enthusiasm now. Music welled up from him as water from a geyser. Two overtures for orchestra, in E minor and F minor, masses in B major and F minor, a quintet for clarinet in B minor, an octet, several pieces of music for plays at the Czech theatre, and the orchestral prelude to Shakespeare's *Romeo and Juliet* followed, one after the other. None of these works will ever be heard, however. Dvořák wrote in 1873 of a composition "which I tore into pieces and burned." How many works from this period he destroyed we can only guess. We know that he wrote three nocturnes for orchestra in 1872, and a three-movement sonata for violin and piano in A minor, but these too were destroyed, along with many others. (However, one of the nocturnes has recently been reconstructed from the performing parts.)

This was a special time for Dvořák. Music was pouring from his creative being, but he could not always fit his ideas into a formal structure. In 1870 he wrote the opera *Alfred,* based on the English legends of the late ninth century. The work shows Wagner's influence on Dvořák's enormous talent, but it reveals weaknesses, too. A second opera, *Kral a uhlir (King and Collier),* brought this comment from Smetana: "It is a serious work, full of many ingenious ideas."

People wondered how this modest violist could be a good composer. Dvořák felt the need to give more time to his work, so he resigned from the theatre orchestra in 1871. In the 1871 *Musical Leaflets* a notice appeared: "Antonín Dvořák, a member of the orchestra of the Royal Czech National Theatre, whose talent for composition is well known, has finished his comic opera and the management is planning a production of the new work." This was the first news of the composer to appear in print; his road to worldwide acclaim would be a long one.

After a few rehearsals, it was alleged that the work was too complicated, that it was unclear, and that it presented "almost unconquerable obstacles for the singers." The author, disappointed and disgusted, took it back. Much the same fate awaited several of his other works.

His first public success was *Hymnus*, a work for mixed choir and orchestra. For the text he used the poem "Dedicove Bile Hory" ("The Heirs of the

White Mountain") by Vitezslav Halek. Success arose in part from its popular theme, the struggle against the Viennese regime. Dvořák's heart must have beat with the patriotic romanticism of the poem. In his *Alfred* opera he had already sung of the need for the subjugated nation to fight its oppressors. This need now became even stronger because it mirrored the Czechs' own situation.

Dvořák's patriotism was not a passing fancy. He felt it from the heart and expressed it fully. (One example is his requirement that his publisher spell his name in the Czech fashion, with a hacek over the *r* and an acute accent over the *a*, just as he signed it in his native language.) In 1887, he wrote to his German publisher Fritz Simrock:

> Your last letter with the nationalistic and political comments amazed me very much. I just regret that you are not familiar enough with this subject. All our enemies speak in the same manner, especially some individuals employed in journals such as the *Kolnische Zeitung*, the *Augsburger Allg(emeine) Zeitung*, etc..... Let us hope the nations never perish which possess art and represent it, however small they are. Forgive me for this, but simply I wish to tell you that an artist also has a homeland in which he must have faith and to which he must always have a warm heart.

Dvořák had begun to think like this long before he wrote his letter, for he had always felt these sentiments. Indeed, the majestic *Hymnus,* set to Halek's words, had been a way for him to express his nationalism in music and to achieve his first public success.

The Czechs welcomed a composition of this nature, especially with the political situation as it was. The young middle class, under the slogan "Homeland, Nation," had begun their struggle against the German regime in Vienna. Dvořák's *Hymnus* not only voiced feelings of nationalism but was musically satisfying, too. The work was presented in the spring of 1873 at the New City Theatre in a perfect arrangement by Dvořák's friend Karel Bendl, choirmaster of the three-hundred-voice choir, Prague Hlahol.

Continuing in this nationalistic spirit, Dvořák now set four songs from Serbian folk poetry as well as six from the Rukopis Kralovedvorsky (Königinhof MSS). In the 1870s it was still believed that this group of lyrical poems, written on medieval parchment and found in the church tower at Kraluv Dvur in 1818, were genuine, perhaps from the fourteenth century. This manuscript was valued as evidence of the early high level of Czech national culture.

Fritz Simrock, Dvořák's publisher in Berlin

Dvořák's settings of these songs were his first published works. At last, in early 1873, his twelve years of hard work began to bring him some reward. (Remember that his Opus 1 bore the date of June 1861.)

Prior to this publication, Dvořák's work had been more or less ignored. Critics had noted his weaknesses, but with *Hymnus* and the Rukopis Kralovedvorsky songs the situation had changed for the better. He resolved to write another symphony (no. 3 in E-flat major) in the same spirit of freedom. It was produced in the spring of 1874 under Bedrich Smetana's direction with the Philharmonia Club orchestra. Dvořák now divorced himself from his past by destroying all his work up to that time; he was making a fresh start.

This resolve applied to his personal life as well, for in November 1873 he married his former piano pupil Anna Cermak, now nineteen years old, the younger sister of Josefina.

Though the two Cermak girls were sisters, their characters differed widely. Josefina, living in a world of fantasy, sought fame on the stage. She had fulfilled her dream and joined a group of the most charming members of the Provisional Theatre. According to Neruda's *Theatre Review* many men found her looks exciting. Josefina had quit her career after her marriage to Count Vaclav Kounic in 1877; after the National Theatre finally opened in 1883, she visited the place as a countess rather than as an actress. Perhaps she took greater pleasure in attending as a member of nobility than if she had appeared in a professional role—who knows? With the Count at her side, and in a box opposite, her brother-in-law Antonín (no longer the obscure violist of the orchestra), she could take pride in her position.

The younger Cermak sister, Anna, was quite the opposite of Josefina. She loved music and possessed an excellent alto voice. When Dvořák's *Requiem* (which had premiered in England) was first performed in continental Europe at Olomouc in 1892, and later in Kromeriz, Anna was the soloist under Antonín's direction.

Anna was a good household manager, who provided a calm environment for the composer and their expanding family. She took charge of the family finances, and she always knew what they could afford and which direction they should take.

At first the young couple lived with Anna's parents in Prague. But after February 1874, they moved into their own apartment at 14 Na rybnicku. Dvořák accepted a position as organist in the Saint Vojtech Church, and held that post until 1877. His salary was 96 zlatys, 60 groschen for the year, but it afforded him ample free time for composing, which he had resumed and at which he was working eagerly and tirelessly. No longer totally unknown in Bohemia, he produced a quartet in F minor and was revising a second string quartet that gave evidence of his movement away from the influences of Wagner and Liszt. He now began to realize the significance of Bedrich Smetana's music in the nation's cultural life.

Dvořák now struggled to establish his own individual voice in the musical world, writing another symphony, no. 4 in D minor (the Scherzo movement of which was produced in 1874 by Bedrich Smetana). Dvořák further surprised everyone by rewriting his opera *Kral a uhlir (The King and the Collier)*. The libretto was based on the puppet theatre work *Posviceni v Hudlicich (The Village Wake in Hudlice)*. Dvořák had condemned the first version of the opera, which he had previously withdrawn from the Provisional Theatre, and he changed it in virtually every beat. Any other composer would have been disheartened at such a task, but Dvořák kept right on working, and his career progressed.

One evidence of this progress is the 1874 stipend granted him by the government in Vienna. Under the conditions of the grant, the Ministry of Culture and Education gave "to selected young, poor, and talented artists" a year's financial support. There were grants for artists, writers, and musicians, and a distinguished jury was assembled for each area. Serving on the Music Commission were Johannes Brahms, Eduard Hanslick, the eminent music critic, and Johann Herbeck, the director of the Court Opera. The winner in Music Dvořák, received 400 zlatys, and such was the quality of the music he submitted that five years later Hanslick wrote these words:

> The majority of the applications coming to the ministry were documented with bulky and extensive scores. They were usually presented by composers who could satisfy only the first two of the three legal requirements—youth, poverty, and talent—and lacking the third. Indeed, we were very surprised to receive examples of the extensive and still growing talent of the Prague applicant, Antonín Dvořák. We remember especially his symphony which showed such a talent that one member of the commission, Herbeck, took a lively interest in it.

Thus did Dvořák gradually establish himself in Bohemian music circles. In 1875 he completed the *Quintet in G Major for String Quartet with Contrabass,* submitting it to the chamber music competition organized by the Umelecka beseda (The Art Club). He called his work *Svemu narodu (To My Nation)* and won first prize with it.

Following this success, Dvořák again seemed instinctively drawn to folk music, this time that of Moravia. Inspired by a collection of folk songs gathered by Frantisek Susil, Dvořák transformed some of them into three duets for soprano and tenor. The texts of these songs were close to Dvořák's heart, always deeply attached to his native land, and to the village where he grew up. He loved folk poetry as well as music, and this period of his work in the 1870s brought with it fame and recognition as one of the leaders of Czech music, the other being Smetana.

Antonín's home situation, meanwhile, was much less happy. His son Otakar, born April 4, 1874, died on September 8, 1877, at the age of three-and-a-half years. A daughter, Josefa, born September 19, 1875, died two days later; and a second daughter, Ruzena, born September 18, 1876, died in less than a year. One can imagine what blows these were to the kindly, family-loving Dvořák.

He answered these sorrowful events by reaffirming in his *Stabat Mater* of 1877 his profound belief in God as well as giving vent to his own grief. The Latin text for his cantata is from the early thirteenth century and speaks of Christ's mother, stricken with sorrow as she views her son's suffering on the cross. The text ends with her prayer, asking that she be allowed to suffer the same fate as a means of redemption and reunion with her son. This story has been used by many composers—including Palestrina, Haydn, Rossini, and

Verdi—both before and after Dvořák, but his music ranks as one of the most deeply touching works. In it the composer relies on the orchestra and human voices to express his feelings, knowing that the Latin text would not be understood by most. It is in the music that he captures pain as well as faith and hope, all in masterly fashion. This work brought him to the attention of audiences all across Europe, but more was needed to spread the young composer's works.

One Marie Neffova, the wife of a Prague merchant and patriot, held salons where artists used to meet. She recalled that

> at the beginning of Dvořák's career, one of our acquaintances, a musician and teacher, recommended the young composer as his substitute. As a result, Dvořák spent many fine evenings at our home with all of us singing and playing. The duets were especially enjoyable, with the composer accompanying. Our only complaint was the limited repertoire—we became tired of Mendelssohn and the other German composers. My husband, an enthusiastic Moravian, asked Dvořák, "Would it be possible to compose something for us based on Moravian native sources?" "Why not?" answered Dvořák. "Find some good texts, and I'll do the rest."

Marie Neffova continued:

> Our governess, Marie Blazkova, went to Naprsteks [a museum] to consult Susil's collection of folk songs. She selected from it approximately fifteen songs, and Dvořák promised to rearrange them for two voices with accompaniment. In a few days, however, he changed his mind. "I won't do that, but if you want, I'll write new music of my own to the poems, not just add a second voice." No one objected, so the young man set to work.
>
> The result was the famous *Moravian Duets,* which he dedicated to me and my husband, who were his friends. When we sang them for the first time, we praised his music but he only sighed and said, "I'm sorry, but I haven't the money to have them printed." My husband reacted immediately. "Wait a moment, that will be my problem. You can have half the copies, and I'll keep the remainder. Each of us will be free to use his own copies as he sees fit." Dvořák agreed gladly, and the *Moravian Duets* were lithographed by the Stary Publishing Company. We kept certain copies for our own use and gave the others to Dvořák.

One day, in the composer's absence, we decided to bind the songs splendidly and present them to a number of the foremost music critics, composers, musicians, and patriots. Naturally, we had to do it without Dvořák's knowledge, so we secretly sent them to Brahms and Hanslick, men of great significance in the musical world. We knew that he would certainly object, so Miss Blazkova took on the task of preparing a cover letter asking each recipient of the songs to accept and examine them. She signed it with Dvořák's name.

This was the beginning of a journey around the world for these songs, but Marie Neffova's account might be a bit romantically exaggerated. The truth, equally interesting, is that though Dvořák did write the songs for the Neff family where he was employed as a substitute music teacher, and did use the Susil collection of Moravian songs for his text, he wrote five songs, calling them *Duets for Two Sopranos,* and published them as his Opus 29. After a month's time, he added Opus 32, consisting of ten more songs. Both groups are poetic and subdued, obviously conceived as a single unit. The composer did not merely imitate folk songs, but in characteristic Dvořák style, created fresh, new songs from the original melodies. Although each song is written in a different style, they are all bound with the particular magic of the composer's personality and have their own musical mood. The simple wisdom of the lyrics combines with his harmonies to convey profound feelings.

After their publication in 1877, Dvořák presented the songs to the musical authorities in Vienna as documents of his creative work. His first application for a stipend, remember, had been approved in 1874, and the following year it was extended with a further grant of 100 zlatys. In fact, Dvořák received the stipend five times, the *Moravian Duets* being one of the works he submitted. The young composer as yet had no idea of what would result from the publication of these songs.

In a letter to Johannes Brahms dated December 3, 1877, Dvořák wrote:

Highly Respectable Sir,

I have just received a letter from the Honorable Professor Doctor Hanslick, who informs me that at the recent meeting in the office of His Excellency, Minister Stremayer, I have received the stipend for artists through your kind recommendation. I am so happy about this that I feel free to send you, Honorable Master, these few words to express my profound gratitude for your exceptional favor. I am most happy for the sympathetic attitude which Your Honor showed toward my modest talent, and also for the pleasure which you, Dear Sir (as Herr Professor Hanslick writes to me), have taken in my Czech songs for two voices. Herr Professor Hanslick suggests that I arrange a translation of my songs into German. He says that this will make it possible, Dear Maestro, to recommend them to your publisher. I turn to you with this request once more, and ask you for help in this important matter. It could become valuable to my country, Dear Sir, whose work is giving so much pleasure to the whole world. With your kind help, I may be introduced to this world, too.

The letter is interesting. Naturally, Dvořák sought to reach a world stage, but he wanted to reach it as a Czech composer for the benefit of his beloved country. We do not know when Brahms received Dvořák's letter, and can only note what Brahms later wrote to his publisher in Berlin, S. Simrock, then one of the foremost music publishers in the world:

Dear S.

In connection with the State Grant, I have for several years past had great pleasure in the works of Antonín Dvořák (pronounced Dworschak) in Prague. This year he sent in, among other things, a volume of ten duets for two sopranos with piano accompaniment, which seem to be very practical for publication. The volume appears to have been printed at the composer's own expense. The title, and unfortunately also the text, are in Czech only. I have advised him to send you the songs. When you play them over you will, like me, be delighted with their piquant charm. It would be necessary, however, to see to obtaining a very good translation. Some of them might already be translated by Wenig (recently deceased). Otherwise, Dr. Siegfried Kupper of Prague would be perfect for the job. Dvořák has written all sorts of things: operas (Czech), symphonies, quartets, and pieces for the piano. There is no doubt that he is very talented. And then he is also poor. I beg you to think the matter over. The duets won't give you much thought and will sell well. His address is: Prague, Zitna St. no. 10,11.

With best greetings,
Yours, J. Brahms

This letter demonstrates Brahms' extraordinary sensitivity for other people's talents, and it also shows his practicality. He knows which string of the publisher's vanity to play in order to reach an agreement, pointing out not only the beauty of the work, but its market value as well. To be "published by Simrock" was a passport to the future.

Simrock decided to examine carefully and impartially the recommended work. After he finished playing the duets, he realized what Brahms was talking about. He suggested publication to Dvořák, but of course the composer had to understand the risk that the famous publisher was taking with these songs. Publication of *Moravian Duets* would have to be without fee. Perhaps next time....

Brahms, unaware that Simrock would send such an offer to the composer, wrote at the same time to Dvořák:

> Dear Sir:
>
> I would like to thank you briefly for your letter and for the great pleasure of having your works. I enjoy them very much. I took the liberty of writing about them (most of all about the duets) to Herr Fritz Simrock (Berlin, W. Friedrichstrasse 171). I see from the title page that the duets are still in your possession. In that case, you would be able to sell them to Herr Simrock. It will be necessary for you to arrange a good translation of their text into German. Can you handle this yourself? Are there any of your songs included in Joseph Wenig's "Marchenschatz" (Leipzig, G. Senf, 1866)? Do you know Herr Dr. Siegfried Kapper from Prague? He might be able to translate your work. In any case, do not act hastily; avoid everything that could unfavorably affect your work.
>
> Meanwhile, can you send manuscripts of your work to Herr S. for his opinion? The rest will be arranged later. I am sorry that this will be all for today because I do not want to delay my letter to you. I hope to hear further good news from you in the near future. With especial respect,
>
> Yours truly, J. Brahms

The relationship between Dvořák and Brahms proved fateful. Both composers were enriching old musical forms with the new wealth of their compositions. Both had grown up in the musical legacy inherited from Beethoven, and both were influenced by Schubert. They became the representatives of "absolute music" at the end of the nineteenth century. Both were composers of great symphonies and creators of chamber music. Brahms, nine years older, was more systematically and thoroughly educated than the less affluent Dvořák.

Dvořák received Brahms' letter just as he was finishing his Quartet in D Minor. He was pleasantly surprised, and went to Vienna immediately to thank Brahms in person and to inform him of plans to dedicate this most recent composition to him. But because Dvořák had not written in advance, Brahms was away from Vienna at that time. In a letter to Dvořák in May 1878, accepting the dedication, Brahms wrote:

> it gives me the greatest delight to be involved with your works. I would be very pleased to discuss all the particulars with you. Your writing is a little bit hasty and you will need to complete it with the many sharp-, flat-, and natural-signs which you have missed. Then you can check the individual notes and the leading voices more clearly.

The evaluation that had been written in Dvořák's graduation certificate from the organ school was still valid: the young composer was "somewhat weaker in theory." Within a few years, however, he would remedy this weakness.

The relationship between Brahms and Dvořák was scarcely that of teacher and pupil. Before Brahms wrote his first symphony (in 1876), Dvořák had composed four, as a seeming preparation for his later masterpieces in this form.

Thus two personalities, two great musicians, became acquainted. The event was marked by their mutual respect, recognition, and interest. Simrock described to Brahms the composers' relationship in this way: "Dvořák feels for you a fanatical respect. This is apparent when he speaks of you. He plans to visit you in Vienna again as soon as possible. He says that nothing else is more important to him."

Brahms regarded Dvořák with the same feelings. Leading the way for him at Simrock's (now it was the Quartets in E Major and D Minor), he recommended that the publisher listen to Dvořák's music carefully. He wrote: "I am sure that the best new music…comes from Dvořák, and all musicians should purchase it." Later, in 1892, when Dvořák decided to go to America, Brahms offered to proofread all the works written during his overseas visit.

Dvořák's financial situation had improved, and he was able to quit his job as organist at the Saint Vojtech church in 1876. He also changed his apartment, moving his family from a simple flat at 14 Na rybnicku to 564/10 Zitna Street. They lived there in a small but comfortable apartment, which remained their home until the composer's death in May 1904.

Dvořák liked it there. He walked to nearby Charles Square, where he could listen to the singing of birds in the mornings. Sometimes he hiked to Nusel Valley, or to the main railway station, then named after Emperor Franz Josef. He could linger there for hours, watching the engines. And then there were the coffeehouses where he went to read the fresh newspapers each day. They were reached easily from his home. Just across the street was the Parizska (Parisian) and a little further, at the intersection of Spalena and Myslikova streets, the Novomestska (New City Cafe).

After Simrock had accepted the *Moravian Duets* for publication, he suggested that Dvořák write at once a series of Czechoslovakian dances for the piano, four hands. "You are gifted with a powerful talent," he wrote. "Why don't you try something like the Hungarian Dances of Brahms?" Simrock did not mention that he had made a goodly sum from the Brahms compositions, and that he foresaw a similar gold mine in the music of Dvořák. The good publisher believed it was his right to make a profit from Dvořák's work so long as the cause of music was advanced. Indeed, thanks to Simrock's challenge, the celebrated *Slavonic Dances* were written at the same time that Dvořák was working on his *Slavonic Rhapsodies*. The two seemed to come almost from the same source. The composer interrupted his work on the *Rhapsodies* for two months in order to comply with Simrock's request. The last dance of the first series of eight was finished on May 7, 1878.

The dances which Brahms wrote represent a stylization of Hungarian folk songs, but Dvořák's dances are different. Brahms had quoted national melodies literally, using them in parts of his compositions. This practice had brought about a journalistic dispute and later a lawsuit. The Simrock firm's copyright was not acknowledged in Hungary, and Hungarians claimed that the melodies were in a kind of national ownership. Dvořák, in contrast, did not simply stylize the Czech, Moravian, and Slovakian folk songs, for his ambitions were higher. Brahms was young when he composed his *Hungarian Dances*. Dvořák's aspiration was to create some kind of model of the Czech dance, ideal in its form and content. He had taken from the folk dances only their rhythms. Everything else, especially the expressive melodies of the dances, was original and characteristic of Dvořák's work.

Simrock published the first series of *Slavonic Dances* in August 1878, and it was a tremendous success. Since the *Moravian Duets* had prepared the way for Dvořák, the *Slavonic Dances* conquered audiences in the cultural centers of Europe. Louis Ehlert, a critic in Wiesbaden who was one of the most influential professionals in international musical circles, spoke for many when he wrote in Berlin's *Die Neuezeitung* in January 1878:

Those who have followed the development of contemporary music in the last thirty years cannot avoid a special sadness about the rareness of fresh and significant talent!

One day, I was morosely buried under a mountain of musical scores. My eyes and spirit were weakened by a horror of empty, indifferent, and insignificant music, and I was almost ready to give up. Suddenly, I was jolted to full attention by some compositions hidden in that mess. These were the Slavonic Dances for piano, four hands, and the Moravian Songs—thirteen duets for soprano and alto from Ant. Dvořák. The composer is Czech and lives in Prague. A few years ago he was still a violist in a local opera orchestra there. Although he has published only a few things, he is most likely ready to submit many of his compositions. Among them are quartets and symphonies. This is all that I was able to discover about him up to now. I can only say that finally again we have here a talent that is whole and absolutely natural. In my consideration, the Slavonic Dances will travel all around the world, as did the Hungarian Dances by Brahms. The originality of Dvořák's work is real. There cannot be any discussion about an imitation; his dances are not at all composed in the style of Brahms. The naturalness of God flows in this music because it is entirely folk-oriented. There are no traces of pose or constraint. The whole thing is so impressive and colorful that it would be easy to arrange it directly for orchestra.

Parenthetically, Dvořák indeed had already orchestrated all eight dances in the summer of 1878. Ehlert concludes his Berlin article (where he remarks, "Dvořák writes such a merry bass line that the true musician's heart must rejoice") with a fair appeal:

I think about the joy we share when a true music composer is revealed—a composer about whom there is no need to argue, just as we do not argue about the coming of spring. Like the finder of a jewel on a public street, I must report this discovery which I recently made. I am asking you to regard this young composer from the same point of view.

Perhaps no other Czech composer had ever received such high praise. This did not escape Simrock's attention and interest. He had already sent to Dvořák the first fee; 300 marks altogether! Considering how much money he made on the *Slavonic Dances,* this amount was paltry. However, it had given Dvořák moral encouragement and an important financial boost. Several years later Simrock asked the composer to write another series of eight Slavonic dances. Although Dvořák satisfied Simrock's request, this time he was fully aware of the value of his music and also of his standing in the world. Simrock was forced to pay ten times more for the same number of dances than he did before, exactly 3,000 marks.

In a response to Ehlert, Dvořák thanked him for his high evaluation of the duets and dances. Ehlert answered on November 27, 1878:

> My article caused a great run on the music stores in Berlin. I can say without any exaggeration that in only one day your name was made. I pray that I was correct in my high opinion of your talent. You can depend on it that I will promote our hope for your success with what little influence I have. Also, I would be glad to have your picture. Please send me one you can spare. It is in my nature to want to know the likeness of a person in whom I am interested...."

Two other occurrences in the year 1878 complemented the favorable atmosphere surrounding the more-or-less-well-known composer Dvořák. Dr. Frantisek Bayer, then professor of the *gymnasium* in Tabor, recalls:

> Smetana was in Prague when the score of the *Slavonic Dances* was published in Berlin, and he showed his open pleasure at the fact that works of our Czech composers could permeate foreign countries. He regretted very much that he did not know this music. He wished that the younger composers would show him their newly published works because he was no longer able to hear them. His wish was fulfilled; the next day Smetana saw the score of Dvořák's *Slavonic Dances*. I was present and could hear his unreserved praise of this work. In addition, he said that Dvořák worked with his themes just the way Beethoven did.

A production of the premiere of another of Dvořák's operas, *Selma sedlak (The Peasant, a Rogue),* in the Provisional Theatre was a success and had pleased audiences. The poet and theatre critic Jan Neruda wrote about the composer:

> I do not know Dvořák personally but I think of him as a real musician. Usually musicians are called impractical because they see very little of what is going on beneath their feet. I see him as a young man with an especially active imagination. We usually connect this with poets, painters, and most of all with musicians. However, if he were too sensible, or just ordinary, there

would be nothing special about him.

He has been accused of having too much imagination and too little common sense, as well as being supposedly very "ambitious." Wonderful! I could embrace him for it! And finally, they say that he is "producing too much." Can we rebuke the ocean for having too many waves? Once upon a time there was a musician whose name was Beethoven. He also wrote a lot of music, a great lot of it, indeed. On his deathbed he sighed: "I have a feeling that I am still just at the beginning." I hope that Dvořák feels the same—that he is just beginning.

Neither Smetana nor Neruda could know that a portrait of Beethoven hung over Dvořák's writing desk. A successful period in Dvořák's life was just beginning, and with it in June of 1878 came the birth of his fourth child, a daughter, Otilie. He was in a favorable position to advance his career: he had composed three Slavonic Rhapsodies that were already being played outside the Austro-Hungarian Empire. His name had been introduced to all of Europe, thanks to Simrock's publication; his third rhapsody was initially played in Berlin, then in Dresden, Karlsruhe, Wiesbaden, Budapest, and Vienna; the Vienna Philharmonic had placed it in their repertoire; in 1879, the *Slavonic Rhapsodies* were published by Simrock in an arrangement for four hands, not long after the *Moravian Duets* were printed in 1878. They were first published separately as the *Klange aus Mahren (Bells from Moravia)* and then as a complete edition in 1880. In the same year, the *Rhapsodies* were played in certain European cities—Nice, France, for example. Also they were performed in various cities of England, and by the Symphonic Society of New York City.

Dvořák's music was being played everywhere in Europe, and he felt an almost childish delight with each new success. In a letter to a friend, Alois Gobl, he wrote about the reception his music was getting:

> I was sitting at the organ beside Brahms [during the Vienna production]...and I must tell you that I got a sympathetic reading from the whole orchestra. Among all the new works which we were rehearsing (and there were, according to conductor Richter about 60), my Rhapsody was the most enjoyable. Richter was ready to embrace me and was also very pleased that we could get acquainted....

More opus numbers were coming. Offers from different music publishers mounted. Besides Simrock, the firm of Bote and Bock, the second largest in Berlin, made approaches. They published a few of his compositions, and all copies sold out in a couple of weeks and had to be reprinted. Other publishers, including one from Leipzig, bid for his music.

Dvořák, now forty, stood on the threshold of world fame. The prospects made him a bit breathless and nervous. Of course, he had been somewhat like this all his life—but now there were all those orders coming in. He could not always satisfy the growing demands for new works, so he started to offer some of his compositions from "off the shelf," where they had been resting for some time now. Many of these had seen only one performance—others none at all. No matter; institutions, soloists, publishers, and just about everybody else wanted to have "more Dvořák." The situation became nearly intolerable for him.

Dvořák gave his new *Waltzes* (two books of them) to Simrock, and devoted his time to composing songs. The *Cikanske melodie (The Gypsy Melodies)* appeared, with text by the poet Adolf Heyduk, followed by a book of mazurkas for piano. Everything Dvořák submitted was welcomed by the publishers because these short compositions could be sold easily. Publishers made mountains of money on them. Thus far, though, the symphonies and operas were not in wide demand.

Dvořák enjoyed a level of success which, up to this point, few European composers had achieved. It would be superfluous to give the titles and characteristics of all his works to date, but his Sixth Symphony in D Major, bright and full of joy, should be mentioned. This work sprang from a consciousness of his Czech roots and from his relationship with his homeland. The composition was produced in London and Budapest in 1882. He also composed his opera *Dimitrij,* and in 1883 was working on a dramatic overture, *Husitska (The Hussite)*. Hanslick wrote, at the occasion of its production in Vienna, that "the orchestral music of the battle scenes was so descriptive that one could almost hear the scythes, flails, and war-clubs." This work was written for the festive opening of the National Theatre in Prague.

The strongest reaction to his work came first from England. Besides the *Rhapsodies, Slavonic Dances,* and the Symphony in D Major, his string sextet in A major and a piano concerto were played in the Crystal Palace in London. A performance of the *Stabat Mater* in the London Royal Albert Hall in March 1883 earned him enormous public attention.

It is interesting that England, which contributed so little to the realm of musical composition in the nineteenth century, should have had such excellent orchestras and such a high level of support for good music. As soon as any important musician appeared anywhere in Europe, England sooner or later sought to bring him over. The English aristocracy and the music lovers of the cities assumed the cost of such presentations. This combination of aristocratic and urban support was greater than the support given to music by the noble houses alone in Germany and France. The composer coming to England was treated royally, and could be assured of audiences of mature and well-trained listeners. After all, Handel had lived and worked in England both as composer and conductor; Mozart had also played in England; the English had brought Gluck and Weber to write operas for them; Haydn had been invited there; and the Philharmonic Society had collaborated with Beethoven in commissioning the famous Ninth Symphony. The English had even invited a Czech from the little town of Caslav, one Jan Ladislav Dusik, some years earlier.

The excitement generated by the performance in England of Dvořák's *Stabat Mater* was significant for the composer's future. The Philharmonic Society now asked Dvořák to conduct his works himself. A few years ago just the thought of such an honor would have made Dvořák laugh; now it was about to become reality. In the spring of 1884 he made his first trip across the English Channel, and on March 8 he entered that city on the banks of the Thames River. His friend, the piano virtuoso Jindrich Kaan, went with him, and later remembered:

> The journey was pure magic. The sea was calm and we arrived on English soil feeling well. The next day we saw Dvořák's name in almost every magazine and paper. Some of the publishers have even gone out of their way to get the type-font letters of *r* and *a* made up in the Czech style.

The composer's letters from England were filled with the excitement he felt at such a reception. Besides *Stabat Mater*, two of his concertos were performed. Moreover, the long-expected overture *The Hussite* was included on a program. Dvořák wrote to his father:

> I have received an offer from England for the next year and also for 1886, which I have accepted. It will be my job to write new compositions for them. You can see how much they like me here, and what kind of respect I get! Some newspapers have mentioned you, too. They write that I was born to poor parents, and that my father, who was a butcher and innkeeper in Nelahozeves, gave all one could give for his son's proper education! God's richest blessings on you for that! I will visit you in Kladno after my return to Prague. For now, God bless you. I

am sending you my best regards and kiss you, Your grateful
Antonín.

In a letter addressed to V. Urbanek, the editor of the Prague musical journal
Dalibor, Dvořák describes in great detail his mood while in London.

> It was my first rehearsal with a choir in that huge building,
> Albert Hall, on Monday. About 12,000 people can be seated
> quite comfortably there! After my appearance on the podium, a
> thunder of long-lasting applause welcomed me, and it took a
> good while for it to calm down. I was deeply touched by this
> cordial ovation and was unable to speak. This was not really a
> problem because nobody could have heard me for the noise. A
> rehearsal with the soloists was the next day in the afternoon.
> My feelings at being in front of such a huge musical organiza-
> tion were really magical. It would be impossible to describe....

The atmosphere must have been shocking for him. It was unbelievable that
only a short time ago he was almost unknown in his own country, and now
he was receiving such tremendous homage in London:

> The general excitement grew from one composition to the next,
> and because the applause at the end was so great, I had to thank
> the audience again. At the same time, the orchestra at my back
> was giving me a cordial ovation. In short, everything turned out
> better than I ever dreamed it would be. I was totally convinced
> that right now, in England, a happier new epoch has just started
> for me. I hope my success will bear fruit for Czech art as well.
> The English are a good, hearty, music-loving nation. It is well
> known that once they love somebody, they stand by him faith-
> fully forever. God help me! I hope this will happen to me
> now....

Other words of Dvořák can be quoted: "They write about me everywhere, and it is said and also written that I am the lion of the London musical
season this year!" All of these words taken together give proof that Dvořák
was stunned by his sudden success. His simple musical soul was not used to
anything like that, and his immediate fame overwhelmed him. He was swept
up by it, but typically for him, he did not forget his relationship to his homeland, nor did he forget his home and family.

These were the years of Dvořák's frequent visits to England, where he
went to conduct his compositions. The cultural society of Europe was well
aware of these trips. Both London newspapers, the *Times* and the *Morning*

Post, praised his conducting highly ("Dvořák is apparently a well-experienced conductor..."). Neither paper knew, however, that Dvořák had never studied conducting at school or anywhere else, and that opportunities for practicing at home were rare.

The press conference after his third concert was successful. An evening reception, organized by the wealthy publisher Henry Littleton, and a huge banquet given by the Philharmonic Society followed. At the latter event, Dvořák made his first short speech in English.

In September of the same year, 1884, he traveled to England a second time. In Worcester he joined in celebrating the eight-hundredth anniversary of the founding of the famous cathedral. He stopped in London first (staying with Littleton) to rehearse his *Stabat Mater* and the Symphony in D Major with the orchestra. Both works were included in the program of the Worcester Festival. Also presented were Beethoven's *Violin Concerto,* Cherubini's *Mass,* Handel's *Messiah*, and cantatas by Bach and Schubert.

"The listeners were electrified," wrote a local newspaper after the performance of the Symphony in D Major, conducted by Dvořák himself. The production of the *Stabat Mater* in the ancient cathedral made an indelible impression.

On his next trip to England, Dvořák was accompanied by the music editor, V. J. Novotny. This visit was also important to Dvořák, but for a different reason. During his sojourn in London, while staying with Littleton, Dvořák became acquainted with Dudley Buck, a composer and conductor from Brooklyn, New York. The American invited him to make a concert tour around the United States. Novotny reported the meeting in these words: "At first Dvořák did not show much enthusiasm for the offer, but then the idea began to appeal to him. If America made the contract attractive enough, the composer would accept."

Eight years were to pass before the tour became a reality. The circumstances of the trip would be quite different from those Dudley Buck had anticipated.

In the fall Dvořák was going to Berlin to conduct in Germany for the first time. On the program were the *Hussite Overture* and his Piano Concerto. He was already at work on yet another symphony (in D minor, Opus 70), the seventh in line, which was intended for England. In the summer the Philharmonic Society appointed him an honorable member, and commissioned him to write a new composition. On New Year's Eve, he wrote to his friend Alois Gobl:

> I have just finished the second movement of my new sym-
> phony, and as usual, I feel happy and contented while I am
> composing. God bless my good fortune; I hope to have the
> same emotions in doing all my future compositions. This is and
> always will be my motto: "God—Love—Homeland!" That and
> only that can bring me to my goal!

When Dvořák went to England the third time (accompanied by his
friend Josef Zubatý) he knew that his success was assured. There was to be a
premiere of his newly finished Symphony in D Minor in Saint James Hall in
London on April 22, 1885. Again came the great celebration and the huge ovations. He stayed a month, and it was indeed a successful visit. *Dalibor* later
published in Czech a column about this concert, based on material from *The
Athenaeum*:

> "[The symphony] does not only and with dignity represent the
> name of its composer, it is also one of the greatest works of its
> kind created in this generation. Dvořák's music is very interest-
> ing to the followers of both schools—the conservatives and the
> progressives. For the first group, it shows the possibility of cre-
> ating a completely new and original work without the necessity
> of separating it from the bounds of form or other artistic rules
> set down in the past by the great masters. On the other hand,
> the devotees of the modern school can appreciate the boldness
> of its harmonies with its rhythmic freedom. Each school found
> in Dvořák's music some aspect of beauty to admire.

After its London premiere, the symphony was produced in the fall of 1885
in Prague. Later it was heard in Vienna, Berlin, Hamburg, and elsewhere. Its
publication by Simrock, however, was attended by difficulties. Dvořák's
English success had increased his confidence, and because Simrock was not
willing to pay him more than 3,000 marks, the composer wrote him,

> I am asking you to consider the fact that you discovered a gold
> mine when you published my *Slavonic Dances*, and don't forget
> you wanted from me no symphonies, no big vocal or instru-
> mental compositions, or dances, and I don't know what else. As
> an artist of my status, I cannot accept your guidance at all!

Simrock agreed on an increase to at least 6,000 marks. But yet another
conflict developed for a different reason. Dvořák had asked that his name be
spelled correctly. He wanted to change his first name on the title page of his
piano sketch from Anton to Antonín or to use the neutral Ant., at least. In

addition, he asked that the title of his work be printed not only in German but also in Czech. Simrock refused. Dvořák's letter to him said, in part:

> Do not ridicule my Czech brothers, and do not feel sorry for me, either. Because of your inability to honor my requests, I must believe that you are refusing me my rights....

Somewhere in this dispute were the beginnings of a separation of the composer from his publisher. Simrock was looking for lively little pieces which could be sold easily. He had no understanding of Dvořák's proud Czech patriotism. Most probably it was the publisher's obtuseness that encouraged the composer, on his return from England for the fourth time, to begin work on his great oratorio *Svata Ludmila (Saint Ludmila)*, with text by Jaroslav Vrchlicky. Let us take a look at that fourth trip to England.

This time he went alone. There was a festival in Birmingham in the summer of 1885. On the musical agenda were Beethoven's Ninth Symphony and the *Leonora* Overture, Handel's *Messiah*, Gounod's Oratorio, and compositions by Wagner and Mendelssohn. Of course, they played Dvořák as well. It was the world premiere of the ballad for soloists, choir, and orchestra, Opus 69, *Svatebni kosile (Wedding Robes)*. The theme, following a dramatic poem from *Kytice (Bouquet of Folk Tales)* by Karel Jaromir Erben, doubtless made an exciting choice. The cantata *The Spectre's Bride*, with its title in English, brought him a gigantic success. Dvořák described it to his friend Zubaty:

> ...a great round of applause first, then becoming increasingly louder and louder until it finally burst into an uproar. Continual cries for Dvořák, without end. The audience and the orchestra shouted with joy. I did not know what was happening to me.

The Spectre's Bride was the second of Dvořák's compositions to take a victorious worldwide route. In addition to being played in London and Nottingham in 1886, it was performed in Milwaukee in the USA as well. Almost at the same time as the festival in Birmingham, the *Stabat Mater* was repeated at Hereford in England, and concerts of Dvořák's work were in preparation in Glasgow and Edinburgh. The Symphony in D Major was rehearsed in Bristol. It must be noted that after the Birmingham Festival, Dvořák was to conduct his Symphony in D Major in London, but he refused. He began to be more conscious of time; he was no longer a composer who would accept with gratitude every invitation. At this time he preferred the little village of Vysoka near Pribram in Bohemia to London. Some may have thought this a strange preference, but it agreed well with the composer's personality. Dvořák liked to go to the estate of his brother-in-law, Count Vaclav Kounic. Surrounded there with wonderful natural scenery, Dvořák's composing progressed very well.

His mind was already occupied with a new composition, the oratorio. Originally, he had wanted to work on the *Svaty Vaclav (Saint Wenceslas)* oratorio or still another oratorio, *Mistr Jan Hus (Master Jan Hus),* but Jaroslav Vrchlicky had sent him a text about the baptism of the Czech prince Borivoj and his wife Ludmila. Thus in September he began an elaboration of this alluring theme. Even though he was a flaming success in England now, he was in a hurry to lock himself in his study in Vysoka, where from the second floor he could observe the countryside and write music. He finished his work in Vysoka at the end of May 1886. Although he was pleased with the news of success accompanying his work abroad (the *Stabat Mater* in Vienna and Australia), he still refused offers to conduct his music at Bremen and Frankfurt-am-Main. He also rejected a request from Leos Janacek to conduct his own symphony at Brno.

In early October of 1886, Dvořák embarked on his fifth journey to England, this time with his wife, Anna. They stayed for some time in London as guests of the Littletons again. The world premiere of the *Saint Ludmila* oratorio was on October 15 in Leeds. The audience came here from many different parts of England according to an item in the *Daily Telegraph.* Many had to travel the whole night to get there. Dvořák wrote home:

> *Saint Ludmila* made a great impression and was the high point of the entire festival. Such a choir and orchestra I have never heard before in England. It was colossal! I am still in a state of the greatest excitement, evoked by this significant production of the 120-piece orchestra, a 350-voice choir, and first-rank soloists, as well as by the magnificent public ovations."

By the end of October, he had again conducted *Saint Ludmila* in London's Saint James' Hall, and at the beginning of November in the Crystal Palace. At the same time, his *Spectre's Bride* was performed in London and Nottingham, always with success and great ovations.

Dvořák's music was played widely now—in Mannheim, Manchester, Vienna, and Budapest. One could continue the list of his successes. The years were flying by, and names of additional cities playing his music appeared. Now it was Zagreb, Berlin several times, Dresden, and Munich. In 1889, a new Symphony in G Major (op. 88, no. 8) appeared, excitingly interesting with its poetic qualities and loveliness. Meanwhile, a new opera, *Jakobin (The Jacobin)* was completed, a work which revived Dvořák's remembrances of childhood in the country. According to his own words, this work was written "for my own pleasure and joy." He also composed the *Requiem;* in March 1890 he went to Moscow, and in April to Petrograd.

On his sixth trip to England, Dvořák conducted his Symphony in G Major in London. Meanwhile, the academic senate of the Czech University decided to grant him an honorary doctorate of philosophy. It was supposed to have been a doctorate in music, but Minister Gautsch in Vienna refused to approve the move. The whole dispute dragged on for several months. A positive decision was reached only when Cambridge University in England nominated him for an honorary doctorate.

At the same time, Dvořák was offered a teaching position at the Conservatory of Prague as professor of composition, instrumentation, theory, and musical form. His decision to accept the offer required considerable thought. The new position would mean a loss of freedom for him. For many years now, Dvořák had lived only for composing; suddenly he was fifty years old and would earn twelve hundred zlatys a year. Would the duties of the new position result in a decrease in his composition? Not at all! He had never learned how to "take it easy," so he wrote and wrote, with the regularity and power of waves beating against the shore.

In the spring of 1891, *Priroda, Zivot, Laska (Nature, Life, Love)*, a cycle of overtures came from his pen. He later renamed these pieces Preludes and changed their individual titles to *V prirode, Karneval, Othello (In Nature's Realm, Carnival*, and *Othello.)* Such program music became for Dvořák a profound statement about his relationship with the world and with life.

Meanwhile he was invited to Cambridge University to be honored with the title of doctor of music. (The minister in Vienna had no power to interfere here). Accompanied by his wife, Dvořák made his seventh trip to England to receive this award of incomparable dignity. Such an honor was accorded to few Europeans, and was an unprecedented honor for the Czech people!

June 16, 1891, was the date fixed for the ceremony. Besides Dvořák, other great men honored with the doctorate honoris causa included the Russian zoologist Ilya Ilich Metchnikov, the English physiologist William Henry Flower, and Indologist Leyell. In place of the traditional dissertation speech, on the eve of this occasion Dvořák conducted his magnificent Symphony in G Major and the *Stabat Mater*. The dean of Cambridge University proclaimed in his ceremonial speech:

Dvořák received an honorary doctorate from Cambridge University in 1891

[P]erceiving the first light of the world somewhere in the remote Czech country and overcoming steep obstacles in his way, he grew tall. He is a genius who has enhanced the reputation of his homeland, showing faithfully what a legacy he inherited from her musical culture.

Listening to these words, Dvořák was silent. He was probably remembering the long journey that had brought him to this point in his life. He listened with pleasure to the word "homeland," repeated many times. He still had no idea of what was awaiting him just beyond the horizon, but he could make a shrewd guess. By the end of spring he had already received an offer from America, which he again refused.

In October 1891, Dvořák was en route to England for the eighth time, to conduct the world premiere of his *Requiem* there. While he was standing on deck, the immense autumn sea around and beneath him, he looked toward the West. The evening sun, disappearing in the waves, drew his thoughts to the distant land of America, a land that knew his music well and had tried to entice him to her shores. What would his answer be?

Journey ⮑ A

T HE FIRST SUGGESTION THAT DVOŘÁK should conduct his music in America came from the Brooklyn composer Dudley Buck, who had met Dvořák in 1884 in London. However, his suggestion was only that, and served to lay the foundation for another later proposal that was clear and concrete.

Let us start from the beginning. In the spring of 1891, Antonín Dvořák received an inquiry from the enterprising Jeanette M. Thurber, founder of the ostentatiously named National Conservatory of Music, about his willingness to accept a position as Director of the National Conservatory in New York City. This request came by way of Mrs. Thurber's secretary, who was then living in Vienna.

The composer's answer was a simple No.

Most people, after such a terse refusal, would have lost hope and ceased negotiations, but not the determined Mrs. Thurber. Jeanette M. Thurber's parents had emigrated from Denmark to America in 1837, but they never forgot Europe, and later sent their daughter to be educated in the Old World. The Parisian atmosphere intensified her love of music, and she dedicated her life to it. After her wedding in 1869, which was for her financially favorable, she could devote her time and energy to the National Conservatory.

Jeanette M. Thurber was a lady of great personal charm; she had many typically American male characteristics, and nothing could stop her once she

Jeanette Meyer Thurber (1852–1940), founder, National Conservatory of Music

embarked on a project. In 1890, when someone described her as "not pretty," she was defended by pianist and writer, James Gibbons Huneker, her one-time secretary and a connoisseur of female beauty. He wrote: "Mrs. Thurber *is* pretty, take my word for it, and girls, *you know* I am a recognized authority!"

Dvořák's fame as one of the greatest living composers in the world made it vitally important for Mrs. Thurber to get Dvořák for her institution. The active Mrs. Thurber wanted the highest possible artistic level of music for her institution, and she concluded that Antonín Dvořák would be the most favorable person for the top position in her school. She hoped that he might establish a classical American music era as well.

The situation for music in America was similar to that in England. Each nation had adequate funds to support music, but unfortunately, each lacked composers of international stature. There was an urgent need in each country to fill this void with someone capable of laying the foundation for a national music. In America, there was a high level of musical performance. American millionaires (later called the American aristocracy by Dvořák) guaranteed financial support of the most prominent organizations, such as the Philharmonic Society of New York.

From its beginning in 1842, the New York Philharmonic Society had tried to maintain high musical standards. In the 1890s the head of the Philharmonic was Anton Seidl, who before his American period had been a close friend of Richard Wagner. There were two other good symphonic orchestras in America — one in Chicago under the leadership of Theodor Thomas, and the other in Boston, conducted by Arthur Nikisch.

Besides the Philharmonic, there was opera in New York City. The Metropolitan Opera Company was founded in 1883, and with its good financial backing was able to present excellent performances of Beethoven's and Wagner's operas in German, Verdi's in Italian, and Bizet's *Carmen* in French. Jeanette Thurber wanted a change. She had asked the opera management to add operas in English to their repertoire, but to no avail. This gave her a good reason for founding her own ensemble, the American Opera Company, later called the National Opera Company. The new group's performances were exclusively in English. About the same time, she made another significant step in the promotion of American music by helping to found a conservatory for young Americans who otherwise would have to travel abroad for musical training.

Her husband, Francis Thurber, eight years her senior, was an interesting man. We may call him a real self-made American. He started his career in 1858 as an errand boy for an import firm in New York. By 1890, he became president of one of the largest wholesale food corporations in America. We can envision the thousands of hours of hard work as well as the ingenuity and dedication that he devoted to this great enterprise. The corporation owned factories and grocery stores in suburban areas, and sold foodstuffs and household supplies in the region. A network of small convenience stores that were owned by the corporation was supplied directly from his factories, and workers in those factories were encouraged to purchase company shares. Always smiling, President Thurber asked the employees to work harder and longer because as shareholders they prospered along with their company. It was also to their advantage to shop only in their own stores and to use their own products exclusively. He made millions this way and soon became one of the richest men in New York. The financial crisis of 1893 caught him unawares and he lost almost everything, but he was not discouraged. He became the oldest law student in America at that time, and completed his studies in 1899, at age fifty-seven. He became one of the foremost lawyers in New York and regained his property.

His wealth enabled his charming wife, Jeanette, to establish the National Opera Company and to hire the famous conductor Theodor Thomas, among others. But sadly, Jeanette—unlike her husband—was not good with figures, and she lost over a half million dollars within two years. She was unable to keep pace with the Metropolitan Opera, and soon had to abandon her opera venture, without much to show for her efforts.

The National Conservatory of America stayed in business, however, and Mrs. Thurber took great pride in the knowledge that none of the other American conservatories could use the word "National" in its title. Although conservatories of music existed in every large American city, the length of study in these private schools was optional, and none offered a systematic course of study over a several-year-long period. Only students from rich families could attend the conservatories, because the fees were quite steep. Even so, the final outcome of their study was usually unsatisfactory.

Jeanette Thurber's actions were more generous and purposeful. Her conservatory was to be well organized. She rented a building on East 17th Street and the first class for vocal instruction was attended by eighty-four pupils. As its reputation grew, the conservatory expanded, and classes in piano, violin, and other instruments were added in rapid succession. Finally, the curriculum offered courses in instrumentation, the study of orchestral instruments, and their optimal use in composition. At the end of the first decade of the conservatory's existence, it had a staff of 57 professors, with a total of 631 full-time students.

Mrs. Thurber was more interested in genuine musical talent than in a student's ability to pay. In her efforts to support music she would often waive fees and tuition. Dvořák admired this trait, recalling that he had been so needy when he was young. Her financial ideas—alien to an American world running after dollars and profits—also attracted the attention of the United States Congress, which awarded her conservatory the sought-after title of "National."

This extraordinary woman understood that the prosperity of the National Conservatory and its leadership in American music could be secured only by an outstanding leader—a musician who was famous in Europe, and accordingly, in the world. From her own experience she knew that the personal approach would be most effective for enticing a famous European musician to come to the National Conservatory, and for that reason she initiated the "Vienna negotiation" with Dvořák.

These negotiations began when her Austrian-born secretary, Adele Margulies, made a visit to her hometown of Vienna. Mrs. Thurber, as president of the National Conservatory of Music, entrusted Adele with a special task: to seek professional advice there as to who might be the most suitable candidate for director of the conservatory. From Paul Stefan we have learned that Miss Margulies' former teacher Anthon Door recommended Dvořák and Jan Sibelius.

Sibelius was twenty-four years younger than Dvořák and just starting on his road to fame. In 1889, he finished his school year in Berlin and went to Vienna, which was then considered a center of musical learning. While studying there with Karl Goldmark and Robert Fuchs, he probably became acquainted with Anthon Door. In 1890, Sebelius returned to Helsinki and composed his first work to receive world recognition, *Kullerwo*.

Mrs. Margulies acknowledged that Sibelius had studied in Vienna and was regarded as a good musician, but it would require an arduous trip to Finland to meet him face to face. On the other hand, Dvořák was already recognized in Europe, so both Mrs. Margulies and Mrs. Thurber decided to concentrate on him.

In her recollection of 1919, *Dvořák, As I Have Known Him,* Mrs. Thurber says clearly, "In 1891 I had the good luck to sign the foremost Czech composer, Antonín Dvořák, for the position of artistic director at the National Conservatory." She had visited Paris in 1891 and from there asked the composer to consider her offer.

Antonín Dvořák's father wrote in a letter to his daughter on June 21, 1891, that Anton

> has received a telegram from Paris, asking him to accept a position as director of the National Conservatory in New York, which is in America. I believe that he is not going to accept that job, because as a good Czech and patriot he knows well how hard it would be for the Czech nation to lose him.

The content of Mrs. Thurber's telegram to Dvořák had been: "Would you accept position Director National Conservatory of Music, New York City, October 1892 also lead six concerts of your works?"

Dvořák's surprise at this offer is revealed in a letter to his friend Alois Gobl, written immediately after his return from Cambridge on June 20, 1891:

I am supposed to go to America for two years! I would be director of a conservatory and conduct ten concerts of my compositions there. I am offered $15,000, which is 30,000 zl. net annual income for eight months' work with four months' break. Should I accept? Drop me a line. I must wait with my decision until my meeting with Dr. Tragy. Write me at Vysoka, where I am going with the family next Monday. Kissing you all in Sychrov, with my respect and best regards,

Yours, Antonín Dvořák

This is the first known mention in the composer's correspondence about the American proposition he had received.

It is understandable that he had to delay his decision because of Dr. Tragy. During the school year 1889–1890, the organ school was finally united with the Prague Conservatory. Dr. Josef Tragy, a Prague lawyer, the president of the juristic chamber, a musical enthusiast, and an amateur composer, was then the director of the Prague Conservatory. Dvořák, wanting to have all his time exclusively for composition, had refused the first Prague Conservatory offer to teach composition and instrumentation. Dr. Tragy, knowing well the real value of having Dvořák at the Conservatory, continued in his psychological campaign until he succeeded. At the board meeting of the Association for Promotion of Music in Bohemia in October 1890, Dr. Tragy could announce that Dvořák had finally agreed to accept the position of professor of composition, instrumentation, and musical form, starting January 1, 1891.

This news was received with great pleasure. The stipulations of this agreement were good: Dvořák would teach seven to eight months a year between October and April or May. His salary was set at 1,200 zlatys per year, or 100 zlatys monthly. (We may recall that he was paid 18 zlatys per month as the violist in the Provincial Theatre orchestra.)

Dvořák began his duties at the Prague Conservatory in January 1891. Mrs. Thurber's offer came shortly afterwards. Dvořák felt that an application for a leave of absence at that time would be judged as improper conduct. It would be different if he had already worked for a year or two, but after coming in January, could he leave in June?

It was a delicate situation for him, complicated by the fact that there were some good pupils in Dvořák's grade-three composition class. Among them were Josef Suk, Oskar Nedbal, Otto Berger (the first violoncellist of the Czech Quartet), Julius Fucik, and later, Vitezslav Novak and several other talented students. Besides, he did not want to be in America as just some kind of decorative prop, using his European reputation for his own benefit. That was not in Dvořák's character. On the contrary, once a work was undertaken, he always fulfilled it with great responsibility and in good conscience.

Because Dvořák lived only for music, he did not mind the time scheduled for lessons. He did not like to waste time, and he taught his students the same kind of attitude. The breadth of his experience impressed everybody. He was strict and obstinate, and he demanded creativity in assignments. Suk stated and Novak agreed: "Sometimes I feel so much pressure that I want to cry, but we're learning a lot."

Dvořák set down the rule in his classes: "Everybody should make an effort to write something new. Any composer who is unable to create original work, cannot be genuine."

We can see now a paradoxical aspect to this situation: On the one hand, he had not sought this position at the Prague Conservatory, but now that he had it, he tackled the work with genuine enthusiasm, typical for him. He enjoyed a pleasant association with the young talents. He wondered, Would it be possible to leave everything here for a distant land beyond the immense ocean? Few artists have loved the Czech landscape as he did, and his identity with his country was always strong. Could he say farewell to everything and go to the other side of the globe? After just a few days in England, he was always pleased to come home to his Vysoka.... Now, he might not be able to see it any more for the next two years! Could he survive it all?

His beloved Vysoka!

This estate had been purchased in 1873 by Count Vaclav Kounic, Dvořák's brother-in-law.

Kounic was an interesting man. Marie Cervinkova-Riegrova, Dvořák's early librettist, wrote about him: "He is a good-hearted man, with a sense of humor. There might be traces of adventurous French nature in his character, but the mode of his behavior is decidedly good." In the 1880s, Kounic became a delegate to the Viennese Parliament, where he espoused radical political views. He fearlessly maintained a defense of Czech rights better than most of his fellow delegates ever could.

Kounic held Dvořák in high esteem. In his manuscript, "The History of Music," which Kounic starts from the fourteenth century, there is a list of Czech composers, which includes Dvořák's short biography. Kounic concludes: "He is one of the greatest composers of our time."

It was with great pleasure that Dvořák had first accepted Kounic's offer to spend a summer in Vysoka. For the first time, he lived with his family in a so-called *Dvorek* (farmstead), several hundred meters distant from a castle, sit-

Count Václáv Kounic, Dvořák's brother-in-law

uated on a meadow in the middle of a forest. There were three buildings, all occupied by employees of the castle, among whom was Dvořák's brother-in-law Jan Hertan, married to Klotilda, Josefa's and Anna's youngest sister in the family of eight Cermak children.

The Dvořáks stayed at *Dvorek* from spring to fall. Antonín loved the direct contact with nature, and was happy there. In only twenty steps he could reach the forest and a romantic little lake, hidden in the woods. The little islands with their trees, the gentle rustle of reeds, and birds singing from dawn till eve, all made a perfect setting to imagine water sprites and nymphs. Nature was such an infinite source of inspiration that Dvořák liked to compose right there, on that enchanted spot. He felt as if he could stay there until he died.

At first, there was room enough for Antonín and Anna, with their one little daughter, Otilka, but gradually the situation changed. The family enlarged with the births of daughter Anna in 1880, then Magdalena in 1881, and life went on. In the winter of 1884, after Dvořák had received a decent payment from Simrock for his piano cycle *Ze Sumavy (From the Bohmerwald)* and for *The Hussite,* he sought Kounic's advice about finding better living arrangements for his family.

Kounic suggested that Dvořák buy something in the same establishment, which consisted of several buildings, but Dvořák could not find there enough of the peace and quiet he so needed for his work.

"And what about *Spejchar* (the Granary)?" asked Kounic.

Dvořák probably considered the idea.

"The Granary?" he asked in surprise.

"Yes, the one on the other side of the village, called *Ovcinec* (Sheepfold). I can sell it to you quite cheap. After all, we are relatives."

Josefa (Josefina) recorded in her memoirs that Dvořák secretly called Kounic *groficek,* the nick-name for count. It was an appropriate and familiar term for him.

As always, Dvořák probably took some time to think it over.

"— if it will not cost too much."

Dvořák's daughters Otilia, *l.,* Magda and Anna, *r.*

Kounic probably laughed: "Not at all!"

A long time before, there used to be a sheepfold alongside, but at the time of the transaction it was in a state of disrepair. Dvořák bought the Granary with its surrounding property, and the masonry from the sheepfold was used to build a little ground-floor house just at the entry of the estate. The house was used by Mr. Hodik, a former miner, who came there to serve as Dvořák's custodian and general handyman. "As a matter of fact," recalled the composer's son Otakar, "Hodik was a great amateur gardener, and being a miner, he had the strength to carry out any task, so he had accepted his new position of custodian with pleasure."

The deal was closed in the summer of 1884. In a diary, preserved among other things in Kounic's bequest, we can see a note written in French, and next to it the date of August 1: "Ovcin sold to Dvořák, Pribram."

A record of the sale (no. 12335) is still kept in the city of Pribram. It has five items, and in the introduction states:

> Today, in the year below, we declare that this contract between two sides, Mr. Judr. Vaclav, count from Kounice at Vysoka, county Pribram, as a seller on one side, and Mr. Antonín Dvořák, music composer from Prague, Zitna ul., no. 10, as a purchaser on the second side, was signed of their own will and cannot be annulled...."

A description of the two-story house and the size of the property belonging to it follows:

> 1 acre and 364 cords of garden and pasture, which is less than three quarters of 1 hectare, exactly 7,063 m2 [square meters]. The total price of this deed is 2,000 zl. in Austrian funds, verbally two thousand zlatys, reciprocally agreed upon in this contract.

Extensive renovations of the property were undertaken by the composer immediately after the purchase, which included restoration of the garden, surrounded by a high masonry wall.

Otakar Dvořák recorded that his father

> had divided the garden into two parts. The upper part, with the newly renovated dwelling, was changed into an English park with ornamental trees. Near the center of the park was a high projecting rock, which was broken up into pieces to be used for a raised circle. Its top was covered with soil, and several steps on

the south side were added to a platform on its surface. In the center of it, father placed a pavilion made of birch wood.

This became the famous pavilion where many guests from Prague, from abroad, and from the whole world sat to converse. In the middle was a table made of a tree stump fitted with legs. On its top even today we can recognize traces of initials carved by guests: O. N. (Oskar Nedbal), J. S. (Josef Suk), H. P. H. (Hopkins), J. N. (Novotny), and others. Near the pavilion father planted rare conifers and foliage trees.... [H]e also planted fruit trees in the lower garden.

The name Vysoka (Highland) came from the elevated plane it was built on. My father liked his walks there, especially during the sunny days. Awarded with a spectacular view of a vast landscape, he observed the clean outlines of the Sumava mountains (Bohmerwald) above the horizon. Quite often he could see Mount Boubin from his studio window.

The serenity of this landscape gave Dvořák great tranquillity. He loved it passionately. From every journey and every corner of the world he rushed back to Vysoka after one day in Prague. How could he leave this place? In the same year of the purchase he wrote from Vysoka to his publisher, Simrock: "For a few days again, I can be in my magnificent forest and experience the most splendid days and wonderful weather. Again and again I must marvel at the enchanting songs of the birds." More superlatives in other letters, show his admiration for his beloved refuge.

The American offer was financially advantageous and even outstanding, but first, he must verify all the details of the contract. From his childhood he had learned well the value of each small groschen. Although he was no longer poor, he had become a good manager, and he never wasted money. For instance, in the spring of 1891 he wrote to Jan Hodik:

> We just received a letter from the Kovars. They mentioned that Vaclav Fencl would like to have my winter coat. Since it is still in good condition, I could sell it to him for 9 zlatys. However, he does not have to pay me in money; I can deduct it from his wages as our gardener. Let me know if he still wants it."

The garden in Vysoka was Dvořák's true love. He knew the Fencl family well. Almost every evening he went to Fencl's inn to drink his mug of beer, to talk, and to play cards with the neighbors. On Sundays and holidays he went to the nearby village of Trebsko to play on an old organ in the chancel of the church. He liked to lead the people in religious songs, and the villagers in the

Backyard of Dvořák's summer estate in Vysoka at Pribram

pews enjoyed these precious moments of his presence. The melodies penetrated through the church windows and could be heard over and beyond the
village green.

In a good mood after the service, he would be invited by the school
teacher, Augustin Forbelka, to visit the village inn for a glass of beer and a
game of cards. Dvořák did not like to lose in a card game, and when he did,
he could quickly change from a cheerful player into a grumbler. He passionately preferred Darda to all other games. It was a demanding card game, and
one must be quite bright and good in figures to win. Every card was worth a
different number of points, and when Dvořák received three cards in a row of
the same color, his face brightened; he had Darda and scored 20. With good
luck he got four cards, and this meant 50. What about five cards? In this case,
he laughed like a little boy. This kind of good fortune was called *fus*, and the
player who got it usually won outright.

Do they play Darda in America? wondered Dvořák, while feeding his
pigeons in the backyard at Vysoka. Pigeons were another of Dvořák's hobbies, which he loved and enjoyed tremendously. He had built a pigeon cote
just above the annex at the side of the house. Mr. Hodik was given ninety-
nine suggestions on how to care for them, what to feed them, and how
much. It was almost a science to be learned. "…and watch out for children;
they might hurt the birds," Dvořák would warn.

Sons Antonín, *l.,* and Otakar Dvořák, *r.*

Most of all Dvořák worried about what to do with his children if he accepted Mrs. Thurber's offer. At that time the Dvořáks had six healthy children of whom they were very fond: Otilie, Anna, Magdalena, Antonín, Otakar, and Aloisie. In 1891, when the American contract was negotiated, the oldest was thirteen and the youngest only three. How could they possibly go away from home with such a small child?

Sometimes he thought it would not be possible to go and he wanted to forget about it, but his practical wife, Anna, could talk of nothing else. Eventually, it was she who mailed the final contract back to Mrs. Thurber. The composer told about his indecision in a letter to his friend Gobl on August 1, 1891:

> Most probably, you would like to know why I have taken so long to answer your letter! I wanted to enjoy every moment of my short visit to Vysoka, and therefore, while leaving my pen dry, I walked in the fields, took delight in our garden, and played with the pigeons for a whole day.

Indeed, his pen had stayed on his desk all day. Instead of writing, he stayed at the window to observe his beloved landscape. The distant horizon, bluish with mountains and hills, stood silent. He was still undecided. The letter continues:

> Now, something about America. I received a copy of the contract yesterday. It is an extensive document, and I do not know yet if I will sign it. It seems that I would teach three periods per day—composition and instrumentation. My duties include the rehearsal and production of four conservatory concerts performed by the students in an eight-month period, plus six concerts of my works in different American cities. Included would be mainly the *Stabat Mater, Spectre's Bride, St. Ludmila, Requiem*, symphonies, overtures, et cetera.
>
> For all this work I will be paid $15,000 per year, which in our currency represents 35,000 zlatys. Half of my salary will be deposited in Prague before my departure; the rest of it will be paid to me in advance at the beginning of each month. There is one more problem: I want to get another $7,500 before the end of May 1893. This would give me a chance to spend my vacation in Bohemia from June until the middle of September. I am going to accept the contract if they will meet my conditions. It is not too good what people are saying about America, but as far as we know, there are always people for and against her

everywhere in the world. However, I can go there myself and see it with my own eyes.

This week I am going to Susice to see Prof. Kopta because he lived in America for a long time. He knows it well and his wife was born there. They will be my best source of information to tell me more about life in America. I do not know if I will be able to come to see you, too. In any case I might drop by during October, after my return from England, and then we will have a good talk.

Dvořák was well aware of the financial advantages this contract would give him. In New York he would get the equivalent of 97 zlatys every day, which was almost his monthly salary in Prague. Without a doubt, Francis Thurber was a generous man, and his wife Jeanette desperately wanted to win for her conservatory this unusual man who was worshiped in England and all over Europe. It was a royal salary, and never before in Bohemia had anybody been paid so well. Not one governor of His Majesty's court could command an official income to equal Dvořák's offer from New York.

No matter how good it looked, Dvořák still hesitated. What if there were hidden loopholes in the contract? He still wanted to discuss it with Kopta, who would tell him the truth. They had known each other from the time they played as young men in the orchestra of the Provisional Theatre. An interesting article appeared in *Dalibor* on October 3, 1891, which explains what happened during Dvořák's visit with Kopta:

Vaclav Kopta

Flora P. Kopta

The writer, Mrs. Kopta, wife of Prof. Kopta from Podmoky at Susice, wrote for the Czech-American journal *Jonas's Slavia* on August 12, 1891:

It might interest you that a week ago we had as visitors Dr. Antonín Dvořák, the music composer, and his wife. Dr. Dvořák is an old friend of my husband, and he brought with him a contract written in English which he could not fully understand. The contract has not been signed yet, and Dr. Dvořák wished me to make a small change in his name, which I did.

I feel it is my obligation to inform you about a few things which might interest the *Slavia*'s readers. Dr. Dvořák holds an 'honoris causa' doctor's degree given to him by Cambridge University in England. He has been offered a position as director of the National Conservatory of Music in New York, in America, with a salary of $15,000 annually for teaching four periods a day for two years. He would start the job on September 28, 1892. Nothing can be certain in this world, but it seems that only a few insignificant changes need to be made in this contract before it is approved. It might indeed happen that my husband too will accept a job as a professor at the same institute in New York.

During his visit Dr. Dvořák mentioned that he intends to set Erben's *Zlaty Kolovrat (The Golden Spinning-Wheel)* in the same manner as he did *The Spectre's Bride* for a musical festival in Birmingham. It has six sections, and I can send you my translation of this poem later.

I believe that all this might be really interesting for American Czechs.

This news was important, and it offers us several bits of information. First, it does confirm the composer's visit with the Koptas and his need to get an exact translation of his contract. Mrs. F. P. Kopta wrote and published her article for the journal *Slavia*, which was read by Americans of Czech descent, and she had sent a copy to the Prague journal *Dalibor*. Understandably, the news that Dvořák had accepted a position in America came out in the next edition.

It is obvious that the composer analyzed carefully what he was signing, and only after the "insignificant" changes had been made, did he accept the offer.

The truth is that Dvořák was very particular in checking the offer. A letter to Mr. August Bohdansky, director of the Cimelice estate, gives evidence that every detail of his contract had to be absolutely clear, comprehensive, and to the point:

> First of all, I would like to thank you for your kind delivery of the feed supply for my pigeons. They relish it with a great appetite! Yesterday, I mailed to London my third revised contract. If my recent revision is approved, I will sign it. There is great speculation in the American press about my arrival, which promises all manner of things from my artistic activity. All this shows that my arrival there will cause quite a commotion. I heard also that the Czech-Americans can hardly wait for my arrival.

We do not know every detail of the contract, which ultimately had four versions. Obviously, Dvořák finally overcame his doubts and accepted the position.

It was said that Dvořák had met Mrs. Thurber during his stay in London. Confirmation is included in a review written for the *New York Herald* on Sunday, December 17, 1893, after the premiere of the Symphony *From the New World*. The article was titled "Dvořák's Symphony a Historic Event." It states, in part:

> Two years ago, Mrs. Thurber telegraphed to a friend in Vienna asking whether Dr. Dvořák would accept the post of director of the National Conservatory of Music. Her friend replied that it was out of the question. Thurber later on visited Paris, and again tried to reach the Bohemian composer through an intermediary. Dr. Dvořák was then director of the celebrated conservatory at Prague. Failing in this effort, Mrs. Thurber telegraphed directly to the composer, who replied that he would meet her in London, where he was going to conduct the initial production of his requiem mass. A few weeks after this, Dr. Dvořák talked the matter over with her and agreed to come to New York as Director of the National Conservatory at a salary of $15,000 a year.

This information is not entirely correct and can be used only with caution. Dvořák was not the director at that time, but rather a professor at the Prague Conservatory. We also cannot verify his answer to Mrs. Thurber that he would meet her in London. However, it might be true, except that the premiere of the *Requiem* took place in Birmingham on October 9, 1891. This means that he met her later, in October. Another error is that Dvořák agreed to accept her offer. His definitive agreement was still far away. Other negotiations were necessary, and not before the end of October had Dvořák sent the third version of the contract to Littleton, who functioned as their mediator.

The publisher Simrock, from whom Dvořák had been estranged for some time because of their disagreement, was curious to know what was going on, and he wrote to Dvořák in November 1891:

> Have you already been to America? Are you going there later or are you entirely dead? Why do I not hear from you any more? Are you not writing something that your German publisher could print?

Dvořák's answer of November 22 was clever:

> Thank God, I am well and working as usual very hard.... My negotiation with America is still going on, but very soon it will be decided whether I go or not.

Only a few days later Dvořák confided to his friend Gobl:

> Simrock would like to get something from me again. However, he must wait and taste the bitterness of my revenge. Since his fees are not good, I am not going to give him any of my overtures: *In Nature's Realm, Carnival, Othello* not even one of the *Dumkas*. He is not going to take advantage of me any more.

The final contract between the New York Conservatory and Dvořák was probably signed in December 1891 or at the beginning of 1892, because at the end of November Dvořák wrote that his "thing with America was still in progress," and in January 1892, he began his tour across Bohemia and Moravia as a "farewell before his journey to America." This tour expressed Dvořák's feelings for his native country, although it became a demanding and exhausting affair. The idea for it had come from Velebin Urbanek, brother of the renowned music publisher. Although he alone had organized the tour, he could count on Dvořák's established popularity to assure its artistic and financial success. He chose to feature only Dvořák compositions.

The tour began on January 3, 1892, and ended May 29. Professor Ferdinand Lachner and Hanus Wihan, friends of Urbanek, accompanied the group, and they visited more than forty Bohemian and Moravian cities while covering thousands of kilometers.

It proved to be a triumphant journey. Dvořák's friends and admirers came to say farewell and wish him a successful journey to America—a country in sharp contrast to Europe—the country of endless opportunity, liberty, and freedom. The Czechs looked upon the American continent with a certain amount of envy because their long fight for equal rights within the Austrian Empire had not yet been successful. Every year thousands of emigrants left their homeland to find better jobs and freedom of speech in the New World. At least one Czech poet, Josef Vaclav Sladek, had evaded the Austrian police by fleeing to America. But Dvořák was not one of these refugees; he had already become a world-famous composer and was going to America to present aspects of Bohemian culture from his politically humiliated nation.

In the summer of 1892 he received a letter from Mrs. Thurber with all the plans for his departure. She had already booked their cabins on the *Saale*, which would sail from Bremen, Germany. Dvořák's wife, Anna, and the two oldest children—Otilka, 14, and Antonin, 9—were going with him.

Final plans had been made—Dvořák wrote to several of his friends that he was leaving on Saturday, September 17, on the *Saale* and hoped to be in New York on September 23. He said that his first concert would be in the Metropolitan Opera House in New York on October 12—Columbus Day in the United States—and that at Mrs. Thurber's request he had written a cantata for the occasion—*Te Deum Laudamus*.

Mrs. Thurber had wanted him to use the text of an English poem, "The American Flag," written early in the nineteenth century by the poet Joseph Rodman Drake. The clear message of the poem mirrors the patriotic mood of the United States after the Revolutionary War against England. The starry flag was gradually hoisted to flutter over the immense land as a symbol of the New World.

Unfortunately, the text was sent first to Littleton, who then had to deliver it to Dvořák, and he received it too late to compose a suitable cantata for the first American performance. He explained this in a letter to Mrs. Thurber on July 28:"It is absolutely impossible for me to accomplish a work of half-an-hour's length before October."

He did promise to work on it in New York. Perhaps it all worked for the best because his using a Latin text for the *Te Deum* helped him overcome the language barrier of his first American performance. He actually found time to start the patriotic work before he left Prague, and he had a sketch of it done when he got to New York.

One of his last duties before he left Prague was to write a letter to the director of the National Theatre, Franz Schubert:

> Before I leave, I would like to ask you to allow my children to
> use our theatre tickets during my absence.
>
> Antonín Dvořák, Prague, Sept. 15, 1892.

Dvořák's American secretary, Josef Kovarik

Besides his wife and the two oldest children, Dvořák was accompanied by a hardworking, faithful, and devoted young man, Joseph Kovarik. We quote from Kovarik's memoir:

> I met Mr. Dvořák during my study at the Conservatory in Prague, which I finished in 1892. I went there from Spillville, Iowa, my birthplace in America.
>
> After my graduation I mentioned to Mr. Dvořák that very soon I would be going home. The Master said simply: "Fine. Suppose you stay here until September, and then we will go to America together." The Master cut short my objection of, "What am I going to do in Bohemia for two months before we leave?" by saying: "You will spend your vacation with us in Vysoka, and afterwards, in the fall, we will sail to America together." Everything happened as planned.

We have a better description of this event, written with dramatic flavor as a story, by Kovarik himself, in a book entitled *Music in Spillville*:

> In 1888 Kovarik started his study at the Conservatory in Prague, which was already well known for its excellent musical education. While strolling through the ancient city, he often wished to meet Antonín Dvořák, who was honored and respected in America as well as in Europe. This did not happen to him on the streets of Prague but it became a reality on another lucky occasion.
>
> Every Monday Kovarik used to go to Urbanek's Music Shop where the Prague musicians liked to gather. Kovarik usually sat in a corner, hidden behind a huge Czech newspaper which was published in Chicago. One Monday, there was a great commotion in the store, and he noticed a respectable, dark-looking man with piercing eyes just entering the shop. Dvořák! Dvořák had just returned from his summer estate at Vysoka to make preparations for his departure to America....
>
> Somebody in the shop pointed in Kovarik's direction, saying: "Behind that paper is a real American!" Dvořák ran directly to Kovarik, grabbed the newspapers from his hands, and said gruffly: "O.K., Red Face, can you speak English?" Kovarik's friends usually described Dvořák as "a bear" or "'whimsical fellow."
>
> After this incident in the shop, Kovarik's idea about him agreed with theirs: "He is quite a queer person." However, when Dvořák asked him to walk home with him, Josef was glad

to go along. Soon Dvořák became fond of this well-balanced, modest young American with whom he could speak English and learn all about American life. In a short time he became indispensible to him. Dvořák, the musical genius, was in many ways like a child.

These two, Dvořák and Kovarik, worked together for almost three years, and this arrangement proved beneficial for both musicians. Kovarik recorded Dvořák's last few weeks in Bohemia and described their journey to the New World, as well:

> Life in Vysoka had a fixed schedule set up by Dvořák from his experience on previous stays. That summer, he was especially industrious. First it was his *Te Deum,* to be finished for its premiere in New York, and when the English poem "The American Flag" finally arrived, he started to work on that cantata as well. The sketches of it were completed before his journey to America.
>
> However, life in Vysoka was quite colorful since the two young composers, Oskar Nedbal and Josef Suk, came to visit and work on scoring for piano several of the Master's compositions. Nedbal, always ready to play tricks, sometimes made Dvořák really angry. "One day, I was playing hide-and-seek with the children, and in the excitement of the game, I got near Dvořák's pigeons which he was feeding. Birds soared and flew up above Dvořák's head. No rough stuff around his pigeons! I was driven off with a few choice epithets — it is difficult for me to figure out where he learned such strong language.

The time for departure was getting short. It was on a Saturday, according to Kovarik, September 10, 1892, when Dvořák said good-bye to his four younger children, and with his wife, daughter Otilie, and son Tonik, started their long journey. Kovarik was the fifth member of Dvořák's group. He was anxious to be in Spillville soon because he had not seen his family since 1888. He did not know how long it would be before he could return there. He remembered:

> On Thursday, Sept. 15 at 3:00 P.M., the Master and his group left Prague. Saying farewell to his friends and admirers, he promised: "See you next summer!"

Kovarik continued:

On Friday we reached Bremen, and on Saturday we boarded
our steamboat *Saale*. The ship left at 1:00 P.M., and on Sunday,
at 5:00 P.M., we reached Southampton, England. The Master
sent a telegram to his children in Prague: "Everything O.K. —
everybody healthy."

Their journey overseas took nine days, and in spite of three
stormy days at the beginning which forced everybody except
the Master back to their cabins, the sea voyage was quite pleasant. The Master was an excellent sailor. Not even the worst
storm could stop him from walking on deck. Sometimes he was
the only passenger who was able to join the captain in the
dining room. After the meal, they smoked cigars and talked. I
believe that our ship cast anchor in the Port of New York on
September 26, at six o' clock in the evening....

Journey ⤳ B

MAGIC MOMENTS IN VYSOKA VANISHED with the sunset, and the electric light gave a new dimension to every object in the room. This would be a good time to search for traces of Dvořák's experiences, enthusiasms, ideas, and disappointments. It would be valuable to find documentary materials and to get the feeling of the atmosphere toward the end of the last century. Later, it might be possible to sit in Dvořák's study in the New York City apartment, walk through Spillville, and spend a few peaceful moments on the banks of the Turkey River. There must be some documents to seek out in American archives and libraries. I was inundated with ideas for work and research in the days following. I realized how much more remained to be learned.

My search in Kounic's archives was fruitful. I found albums of actors, writers, and politicians as well as Dvořák's little box with dozens of photographs, some of them not yet published. There were pictures of the children—little Otakar, Tony (Tonik), the three daughters, Otilka, Anna, and Magda; Dvořák in his ceremonial Cambridge University doctoral robe; Dvořák as a housekeeper wearing a cap; Dvořák with children, lying down in the grass; and a last picture of Dvořák that showed the tired, aged composer leaning against a chair in the garden at Vysoka. There were pictures of Count Kounic and his wife, Josefina, along with their diaries.

The search through the archives also produced a detailed biography written by Vaclav Kopta near the end of his life. He had studied at the Prague Conservatory, and later wrote:

> [I]n the fourth year of my study, I was privileged to know the best Bohemian composers, Bedrich Smetana, Antonín Dvořák, Zdenek Fibich and Karel Bendl. With permission of the Institute authorities, I played as a conservatory student in the orchestra of the Czech Provisional Theatre at the second desk of the first violin section.

Dvořák at that time played in the same orchestra, and they became colleagues and friends. In 1866, Kopta went to America and gained fame and success as a violin virtuoso in concerts throughout the country. He accepted a position as professor at the Philadelphia Conservatory. There he met his future wife, Flora Pauline Wilson, an American who was related to the future President Wilson. After their wedding in 1872, the Koptas returned to Bohemia. While he was performing in Europe, Kopta had bought an estate in Podmoky near Susice in South Bohemia. Dvořák went there to consult with them about his post in America. (Flora Pauline was encouraged by her husband to become a translator from Czech to English. She translated poetry mostly, and among other poems, there was a series of ballads written by Czech poets. Although her book was printed in Bohemia, the whole edition had to be sent to America before an Austrian censorship order for confiscation could be issued.)

I do not know what kind of advice Dvořák received from the Koptas. I suppose that Flora Pauline carefully and accurately translated the contract, and supplemented it with all the additional details suggested by Dvořák. Since their diaries were not preserved, I could only get information from the articles in the paper, for example in the journal *Uhlavan*, vol. 1, no. 13, August 8, 1891:

> Dr. Dvořák in Susice,
>
> The Thursday afternoon train brought to Susice our foremost musical composer, Antonín Dvořák. From here, he went to Podmoky to visit Prof. V. Kopta. As soon as the news about his visit reached Susice, a friendly welcome was organized for him. City Mayor Mr. K. F. Uhl, with a deputation of patriotic ladies, the Citizens' Club, the St. Vaclav Choir Association, and students came to meet him.

There is no mention of a discussion with the Koptas, and without Flora's article reprinted in *Dalibor* we would know nothing about the event. Indeed, on August 5 an important matter was dealt with in the little village of Podmoky in the Bohmerwald. This matter concerned the true origin of Dvořák's Symphony *From the New World*. It would eventually be written on the other side of the world in the middle of a human anthill, in an ordinary, narrow two-story house on 17th Street in New York City. This symphony would win the world, but who could have foreseen it then?

The Dvořáks were probably entertained with desserts, wine, maybe coffee. Professor Kopta must have talked about America and life at the conservatories while Flora Pauline was bent over the text of the contract, reading it word for word. Dvořák listened attentively, his wide-set, restless eyes wandering from face to face. When he said good-bye to the Koptas a few days later, he still was not convinced to go to America. His inner turmoil had not left him.

Dvořák's grandson once loaned me some unpublished memoirs of his father Otakar which described the period of Dvořák's life at the end of 1891. Otakar wrote:

> I can remember the stubbornness with which my father reacted to the offer. He proclaimed with certainty that not even twice the money could move him to go. Indeed, he rejected it from the very first. Nevertheless, the persistent Mrs. Thurber requested the signing of a contract, and again raised his salary. He had explained with his original rejection that he would lack time for his own composition. She promptly reduced his responsibilities and increased his income.
>
> My father was not too impressed by the salary which he felt was bigger than necessary for maintaining a good living. His ideas of income were that no man should be paid disproportionately to the work he did. This idea had been demonstrated when he was a young man composing continually without any hope for financial reward. My mother, the better financial manager in our family, in a desire to increase our standard of living, urged father to accept the improved offer from New York. I can remember her presiding over a discussion about the American journey at the table in the presence of all eight of us. Father patiently agreed that we children could vote on it too.
>
> Although a few of us disagreed, the majority voted for the trip. The contract was on the table in father's study just ready to be signed. After the vote we interrupted our dinner, and mother

grabbed father's hand to escort him to his room. There she pressed a pen into his hand, forcing him to sign. After their return to the table, father remarked (to his own satisfaction and those who had voted against the trip) that the signing of a contract does not mean anything definitive, at least not while the contract was kept at home. My mother dismissed this argument, hid the contract, and then, on her own, mailed it. This meant that the journey to America was definitely settled.

This remembrance of Dvořák's son Otakar enables us to look deeply into the working of Dvořák's family. The father, an inspired musician who lived first and foremost for music and his work, depended on his wife when it came to other responsibilities. She had to take care of everything: feed the family (an important task at the beginning of Dvořák's career), and provide the comfortable, peaceful atmosphere in their home so much needed for a composer's creative work. This was no easy task for her, but Anna was equal to it.

Otakar's memoirs are a trustworthy source of information, and one can find in them many similar moments when the mother's intervention was necessary. It is well known that the third Dvořák hobby (besides Darda and pigeons) was engines. Very early in the morning he would walk to the Franz Joseph railway station to examine those miracles of technology. He knew personally many engineers, and it is said that he even proclaimed: "I would give all my symphonies away for the chance to invent an engine...."

Otakar recorded:

> My father was not fond of writing letters, and therefore he stayed in touch only with his closest friends. Of course, amongst them were the engineers. I can remember that my mother had once insisted that he answer Simrock who was waiting impatiently for a letter. Never in my life had I known my father to lie; however this time he told my mother that his letter was finished and sealed in an envelope, only lacking the address. After my father left for the cafe, mother hurried to add the address, and she mailed the letter to Simrock. Later on, when father tried to find the letter on his desk, he had to ask mother for help. She simply said that she had addressed and mailed it. Now, my father had to tell her the truth. He had not intended to send this letter to Simrock but had written it to one of his friends, an engineer.

There are two things to be deduced from Otakar's memoirs: First, that Anna, when having a goal in mind, influenced Dvořák's decisions in practical life; and second, that an accurate account of Dvořák's life in America can be learned from the contents of his correspondence, at least the fundamental part of it—what he wrote, and who wrote him back.

How to start? In 1981 an extensive work *The Inventory of the Antonín Dvořák Foundation* was published by an employee of the Museum of Czech Music. In the introduction it is stated that

> The Antonín Dvořák Foundation includes three units:
>
> 1. The property, acquired on May 30, 1980
> 2. The materials from the former music department of the National Museum
> 3. The materials from the former Museum of Antonín Dvořák
>
> The foundation includes a total of 1,769 inventory units, deposited in the safes of the Czech State Bank in 34 bound sets, 24 semi-leather albums, and 24 bound sets of atypical formats, deposited individually.

It would be a formidable task to examine and analyze more than one thousand seven hundred inventory units (the official term for all the materials, letters, and scores). Such an analysis could become quite a useful tool for musicologists, researchers, and writers, too.

My search took me to an ancient museum building, surrounded by the romantic Mala Strana (old Prague town quarter). I parked just in the front of the house where Beethoven had once lived. First, I had to fill in the application and present a statement from the Czechoslovakian Writers Union showing their approval of my plan. In one room were big tables with little lamps; along the wall were shelves with music reference books.

The silence and peace here were typical of this almost forgotten world. While I studied the chief characteristics of each item included in the inventory catalogue, I made my notes. The list of materials necessary for my study was slowly expanding.... Some items were already awakening my curiosity. For example, inventory no. 1,298, a letter of Josef Kovarik (a relative of Josef J. Kovarik) to his brother Karel inquiring about the possibilities of renting an apartment for Dvořák. The letter is dated "Chicago, January 23, 1892" and was written immediately after the composer had signed Mrs. Thurber's contract. It says:

Dear Karel!

Thank you for answering my letter. As soon as I received your information, I wrote to New York in order to find out more about the matter. I just received the answer and am sending it on to you.

The prices and methods of renting apartments are different from those in Europe. It is possible to rent either a whole house priced according to size, an individual floor of the house with a private entrance, or an apartment, as found in European cities.

It will be the best for Dr. Dvořák, I think, to rent one individual floor which usually has 4 to 7 rooms. In his case it would be no problem to rent a five-room apartment with private entrance, completely furnished. Such an accommodation costs $25 to $45, depending on the area in which it is located. There are streets in New York where only millionaires live; there are also streets for people worth $100,000 or less; and then you see sections so impoverished and dirty that in comparison, the Jewish ghetto in Bohemia seems to be paradise. The property in wealthy areas is three times more expensive, so one must pay higher rent. A narrow-minded spirit of caste puts rich man beside rich and poor man beside poor. One street is splendid, looking clean and wealthy, and sometimes another one nearby is very poor and dirty. Most often, there are transition streets adjoining both, and in such an in-between area would be the best place for doctor to stay. The Academy of Music is in the center of the city.

My friend Janacek, a banker in New York, whom I had asked about the cost of an apartment in the neighborhood of the Academy of Music, informs me that a five-room apartment might cost 5 or 6 hundred dollars per year. Together with the household it would take about 2,000 to 3,000 dollars per year to run. I also asked his opinion about renting an apartment already furnished. I suppose this idea is the best one. It would cost about 20 to 30 dollars monthly, and buying the stove (apartments are not equipped for heating, except that in the living room and dining room there is usually a fireplace), carpets, curtains, wardrobes, etc., could cost 6 to 7 hundred dollars.

There is another possibility, renting an unfurnished apartment and paying monthly rent to some firm to furnish it for eight months. I regret that, not being in New York, I cannot be of better service to Dr. Dvořák in this matter. However I believe that any decent Czech would accept the honor of helping him with advice and doing a good deed.... This is certainly an important matter because Americans notice everything while judging a man's life-style, and behave accordingly.

I have tried to describe everything to you clearly. It would be an honor and pleasure for me to be able to offer further service or help to the Doctor if needed. Every Czech in America would do the same.... Did you receive the two newspapers which I sent you? I will write again soon. Best regards and kisses from

your brother Josef

It became obvious to me that this matter was not easy and simple for a fifty-year-old man whose roots had grown deeply in the soil of his homeland, whose habits and hobbies were set into their everyday schedule, and whose work and rest followed in a regular rhythm comfortably settled for years. Moving overseas, looking for an apartment, making decisions about renting a furnished or unfurnished accommodation—all this called for lots of courage and will.

Dvořák's constant traveling was quite unusual for his time. He had left home to conduct his works around Europe many times during the last years. The American journey, though, could turn his life completely upside down. Everything over there was different, and most important of all, who could give him a guarantee that this radical change, touching directly on the sources of his creativity, would not influence it in a negative way?

Perhaps this point in our story would be a good place to insert a few things about the Kovariks who took in the composer's family during their famous vacation in Spillville in the summer of 1893.

The patriarch of the family, Jan Josef Kovarik, was born in Vsetec at Protivin in South Bohemia, which he left in 1869 to join his countrymen in Spillville, Iowa. These Czech people had arrived in this northeast Iowa community around 1850 to establish their new homes. The young Jan Josef Kovarik, besides being a teacher who could play organ and violin, soon became the center of all his countrymen's activities and lives. In a year, the first Kovarik son was born—Josef Jan, and five more children came later. Every child was musically gifted, and their father, as a rigorous and demanding teacher, made them play all day long. Why not? They had a violin, viola, violoncello, and piano at home, and an organ available for use at any time in a local church.

Four of the six children became professional musicians, and Josef Jan was one of them. When he was thirteen, his father sent him to Milwaukee in the state of Wisconsin, where a Czech-American, Josef H. Capek, had a school for musical training. Josef used to participate in the various concerts there, but when he became eighteen in 1888, he left for his father's homeland. He wanted to learn more about it because his father assured him that the family had never lost their nationality, and would always be Bohemian. Besides, he could study music at the National Conservatory in Prague.

In Prague he found a room in an old house with an odd-looking gable, and no less odd name of "At the Gold Skeleton." He stayed there with the family of a worker. They fed him well, enough to keep him comfortable for his musical study. We already know the rest of his story—about his frequent visits to a store on Ferdinand Street in Prague owned by the music publisher, Frantisek A. Urbanek. Czech newspapers published in America were smuggled in illegally, wrapped together with shipments of music materials from a company in Leipzig. Here he met Antonín Dvořák who hired him as his private English teacher. After a vacation in Vysoka during the summer of 1892, Kovarik accompanied the Dvořáks to America.

While I was sitting in the Museum of Czech Music, I needed to go through numerous yellowed materials of a collection. Despite the two sweaters I wore, and a large thermos of hot tea standing on my desk, I felt terribly cold. There were many interesting documents, scores, and letters, several from Jeanette Thurber. This energetic woman did not shrink back from any difficulties and obstacles in her way. She had written many letters to the composer, and four of them were available in the Museum. They were written in the period of negotiation over the exact spelling out of the contract, which, as we know, was not easy and smooth. Here is the first of these letters, dated "Paris, September 3, 1891."

> Dear Doctor Dvořák,
>
> Last Wednesday I sent you a telegram to let you know that I accepted all your changes. Mr. Littleton will have a contract ready for you, revised according to your notes, and I will send it to you to be signed.
>
> Please be so kind as to return it without delay. I hope that you and Mrs. Dvořák will enjoy teaching the Americans now as you did Englishmen before. With my compliments and cordial regards, Yours, Jeanette M. Thurber, President of N.C.M.A.

This brief letter shows how much Mrs. Thurber wanted to hire Dvořák. Its date suggests that the composer's changes created during their visit at the Koptas' had already been included in the contract. The beginning of this letter proves that the news of Mrs. Thurber's visit to Paris in the summer had been published in the *New York Herald*. She had written her second letter, dated September 17, 1891, from there:

> Dear Doctor Dvořák,
>
> Included are two copies of a contract which contain your changes—written in English and German—sent to me just now by Mr. Littleton. Please, kindly sign both copies and mail them as soon as possible to me. After their receipt, I will send you back both our copies, signed and certified.
>
> In case further changes are necessary, please meet with Mr. Littleton again during your stay in London but I do not doubt that you will be satisfied with this contract now. Do not hesitate to ask me for further information about your children's education and about life in New York, etc. I suppose that the gentlemen from Novello and Company (music publishers in London) will be pleased to give you a letter of recommendation to their representative in New York to help you to find a home for reasonable rent.
>
> With my best regards to Mrs. Dvořák
>
> Cordially Yours, Jeanette M. Thurber.
>
> P. S. I have telegraphed America to announce your acceptance.... I will send you any news which appears in the press.

We know the course of the next events. Dvořák went in October to Birmingham to conduct the world premiere of his *Requiem,* and he met Mrs. Thurber for the first time in London. We have no idea of the composer's impressions of "Madame," as he called her in his letters. He recognized her as his rich employer with good connections in New York society, but that did not change him. And Mrs. Thurber? She wrote about him in her recollection, *Dvořák, As I Knew Him*:

> There is a characteristic sentence in one of his letters which shows his dignity and naivete so well (he was as free of vanity as his idol Schubert had been) that I cannot resist citing it here: "Mrs. Dvořák and my oldest daughter Otilka are very anxious to see America but I am a little afraid that I shall not be able to please you in every respect in my new position. As a teacher and instructor and conductor I feel myself quite sure but there (are) many other trifles who [*sic*] will make me much sorrow and grieve [*sic*] but I rely much upon you[r] kindness and indul-

gence, and be sure I shall do all to please you...." He kept his
promise well.

We can summarize: Mrs. Thurber wrote in her letter of September 17 that all
Dvořák's conditions were included in the contract. After that she went from
Paris to London and met the composer there. This resulted in further discussion and more changes. This is shown best in the letter Mrs. Thurber wrote
from New York City on November 20, 1891:

> Dear Doctor Dvořák,
>
> Because I would like to have our agreement signed as soon as
> possible, please, kindly send me the contract with all the
> changes you wish to have made. Many regards to Mrs. Dvořák,
>
> > Cordially Yours, Jeanette Thurber

Finally, came the day when all the problems were solved and every obstacle removed: Mrs. Thurber mentioned it in her memoirs of December 12 after
Dvořák had definitively agreed to all conditions of the contract.

Another letter from the Conservatory Director was dated December 29,
1891 and represented accurately Thurber's characteristic attitude. She moved
quickly ahead, never looking back. Why not? The most important events
were yet to come, and they were going to fulfill her plans. Therefore she
wrote:

> Dear Doctor Dvořák,
>
> Would you be so kind as to send me your latest photo, auto-
> graphed, showing your face from two different angles. Also,
> include a few little details of your life which are not included in
> the Musical Dictionary. In addition, we would be obliged if you
> could send us two of your manuscripts, each about one page
> long, also bearing your signature. All of these will be used for
> publicity, and I would appreciate it if you can include your ded-
> ication with each picture and manuscript. Please address all this
> to the "National Conservatory of Music in New York City." For
> best results, please, kindly mail it to us before February 15 if pos-
> sible.
>
> I am enclosing a list of the textbooks used at the National
> Conservatory. Please feel welcome to ask for any changes you
> require. Do not hesitate to make your request known. We
> Americans can be very flexible. Please do not worry about any-

thing. With best wishes for a Merry Christmas and Happy New Year to all of you, to Mrs. Dvořák and the children,

Cordially yours, J. Thurber.

So Dvořák left to begin his artistic tour across Bohemia and Moravia and his wife started to prepare for their journey. She had to make arrangements for someone to take care of their four children remaining in Prague. She was busy going through closets to find out what to buy, and what they could do without in New York City. Every week brought the moment of departure and farewell closer and closer.

A final letter written by Mrs. Thurber during this period was found in the composer's papers. It was undated, but in any event not written before July 10, 1892:

Dear Doctor Dvořák,

I would like to answer your kind letter from June. I take the liberty to inform you that Mr. Staton, the Secretary of the National Conservatory, has asked the ship company in Bremen to make direct contact with you and answer any questions you may have. Do not hesitate to write me for any additional information. About your cantata, "Columbus" [the work written to celebrate the explorer's 400th anniversary], I hope that you will be in favor of composing the "The American Flag" for October 12. The text has been sent to Mr. Littleton, and should be most appropriate.

With regards... Jeanette Thurber

As darkness fell outside the Museum of Czech Music, I finished my reading, and while sipping the warm tea from my Thermos, started to think of the Dvořáks as their departure came nearer and nearer.

I spent all my time searching for all sorts of information. I collected data, facts, articles, and notes; I spent long hours listening to Dvořák records. I asked many questions. First I interviewed the great-grandson of Antonín Dvořák, Josef Suk. He was the violin virtuoso who spent a few hours several years ago in Spillville. He still had the booklet of the Spillville Clock Museum given him there. He explained, "Spillville is famous for the Bily Clocks made by farmers of Czech origin in their spare time.... Their museum is located in the house where my great-grandfather lived."

The flyer, inviting tourists to visit distant Iowa, stated: "Visit Spillville— Home of Antonin Dvorak—and the Bily Clocks." The front page of the booklet showed the picture of a wooden clock shaped like a violin in the upright position. Its lower wood-carved section represents Dvořák's face. In the background are the first six notes of the popular Humoresque.

The brochure gave more information:

Joseph C. Bily (1880–1964) and his brother Frank L. Bily (1884–1965) had a special hobby. They carved clocks, dozens of them. They both owned farms in the Spillville area, and at the time of the composer's appearance in town, were just boys. Still other brochures said: "Visit Home of Antonin Dvorak," "Visit the Czech Inn," "The Czech Restaurant—open seven days a week." Here too was a photo of the composer's stone memorial in the local park. There was an interesting monument on the little square, dedicated to the "war veterans." On the top of the little hill above the settlement was the church of Saint Vaclav where Dvořák had played the organ almost every day.

During a discussion, a piano virtuoso who had given concerts in New York City, described 17th Street where Dvořák had lived. He said that one of the buildings still bore a commemorative tablet saying that the composer had lived there from 1892 to 1895.

More inquiries were made and more clippings examined. Useful information might be anywhere. I talked with a diplomat, our former ambassador to the USA, and I borrowed numerous books, Baedeckers, tour guides, and maps. The director of the Prague Museum of Antonín Dvořák recalled that two buses had brought Japanese tourists there. He added that numbers of visitors ask for details of the origin of the Symphony *From the New World.*

All the things I considered had to be examined again and again. However, there were other important decisions to be made. First of all, when (and, since two heads are always better than one, with whom) would I travel to the USA? The choice for a companion would probably be a photographer. My notes multiplied, and the amount of collected materials was growing. The other important matter was to get the addresses of people who might be willing to help me should the situation there for some reason become desperate. The employees of the Institute of Foreign Affairs gave me useful advice, names, and telephone numbers. The director of the Museum of Czech Music came up with important suggestions, too. My meeting with a collector of articles about Dvořák, and another with a musical theorist-scientist who had dedicated his life to researching Dvořák's work, was inspirational. The departure was near.

Photographer Jan Einhorn (Honza), assistant professor of photography at the Academy of Music and Arts, was to go with me overseas for two months of investigation and documentation of Dvořák's American visit. I hoped to discover something hitherto unknown, the typical ambition of every researcher.

The last details of our tour were discussed. Sitting together, we planned everything that was necessary for travel. All our documents were finally in order, and we were ready to go. We would meet at the airport.

Two long months—or will they be too short?

It was March, springtime in Prague, with the sky seasonally appealing. While we were saying farewell, our friends and relatives wished us happiness. Special feelings overwhelmed me, and I had to fight for strength to stick to my plans.

My seat was at the window, and in a while the Prague airport vanished. Only a marvelous blueness surrounded the plane. I loved it; there was a good omen in this wonderful color.

From time to time announcements let us know what was beneath us: Frankfurt, Amsterdam, then, across the Channel, Britain. This was the country which had invited Dvořák many times. Now London, Glasgow, and Europe were growing distant behind us, and only a few scattered islands remained surrounded by white crested waves dashing on the rocks.

We were seeing the same picture as it had been hundreds or even thousands of years ago. A vast, grayish expanse, without end, stretched from one horizon to the other. What had forced a man like Columbus toward an unknown destination? He could not anticipate what waited for him beyond the horizon. The same vastness had surrounded Robinson Crusoe, the sailor from York, and Antonín Dvořák, the native of Nelahozeves, in Bohemia. He had not been seasick, not at all, and standing on the ship's foredeck, observing the waves, he immediately felt that the ocean inspired him to write a symphony. What excitement would he have felt at the sight of the silver body of our plane in its speedy chase of the sun! The proud ship *Saale* would have been ashamed to stay behind, almost motionless. The steamships from our window looked like little barges.

Our eyes wandered across the calm ocean, suddenly discovering a wonderful land on the right-hand side. It looked cold; we could see the snow-locked fjords. "Greenland," reported the stewardess, and I was sorry that Dvořák had not seen it, too. We were absolutely enraptured with the beauty of the deep fjords, with the mountains and the white beaches; with the majestic and uninterrupted peace. There were no traces of man, only grandiose, cruel nature.

Continuing in our pursuit of the sun and almost catching up to it, we came near to the Canadian coast. Just underneath us was Newfoundland, and because the dusk was changing rapidly to darkness, most of the travelers slept. The window became blank, and only an occasional glow indicated the presence of Quebec beneath us. We landed in Montreal. We had left Prague in the spring, on March 11, 1982, but here winter was still reigning in full force. New York City was closed to landing because of fog, and we had to wait patiently here in Montreal for several hours.

So we strolled through the huge, coldly elegant airport halls. Most of all, I liked the Eskimo statues in the souvenir stores. It was already evening but the bars were open all night for people with indifferent faces, waiting for the plane, and maybe, for their destinies. These are the crossroads of the modern world, with their overwhelming estrangement. Maybe the passengers of the *Saale* had not talked with each other either. It is a pity that Dvořák did not write a diary.

Before our landing in Montreal I asked for the flight schedule. We were above Frankfurt at 14:20, Amsterdam 14:50; at 15:25 we saw Newcastle, and 15:50 Glasgow. We left the European coast at 16:10, and landed at the Mirabel airport in Montreal at 22:35.... Does it really matter? "Usually we take a course along the fifty-third parallel," the captain informed us, "only sometimes we can be directed to the sixtieth, at which time we can see Greenland." What kind of route did the *Saale* take, with all the Dvořáks on board? But this was not important now.

What did really matter? Captain Rinck did not know that his boat *Saale,* with every nautical mile, was approaching the continent on which would be written a masterwork to enchant all people of all colors of skin to the ends of the world.

During the last weeks of preparation, I could hear this symphony ceaselessly sounding in my head. Even then, when our airplane was taking off from Montreal for the flight to New York City, at three A.M. Middle European time, it was in my ears again.

I was not sleepy any more. There were snow flurries outside, with occasional gales. Mrs. Dvořák had been seasick on the boat; I wonder how she would have felt in the plane. She had seen their voyage and their stay abroad as necessary for the family's financial welfare. She had left their four younger children behind in Prague with one of her sisters, Reza Koutecka, who promised to take good care of them with the help of her mother. She was just afraid that something bad could happen. Was their good income worth taking such a chance? This question would come to her mind again later, but now, she was waiting to see New York City.

While I was thinking of Anna and her problems, the airplane was bouncing a bit and recalled my own problems. The Czech Airlines had given us the latest Czech newspapers, and over the Atlantic I had read the column in *Mlada Fronta* based on my interview before the departure:

> Dr. Miroslav Ivanov, the writer from Prague, answered our questions about his trip to the USA where he will stay for several weeks, and about his reasons for going there. He says that he wants to get information about the sojourn of the great Czech music composer, Antonín Dvořák, who worked and became influential in that country from 1892 to 1895.
>
> After the description of his plans, he continued: "Do you know that Antonín Dvořák earned for his work at home 1,200 zlatys yearly, and in America he was offered a salary which could be calculated as 34,000 zlatys, but in spite of that, because he loved his country so much, he returned home?"

My last sentence in the article was needlessly overstated, but there was no way for me to change it now, it was too late, I was bound for America and had an inexpressible feeling about leaving my country. I was already above the continent. This little article in the paper made me nervous. How could I be sure that the reason for my trip—to find new Dvořák documents and correspondence here—would be fulfilled? I might even find a different reason for his return home. I might be wrong, he had returned because of...? The answer to the question could become crucial because of the many possibilities involved in his decision—and I was to find the only correct answer after all. Would I succeed?

There was a snowstorm below, and somewhere beneath that was Boston, where he had conducted several of his concerts. It was the home of the outstanding Kneisel Quartet which had played two of Dvořák's compositions in their world premieres. Those two works had been composed during the summer in Spillville. In a short time, we were approaching New York City.

I must remember the Dvořák family voting at the dinner table a long time ago; should they go or not? Kovarik might have been anxious, too. He went home—to Spillville. What is the meaning of this word 'home'? In his case, father Kovarik left his homeland for the USA, and this new place became the true home for his son.

As if by a miracle, the snowstorm vanished, and there was a flood of millions of lights, sparks, and flashing dots beneath us. It resembled an endless, fantastic Milky Way reaching from one horizon to the other as far as the eye could see. The sight of a composition of fantastic pictures, planes, circles, ovals, straight lines—everything penetrating and intersecting everything else—was overwhelming. This flood of brightness into which we flew swallowed us, and I felt the same kind of excitement which had filled me in the Valley of the Kings years ago in Egypt, or at Mamajov's mound in Stalingrad, or in my own country, at the springs which are the cradle of the Vltava river (Moldau).

At half-past four Greenwich time, the airplane wheels touched the ground and we landed at the John F. Kennedy airport in New York City.

First Steps ∽ A

S O, HERE WE ARE — in America…!
    What kind of country is it?
What is it like?

A variety of thoughts and memories of the last few weeks were running through Dvořák's head. How many times had he imagined this very moment?

Edvard Valenta movingly describes the scene of Dvořák's arrival in New York City in his 1963 radio play, "From the New World":

Kovarik: (quietly, still very touched) America!… (Boat siren, joined by a second siren, and a third, gradually the whole mass of them, with all kinds of pitches and intensities — like thunder coming from all sides.)

Dvořák: Why do they wail so much, almost non-stop? — and all together at once? Is New York always so noisy?

Kovarik: Not at all. I've never heard anything like this.

Dvořák: Oh my God! So many people, it's a madhouse — we're going to be lost. Nobody knows me here. Who cares?…

(One of the sirens blows directly beside them.)

Dvořák: Ask that fellow. Call to him. Why is he making all that noise?.

Kovarik: (Cupping his hands) Hey, why are you blowing the siren so much?…

Voice: (From a distance) They gave us an order, so we do it…

Kovarik: Why do they want it?

Voice: (From distance again) They told everybody to blow a blast when the *Saale* showed up. The world's greatest musician is supposed to be on the ship.

The writer, Edvard Valenta, described this moment in a pleasant and sympathetic way. He wanted to please any anxious Czech ear willing to believe that this story from that September eve in 1892 had really happened. The facts are not known. Only the notes by Dvořák and Kovarik, plus Jan Lowenbach's biography of Kovarik can help us.

Kovarik's record is the briefest one:

> On Monday, I think in the evening of September 26th our boat anchored in New York harbor. Mr. F. [*sic*] C. Stanton, secretary of the National Conservatory made contact with us. After the usual customs examination, Mr. Stanton took us to the Clarendon Hotel where a suite of several rooms with a concert grand piano had been reserved. Unfortunately, this arrangement did not fulfil Dvořák's request for calm and peaceful accommodations, and soon after his arrival he was anxious to find a private apartment.

Jan Lowenbach, Kovarik's biographer, wrote in *Josef Jan Kovarik, Dvořák's American Secretary*, Prague, 1946:

> The boat sailed from Bremerhaven to New York for nine days. Kovarik still keeps several of Dvořák's cards, the size of a calling-card, which the composer used for ordering beer for supper. Kovarik states that, despite two stormy days, their journey was wonderful. He remembers it with joy, and still cannot forget a very funny episode when he found out that Dvořák was secretly smoking his (Kovarik's) foreign cigars. However, the first days in the Clarendon Hotel were unsettled ones.

There is very little we can learn from this narration, and only Antonín Dvořák's letters can open the door a little wider for us and give some information about his first days on American soil. Up to the present time four letters have been found which could clarify the situation. He wrote in a letter dated October 1, 1892 to Antonin Rus of Pisek:

> ...[M]ost probably you have read in the newspapers that we arrived safely in an American harbor where we had to stay for one day in quarantine. The next day our ship *Saale* took us to Hoboken, a suburb of New York. (Thank God.) We are staying in the Clarendon Hotel for the present, but we hope that in a

few days we can settle into some permanent apartment. Such lodgings aren't scarce here.

I hardly know what to write about first because everything is so interesting, and we are having such a wonderful time here. Therefore, I will begin with our trip. We were on the ocean for 9 days, and with the exception of one day, we had very nice weather. A powerful storm hit us on September 21st, and it took more than 24 hours for the ocean to calm down. After that we had wonderful weather all the way to New York. My wife Anna, the children and Mr. Kovarik were all sick and couldn't eat for two days. Thanks be to God, nothing bothered me and I stayed in good health. During our quarantine near New York, little Tonik amused himself by watching the numerous boats around us, especially the unfortunate, cholera-ridden *Normandy, Bohemia, Moravia,* and others. In a moment of excitement he lost his hat when the wind tossed it into the water. The unhappy boy arrived in New York without it....

This description again shows the typical, charming openness of Dvořák. In a letter to his family in Velvary, dated October 3, he wrote:

Because I promised to write you as soon as possible, I'm in a hurry to let you know that we have happily arrived in America. We left Bremen by the ship *Saale* on September 17th, and entered the New York harbor on Monday, Sept. 26th, at half-past four in the afternoon, local time (it was already eleven at night in Bohemia, because there is such a difference between your time and ours here). We can say that we like it here. Just now, I am sitting in the school, giving exams to students who would like to study composition. This experience makes me quite anxious, but pretty soon I'll know how many and what kind of students will be enrolled in my courses. I suppose that this is not very interesting for you, so I'm going to write about myself:

The next day after my arrival every local English, Czech and German paper wrote a lot about me, and with great enthusiasm. I was welcomed as the world's-greatest-composer, and because of their big expectations, I'm very anxious to see how efficient I can be while I am here.

Valenta's description of Dvořák's arrival in New York City was probably taken from this part of the composer's letter. He tries to show that Dvořák's arrival was a first-class cultural event at that time. This is confirmed in the

composer's letter to his friend, Vicar Jindrich Geisler (from Olomouc), written on October 6:

> The press all across America welcomes me with loud acclama-
> tion as if I were some kind of a savior. I cannot write you every-
> thing they have said about me since I arrived. It would take a
> long and tiresome letter to cover it all. The people here know
> everything about me — every detail of my youth in Bohemia,
> but this is not enough for them, they always want more!

We can read much the same news in a letter written on October 12 to his
friend Dr. Emil Kozanek, after several experiences with the American press:

> It is terrible what the American press is writing about me — they
> seem to see me as some kind of music savior, and I don't know
> what else! All the musicological and political papers have writ-
> ten about me, and are still writing non-stop..."

He also describes his arrival in New York:

> "...Our voyage was very smooth, only one day was miserable —
> every other passenger on the boat was sick but I was not at all.
> Despite a little quarantine we had to go through, we arrived
> here in good spirits– into this promised land — America.
>   The view from Sandy Hook (a harbor city) toward New
> York and its magnificent Statue of Liberty (a banquet for sixty
> people could be served just in her head) is really ravishing! Just
> think, a banquet, etc. The multitude of boats from every conti-
> nent in the world is very impressive, too! Indeed, as I say, every-
> thing is enchanting here. On Tuesday the 27th we luckily came
> to Hoboken, the port which accommodates all incoming and
> outgoing ships. At the local railway station Mr. Stanton, the
> secretary of our Conservatory, awaited us. I was especially
> pleased to see a deputation of Czechs led by Mr. Fialka, the
> brother of your Mr. Fialka. Greetings followed, and afterwards
> a few speeches– Hurrah! A coach was waiting for us, and in a
> short time we entered New York City. Since then, we have been
> living in a hotel.

Dvořák's friend Kozanek from Kromeriz, was chairman of the "Moravian" musical club, and had known the composer since their student days in
Prague. He later became a zealous promoter of Dvořák's music in Moravia.
    This is all that can be found in Antonín Dvořák's correspondence con-
cerning his arrival in New York. He had come to a city of immeasurable mag-

nitude which was incomparable to anything the composer had seen before, Dvořák had already been in many cities; he knew the metropolises of England, Germany, Russia, and Vienna...but what he saw in America looked different. He had nothing else to compare it with. Even the spirit of the people was nothing like that found in the Austro-Hungarian empire.

He made his first critical, concrete remark about America to Geisler: "New York is very beautiful—we like it very much–but living here is expensive." He seems to be surprised, astonished and charmed by the city which showed him its negative side as well as its positive. Compared with the prices in Prague, living here was very expensive. His more concrete analysis is found in his letter to Kozanek, written after two weeks in New York City:

> The city is magnificent, beautiful buildings and streets, and cleanliness everywhere. Everything here costs too much. What a zlaty buys in Bohemia we pay a dollar for in New York. We pay 55 dollars per week for three rooms in a hotel which is located in the main part of Union Square City. It is not too bad for us, indeed, because we cannot spend here more than 5,000 dollars. Thank God! We will be able to save some money to take home....

Now we return to the letter written by "brother Josef" from Chicago. There was information on the possibilities of renting apartments in New York City. It seems that either the prices were not right, or the owners wanted to make money on the famous composer. We quote from a letter to Geisler on October 6th, 1892:

> As soon as we arrived in New York, I sent a telegram to our children in Prague. You have probably learned that from the newspapers. We are still living in a hotel, my wife searched around the city in order to find a convenient apartment, and she finally found one today. We have to buy furniture. The apartments are extremely expensive here, especially in the downtown area. We pay 70 dollars per week for six rooms with a beautiful view of a park but it is not the best arrangement for us because the price is too high.

His complaint was understandable since in his youth he had a very limited budget, and this had made him thrifty. Before his departure to America, as a professor of the Prague Conservatory, he had been earning about 40 dollars or less per month! He was able to live in Bohemia with his wife and the six children on this amount. Now he would pay more money than this just for weekly rent! He was still reorganizing his thoughts, and everyday affairs were crowding out any ideas of composing. With the many journalists questioning him everywhere he went, and with the visits of his countrymen, not to mention Mrs. Thurber, who was already waiting for him to take up his duties, there was no rest.

He wrote to Antonin Rus on October 1:

> Today I would like to write you about the city. It is huge, almost as big as London, and the street-life is very colorful and lively. It pulsates from morning until evening, and almost all night long. Today I was introduced to the professors of the Conservatory, both male and female, and received their cordial welcome. When I made a speech in English, everybody was surprised at my fluency...

Dvořák was right. At the beginning of the 1890s, London, a city with a population of 4,232,000, and an area of 1062 square miles, was still larger than New York City with its 1,515,000, and 563 square miles. However, very typical of America was the rapid tempo of development; this city had just started its tremendous growth at the time of the composer's arrival.

The welcoming reception prepared by Mrs. Thurber at the Conservatory was splendid. She actually arranged everything for Dvořák's publicity—press, interviews, celebration—everything was the result of her action. In her letter to him when he was still at home, she had asked Dvořák to send his "curriculum vitae." She gave it to every editor's office, and journalists had used it in their typical American way.

Still, in 1919, when the reminiscences of Dvořák's pupils was published along with those of Mrs. Thurber, there is an introduction which (with a few errors) states that

> ...his father predestined him for the butcher-trade. The strolling bands coming through his village became his first musical inspiration. He persuaded his school-teacher to teach him singing and violin. Later, he sang in church, and on special occasions played violin solos. Eventually he gave up all this (including his butchering career, the ambition of his father), and enlisted in the three-year course for the organ and composition study in the capital city of Bohemia, Prague. After his graduation he had to provide for his own livelihood. He played in cafes and with various orchestras. The latter introduced him to the composer Smetana, then a conductor of the theater orchestra. Smetana and Karel Bendl, who was a choir conductor,

helped the young composer all they could to bring his art to perfection.

The American public appreciated anybody who was able to make it to the top on his own. Dvořák's biography could, in the "land of unlimited opportunities" stir up a real interest, and Mrs. Thurber was able to feed this growing interest shrewdly. The composer wrote to Geisler on October 6th, 1892:

> The Conservatory has announced a competition for composers with awards of 1,000 dollars for operas, cantatas, symphonies, etc. This competition is in my honor since I have taken over my new job of heading the conservatory. I am sitting at my desk, and in front of me is a mountain of various scores. I can see that most of the works are good-for-nothing, so I think I will be finished very soon. Talents here are terribly neglected, composers seem to know very little, and I suppose that this was the reason for hiring me. They need me to show them, if possible, what direction they should take. I have about two talented students in my class. This makes me happy, otherwise, I would become desperate...

Here was the real Dvořák again. He was longing for good achievement from his students as the reward for his teaching efforts. He was quite content The new experience and obligations fully occupied him, as he wrote to Dr. Tragy (Director of the Prague Conservatory) on November 28:

> As for my composition class, I am satisfied with it. At present time I have eight pupils and among them are exceptional talents. Thank God for them; otherwise nothing could comfort me here...

He wrote in more detail about the situation to the President of the Czech Academy, Josef Hlavka (from the "Parker House" in Boston). The date was November 27th:

> The most important thing is, thank God, that we are all in good health and that we like it here very much. Why not? Everything here is very beautiful and unrestricted, people can live more peacefully and comfortably– and this is what I need. I have no worries, only duties that must be done, and everything is good then. There are many things here which one must admire, but there are other things which I'd not wish to see at all. However, what's the use? Unpleasant things can be found everywhere. In general everything here is different. If America continues to

make such progress in everything, she will beat everybody.

Just imagine how much the Americans work for the benefit of people and the arts! For example, yesterday I went to Boston to conduct the obligatory concert arranged for me by our honorable Madame President of the Conservatory, Mrs. Jeanette Thurber. It will be my *Requiem,* and several hundred musicians will be involved. The concert will be on Wednesday, December 1st, and it will be produced for a rich and intelligent audience only! However, a day beforehand, my work will be given for the "poor laborers who only earn about 18 dollars per week". Thus the poor and uneducated people here also have an opportunity to listen to musical works of all periods and nations! Isn't that something? I am looking forward to it with a childish pleasure.

Dvořák sent similar information to Dr. Emil Kozanek the same day:

> …I am here in Boston. The occasion is the production of my *Requiem*. The first performance will be for the poor laborers and then, on Wednesday for the rich. This is the American way…

He repeats almost everything he wrote before to Dr. Josef Tragy, word for word; only a short bit of information is original in this letter:

> …Very American! but indeed I like it. Why should not a poor laborer, who has to toil for a whole week to earn just a loaf of bread, know the music of Bach, Beethoven, Mozart…?

Dvořák's sense of social justice was sound. Poverty in his youth had taught him economy, and wealth could not excite his admiration. He was a profound Christian believer, and it seemed to him that American Democracy fulfilled the Christian claim of equality before God, regardless of wealth or property. The composer, being closed off in an enclave of his artistic world, did not then have any opportunity to take a close look at the wrong side of that kind of democracy, with its love of the dollar. However, after little more than two years, he started to see certain things differently, and later on, back at the Prague Conservatory he characterized the Americans to his students:

> There is no class distinction in America. The millionaire uses the same form of address to his chauffeur as the chauffeur uses to him. Indeed, the only difference between them is the millions…

Dvořák continued in a letter to Josef Hlavka:

> The Americans expect great things from me, and what is more important, they want me to show them the right route to the promised land, to the empire of new, independent art. In short, they want me to create for them a national music! Their land is large and the people are numerous. Should they too not have their own great musicians as the smaller, poorer Czech nation has?

In the second part of this important letter, Dvořák mentioned the competition announced just recently by Mrs. Thurber:

> A whole mountain of scores has arrived from all corners of America, and it is my obligation to check them! However, it will be easy for me. Just one look at the first page tells me enough about each composer and enables me to separate a dilettante from an artist.
>
> As for the operas, these are miserable, and I don't know if any of them could be awarded prizes at all. Besides me, there are other members of the jury– five jurors for each kind of composition. I can say that the other compositions—the symphonies, concertos, suites, serenades, etc—are quite interesting to me. The young composers are much like those in our country—educated in the German school of composition, but here and there, one finds a new spirit, a flash of different color from American Indian music. Therefore I am very anxious to see how things develop…

The perceptive Dvořák understood that the music of America consisted of elements unknown in Europe. But could it be called "Indian"?

"To refer to my schedule of activities"—Dvořák informs Hlavka,

> Monday, Wednesday, Friday, 9 A.M. to 11 A.M.—composition; twice a week, 4 P.M. to 6 P.M.– orchestra; the time left, I can schedule for myself. You can see that it is an easy schedule. Mrs. Thurber is very "considerate" and acts according to her promise given to me earlier in Europe. Therefore, a part of the administrative work is managed by her and by her secretary, Mr. Stanton, a very rich man and a confidential friend of Mr. Cleveland. It does not matter that Mrs. Thurber is a Republican, they both agree in everything that concerns art. They would do anything for the benefit of our not-yet-developed institute, and this is

very good. Another secretary of Mrs. Thurber is Mrs. MacDowell who is responsible for all correspondence.

"Now a little bit about our domestic matters," continues Dvořák:

> ...We live only four minutes from my school in a very pleasant
> house. Mr. Steinway immediately sent me a gorgeous piano,
> free, so we have one good piece of furniture in the parlor.
> Besides this room, we have three other rooms and one more
> small one which is furnished. The rent is 80 dollars a month, a
> lot for us, but a normal price here.
>
> We eat breakfasts and suppers at home but we go to the
> boarding-house for dinners. The meals are delicious (not
> English), and very cheap. We pay 13 dollars per week for five
> persons, and that includes soup, a different meat every day: tur-
> key, poultry, and desserts, sometimes dumplings, too, pancakes
> (a bit different), compote, cheese, coffee, wine and beer. All this
> for $1.70.
>
> Because we are spending little money here, I hope that
> besides the 7,500 dollars in my account in the Land Bank in
> Prague, we can still save half of the salary I am paid here—at
> least 400 additional dollars! Everybody tried to discourage me
> by saying that things are very expensive in America, but after
> two months here I can see that you don't need big money to
> achieve success. Besides, I am keeping the rest of my family in
> Prague. I am sorry to annoy you with such things, but the dis-
> tance dividing a man from his friends and acquaintances makes
> him babble!

Again, the typical Dvořák openness and sincerity is obvious here. He
writes without hesitation about the cost of food or about the piano "for free,"
which after all was "a good piece of furniture."

In his time he was one of the most popular men in America, but his fame
did not change him at all. The apartment to which the Dvořáks had moved
from the temporary accommodation in the hotel was an important change for
them. After the restless, uneasy time when it was hard to concentrate on anything really serious, the composer felt relieved. Kovarik remembers:

> Dvořák yearned for a private apartment. Finally, one was found
> on East 17th Street, No. 327, just across from Stuyvesant Park.
> The owner of the house was Mrs. Drew. Since the Conservatory
> was on the same street at No. 128–130, the master was able to
> walk the short distance to school. Dvořák stayed in the same

apartment until his contract came to an end. This house still exists– it has resisted all the feverish development around it. But how much longer can it last?*

This comment was written by Kovarik in 1929.

*A news item in the New York Times Metropolitan section on February 27, 1991 stated: "[Yesterday] the house was designated a landmark by the Landmarks Preservation Commission." However, the Manhattan Council decided [in 1991[that the Dvořák House in New York City will be razed and will cease to exist." —Translators note.

First Steps ✂ B

I T WAS COOL OUTSIDE THE PLANE. A March shower had ended just a moment before I stepped down onto the soil in New York. Passengers, under a flood of light, were advancing in disciplined lines waiting for customs. As I reset my watch, I couldn't avoid the strange feeling that I was now *really* in the New World. Almost lost in the spacious hall, I could see numerous signs, advertisements, and other evidences of the commercial world everywhere.

The photographer Honza pointed out that our luggage must be somewhere there. After our declaration, the line moved, and the customs officer waved his hand sending us into America.

I asked Honza, "Do you have all your boxes, paraphernalia, and bags?"

Honza, laughing as usual, with both hands occupied, pointed with a nod to all his photographic equipment, and we moved to the exit. The hall space, half empty at close to midnight, seemed to be even more gigantic.

A waiting diplomat from the Czechoslovakian embassy to the United Nations, instead of complaining about our delay, only gave us his diplomatic smile. After introductions, he started to ask us about our trip. We talked proudly of seeing Greenland, which the Dvořáks had missed. Their experiences must have been much different from ours. We came here to collect every possible bit of material about the composer's visit to America.

For a while we were to be the guests of our embassy, which gave us a temporary shelter.

The maze around us became less frustrating, since our guide seemed to be a magician leading the way. Sitting comfortably in his car, I could feel that the heavy weight pressing on my heart was becoming lighter and lighter, and finally a new sense of curiosity helped me to lessen the stress.

The gigantic buildings amazed, astonished, and shocked me. Though not technically inclined, I felt that I would like more information about all these miraculous architectural works. What would Dvořák think if he were in a car with us, seeing New York in its late night splendor, flashing with radiant lights? It was stunning and colossal to the point of dizziness.

"How does the city look in daylight?" I asked the guide.

"Different," he answered, "but in some way the same as now.... You will see it for yourself soon."

After two or three weeks, I realized how right he was. His skillful driving astonished me. How could he be so self-assured? Overpasses, tunnels, curves, all the sharp turns and intersections, expressways with several lanes, left and right—how could he see all these? I could really appreciate his driving. A week later, going with him across Harlem, it became obvious to me that our night drive had been only an easy trip across the sleepy city.

Our eyes could hardly register every change in traffic, and names on signs were coming at us in an incomprehensible blur of syllables without sense or meaning. Our guide explained that after crossing the East River, we would be in Manhattan. I had read somewhere that Manhattan has a population of about two million, and it is here that Wall Street, famous for its banks, is to be found. It is as well known as Broadway. The United Nations' home is here, too, and somewhere there must also be a street with a house where Antonín Dvořák lived.

Soon we stopped in front of a building of several stories, the home of our Mission in the USA Before going to bed, I stood at my sixth-floor window for some time and observed the street beneath me. I saw the cubical houses of different sizes and watched the flashing of the neon signs. As I thought of tomorrow's task, I had a feeling that everything would be fine. But what about the days to come?

Several weeks before the trip, I made plans for my mission. First of all, I would do research in the local libraries, archives, and collections, looking for Dvořák's autographs—the letters, notes, and everything he wrote by hand. The other task would be to go through newspapers and journals from 1892 through 1895 and find all articles written about Dvořák. There might be reviews of his concerts, probably interviews with the composer, and his own articles, too. Finally there would be a tour, following Dvořák's trail everywhere he went. First of all, 17th Street where he had lived, then the National Conservatory where he had worked. Close to it was the Hotel Clarendon, the first shelter of the Dvořáks in America. It was going to be a busy schedule!

Next day, for my convenience I made a little chart of Manhattan, and gladly accepted the idea of the ambassador that we could always turn to our cultural attaché for help. Later on, he helped me with checking my first job on the project. I wanted to begin with a study of the newspapers from the nineties. Dvořák had arrived here at the end of September 1892; this meant that in the second half of September, the first news and notes about him found their way into print like the first of the swallows announcing the coming of spring. This metaphor came to me from Valenta's radio play "From the New World." I just needed to know where to look now, in 1982, for the old newspapers.

We made many telephone calls, asked many questions, and considered what we had learned. The Main Library was located on 42nd Street but the newspaper files were stored in a building at the intersection of West 43rd Street and 11th Avenue, about six hundred feet from the Hudson River. I was to do most of my research in this building.

Checking our map, we could easily see that it was too far to walk there so I would have to take the subway. The nearest station was on 86th Street. My assistant showed me the routes, and instructed me how to travel to the Branch of the Main City Library where the papers from the 1890s were stored. Very well, it seemed to be quite simple.

The reality was less pleasurable. The subways do not look too nice. I think that the one I took was the dirtiest subway I have ever seen. All the walls were painted with graffiti, sprayed with an irremovable paint, even on the ceilings, corridors, and everywhere. There was not one blank place without these scrawls. This is seen as a special kind of protest for some, for others as sheer vandalism. Especially at the beginning, the subway had a confusing look about it, and for some time I had a problem in choosing the right train for my destination.

Nevertheless, the first day of my search was quite successful. A pretty, young black girl, in fashionably worn-out jeans, brought me rolls of microfilm, and with a pleasant smile started to teach me how to use the projecting device.

I began the search in an independent paper, the *New York Herald,* which often showed sympathetic coverage of Europe and of Mrs. Jeanette Thurber, too. While looking carefully through each column, I suddenly gave a shout. The library assistant came in a hurry ready to help me.

"What's the matter?" she asked.

"I have just found my first article about Dvořák."

When she saw how happy I was, she forgot to be annoyed with me for making noise, and returned to her desk. The copy of the *New York Herald* was dated September 28, 1892, and a headline on the sixteenth page proudly announced: "Dr. Antonín Dvořák Ready for Work." The subheads carried more details:

> The Composer Lands from the *Saale* and Will Assume the Direction of the National Conservatory To-Day.
>
> . . . .
>
> To Lead a Concert of His Own Music Next Month and a Symphony at the First Philharmonic.

More information, somewhat exaggerated and inaccurate, followed. Some of the items were quite charming. For example, there was a story giving the average American citizen, at the end of the last century, his first information about a musician who made his homeland renowned worldwide:

> Dr. Antonín Dvořák the distinguished Bohemian composer, who comes here as the director of the National Conservatory of Music, was one of the first to leave the steamer *Saale* when she reached her dock at 1 o'clock yesterday afternoon. With his wife and two children he went to the Clarendon Hotel.
>
> Mr. F. [*sic*] C. Staton, the secretary of the National Conservatory, tried to arrange a little reception at which some musical and newspaper men might meet the composer last evening, but Dr. Dvořák asked for a night's sleep before meeting anyone, and he looked tired enough to need it. The composer is not however the ferocious personage, very Cossack in type, that most of his pictures make him out to be. He has a pleasant face and an affable manner.
>
> Dr. Dvořák Speaks English
>
> "If you can only come tomorrow," he said to me in excellent English, "I shall be glad to answer any questions."
>
> Dr. Dvořák's knowledge of English, by the way, has been acquired by several lengthy visits to England. He has been in London almost every year since 1888, when he first conducted his *Stabat Mater* there, and has written many of his most important works for the great English festivals. For Birmingham in

1885 he composed *The Spectre's Bride,* for Leeds in 1888, *St. Ludmilla,* for Birmingham in 1891, the *Requiem Mass.* In England he is better known than in Germany. It was in London last year that Mrs. Jeanette M. Thurber first met him, and made the contract for the National Conservatory of Music.

The proper pronunciation of Dr. Dvořák's name is Dvorshak, with the accent on the first syllable. The Bohemian language contains a sibillated 'r,' pronounced like 'rsh' in German words.

A Fight With Poverty

Dr. Dvořák's career began in poverty. His father, Franz Dvořák, was the village butcher and innkeeper at Nelahozeves, in Bohemia. The child learned from wandering musicians to play the fiddle, and showed such aptitude that in 1850, when nine years old, he was sent to Zlonice where the village organist taught him the rudiments of piano playing. In 1857 he began to earn his own living by playing viola in a band that played in cafes. He was at this time so poor that once, when an opportunity presented itself of hearing *Der Freischutz,* he could not spare the necessary four cents. His earnings then averaged about $9 a month.

In 1862, a Bohemian Theatre was opened in Prague, and the band to which Dvořák belonged was engaged to furnish the music. This enabled him to hear operatic music and he began to compose. In 1865 he had finished two symphonies and part of an opera. In 1873 he composed a patriotic cantata, *The Heirs of the White Mountain,* which was produced in Prague with much success. It was followed in 1874 by a symphony (E flat) and two sketches for orchestra.

His First Opera

Prague was so well pleased with Dvořák's music that the municipal authorities commissioned him to write an opera. *The King and the Collier* was the result, but it was not a success until rewritten some years afterward.

More important however than this recognition was the award to Dvořák of a grant or prize of $240 by Brahms, Herbeck and Hanslick for a book of vocal duos, *Sounds from Moravia.* Hanslick then induced the publisher Simrock to print some of Dvořák's music, and in 1883, the London Musical Society performed his *Stabat Mater.* From that time the road was easy.

Mr. Thomas, Herr Seidel and Herr Nikisch have performed most of Dvořák's cantatas here during the last ten years.

The contract between Dr. Dvořák and the National Conservatory of Music is for three years, at a salary of $15,000. Dr. Dvořák is to have general charge of the institution, and personal direction of the class in composition. It is probable that he will also direct the choral music and orchestra concerts.

Earlier this last summer, Mrs. Thurber sent to Dr. Dvořák Drake's poem *The American Flag* as the text for a Columbus cantata. The music for this is now sketched out, and will be finished for rehearsal early this winter. In the meantime, Dr. Dvořák wrote a short *Te Deum,* which is now under rehearsal and will be heard at the Carnegie Hall under his direction on October 21.

To Lead at the Philharmonic

At the first Philharmonic concert this season, Dr. Dvořák will conduct his "Symphony in D minor." This invitation was made by Mr. Hyde, the president of the Philharmonic Society yesterday, and accepted by Mrs. Thurber upon Dr. Dvořák's part. It is probable that the Liederkranz and Arion singers will unite in giving one of Dr. Dvořák's cantatas at the Carnegie Music Hall in December if the composer can be induced to lead it.

At the concert of October 21 an oration of welcome will be delivered by T. W. Higginson. The program will contain, besides the *Te Deum,* Dvořák's *Triple Overture.* On the 15th of November, a reception in Dr. Dvořák's honor will be given, to which leading musicians from all over the country will be invited.

Yes, many inaccuracies can be found in the news reports, indeed. Dvořák did not start to write music as late as 1862, and the City Council did not purchase his opera at all. Also the dates of his contact with England are incorrect. However, these errors were much less significant when compared with the true respect shown for Dvořák, a man who had risen from the ranks. It was this aspect which really fascinated the American people; they accepted him with fondness and admiration.

While I was using the copy machine, a very modern one, I met researchers and students. I was glad that for a short time I could belong to this group. The next day I found other news about Dvořák. It was printed in the *Herald* on the 29th of September, 1892, page sixteen, and in it the author tries to correct the errors in the previous article. The main title of this text is:

Composer Antonín Dvořák Walks and Talks

He Gets an Idea of the City and Has Something to Say on Musical Matters.

Dr. Antonín Dvořák, the composer, was not able to visit the National Conservatory of which he is now director, yesterday, owing to the number of callers who came to him at the Clarendon Hotel. He has decided not to enter upon his duties until next Saturday, when the year begins at the Conservatory.

In the meantime, he will see as much of New York as he can, and he began by taking a five mile walk yesterday, wandering along Broadway and of course getting lost. At the hotel last night he chatted about what he had seen, and seemed to be much pleased at his glimpses of the city which he hopes will be his future home.

"My work for the next few months," said he, "will be almost wholly devoted to the composition class at the Conservatory, and the organization of the chorus and orchestra by which I can illustrate what I mean. It is difficult to teach symphonic composition unless you can show with an actual orchestra what is right and what is wrong. In the Prague Conservatory we have three hundred pupils this year and quite a respectable orchestra from among the pupils. With so large a number of pupils as you have in your National Conservatory, it ought to be an easy matter to organize an orchestra capable of playing every kind of music. Our course in Prague, however, lasts for six years, which is longer than we can give here, and we recruit our orchestra from the pupils in the last three years only. I see no reason why we should not have orchestra rehearsals twice a week at which the pupils in composition can hear illustrations.

"As to the number of pupils who may apply for my composition classes, I know nothing, of course, I take only young men who show decided promise. In Prague I had a class of eight, of whom two will be widely heard of, if early promise is any indication. If I get even two pupils of genuine promise every year, I shall be satisfied. Just at present, there seems to be a dearth of rising composers in France and Germany, and I shall not be disappointed if the same is true here. The best we can do in the case is to teach people to love the best music that can be played, and to play it for them."

"From what I hear, I understand that you have several large permanent orchestras here, and nothing will delight me more than to give them the ideas as to my own music. I shall lead one of my symphonies at the first Philharmonic concert with the greatest of pleasure."

The girl in jeans who helped me before now noticed my puzzled look, and with a gorgeous white smile on her black face, and swaying her hips (knowing well that even respectable researchers need to straighten their backs once in a while and switch attention to other subjects), asked:

"Copy machine?"

"Exactly so," I nod.

"Do you have a token?"

Of course I didn't. She took me to the cashier, and after I bought what I needed, she instructed me how to operate the copier, and the first copy of the microfilm finally slid out.

Time went by, and while New York outside pulsated vigorously with the fast pace of modern times, I was still in the grip of the last century, far away from today.

It was almost evening when I found on the thirteenth page of the *Evening Post* from Saturday, October 1, 1892, an interesting interview with a simple title:

A Discussion with Dvořák

His Opinions About Musical Affairs—His Insights About Mascagni—The Suitability of English in Songs—*Ode to America.*

I must admit that I was a little surprised by Dvořák's opinions in this article, which seemed to me quite unusual. However, Dvořák himself often complained in his letters home that the "Americans" wrote things he never said or that they had changed the meaning of his statements slightly. The majority of the journalists did not trouble to check their texts with Dvořák; they just listened to him, and rushed to the editor's office to write the most interesting story from their notes. Therefore, besides the believable statements, we can read things which probably astonished Dvořák when he saw them in print. He wrote his friend Kozanek about one example: the references to him as a musical "savior."

Now back to the article in the *Evening Post:*

Dr. Dvořák, the new conductor of the National Conservatory who came to our country last Tuesday, spoke with our reporter about his experience and opinions related to his art. When questioned about the composer Mascagni, Dr. Dvořák explained with a smile:

"He has talent" he said, "I expect him to write many operas, certainly, and it is hoped that he will develop a more individual style. My first works were also lacking in originality. However, there is one difference between us. Signore Mascagni was successful from the first but his *Amico Fritz* was far less original than was his earliest work *Cavalleria Rusticana.* His music is light and Italian. It remains Verdi. I do not mind. I like music which preserves its national features. I like Verdi's *Aida* and *Othello,* I can even enjoy *Il Trovatore.* Of course, I prefer Wagner. All his operas except the *Ring of the Niebelungs* and *Parsifal,* are often in repertoire in Prague, both in German and Czech.

"I prefer Wagner sung in German because it is his own text, and it is more suitable to his music than Czech. The same could be true about English. In my opinion, the English language is exceptionally suitable for musical compositions. As long as you have good translations, it would be better to sing operas in English. It is a pity to leave the audience without the poetry of a text, and make them dependent only on the art of the actors. I discovered the musical values of the English when I worked on the composition of *The American Flag.* I have still written only a part of it but it will be no problem to finish."

Dvořák's modesty made it hard for him to talk about his own work. However, at the end we were able to persuade him to show us his latest version of the *Ode to America* in order to demonstrate the advantage of English when compared with Czech. During our discussion, when Dr. Dvořák could not find a correct expression in English, he usually turned to German. Once in awhile he used a Latin word, similar to its English equivalent.

"English," the composer explained to us, "has, as you know, many monosyllabic words. The stress should be on each of them or, which is even better, every second word could carry a musical stress. For example, in these iambic versions:

"When Freedom from her mountain height
Unfurled her standard to the air.

"It is very easy in English, but in Czech, the words have two, three, four, six, and sometimes seven syllables. What can you do with these kinds of words? It is especially hard, because the stress is always on the first syllable. If I could find a suitable libretto, I would like to try to write an opera in English. I am a great admirer of English poetry."

"As far as I know, contemporary American composers produce a lot of songs," continued Dr. Dvořák. "As for me, I consider that music culminates in symphonies, concertos, and chamber music—for example Beethoven's work."

"Chopin avoided these forms, but in spite of that, he achieved greatness. There was also Franz Schubert who wrote only songs. I assume that your national songs are the songs of the negro. A folk song is, I think, the most beautiful of all."

While Dvořák was speaking about the Slavonic national songs, his eyes sparkled and his voice became gentle, most of all when he said: "Our songs are beautiful, really beautiful, the most beautiful, indeed!" He paced the room without a word, sat at the piano, and a song in waltz-time about a girl who laughed at her boyfriend flowed from the keyboard. It was reminiscent of songs of the Austrians. "This is a dance, see!" remarked the composer, and played something in the craziest kind of swirling rhythm, suggestive of the dances of Irish sailors. "This is our most favorite Czech dance, the "furiant" (swaggerer). I incorporated it into my *Dumka and Furiant* in Opus 12, and also Opus 42. In the *Slavonic Dances* there is something that reminds us of the Polish *Mazurek,* which Chopin was able to capture to perfection in his mazurkas.

"I am going to play you our most beautiful song of all," added Dr. Dvořák, still sitting at the key-board. Then, in a waltz beat he played the tender confession of a girl in love. This song reminded me of the songs of South Germany.

"She is longing for the distant mountains where her lover dwells. This is the most beautiful song I know," repeated Dr. Dvořák, and he raised his head from the keyboard, "and these songs are dying out because of those terrible operettas. In Bohemia, the same things happen as everywhere else in world. The folk songs are disappearing and the newest musical farces from Vienna are replacing them instead. The beautiful folk costumes are replaced by tedious fashions of city people. The country people are becoming emancipated from their old life."

Dr. Dvořák spoke about his future career as a teacher of American students:

"Nothing could please me more," he said, "than having a

talented student. I hope that I will succeed in implanting in the minds of the conservatory students the most important concepts of all—faithfulness to one's own national culture and the importance of originality."

Although many sentences of the composer were probably quoted inaccurately, this last phrase sounds like pure Dvořák: "to preserve faith in one's own national culture...."

First Weeks ᴄ A

SOON AFTER MRS. THURBER INTRODUCED Dvořák to the professors of the Conservatory as the new Director on October 1, life settled into a routine for him. Actually, he still had more "vacation-time" left, but now he needed to start preparing for the celebration of the Anniversary of the Discovery of America. Every paper of the day was flooded with articles and news about it, recalling the life of the famous native from Genoa, Italy—Christopher Columbus. The air was charged with confidence and power.

Dvořák, a newcomer, was quite interested, and followed all the special plans for the celebration. He could not, however, easily fall into the general excitement in New York. It was most important for him now to become a true part of this new and interesting city, which attracted him by its unusual charm. He wrote about it in many letters, some of which appear earlier in this book. In a letter to Jan Hodik, his caretaker in Vysoka, he wrote:

> Hodik,
>
> With the protection of God, we have happily arrived in this gigantic city. It is huge and beautiful, more than anything I have ever seen before! Because there are many Czechs here, we cannot complain of loneliness, for time goes very fast; you really have no idea how fast.

Josef Kovarik's memoirs give us an insight into these days more than a half-century later. He recalled:

99

After we arrived in New York, I expected to go home, directly to Spillville. I had not seen my family for five years. Dvořák's reluctance to let me go, however, changed my plans. I stayed, and I can see now that it was a good decision. We were just getting settled when Mrs. Thurber, the very beautiful and energetic lady who supported the National Conservatory in New York, asked Dvořák to conduct the first concert of the New York Philharmonic that season featuring his work. Maestro was not too excited about the offer but he had accepted the unavoidable invitation more or less graciously. After all, it was in his contract.

Before each concert, Dvořák felt sick. The day before the last rehearsal was the most difficult, not only for the composer but for everybody in the household. He could not work or read, and became incurably restless. To relieve the tension we would go for a walk together but when we had made two or three trips around the park just outside our house in Stuyvesant Square, he would be in a hurry to return home.

Since this routine might be repeated several times, I had to be with him all day long. While helping him with his musical scores, I tried to turn his attention away from the coming concert. Sometimes, he chased me out, sending a barrage of unflattering epithets after me. But soon afterward he would try to locate me again, and I had to slip back pretending nothing had happened. Fortunately all his desperation left him on concert night when he walked on stage to the podium. From the first downbeat he took absolute charge, and his nervousness was gone.

Kovarik also wrote: "…and after everything was done, we went home." In his naive way, he believed that Dvořák's apartment on 17th Street was his home, too, and in some ways this was true. In the Hotel Clarendon, where the Dvořáks had stayed for almost four weeks when they first came to New York City, their days had been broken up by numerous visits. After all that turmoil, their abode at No. 327 East 17th Street, just across from Stuyvesant Park, "was an oasis of peace."

Kovarik continues: "The apartment was furnished but they needed a piano. This proved to be no problem since Master visited the Steinway firm, selected a piano, and in half an hour a concert grand was delivered to the door."

Interior of Dvořák's apartment in Manhattan

Dvořák rented the apartment from Mrs. Drew, and he lived there until he left America in the spring of 1895. It was close to the Conservatory of Music, just a short walk for Dvořák. They now lived in a three-story building, requiring one to walk ten steps down to an entresol where there was a living room with two windows facing the street. It was here that Dvořák received editors, musicians, and other professional visitors.

The second floor—again with windows facing the street—was used as Dvořák's study, and beside it was Kovarik's room with a window facing the yard. The building was just wide enough to have three windows in a row. The two bedrooms of parents and children were located on the opposite side, with a yard view.

The third floor of the house was not rented out, but according to the composer's biographer, Otakar Sourek, "during the second year of Dvořák's sojourn in New York, the dining-room together with a kitchen on the second floor were rented by the Dvořáks, as an addition to their apartment."

This means that, after their return from Spillville, where they spent the summer vacation, Dvořák's apartment had a living room on the mezzanine, four rooms on the first floor, and a dining room with a kitchen on the second floor.

In the summer of 1894 the Dvořáks went back to Bohemia for their vacation, and returned to New York City with a maid. Barbora Klirova was a
simple girl whose brother, Karel Klir, was a subtenant of the composer's
mother-in-law in Prague. Barbora managed the Dvořáks' household, cooked,
shopped, and did all domestic jobs which were not, according to the social
customs of New York Society, suitable for Mrs. Dvořák.

The recollections of Barbora Klirova reveal many as-yet-unknown details
about the Dvořáks. Sometimes, this information is indirectly in opposition to
the established facts about Dvořák's days in America. For example, she said
about the apartment on 17th Street:

> Although they had three rooms and a kitchen, there was noth-
> ing that would make it luxurious. Everything was equipped
> with taste, however, and comfort and coziness made it very
> beautiful. The apartment was on the first floor, with only
> Dr. Dvořák's studio on the second. Occasionally, Dr. Dvořák
> would change his mind, and come back downstairs to join us.
> He said that he was feeling lonely up there. He did not like to
> be alone, not at all. The only exception was the time needed for
> composing.

This recollection of Barbora Klirova is in contradiction to everything
known by Dvořák's biographers about the New York City apartment.* It
throws doubt on the reliability of much of the information about Dvořák's
visit. The composer, too, helped to increase such doubts when he wrote in a
letter November 2, 1894 (according to Sourek, just after the dining room and
kitchen were rented): "We have a very beautiful piano in the back room
which belongs to Mrs. Drew. It is a nice room—so quiet that I cannot hear
the little Misses playing upstairs, which would be quite hopeless for me, otherwise."

Heinrich Zollner, the choir conductor of the "Deutscher Liederkranz
Club of New York," himself a composer, wrote in his memoirs about Dvořák

---

*Much of the confusion surrounding the layout of Dvořák's house stems from the differ-
ence in the way Europeans and Americans number the floors. In America, the first floor is the
ground floor, while in Europe it is the one immediately above the ground floor. Thus what Barbora Klirova would call the first floor, Kovarik would call the second floor. From this we see that
the extra room which the Dvořáks added to their apartment was not on the second floor, but on
the first. Upstairs, as we already know, were only Dvořák's study and Kovarik's room, with two
bedrooms shared by the parents and children. That there was one other room, a back room originally used by Mrs. Drew, is inferred. It really does not matter too much any more. The most
important fact about that building is the compositions which were created in that narrow, two-
story house on East 17th Street. —Translator's note.

that the composer's apartment "looked almost modest." Kovarik did not agree with his statement, but Barbora Klirova remarked that "there was nothing which would make it luxurious."

After they settled in, the Dvořáks began to make their first contacts with the city area to which they had moved. It was a modest area, indeed. Only the street number — 17th — suggests that the apartment was somewhere in the lower end of Manhattan. The curved, narrow streets here remind one of European harbor cities. For this reason, it was originally named New Amsterdam.

In 1609 the British explorer, Henry Hudson, in the service of the East India Company, had discovered a river here flowing into the sea. He immediately understood that Manhattan Island would be a very important strategic point. His discovery was also taken seriously by his employers, and in 1624, they founded a settlement here for trading furs with the local Indians. These were the ones who had sold their island to the first Dutch governor for 20 dollars. He gave it the name of the capital city of his homeland. Around 1650, New Amsterdam had a population of 1,000, and its last governor before the city was taken by the British was Peter Stuyvesant.

A square near Dvořák's apartment was called Stuyvesant Square. When Dvořák went there, New York City was growing with incredible speed — from the south point of Manhattan toward the north there was one crowded street after another. At that time, instead of the 220 streets we have today, only 160 were in existence.

Seventeenth Street and its surrounding area joined New York City's past with its future. Everything north of this street was built there in the nineteenth century, and was modern and elegant: the theatres, Carnegie Hall, and the Metropolitan Opera. The latter building unfortunately burned down in 1892.

In the evening Dvořák preferred staying at home. He did not care for social gatherings, and the glitter of fame had always remained insignificant for him. Mrs. Thurber assigned one of the professors of the conservatory the task of showing Dvořák the 17th Street neighborhood and helping him get his bearings. James Huneker said later:

> When I was on the professional staff of the National Conservatory — the only musical institution in this country that deserved the appellation — I was intrusted by the President, Jeanette M. Thurber, with the care on his arrival of Dr. Antonín Dvořák, Bohemian composer and musical director of the Conservatory...."

With "Old Borax," as Horatio Parker the composer affectionately called Dvořák, in tow I assured Mrs. Thurber that he would be safe in my hands, and then I proceeded to show him certain sections of our old town, chiefly the near east side.

As he was a fervent Roman Catholic, I found a Bohemian church for him; he invariably began his day by attending the first mass. Jauntily I invited him to taste the treacherous national drink called whisky cocktail. He nodded with that head which looked like an angry bulldog bearded. At first he scared me with his fierce Slavonic eyes, yet he was as mild-mannered a musical pirate as ever scuttled a pupil's counterpoint. I always thought of him as a boned-pirate. But I made a mistake in believing that American strong waters would upset his nerves. We began our rounds at Goerwitz's, then, as now, Scheffel Hall, which stood across the street from the National Conservatory. Later we went down to Gus Luchow's; for a musician not to be seen at Luchow's argued that he was unknown in the social world of tone. We traversed the great thirst belt of the neighborhood. At each stopping place Doc Borax absorbed a cocktail or two. He seemed to take to them as a prohibitionist takes to personal abuse.

Now, alcohol I abhor. Therefore I stuck to my usual three-voiced invention of hops, malt, and water. We conversed in German, for he knew no English, and I rejoiced at meeting a man whose Teutonic accent, above all whose grammar, was worse than mine. Yet we got along swimmingly—an appropriate enough image, as the thirst-weather was wet, though not squally. He told me of his admiration for Brahms and of that composer's admiration for Dvořák. I agreed with Brahms. After he had put away about nineteen cocktails, maybe more, I said, rather thickly: "Master, don't you think it's time we ate something?" He gazed at me through those jungle whiskers, which met his tumbled hair half way. He grunted: "Eat! I no eat. We go to Houston Street. You go, hein! We drink the slivovitch. It makes warm after beer." I didn't go that evening to the East Houston Street cafe with Dr. Antonin Dvorak. I never went there with him, for I not only feared the slivovitch, but also that deadly Humoresque played by a fake gypsy fiddler, attired in a red coat and wearing an ineffable grin. Such a man such as Old Borax was as dangerous to a moderate drinker as a false beacon to a shipwrecked sailor. His head was like iron. He could drink as much spirits as I could beer, and never torn a hair.

I tell this anecdote, not for a moral purpose, but as one of the rapidly vanishing specimens of rum-lore, soon to become legendary.

The last sentence in James Huneker's memoirs suggests that it was written many years after Dvořák's sojourn because there is a mention of prohibition which actually started several years after Dvořák's return to Bohemia.

James Huneker was a musical theorist, critic, composer, and a whimsical columnist and writer. He is interesting to us because he worked under Dvořák at the National Conservatory in the 1890s, and became his collaborator when Dvořák was planning to write his cantata based on Longfellow's poem *Hiawatha,* as Huneker recollected later. In one of his books Huneker wrote: "For Dvořák there was a musical god, and he was Bedrich Smetana; Bohemia's greatest musician."

On another occasion Huneker remembered how profoundly he was touched after listening to Smetana's work *Moldau.* He had asked Dvořák about the Czech name for the "Moldau," and Dvořák answered with apparent pleasure: "Vltava." Huneker continued:

> And from sounding Vltava to myself I longed to see the precious river and the historical city of Prague, built on both its banks. I often sought a verbal setting for Prague: Prague, the picturesque; poetic Prague; but after I had lived there I found the precise combination — Prague, the dramatic.

His words are adequate, and represent a well-understood characteristic of Prague as seen by a foreigner. What he wrote about their "drinking adventure" when he and "Old Borax" navigated the pubs of Manhattan, was probably more than a little overstated. The same could be said about his other recollections of Dvořák's sojourn in America. Nevertheless, these things do usually happen in talking about a celebrity, and often become legend. It is true that Huneker overstated Dvořák's inability to speak English because on the occasion of his installation in office, his introductory speech was in English, and he spoke English with the journalists, too. True, he made mistakes, and his vocabulary was not so good that he could speak with absolute confidence.

Josef Kovarik recalled:

> He was always a hard-working man, whatever he did. For example, when he read a New York paper, he would spread it on a table with a dictionary always at hand. Any word he could not understand (he called them "obstacles"), he looked up.

Then he would use that word again, even sometimes intention-
ally preparing a situation for the special purpose.

Kovarik's recollection describes Dvořák's relation to English more adequately than Huneker, who was trying to have fun at the composer's expense.
Also Huneker's fancy remark that he never went with Dvořák to East Houston Street because he had been frustrated by their slivovitch and by the
Humoresque played there by the "fake gypsy violinist," was something other
than witty. The famous Humoresque was written in the summer of 1894
during Dvořák's vacation in Bohemia. It could not have been heard in Houston Street before October 1894, and by spring 1895 Dvořák had left America
for good.

Many similar mistaken ideas existed about Dvořák. For example, as late
as 1933, a columnist from the Czech-American-Countrymen press, calling
himself "Musicus," wrote to Kovarik with a question concerning unpublished
compositions which Dvořák might have left with Kovarik before his final
departure from America in April 1895. Kovarik answered later in *Hlas* (*Voice*)
on June 23:

> Dear Sir,
>
> Antonín Dvořák did not leave any manuscript of his work with
> me at all. Before he left for Europe, he had sent me a composi-
> tion *The American Flag*, published by Schirmer in New York.
> This composition is a cantata for choir, with bass- and tenor-
> solos, and orchestra, using a text written by Joseph Rodman
> Drake. Dr. Antonín Dvořák wrote to me on the front page of
> his composition:
>
> Dear Mr. Kovarik! New York, April 15, 1895
>
> Please accept this token in remembrance of me. It is a composi-
> tion which should have been performed in Carnegie Hall on the
> occasion of my first public appearance in New York on October
> 12, 1892. I started this work before my arrival in America, but
> was not able to finish it in time for the performance. However, I
> substituted another work for that occasion. This was the *Te
> Deum,* performed on October 21, 1892, which became my intro-
> duction to the New York audience. Only this year, after my wife
> insisted on it, did I take the step of publishing *The American
> Flag* with a local firm, Schirmer. I will also send you a copy of
> my *Te Deum* after it is published. However, I have to wait until

some publisher takes pity on my composition, and you will have to wait for it, too. With friendly greetings

Yours, Antonín Dvořák
Written before departure to Europe, on the ship *Saale*,
April 16th.

This means that Kovarik did not get an original Dvořák work, but just a copy of one, on which was written the dedication which we have quoted. The passage also shows the considerable influence of the composer's wife Anna, and makes it obvious again what a big role she played in his life.

Kovarik's letter, quoted above, was written to a "Dear Sir" (perhaps to W. A. Dostal or J. Rynda), who was using the pen name Musicus. This letter also disproves another chimera: "I had even read in one article," says Kovarik, "that he (Antonín Dvořák) went with his pail-ek* every day to buy himself a beer! This is vulgar gossip — he never did anything like that."

Musicus remarked about it, "I also read the story in a Chicago paper and it made me wonder a bit — whoever wrote it must have imagined Dvořák to be like himself."

On the contrary, it would be difficult to imagine anyone whose life was more sober and temperate than that of Antonín Dvořák. Direct evidence came from the pen of Josef J. Kovarik, who was the best confidential witness of all. He said:

> Master lived in New York very peacefully, even more peacefully I suppose, than he had lived in Prague. I can remember very well that sometimes in Prague, the Czech-Austrian or better, Austrian-Czech politics could upset him. This situation did not exist for him in New York. At the beginning, now and then we went to the Cafe Boulevard on 11th Avenue and East 10th Street. There he could read a Prague paper *Narodni listy* (the *National Newsletter*). We usually stopped there as soon as a ship from Bremen or Hamburg arrived in New York. After reading a few of the political news items, Master would start to "grumble." However, before we had returned home, he had forgotten everything about it, especially since the paper was already two weeks old. Shortly after that, the *National Newsletter* ceased to come, and since Master did not have any further political news from Bohemia, he lived in perfect peace. American politics he

---

*The Czech words "vedro," "kbelik," and "konev" in Czech mean "pail." With the diminutive ending "-ek," we get a new Czech-American expression used often by the Czech country folk.

could not understand, so he did not get upset about the American political situation.

Master did not leave home very often. He was a regular visitor to the concerts of the New York Philharmonic. Besides these, he went only twice to the Metropolitan Opera, twice to hear the Kneisel Quartet, and twice to a concert of the Boston Philharmonic. That organization, the same as now, came five times to New York during the season, giving ten concerts.

Master very seldom participated in social activities. When he received an invitation, he often made excuses. He did not have the same kind of acquaintances here as he had in Prague. Besides, American social life is not like that of Europe. The American, employed all day long in his business, likes to be at home in the evening to stay with his family. Besides, all the concerts and theatres in New York started at half-past nine, with the exception of operas, which began at eight or occasionally at half-past seven. This meant that performances ended not sooner than eleven, even later. All this was not convenient to Master, who enjoyed getting up and working during the early hours. Therefore, he preferred to stay at home.

This Kovarik recollection was printed in 1929. In another extensive article, published in the Almanac for 1934 (previously published in the journal *Nation and Catholic*), he talks about Dvořák's first weeks in New York City:

Very soon after he got settled, Master started to work on the instrumentation for *The American Flag*. He had finished a sketch of it before he left his Vysoka but the instrumentation took him longer than usual. He could easily have finished it in a few weeks if he were not working every day from half-past nine to four, and twice a week until six at the conservatory. There was another reason for his delay; his mind was already working on ideas for his new, large work.

To be exact, I have to say that Master never worked in the evening. He got up early in Prague, and also in New York. At five A.M., he was already at his desk. In Vysoka, and later in Spillville, he got up even earlier, went for a walk, and then started to work. Evidence can be found in comments which he made directly in his compositions. For example: "Sunrise is very beautiful at half-past four," etc.

In the evening Master took a rest, and as always, when overcome by his only "sinful addiction" he played his beloved "Darda." However, we cannot take his passion too seriously. He played the game mostly for passing time, and for fun. Despite the fact that they played only for "buttons," he could get very excited, especially when he had lost two or sometimes three games in a row.

At first, when we were staying in the hotel "Clarendon," Master used to play Darda with his wife. When they moved to their private apartment, and I (Kovarik) unpacked my numerous books, Master's wife, a very eager reader too, became absorbed in reading from my collection, and Master became an orphan. For two evenings he kept himself occupied by going through the scores, but on the third, his "passion for Darda" overcame him. Master could not resist his desire any more, and called me in: "See, you little Indian," (he always had called me a "little Indian" when he was going to beg me, otherwise, I was just an "Indian"), "my wife is sunk in a book and nothing is going to move her — come here, I am going to teach you Darda."

Master was a very conscientious teacher. Only once in a while, when he lost his temper, did he swear at me. However, later on, while initiating me into the rules of Darda, he recovered his patience, and this stayed with him until I learned the game.

The game was usually over by nine, and there was time for one more hour for discussion before the Master went to bed.

Kovarik's recollections are priceless. I found in America that his narration exists in three versions:

(1) The English version was an article entitled "Dr. Dvořák as I Knew Him," which *Fiddlestrings* published it in installments in 1926. "Musicus," still using his pen name, later used this serial which he edited and published in the Czech journal *Ceska zena* (*Czech Woman*), in Saint Louis.

(2) The first Czech version, titled "Dvořák and Spillville," also originated in the 1920s. Kovarik had it published in various local newspapers and magazines over America. It is not identical with the English version, and some parts of it were sent by Kovarik as letters to a Prague researcher Otakar Sourek. He first published them in magazines, and later used them in his book.

(3) The second Czech version originated in 1950 and was published as a booklet in New York City, in 1963.

Another good source of information is Kovarik's biography, written by Dr. Jan Lowenbach. It is understandable that some items in these materials get tangled up, and once in a while they could be wrong, but they never contradict Kovarik's writings about Dvořák's hobbies:

> What did Master miss most in America? His pigeons and the engines. He was always longing for these hobbies, even after he found a little substitute here. One day we left with Master for Central Park where there is a little aviary with various birds, and suddenly we came to an enormous cage which contained two hundred pigeons. That was a surprise for Master, and he was really happy. Although none of these pigeons could match his pigeons at home, we went back to Central Park at least once a week after that, and often twice. (1929)

Kovarik wrote there about Dvořák's second passion — engines:

> However, to find a substitute for engines was more difficult. At that time there was only one railway station in New York — the rest of them were on the other side of the river. The main railway station was run with strict rules then. Only the travellers could enter a platform, and all our requests to get permission for a visit to the "American engine" did not help. The adamant doorman would not let us in, so we had to look for another way. We took the elevated railway to 155th Street, a good one hour distant from Master's home, and there, standing on a hill, we waited for a passing train from Chicago or Boston.
>
> Nevertheless, this trip took too long, and was not worth it just to see a few trains coming our way. Never mind, Master had discovered another hobby. Instead of train engines, now it was steamships! The distance to the harbor was much shorter, and besides, it was the general custom for visitors to board the ships, and Dvořák took full advantage of that.
>
> Since then, there has been no ship which we have not explored thoroughly. First, Master would speak to the captain, then to his assistants, and in a short time, we knew every ship, each captain and non-commissioned officer by name. We left just before the ship pushed off from shore, and waited there until it was completely out of sight. In case the Master had to stay longer at the conservatory, or was absorbed in his work at home, leaving us little time for a trip to the harbor, we took the elevated-railway to Battery Park (the very southernmost point in the city) and from there, we could follow the ship on her way to the Atlantic, until she was no longer visible.
>
> In the evening, after a round of Darda, we would discuss

with Master how many nautical miles the ship had already made; where she might be now, etc. The first thing the Master did the next morning was to read everything in the "Shipping News" column in the *Herald*. I still continue to read the shipping news, despite the fact that not even one ship from Master's time is left.

This is Kovarik's recollection in the first Czech version. Twenty-five years later, when asked about the same material, his description was even broader:

The second of Dvořák's hobbies was engines. While still in Prague, he often used to stand above the tunnel, leaning over the guardrail, and observe the engines coming in and out from the tunnel near the Wilson Railway Station. He knew the numbers of every engine, their schedules, and even the names of the engineers. Dvořák, too, was well known at the railway station, and could move about there freely without restriction. Dvořák awakened in me the same kind of delight in this hobby and I always took part in his trips....

Soon after his arrival in New York, Dvořák started looking for his old friends, the engines. But this time he could not get permission to move freely about the railway station. Therefore, he found an alternative, his own observatory on Washington Heights. He used to go there about three times a week. However, after a while, his interest slowly changed to oceangoing steamships. We obtained permission to go on board and observe everything that we wished. We stayed on deck until the very last moment before the ship's departure.

In his previous recollection, Kovarik spoke about 155th Street, which they had reached by the elevated railway to observe the engines. In his last version, he talked about the composer's "own observation on Washington Heights...." However, the conclusion is approximately the same. Dvořák's hobby broadened, and its significance became more serious because every ship was heading to the Old World, to Europe. There, his children and friends lived, in his Bohemia.

His new interest also showed up in his American correspondence. As soon as he became better oriented, in his many letters could be found some additional information about the ship which was going to take his letter to Europe. For example, in a letter to Antonin Rus from January 2, 1893, he wrote:

> I have to finish this letter soon because tomorrow morning, the
> ship *Lahn* is going to Europe, and I hope that you can get my
> letter on the fifteenth. The ship which brought your letter here
> was in a big storm, and it took her 15 days to arrive.

Similarly, he wrote to Marie Bohdanska at Cimelice, on April 12, 1893:
"Tomorrow the English ship *Majestic* will take your letter."

Also to Dr. Kozanek, on April 12, 1893: "Tomorrow the ship *Columbia*
from Hamburg is going to leave, and I hope that she can bring you our letter
earlier."

These pieces of "shipping information" multiplied when he began to feel
more homesick. The ship became a symbol (and a reality) of his contact with
home. For example in his letter from November 3, 1894, he wrote:

> My dear children and grandma:
>
> Tomorrow, on November 3rd, the *Elbe* and *Luciana* are going
> to Europe, and one of them will bring you this letter. Our first
> letter was sent by the ship *Saale* on October 27th, and the
> second one followed on the *Spree* the following Tuesday. I hope
> that our first letter has already reached you... Today, the *Lahn*
> came (from Bremen, October 23rd), and we thought that she
> would bring us something, but she did not. The *Columbia* from
> Hamburg is supposed to come, too. Maybe she will bring your
> news tomorrow. I do not have to write you that we are thinking
> of you all the time, and therefore, I wait anxiously for any news
> from you. You can write about anything; what you do, and how
> you are...

Of course, this was a letter from November 1894, and thus far we have
covered only what had happened up to the autumn of 1892.

Dvořák's letters to his children and relatives from that period have not
been found. It is possible that they were lost, or are in some private collection.

The first known letter comes from February 7, 1893. However, the letters
written by Dvořák's sister-in-law Josefina were preserved, and the first of her
letters bears the date October 13, 1892. She confirmed that she had received
the letter from Dvořák, and also she rebuked his negligence in not writing
about his wife Anna and the children. She continued:

> Nothing is new in Prague, except that Tchaikovsky was present
> during the production of his opera, *Queen of Spades*. It is
> difficult to judge his work from what the critics wrote about it.

The opera seems to be vague. I suppose that Mr. Kovarik went directly home to Spillville, or did he stay with you?

In another part of her letter she tried to assure Dvořák that the children they left in Bohemia were healthy, and everything else was all right.

A second letter from Josefina was even more interesting. It shows the date of November 8, 1892, and she addresses them as "Dear Friends." After she had informed them about their children, who were doing well, she wrote:

"Andula can think only about America, and is pleased that she might join you."

This is important news. It indicates that during October, Dvořák wrote a letter to somebody in their family, probably to his mother-in-law or one of his sisters-in-law, Terezie Koutecka, or perhaps to Marie Anna Stepankova, and was planning for someone from the family to come to New York City. Why? What were the reasons for this remark?

Josefina stated later:

> ...in the journal *Zlata Praha* [*Golden Prague*], I saw a picture of the bouquets which you received after your arrival, but I cannot tell if it was when you had just come, or during the welcome party. There was a long article in the *Narodni listy* [*National Newsletters*] yesterday about that Czech evening with the summaries and criticisms gathered from your New York newspapers. How is Antonín's directorship? Actually, what kind of job is it? Does he also teach there? It was said here that he has already signed a new contract for another eight years; that Mr. Kovarik has been his secretary, or how do you call it; and Otilka is engaged, and I don't know what all. Someone of our people there supposedly wrote about it to one of our local "Americans" [Czechs who had come back from the U.S.A.].

Speculation was running riot across the Ocean. The composer commented in his letter to Dr. Kozanek, on October 12, 1892, about that Czech welcome evening for Antonín Dvořák, mentioned by Josefina:

> On Sunday the 9th, there was a big Czech concert organized in my honor. 3,000 people were in the auditorium, and the cheering and clapping were endless. The speeches were in Czech and English, and I, poor-fellow, was obliged to climb onto the stage to thank them. Holding the silver wreath they gave me, I felt quite miserable. Nevertheless, you will read about it in your newspapers, anyway. What the American press writes about me

has been terrible. They see me as a kind of savior of music, and God knows what else....

Such dizzying fame pleased Dvořák. We read about it in the notes, scribbled on the sides of his letters, but his fame did not go to his head. For example in his letter written from Boston on November 27, 1892, to Kromeriz, he says:

> All the foremost artists and musicians want to welcome me today, and tomorrow too, (this is called a "reception banquet" here) and it will be a great event for me. Just now, I'm waiting to be picked up at the hotel—and then I have to go along and let them show me off!

Dvořák clearly understood that such parties belonged to the American lifestyle. His first concert here, on October 21, was a great success, both musically and socially. The composer wrote about it in his letter from Boston (November 27, 1892) to Josef Hlavka:

> Today, Sunday, 3 P.M., I have a rehearsal which I am very anxious about. I have heard this orchestra before, in Brooklyn, and it is an excellent ensemble, indeed. It was founded by a local millionaire, Colonel Higginson, who also gave a big speech on the occasion of my first concert in New York. This speech was an event never known here before. He talked about my arrival in America, and described the purpose of my visit. The Americans are expecting great things from me. It will be not only a big task, but also a pleasant one, and I hope that with God's help I will succeed. There is enough material here for me to work with, and plenty of talent. I even have students from San Francisco! Most of them are poor, but the education at our institute is free for those who can show evident talent—they pay nothing in that case.

It was true that Dvořák's first performance in New York City was widely heralded. The concert was performed on October 21, in Carnegie Hall. On the program were his compositions *In Nature's Realm, Carnival,* and *Othello.* After the intermission came *Te Deum,* which he had composed in Bohemia, just before his trip to America. The choir had 250 singers, and Col. Thomas W. Higginson made a speech.

Dvořák received floods of applause; who could wish for anything more? In a few weeks, on November 17, the New York Philharmonic, conducted by Anton Seidl, played Paul Gilson's symphony, *Sea,* and Karl Goldmark's Overture, *Prometheus Bound*. After intermission, Antonín Dvořák took over the orchestra, and the tones of his Symphony in D Major resounded in the auditorium.

His success was unexpectedly overwhelming. The composer wrote about it to Antonin Rus (January 2, 1893):

> You know mostly everything about my earlier concerts. In New York I conducted my Symphony in D Major, and the result was magnificent. In spite of the fact that my work was the last one on the program, the audience in the seats and boxes gave me a standing ovation with endless applause. They called me back— but I threw my fur-coat over me, and hurried home. I was very tired, and it was already eleven; the concerts here begin at a quarter-past-eight and sometimes are very long and slow. Later I also conducted my *Requiem* twice in Boston. It was as well-received there as in New York, and I was presented with a wreath.

He enjoyed writing similar letters to others, his friends and relatives. His success encouraged him and he found complete satisfaction in his creativity. He wrote to Josefina, too, but these letters have not been found. We do have her answers, which are very typical for a woman of her character. She wrote from Vienna, on November 17, 1892:

> ... I wish you success with all my heart. I hope that you will be able to earn substantial wealth over there, and that you will remember your homeland again and return to us. Other places can be fine, but "There's no place like home." This proverb is very old but true. According to your letters, Mr. Kovarik is still with you; that is good, isn't it? It was an easy way for him to make his way into the world. You don't write about him. What kind of job did you arrange for him, is he a professor, or something else? Does he have a profitable job? How much does he make? It must be a great advantage for you, too, that you aren't lonely there, and with his help, communication must be easier for you.

So much for Josefina's letter. We can find more about it in Kovarik's recollection published in 1926 in the journal *Fiddlestrings:*

> ... upon our arrival to New York I intended to go right on to my home in Spillville, but Dr. Dvořák frustrated all my plans by saying: "Man alive, would you have the heart to leave me all

alone in this strange city, with no one to talk to, no one to argue
with, and no one to play Dadka [*sic*] [Darda is the card game]
with?" Remarking that I hadn't seen my folks for four years, he
replied:

"Why, couldn't you wait just three months more now, and
then run down for Christmas, or wait till June, and then spend
the whole summer?"

So I decided to postpone my trip till Christmas, but just
about the time I expected to leave, I was offered an engagement
which I couldn't very well refuse.

It was through Dvořák's influence that the President of the Conservatory,
Mrs. Thurber, hired Kovarik as the violin teacher for her institute.

Now, we go back to Josefina's letter, which was filled with spontaneous
comments. She continues:

What about Anna? Is she able to do her shopping without help?
And what about your social life, are you going somewhere
every day? Doesn't she spend too much money for her party
clothes? I know that Otilia does not regret that she went along
with you for she will see a great deal of the world. What if one
of the numerous millionaires over there would make the mistake of taking her for his wife? This would be something for
her! It would fit her very well—nothing to do but have a good
life, just fun and reading those romances as she does all the
time. Before such a thing happened, it would do her no harm if
Anna would keep her at domestic work for a while. It is what
Otilie least cared for. Domestic work would never enter Otilie's
head. Nothing new to report from Prague, only that everybody
would like to go to America.

Some news about the political situation and the session of Parliament followed:

Everything those legislators do is slow and monotonous, and
there is nothing for you here to miss during your absence, nothing at all. Things don't change here as fast as where you are
now, in the New World.... How much I desire to see you there,
to go for a visit, Only I am afraid that it would be absolutely
impossible for me to survive the first attack of seasickness.

Best regards from my husband, and from your—always
been devoted to you—kissing you all   Josefina

In many of Josefina's letters were complaints of her being ill and permanently weak. For example, on January 9, 1893, she wrote: "Speaking of me, I am always ill, especially when I come to Prague. I do not think that this will change, and God knows whether you will see me when you return to Bohemia! Everything is in the hands of God!!! No help."

In February 1893, she wrote again about her condition:

> ...I have been sick continuously since Christmas.... It seems to be my fate that I can no longer recover, and will suffer much until the end of my life. I only wish that if I cannot recover, my suffering will be very short!
>
> However, it is not my intention to get sentimental about it. What is the use of that? Everybody has to go, sooner or later.

In the preserved correspondence of the countess Eleonora Kounic were similar remarks about her daughter-in-law Josefina's health. Eleonora never forgot to inform Dvořák that "Dear Josefina came down with a bad cough" (January 3, 1893) or: "Dear Josefina is a bit sick..." (January 9, 1894).

Josefina's openness (her wish that Otilie would marry a millionaire, or her mention of Otilie's lack of interest in household duties) was sometimes teasing or taunting. For example, she wanted to know if Anna did not spend "too much money for her party clothes"—as if she would not know her sister! Anna was never attracted to the social life as Josefina was; this made them different. The Dvořáks were somewhat indifferent to the idea of making their way into New York Society.

Once in a while, Dvořák accompanied his wife somewhere, or they received an invitation for a visit which he always enjoyed. However, very soon he started to miss his evening relaxation within the family circle, and his card game, too. He was very glad when the visit was over, and they could return to their American home. For example, in a letter to his children from January 11, 1895 (Dvořák misdated it as 1894) he relates that:

> Yesterday afternoon at 3 P.M. there was a concert at Mrs. Thurber's in honor of me and your mother. The most distinguished company was invited there, and the *New York Herald* today carried the news about it. I am sending it to you. Otilka, you should read it because you probably will remember many names in the article, for example, the millionaires, Peabody and Douglas, Dr. Parkhurst, etc. In short, the so-called American aristocracy was there. None of the teachers was invited, nor was Mrs. Margulies there. After the concert, Mrs. Thurber intro-

duced me to all her guests, which was not very pleasant for me, as you know. Everything was over by half-past-five.

The Dvořáks would be in a hurry to get home. There was his piano waiting for him, maybe a letter from Bohemia from friends, perhaps from the children, and a few games with Kovarik after supper. He would not forget "Darda," after all. And once in a while, he could hear a thrush singing. Barushka (Barbora) Klirova recalled:

> For their enjoyment, the Dvořáks kept a thrush in a cage, and it was usually in care of the Perina family during the Dvořáks' absence from New York. The Perinas owned a cigar-making business then, and we bought cigars from them for the Doctor. Besides, they made Czech liver-wurst, which Dr. Dvořák liked very much, and he went there often to order a much-longed-for meal. The thrush was another of Dr. Dvořák's favorites. Nevertheless, one night he got angry because the thrush, probably disturbed by the street lamp in the window, twittered and chattered without a stop. One could take the noise only so long, so when the bird continued its clamor, Doctor Dvořák grabbed Otakar's shirt, and draped it over the thrush cage. It became quiet in the dark, and we were able to sleep.
>
> Doctor Dvořák got up very early every morning, and while the rest of the family still slept, he was already working. Later, he left for the conservatory.
>
> When he first arrived in New York, he received a tempestuous welcome from the conservatory staff, with whom he later became very popular. When the weather was bad, some of his students came to our apartment. These students were usually older men, and as Mrs. Dvořák said, they came from Boston, Philadelphia, Washington, and I do not know from where else. I still can picture their fur coats, which were not yet known in Bohemia. After they finished their lessons, they stayed for a brief discussion. On one such occasion, they asked the Master to play a song for them — our present national anthem *Kde domov muj?* [*Where is My Homeland?*]. Despite his kindness he denied their request. Professor Kovarik played it instead. The remembrance of his homeland affected Dvořák very strongly so that he had to turn away from them and look out the window.
>
> After he returned home from the conservatory, sometimes he composed, and when he had somebody to go with, he went for a walk. It seldom happened that he walked alone. He did

not like loneliness, and therefore, Mrs. Dvořák or Prof. Kovarik
went with him. Once, Dr. Dvořák wanted to go to "Perinas" to
get his cigars. That was quite far from us, and Mrs. Dvořák was
not available, so I offered him my company. On the way home I
wanted to stop to see some friends who had emigrated years
ago to New York from Kozlany in Bohemia.

When we got the cigars, on our way home Dr. Dvořák
advised me that it was time to leave him. However, because I
knew how much he disliked being alone, I decided to accompany him back. His pleasure was apparent when he gave me a
big smile as a reward. All the same, he instructed me that I was
to explain this to his wife. She would probably be upset that he
did not allow me to leave him. And indeed, when Mrs. Dvořák
opened the door, and was welcoming us, she smiled, and said to
me: "Of course, Barushka, I had a pretty good idea that you
would be coming too." They knew and understood each other
very well, and it helped them with such problems.

Another time Dr. Dvořák, who had just returned from the
conservatory, sat down at his piano and played and played.
Always a stream of new melodies sounded from his room, but
suddenly there would be silence when he tried to sketch them
on paper. None of us had the right to enter his room at such a
time. It was very interesting to watch how greatly he changed in
those days. There seemed to be a mountain of thoughts and
ideas whirling in his head, and radiating out, and he might say:
"If I could give my head to Oto" [the nickname for his son
Otakar]. Once, Mrs. Dvořák called me to a window to see
something. I looked out, and there was Dr. Dvořák, walking
along the street, as if he was lost in his ideas, with a cane stuck
under his forearm, and his fingers running over his coat if it
were a keyboard. He entered the house quickly, and in no time
he was completely absorbed with his work.

Once, he became very lonely in his study, and with an
armful of sketches, he came downstairs to work among us....

He became very popular, and not only the Czechs but also
the Americans respected him greatly. They expressed their love
and respect for him in different ways—most often, they sent
gifts and gave him other courteous favors. Everybody sent what
he could, because they knew well that Doctor would be as
much pleased with a small gift as he would be with an expensive
present. For example, all of the time we lived in New York, we
did not have to buy a piece of pastry because there was a compe-

tition among the bakers there, as to who would supply our
kitchen with the best. Everything was free. It made them proud
that the Doctor accepted these gifts. Similar arrangements were
made with meat, and with other things for the kitchen. Besides
the food delivered to us, some other things came with it, too....
Once, I saw a young man following Dr. Dvořák, showing great
respect for the composer. He stayed behind him, waiting for the
Doctor to enter the house. Then, he walked three steps down,
and standing at the main door, he kissed the knob, which just a
while ago had been touched by the Master....

As the weeks and months passed, Dvořák got used to his new environment and work, and he received a great deal of satisfaction from it. He always worked strictly according to the daily schedule he set up for himself. Kovarik recalled that, after conducting in Boston, he worked on routine instrumentation of his composition, *The American Flag,* as if he wanted to isolate himself from that kind of activity. He listened with all his soul to the heartbeat of the city. He absorbed the noises of the harbor, and the contrasting quietness of the landscape. These he learned to know from his explorations in the surrounding area as well as his trip to Boston. He could hear the throbbing, pulsating heart of this unusual, intoxicating, and very exciting new country. He used a large amount of his free time to gather the energy and the themes for his next work. This does not mean that his name had disappeared from the American newspapers. On the contrary, his popularity was entrusted to the good care of the President, Mrs. Thurber. The New York Philharmonic conducted by Seidel performed Dvořák's Suite in D Major (Opus 39); and the Beethoven String Quartet played his Piano Quartet in E-flat Major (Opus 87). Many other performances were to come.

His first steps were already successful, and the beginning of his sojourn in America had produced a visible ruffling on the calm, untouched surface of American music, which had waited patiently for what might come later. What kind of composition would originate from the soul of such a special man? Dvořák was beyond the scope of their original image of the "devilish Cossack type personality," whose head, according to Huneker, "looked like an angry bulldog bearded...with his fierce Slavonic eyes."

Yes, the first weeks and months had passed when they received a letter from Josefina in Vienna dated November 29, 1892:

I wonder what your Christmas Eve will be like there. Where
will you celebrate it, and how? Let us hope that we can meet
again in good health and happiness. I trust that you will not

forget us, and despite your intention to move the rest of your family from Bohemia to America the next spring, you will return here after all. I received this information in a letter from Reza yesterday—she only mentioned what you had asked in your previous letter—if grandma would take the chance, and come with your children to New York. However, before spring you still have time enough to change your mind. Perhaps, you will have another opinion, etc. Maybe after the first excitement is over, and new obstacles and adversities arise, it is quite possible that you will change your mind. As we say in our old proverb—"We can feel fine everywhere, but there is no place like home..." Nevertheless, I wish you both the most happiness. Let Our Lord present you with plenty of money, and grant that you will be able to make good use of your wealth in good comfort, back home again. I wish for Otila, as I already wrote, a millionaire; to Tonik—a very nice and expensive surprise for Christmas; and also to Mr. Kovarik that he, besides his excellent artistic career, would find some good and very rich American girl....

> With kisses Yours, Josefina."

This letter is absolutely typical of the Countess Kounic: all about wealth and property—her head was full of it. We can cite from the letter which she wrote on January 9, 1893:

> ...and then, you should use a chance offered to you by this exhibition, and try to earn from it as much as possible. The popularity comes first, then the money. If you can trust yourself to finish the work offered to you by those gentlemen on time (as you mentioned in your letter), you must certainly accept this opportunity given to you. It is quite possible that you could earn much money in a short time, a sum which you could not earn in your present job in many years of service. You cannot expect to grow as a little violet: In America, with all her advertising, the most important thing is how much people talk about you, this determines the degree of success you can expect to attain.

Dvořák's ideas were never like hers. The business of running after profit and money did not impress the composer, and always was strange to him. Indeed, it took him a long time to make a decision before he signed his contract to go to America. Only after his wife had initiated a vote about it at the family table had things changed.

The first problem mentioned in Josefina's letter was the possibility that the Dvořáks might emigrate. The rumor might have been related to Josefina's early remark in her letter from November 8, when she talks about "Andula" who hardly could wait to join them in America.

Later, in another letter from November 29, there is a similar mention; the sister Rezi had written to her that next spring grandma should take the rest of the children to the Dvořáks in America. It is obvious that this information had prompted Josefina to accuse Dvořák of planning to stay in America.

What was the truth? Dvořák's son Otakar wrote about it in his memoirs:

> As soon as he (father) arrived to America, he sent many, many letters to us, his four children left at home. I am sorry that some of the letters from father could not be included in a section which I dedicated to letters only. In most of them, addressed to his mother-in-law and to us children, our father recalled his early splendid impressions of sightseeing in New York; the streets; Hoboken harbor; and on another occasion, Central Park, which has the largest zoo in the world. He described his close observation of transatlantic ships. He also wrote about his teaching at the conservatory; how many, and what kind of students he has; even a few blacks attended his classes. One letter followed the other. I could hardly understand where his opposition to writing went. Besides the letters to us, he sent numbers of them to his friends in Bohemia. Today, I know why he did it. This was his way to draw near his beloved homeland, his friends, and most of all, his children. By writing so many letters, he was able to relieve his enormous homesickness.
>
> That it was homesickness, we can see in one of father's letters. He announced to us that he had decided not to be without us across the big pond any more, and asked us to join him. He also suggested that his sister-in-law, Rezi should escort us to America.

Otakar's explanation is quite simple and clear. His father's thoughts were not of emigration but of his mighty love for his children. After only one month in New York City he wanted to invite the rest of his family to America, not to stay there for good, but to be together until the period of his contract ended. A few weeks later his idea became clearer. Christmas influenced him so strongly that nothing could change his decision. This holiday did not bring them any joy, but they knew that their children left in Bohemia were with the Kounics for Christmas Day. They learned every detail about it from Josefina's letter of January 2, 1893. Nothing helped them, and there was the anguish of sadness on 17th Street, as described in Dvořák's letter to his friend Rus on January 2, 1893. However, New Year's Eve turned out to be a little different, and going back to Dvořák's correspondence, we find that he wrote:

> We were in "Ceska Beseda" on New Year's Eve until 1 a.m. The streets were still very busy, lots of folks there—the young boys and young ladies, blowing trumpets, sang and made such a noise that it was terrible. This is how they celebrate the New Year. In addition you could even hear shouting in the streets, and in general, the things here are not as anywhere else; everything is entirely American, in "American style."

Because the letter was written on January 2, 1893, its mood could convey more accurately the truth than Kovarik's sentimental recollection of that New Year's Eve, written in 1950:

> Our first evening of the New Year's Day in New York was a peaceful one because we stayed at home. At midnight, we heard some beautiful singing, which left Dvořák quite touched. When he looked out from the window, he could see a choir standing on the side-walk, not too far from our house. They had been singing to their priest. "Imagine this!" exclaimed Master, "In the middle of the city! They came to sing Foster's 'My Old Kentucky Home'! Only here could this be possible! Do you think that such a thing could happen in our country, too? I don't think so.—This is beauty, true beauty! That Foster has done a lot for America. Maybe one day the people will realize what a great musician he was...."

Summarizing the experience of Dvořák's exciting first weeks in America, we see a mountain of impressions rolling over him. This foreign environment was flattering to him, sometimes promising more than he was used to in Europe. Nevertheless, the American social lifestyle did not overwhelm him, and Dvořák kept himself as far from it as possible. His presence at most social events was for satisfying the needs of the school, and of the President, Mrs. Thurber. His inner life was similar to that at Vysoka: he had his hobbies which could satisfy him, his evening Darda, and most of all, his work which could fulfill him best and give him the greatest possible stimulation. He described it well in correspondence written on paper with the letterhead of the National Conservatory of Music of America in the upper left corner and with his office address "126/128 East 17th Street, New York" on the right. Dvořák's handwriting shows the date of January 24, 1893. The addressee of this letter was Vicar, Jindrich Geisler, in Olomouc (Moravia).

> Dear friend,
>
> …Considering my job, if everything continues as it is now, I will be fine. My work which I was afraid of a bit, is not too strenuous, and really pleases me…. *The American Flag,* Hymnus for choir and orchestra, is finished and now I am working on my new Symphony. I feel that the American soil will have a beneficial influence on my mind, and I can even say that you should be able to hear something of my new experience in my new symphony.

The Symphony *From the New World* was coming to life. Dvořák's right-hand man, Josef J. Kovarik, remembered:

> On the eighth of January, 1893, the Master finished the instrumentation of *The American Flag*. After that, he asked me to recopy its score—and two days later, on January 10th, he began on a sketch of his new, monumental work, which he has named "The Symphony in E Minor, Number 8."

One of the most renowned symphonies of the ages, the culmination of Dvořák's work, the Symphony *From the New World* was about to take shape.

First Weeks ⮑ B

AFTER A RESTLESS NIGHT I WOKE UP in the strange surroundings of my temporary shelter at the Mission. My eyes, carefully examining everything in the bedroom, were filled with wonder. I had great expectations of coming events. New York City was getting up early; its heartbeat was quickening minute by minute with each traffic noise. I gazed out the window observing the cars and the crowds and the neon signs that rarely go out. The sidewalks were lined with garbage containers, ready to go since last evening.

In my view this is the typical scenery of the metropolis: boxlike buildings of various sizes covered with signs; iron fire escapes, installed decades ago, still hanging ugly and useless at the sides of the old houses, which by some miracle have survived the demand for land so much needed for the mushrooming skyscrapers.

The single houses, whole blocks of them, made me humble, and I could feel my growing admiration for the sight. This view of the city shocked, attracted, and enchanted me all at the same time. I felt the same emotions one might feel on meeting a well-groomed woman, unusually dressed in the latest style, and who is unbelievably beautiful. She could take your breath away, but you fear the coldness of her insensitivity, oblivious to other peoples' needs. She lacks an understanding of human existence, of the hardship of people's lives—their worries, sorrows, and ordinary joys.

These thoughts and observations came back to me every evening, helping me to gain some perspective on my latest achievements. I slowly became accustomed to the route which took me to the branch of the City Library in New York where all the photocopies of journals and magazines were stored.

I also became familiar with the main streets and quarters of the city. About two in the afternoon my library studies usually ended for the day. After a quick late lunch, I began to explore the lower end of Manhattan. Aimlessly wandering, I let my eyes, heart, and mind discover the past and present secrets of this enormous city.

I saw blocks of streets where the rich people lived. These areas were well kept and groomed, smelling of perfume and flowers. But I also found streets, where there were sex shops, dirt, crumbling plaster walls, and noisy squalor everywhere. These sections were not settled by just the Southern poor, or by Chinese, or Italian immigrants. The same conditions could be found in other areas, too.

Besides looking for the soul of the city, I was aware of my main goal here—to find Dvořák. The detailed schedule for my research was a "must." I would have to go through all the newspapers from the period of Dvořák's visit of several hundred days. My next visit would be to the archives of Columbia University, and then to the City Museum of New York where it would be possible to see a model of Manhattan Island in the 1890s. This would help me to get a good picture of the city at that time, and of all the changes which have been made since Dvořák left.

In Kovarik's memoirs and in the composer's letters are recollections of many localities related to Dvořák's sojourn: Central Park with its flocks of pigeons and its little aviary; 155th Street and Washington Heights where he used to have his private spot for observing trains; Hoboken Harbor, important to his latest hobby—the transatlantic steamships; and Battery Park, the southern tip of Manhattan, where he could follow the ships sailing to Europe if he had missed them in the harbor because he was composing at home, or was detained at the conservatory.

The list of the places more or less important for my story is long, but the significance of each location may be changed when the truth is known. So, the list continues: the restaurant where Dvořák liked to go to read Czech newspapers; the Metropolitan Opera; Carnegie Hall, where the world premiere of his Symphony *From the New World* took place; something could be found in the Lincoln Cultural Center; the Hotel Clarendon, where the Dvořáks lived after their arrival in America; the National Conservatory of Music of America should be visited—but first of all, I would have to find 17th Street and the narrow, three-story house where Dvořák lived and composed his music.

It was half past eight in the morning, and although the trees in Central Park were still in a deep winter sleep, the sky was blue, and spring was evidently in the air. My plan for today took me to the southern section of Manhattan where many points of my research were located.

The subway took me to the west side of Manhattan where my map showed the harbor docks on the Hudson River and the railway station. Hoboken was on the opposite bank. I found the railway station but when I went closer to the docks, I could not believe what I saw: half-destroyed buildings, some of them empty, others still in use but showing that they had served their time. The main building of the harbor and its management office did not exist here any more. There were only the ugly remnants of the past, of a world no longer there. Was this the famous New York Harbor, the Gate to America, through which millions of emigrants had rushed to enter the promised land?

This part of the city was permeated with a special sadness. The run-down wharves jutting out into the sea held devastated buildings which had ceased to function a long time ago. Everything had changed; the circumstances, the conditions, even the value of time had changed since Dvořák's visit. In 1892 the trip from Europe took approximately 200 hours. Today, the same distance can be covered in 10 hours by plane. The huge public harbors became orphans, and models of the transatlantic steamships are shown today in technological museums as evidence of human achievement in a previous era. Today's shipping is limited to the transportation of products, while people mostly fly. One must have enough money and time to sail from America to Europe these days. Now and then, a gigantic ship like the *Queen Mary* offers a trip which costs a lot, and takes quite a while to reach its destination. This kind of travel seems to be more for social and recreational purposes than for tourism or business. Airplanes are faster and cheaper, and much more practical for people at the end of the twentieth century.

As I stood on one of the docks, I had to think that somewhere there on the other side, the ship *Saale* with Dvořák and his family on board had reached the coast. As the map shows, there are ninety-nine steamship docks in the harbor, but only three of them are used for public transportation.

The harbor was almost empty, except for a couple of cargo ships and the little Circle Line ferry which had a heavy load of tourists on their way around Manhattan Island. Nothing else interrupted the calm isolation of this no-longer-busy water. At one of the docks which was repaired and modernized, the white colossus *Oceania* cast its anchor. This large ship had several decks, seven or eight lifeboats on its sides, and the Panamanian flag fluttering above the prow. Not too far from *Oceania* another ship was anchored, and a few cranes projected against the sky. The harbor, which at the end of the last century could receive approximately 5,200 ships of all types, and had a total capacity of as much as 6 to 7 million tons estimated weight, was quietly slumbering, as if put to rest. The traffic so busy here before was moved to the two airports, J. F. Kennedy and La Guardia, and to other airports in the area.

This harbor was considered to be the gateway to the New World when Dvořák came to the USA, and as his son Otakar recollected:

> We often went to Hoboken Harbor to welcome the ships arriving from Germany such as those of the North German Lloyd Line and the "American Line," the "White Star Line" and the "Red Star Line," To share his great hobby with everybody, father invited the conductor Seidel to come with us, and very professionally described to him the capacity, horse-power and maximum speed, the name of the Captain, and the interior plan of each ship.
>
> Father's love of ships and his knowledge about sailing were passed on to me. Quite often, when father was busy in other ways, he sent me to the harbor, and I had to find out everything about a particular ship—its time of arrival, weather conditions at sea, and what interesting incidents occurred during the trip.
>
> It might seem doubtful that a young boy would be able to investigate all this but I was used to frequent participation in father's daily visits to Hoboken, and from listening to his discussions with captains I learned what I needed for such a task. He knew every engineer on the express-trains in Franz Joseph Railway Station in Prague, and he became equally familiar with the captains of transatlantic steamships.
>
> It was easy for me to become as popular in the harbor as my father was, and I learned how to find out without much difficulty what he wanted to know.

Everything that Otakar spoke of is now long gone. My next stop was Battery Park in the very southern corner of Manhattan. According to Kovarik, this was a place from which Dvořák could follow the ships sailing to Europe. He watched them steam past the Statue of Liberty, and disappear slowly into the vastness of the ocean.

On my way there I observed the construction of a new expressway around Manhattan, and there were the "Twins," the American name for a quite surrealistic-looking pair of skyscrapers which, until a Chicago skyscraper exceeded their height, were the tallest buildings in the world. It is in human nature to reach higher and higher, and it matters very little that we might possibly burn our wings. In any case, these "Twins" became the unparalleled attraction of Manhattan, and had outdone the previous world's-highest-construction, the Empire State Building. Nevertheless, height is only relative, and can be measured either to the top of a building, or to the top of an antenna above it.

The Empire State Building is situated at the intersection of Fifth Avenue and 34th Street, and, from street level to the top of its antenna, measures 1,469 feet. When the building was finished, it was supposed to be the "eighth wonder of the world." Two of its stories, the 86th and 102nd, the latter being 1,250 feet high, were built as observatories. Honza and I visited there two days ago, and our impression of the city beneath was overwhelming.

The "Twins"—officially named the World Trade Center—are eight stories higher than the Empire State Building, and the last floor, the 118th, is 1,348 feet above the ground, with walls of glass. There is an observatory equipped with telescopes, a restaurant, and gift shops. Although its structure is 98 feet higher than the Empire State Building, the latter has an antenna which surpasses the "Twins" by 121 feet. Such competition is typical of Americans.

We went up to take pictures of the spectacular view from the observatory on the top. As one who admires clean, blue sky and sunshine, I was perfectly happy taking pictures with my own camera up there. The real professional, Honza, was not so happy. He wished to see at least a few little clouds covering the spotless, ultramarine sky for his perfect shots. But no matter how much he complained, I fully enjoyed that completely new experience: the cars which from up here became just small, insignificant spots; the huge body of *Oceania* now the size of a child's toy; and the Statue of Liberty on a distant island, no bigger than a matchstick. I could not wait to find the locations below which were important for my research. Almost at the foot of the "Twins" were Battery Park and the Brooklyn Bridge, built before Dvořák's arrival in New York City. His impressions of the city were probably the same as mine today. Although the skyscrapers, as we know them, did not exist yet, the buildings then already represented a completely new quality in architecture, and were absolutely incomparable to the circumspect styles used in Old Europe. Life here was more colorful, and Dvořák, his heart beating with excitement, was overwhelmed. However, he seldom missed any departure of a ship sailing for Europe.

Battery Park, spread over 21 acres, is the oldest part of Manhattan, and its point juts far out into the harbor. The fortress there, called Castle Clinton, was built at the beginning of the nineteenth century. It was named for the then governor, De Witt Clinton. Close by were the city military headquarters, which were moved later to an adjacent island. From 1824 to 1855, this place served as a kind of public tribunal used by politicians and other speakers. For example, President Jackson, the great Hungarian patriot Kossuth, and many artists, soldiers, and citizens once gathered here. As the United States grew, and development accelerated, more immigrants were needed, and the Battery fortress acquired yet another purpose; it became a "Gateway to the New World." Over seven million newcomers entered here between 1855 and 1890. In 1950 a large monument consisting of eight granite commemorative tablets was erected over the very point of this park. Engraved on these tablets were 4,596 names of the sailors who had perished in the Second World War.

The park sidewalks are bordered by numerous benches, and the area is occupied by pigeons hopping on the paths. The balustrades, separating lawns from beach, belong to the seagulls. The round, red fortress is surrounded by trees, and five or six houses survive from the last century. Overshadowed by the massive skyscrapers, they look like fantastic dwarfs among giants. Dvořák met the same ten-story dwarfs on his way to Battery Park, where he observed the ships sailing to Europe. He must have been overwhelmed by the sky- scrapers' magnitude, which now—many times surpassed by the progress of a new technology—has become a monument to nineteenth-century grandeur.

The scale has changed but not the character of this city. Only a few min- utes from here is narrow Wall Street which hides its ugliness in the shadow of its superficial fame. A little way from here is the renowned New York Stock Market which in the eighteen-nineties was prepared to govern the financial world. Dvořák, fully occupied with music, with his strong faith in God and his great affection for his family, cared little or nothing for these insignificant (for him) features. This gifted, talented genius could become quite absent- minded, showing little interest in American, or even in Bohemian politics. He paid no attention to his brother-in-law Count Kounic's complaints about happenings in Austria—Antonín's world was different and special. Each time he came here to observe another ship sailing, he could hear the sounds of the harbor, the breathing and bubbling of its rapacious life. Everything was absorbed by his perceptive soul to become processed into music which would characterize this outstanding city. He was subconsciously collecting and stor- ing all these sounds, not knowing yet how he would use them, or when.

This was a crucial time for his work, a time for letting ideas grow and ripen. He walked down the streets and went to the Brooklyn Bridge, observ- ing and listening to everything.

The renowned beauty of the Brooklyn Bridge was worth Dvořák's effort, and it is still well preserved one hundred years after his sojourn. It took 14 years to build—too long for American know-how. Nevertheless, several technical problems in its construction had to be solved before this first bridge could join Manhattan with its neighbors—at that time, the suburban area of Brooklyn. The bay called East River was too wide, and the bridge had to be hung on steel cables which create a wonderful, decorative, lace pattern. The opening of this great bridge on May 24, 1883, was organized as a great ceremony with many speeches and proclamations celebrating its technology and achievement. There is still a tablet at the approach, stating that the bridge was "originally built for pedestrians and teams of horses." Only later was the new exterior finished, and automobiles took over. The central path for the pedestrians was raised and made wide enough for comfort. The gigantic constructions of Manhattan—the Chrysler Building along with others—could easily be seen through the lacy cobwebs of steel cables hanging everywhere.

As I was standing in the middle of the bridge, I suddenly remembered its great admirer, the famous Walt Whitman. My eyes tried to find the port from which the ferryboats, linking Manhattan with its nearby islands, usually leave. In his recollections, Dvořák's son Otakar relates:

> Almost every Sunday in the early afternoon, father and I took
> the elevated railway from 1st Avenue, and went to Long Island.
> We watched the surf and picked up shells. Father intently
> observed the numerous coastal ships in view.

The elevated railway was now replaced by a subway, and the coastal shore had changed, too. There are twenty bridges now, and several submarine tunnels as well.

Our tour with the Circle Line around Manhattan was very good for many reasons. It began on the West Side, and took us along the decayed docks with the "Twins" on the left-hand side. Suddenly, Battery Park appeared ahead, and we went under the Brooklyn Bridge. Then came the Manhattan and Williamsburg bridges, the landscaped buildings of the United Nations, and more bridges above our heads. Manhattan Island's unrealistic beauty, observed from the water, helped me to understand better Dvořák's passion for taking his customary Sunday trips to Long Island.

The North area of Manhattan was getting less congested; the skyscrapers became smaller, and had fewer floors. The stony shores changed to lawns, sometimes touching the edge of the water. At 130th Street we left the bay and entered Harlem River. With the Bronx on the right-hand side, and narrowing

Manhattan island on the left, we came to the very point of the island, and we turned again to the wide, majestic Hudson River.

Manhattan was now on our left side. The shore became steep, and featured an unusual edifice; the tomb of General Grant, President of the United States. We should be near the heights where Dvořák and Kovarik had observed the trains. Where was the railway? I hoped for a train to come while we were there, but no trace of railway, no train in view—we would have to get there on foot, overland.

In the evening after our Circle Line trip, I had supper with a friend in a Chinese restaurant which was called "Empire Szechuan Balcony" and was on Third Avenue, between 27th and 28th Streets. Although its name told me nothing about the place, the atmosphere there was pleasant and the service excellent. Our discussion turned very soon to the purpose of my visit to the USA, the task of finding enough new materials for my research about Dvořák, his life and activities in New York City, and later in Spillville.

I also told him about my hope of discovering some new compositions in the possessions of the late Henry Thacker ("Harry") Burleigh, who died in 1949. It is known that Dvořák had arranged "The Old Folks at Home," a song written by the American composer Stephen Foster, and dedicated it to Burleigh, who was a devoted pupil. This Black musician was one of the main speakers during the ceremony of the "unveiling of the Dvořák memorial tablet" on the house on 17th Street in 1941. This was part of a program for the "celebration of the one hundred year anniversary of Dvořák's birthday." Burleigh died of mental illness eight years later, and this arrangement had been temporarily lost. However, it was discovered again in 1990 and published. Some of Dvořák's letters to Burleigh have become valuable collectors' items.

My friend wondered: "Do you have any idea what you are getting into?"

"Never mind," I laughed. "It was always in my nature to go after a difficult task."

At the end of our supper, in accord with a thousand-year-old Chinese tradition, the attentive waiter brought us fortune cookies. Mine carried the following message: "The world envies the man who can smile when it's hard to." It was probably only a coincidence, but I took this little narrow piece of paper home anyway, just for a keepsake.

Our Ambassador invited me to the United Nations Organization. I will always remember what I saw there. The halls beautifully displayed the peaceful nature of the assemblies. The symbolic painting by the Norwegian Pere Krohg gives its character to the overall space. The color blue, dominating the hall, awakens hope and brings profound thoughts. For example, I thought about the role of music, which is to give wings to people; and I thought about death, which takes them away. The Hammarskjold Library there, decorated with glass and white pine ceilings, offers modern studies and reference rooms. The themes of their collections, however, were far away from those necessary for my research on Dvořák in America.

My next inquiry at the New York City Library on Fifth Avenue took me to the manuscript department. After a few days I was able to find only one letter, written by Dvořák to Littleton in 1887, which has nothing to do with his American period. Therefore I returned to the Branch Library on 43rd Street where I found the journal collections most useful. The same young Black girl whom I met before, asked me, smiling, whether I wanted the microfilms of the *New York Herald* which I had before, or the *New York Times*. In a short time I was sitting at the reading machine again, looking for more information about the festival prepared for Antonín Dvořák by Czech-Americans in October 1892, welcoming him to America. The composer wrote about the event in his letters to Prague. It took place not long after the reception party for Dvořák, and the first article to carry the news on October 10 was captioned, "Bohemians Honor Dr. Antonín Dvořák." It stated:

> More than thirty-six hundred Bohemians gave greeting at the Central Turn Verein Opera House, Sixty-seventh street, near Third Avenue, to Dr. Antonín Dvořák last night. When the new director of the National Conservatory of Music entered the hall, accompanied by his wife, son and daughter, the whole audience arose and wildly waved and shouted welcome to the Bohemian composer and his family.
>
> Dr. Dvořák was escorted to a box and there was some good choral music under the direction of by Mr. W. Raboch.
>
> In an address of welcome spoken in Bohemian Mr. V. Truna [*sic*] congratulated America upon having secured "the greatest master in the realm of [*sic*] musical composition" and predicted that Dr. Dvořák will become the "creator and master of American national music."
>
> "He it is," said the speaker, "who has spread the Czech musical art among all nations." An address of a similar nature was delivered in English by Mr. J. Janacek.
>
> Dr. Dvořák was then invited to go on the platform, and after speeches by Messrs. J. Castka and J. Belsky, was presented with a magnificent silver wreath bearing the inscription, "To Dr. Antonín Dvořák, from the Bohemian people of the city of New York."

Responding, Dr. Dvořák spoke with much feeling. He had never dreamed of such enthusiasm in America, where, to his great astonishment, he had found his work better known than abroad. He paid a high tribute to America's wonderful progress, and said that it would be the crowning ambition of his life to add to the lustre of America's great fame. He had never expected such a demonstration in his honor and could not find words to convey his heartfelt appreciation. Dr. Dvořák spoke in Bohemian.

A banquet followed at which speeches were made by Professor J. Reindl, W. Habach, Joseph Janacek and Frank J. Brodil, chairman of the Reception Committee.

That was a glorious day, and Dvořák became a symbol of the homeland for the Czech immigrants who had to leave their homes behind for the opportunity of a better living. They had come as nobodies to America, while the composer was already well recognized throughout the whole world.

In Vojtech Tuma's late-nineteenth-century stylized speech, he described everything about the life and feelings of the Bohemian ethnic group in New York:

Honorable Assembly! Dear Friends!

This is a rare, indeed, a very rare occasion which takes place today, an occasion that enables us to welcome into our circle and pay our respects to a genius—one who is highly respected and renowned throughout the length and breadth of the whole world. It is our pleasure to bestow our open-hearted, meritorious gratitude on the grand wizard of musical art—and according to our old national tradition, to respect all the individuals who helped to elevate the name of Bohemia, and as the sons and daughters of this hearty nation, we salute our esteemed guest of honor—Dr. Antonín Dvořák!

The significance of this event is very important because only rarely was such a genius born in such a small nation as Bohemia. Bohemia was for long centuries a nation pursued by an unfortunate destiny, a nation which, in spite of its venerable age, could never rest in comfort and enjoy peacefully the harvest of fruit ripening on the tree of art, a tree which had been planted ages ago in our ancient, celebrated kingdom to be nursed and improved with our care.

You came here in large numbers, and your eyes shining with pleasure and excitement show how proud you are of this man who has passed all the tests of world criticism, and acclaimed by all, became the man whom we see today. If you have heard the public voices proclaiming that free America is going to be host to the greatest Maestro of the empire of sound, you have also read that he will become the founder of the national music of America, too. Touched deeply, we would like to claim our rights that this man belongs to us! Yes, dear friends, we are proud of him. There are nations free enough to progress and have their Mozarts, Beethovens, and many other composers.

As for our persecuted, discriminated-against and subjugated nation, we have answered them with our Dvořák. What man is there who would not be pleased and feel joy that our Dvořák has been recognized in a foreign country so far from the borders of his homeland; a man whose temples were decorated with the laurel wreath for the acknowledgement of his victory. His glory did not render him haughty, even in this foreign country which lies down in the dust at his feet and worships his great spirit. It shows him its respect and recognition, which is bigger than his own small nation was able to give him, because his nation was deprived of everything it ever held. Regardless of America's attempt to lead him astray from the way he had already chosen, his heart, filled with an extensive love of his nation—his dear Bohemia—could not be denied!

For these reasons we can only respect his pure character, and share with him his joy, not for our sake only, but for the sake of our beloved Bohemia!

As the enthusiastic speech went on, Tuma continued to express similar feelings on the part of the other participants in the reception for Dvořák. During the composer's grateful answer, the audience rose again, giving him another standing ovation, wanting to show him their reverence and love.

Then came the reading of the telegrams which had come from every corner of America: from the Bohemian Committee in Cedar Rapids, Iowa; nine from individuals in Omaha, Nebraska, showing great feelings of nationalism. A few of them were in rhyme, and all of them expressed recognition and respect. Six telegrams were sent from Cleveland, Ohio; one of them was signed, "35,000 Bohemians." The many Unions and Clubs, bearing names like Lumir, Sokol, Thalia, Rovnost, Hlahol, and so forth, wanted to acclaim Dvořák, too. Countrymen from Milwaukee, Wisconsin, sent their greetings; and many, many more—all of them saluting and honoring Dvořák in their proud, poetic, and metaphoric way. The endless flood of high-flown words demonstrated the love and pride of Dvořák's countrymen.

The celebration organized for Dvořák not only touched the composer's heart, but every heart in the audience was impressed that evening. Mr. V. Tuma, several years later, recalled the dinner organized after the concert. He also recollected how much Dvořák liked to visit the "National House" on Fifth Avenue for he had played the game "bulka" there, smoked from his black gypsum pipe which he nicknamed "gypsovka," and drunk "a few pilseners" with his countrymen.

Tuma never forgot Dvořák's ability to demonstrate his Bohemian identity. "Once Dvořák, while walking past a music firm on Cooper Union, noticed that his photograph was on display with his name as 'Anton Dvorak'. Dvořák entered, asked for the picture, and after striking his name out with a pencil, wrote correctly under it in bigger letters: 'Antonín Dvořák,' with thick, ostentatious marks over the *r* and *a*."

I brought with me to the States a file of various articles documenting Dvořák's years in America, but I still lacked firsthand evidence from the American press, and that was one of the reasons for my trip here. Therefore, I scanned every column in the *Herald,* repeating to myself, "Don't hurry, don't hurry." At the same time, the spring wind was raking the face of the Hudson River, tearing off hats, and lifting the skirts of the female pedestrians.

In the same newspaper on Monday, October 10, 1892, I found a note in a column:

> Bars of Music:
>
> Dr. Antonín Dvořák, who has now entered upon his duties as Director of the National Conservatory of Music, will under the auspices of that institution, make his first appearance in a concert to occur at the Music Hall on Friday evening, October 21st. The programme arranged for this occasion will include two new works by Dr. Dvořák, and the performance will enlist the efforts of Mr. Anton Seidl and the Metropolitan orchestra of eighty, a chorus of 300 voices and of Mme. Clementino de Vero-Sapio and Mr. Emil Fisher as soloists.

Time went fast for Dvořák. He knew that his countrymen had praised him to high heaven; but now a more difficult question arose—how well would the musical world of America receive him? I had already gone through every issue of the *New York Herald* from Monday, October 10, to the end of the month. Did I overlook anything? I went back, searching page by page

OURTEEN PAGES.

ANTONIN DVORAK
LEADS AT MUSIC HALL.

American Debut of the Famous Bohemian Composer Before an Enthusiastic and Brilliant Audience.

COLONEL T. W. HIGGINSON'S ORATION.

Initial Performances of the "Triple Overture" and the Specially Composed "Te Deum" by the New Director of the National Conservatory of Music.

Dr. Antonin Dvorak had good reason for satisfaction with both the quantity and the quality of the reception accorded him last night at the Carnegie Music Hall, upon the occasion until the library clerk announced closing time and chased me away. Tomorrow would be another day.

On 43rd Street, a man was hawking warm pretzels covered with salty flakes; neon signs announced that a musical *Evita,* about the Argentinean President's wife, Eva Peron, was tops; somewhere else, the same thing was said about the musical *Amadeus;* and a sexshow, which could excite even the coldest in the audience, was advertising its attractions. In front of the Museum of Modern Art, I learned that an exhibition of Giorgio de Chirico was in preparation, and was to be open April 3 through June 29, 1982. Although I did not really like his work, I was moved by it and I knew that I would be going to see his exhibition anyway.

In the evening, after my library work, I stopped at the home of an embassy attaché where we talked about our homes, and about America. They showed slides from their American holiday. I commented favorably on their cheese sauce, and got a recipe from them to take home. When I praised the whipped cream, I learned that it did not come from a cow but the ingredients were only water, coconut, palm oil, sugar, corn syrup, and xanthein gum. Because I was planning more trips to follow traces of Dvořák's life in America, we next discussed what kind of arrangement should be made for getting the best results in my work.

The next day at the branch of the City Library, perhaps because of a more intensive search and as a favor of the gods, I found an article—"Antonín Dvořák at Music Hall"—from October 22. How could I have missed it? The subheads were truly American:

> American Debut of the Famous Bohemian Composer. Before an Enthusiastic and Brilliant Audience.—COLONEL T. W. HIGGINSON'S ORATION.—Initial Performance of the *Triple Overture* and the Specially Composed *Te Deum* by the New Director of the National Conservatory of Music.

The article is interesting for several reasons. It contains a few errors (Dvořák did not leave "his own country because he wanted to emigrate..." and the journalist forgot to mention that his contract was drawn up for only two years), but the other descriptions carry a lovely, somewhat naive mood. The critical evaluation of the *Triple Overture* (Dvořák still called it *Nature, Life and Love* and changed it later to *Nature's Realm, Carnival, Othello*) sounds more like some kind of misunderstanding. The critic said:

> Dr. Dvořák had good reason for satisfaction with both the quantity and quality of the reception accorded him last night at

Carnegie Music Hall, upon the occasion of his first appearance before an American audience. As a composer whose works have already become classical he was hailed with an enthusiasm which knows no difference of clime or or [*sic*] nationality, while as the man who had forsaken his own land to adopt another, and give to its National Conservatory the impress and power of his musical genius, he was greeted with a royal welcome such as is not often accorded to an individual.

The audience was immense in point of numbers, and representative of the best elements of artistic and social New York. Almost every musician of local prominence was there. Mme Camilla Urso, though suffering from a painfully sprained arm, listened to the music of the great Bohemian. Signor Campanini elbowed his way to standing room in the rear of the densely crowded hall. Signor Agramonte and Adolph Neuendorff crowded into very small space behind the last row of seats in the parquet and applauded vigorously after the *Triple Overture*.

Dr. Dvořák will not soon forget his reception. When he advanced to take his place at the conductor's desk, the members of the orchestra rose as one man and played a tusch,* while the audience cheered the composer to the echo. Even more sedate occupants of the boxes waved their handkerchiefs in greeting, and it was some moments before the composer was allowed to proceed.

Scenes Before the Concert

In the outer lobby a magnificent array of flowers claimed the first attention of the crowds. There were tributes to Dr. Dvořák and Anton Seidl from their many admirers. People lingered to look at the flowers and the lobbies soon became densely packed. Before 8 o'clock every seat in the vast auditorium was occupied, and even standing room was at a premium. Mrs. Jeanette M. Thurber, with a party of friends, arrived early and went to a box on the right of the stage. The Rev. Dr. Parkhurst, with his wife and brother, occupied a box in the centre of the tier, and was the observed of all observers. Anton Seidl held conspicuous place in a box at the extreme left of the first tier, and Mr. and Mrs. William H. Vanderbilt were also prominent among those in the boxes.

---

*"Tusch," as defined by Webster is "a flourish of brasswind instruments of an orchestra signifying applause." —Translator's note.

Chorus Master Richard Henry Warren opened the concert by leading the orchestra, chorus and audience in the national anthem, *America*. He earned golden opinions by the skill with which he conducted. The anthem was never more impressively sung, the audience standing while *America* was sung. Dr. Dvořák stood at the door leading to the stage regarding the spectacle with interest.

He seemed unconscious that every soul in the audience was principally concerned with a mental inventory of his own personality. After it was over Dr. Dvořák expressed himself as mightily impressed with the vigor and enthusiasm of the singing.

Colonel Higginson's Address

Colonel Thomas Wentworth Higginson delivered the oration of the evening, entitled "Two New Worlds—The New World of Columbus and the New World of Music." He spoke in part as follows:

"Over all this wide land today men and women have been celebrating the finding of this continent with such zeal you would think that each one had a hand in the discovery.

"It is fitting that music should take her part in the great festival, because music is the only art which, since Columbus, has also discovered a new world. We meet to celebrate that newer discovery, to lay upon the bier of Columbus the only wreath that has wholly blossomed since his time, the one art that is post-Columbian."

In concluding Colonel Higginson said:

"The triumphs of own our land in music, like most of our artistic triumphs, lie in the future, if anywhere. If we were all made of unmixed English blood, we might have long to wait for them. Moreover the material success must come first. If you choose the picked young men of each college class and send them out on railroads, art must wait, or if a man of commanding genius give half his energies to the building of steam engines and only the other half to making symphonies, the chances are that the steam engines may go at high pressure, but the symphonies will not.

"And we draw to-night on that wondrous country where, it used to be said, every child was tested early in the cradle to see whether he would choose the violin bow or the rifle with his baby hand, the country which has so identified itself with the fire of genius that Boyle O'Reilly makes the burden of his best lyric run thus:

'I had rather live in Bohemia
Than in any other land.'

"Let us hope that our guest of to-night will at least not share this opinion, that he may consent to transplantation and may help add the new world of music to the continent which Columbus found."

What Musicians Thought

These are a few of the opinions I gathered:

Herr Anton Seidl—"Dr. Dvořák is a great accession to the musical art of this land. We have reason to rejoice in his coming as the earnest of fresh conquests is for us all."

Herr Emil Fischer—"He is a great master and a great man."

Mr. Edmond C. Stanton—"Dr. Dvořák has made us all his debtor by making New York the theatre of his future triumphs."

Signor Campanini—"I am a great admirer of Dr. Dvořák's works. They breathe all the restless power of what is best in modern music."

Signor Emilio Agramonte—"It is hardly necessary to add my little tribute to this great acclaim of admiring homage. Dr. Dvořák's coming among us means much for the musical future of New York."

This was how it was. I cannot keep from rereading "The Scenes before the Concert," and also the address of Colonel T. W. Higginson, the million-aire who had founded the Brooklyn Symphonic Orchestra. When he said that the arts must wait because the steam engines and railroads cannot, he sounded like a clairvoyant. The verses of the lyrical poet Boyle O'Reilly could be judged with a smile, but their content is interesting, indeed. J. Thurber, who came to the concert with a "party of friends," knew well what she was doing when she invited Dvořák to America.

Of course this was the enterprising woman, Mrs. Thurber, whose traces I was to discover several days later. I was sitting in the Branch Library on 43rd Street, this time in a low study located in a special building where the Morgan Library's musical section with the Mary Flagler collection could be found. This area reminded me of Old England; the patriotic look of the study with its antique desks and bookshelves breathing of the past, made me whisper.

Finally, I received a file with Dvořák's letters, and an album with more souvenirs. What I found in it was unbelievable—three letters which Antonín Dvořák sent to Mme President of the National Conservatory in New York City, one of them with the original envelope, and a Czech-German stamp from the post office on Charles Square in Prague, dated December 7, 1891. Dvořák wrote there in English:

> Dear Madam Thurber
>
> I have to thank you for your kindly letter in which you ask me for sending you the contract with all the alternations which I found to be made, but I don't know if you accept all of them. I suppose Mr. Littleton has forgotten to send you the new contract. Some days ago I wrote to Mr. Littleton about this matter and I am awaiting every day for it. It was necessary to be made a new translation into English an I don't know if Mr. Littleton has done so or not. Mrs. Dvořák and my oldest daughter Otilka are very anxious to see America but I am little afraid that I shall not be able to please you in every respect in my new position.
>
> As a teacher and instructor and conductor I feel myself quite sure but there many other trifles who will make me much sorrow and grieve [*sic*]—but I rely much upon you [*sic*] kindness, and indulgence and be sure I shall do all to please you.
>
> Can you tell me Madam which which [*sic*] books you use for teaching the pupils in composition and instrumentation? I have two very good books from Richter and Mathiew of New York. You will oblige me in telling me about something about this.
>
> For the present I must finish one other day a little more.
>
> Meanwhile I am your obedient servant
>
> Prague, 18 7/12 91   Antonín Dvořák.

The letter, which was not published in Czechoslovakia until the spring of 1982, supplements the existing information about the negotiations between Dvořák and Mrs. Thurber. She had cited a short passage from this letter in her recollections of Dvořák, as I mentioned previously. Her recollection starts with the following words: "Mrs. Dvořák and my oldest daughter Otilka...." Mrs. Thurber made an error in the date of this letter, then.

Similar information is in Dvořák's next letter, which was written in a hurry on April 30, 1892. After several months of negotiation, the contract was finally signed, and only a few details concerning the trip were supposed to be dealt with:

Dear M. Thurber   Prague 18 30/4 92

Will you kindly accept my best thanks for your letter a [*sic*] for sending me the contract with your signature, and I only will hope that we all with united powers shall have much success and that your institution may flourish as much as possible.

Now we are making great preparations for our journey—which make us very anxious. Md. Dvořák and my eldest daughter are learning English but it does not go well—perhaps they will improve. Can you give me some advise [*sic*]?

We do not know and are not decided yet, whether we should take with us all our 6 children or not—it makes much trouble to M. Dvořák and I myself don't know which would be the best. On the other side we are very anxious too about the lodgings in New York. Should we take a boardinghouse—or a private house. Please can you give us some informations [*sic*] about this matter of importance? Further we don't know where to procure our tickets when we leave from Bremen via Southampton for America (Nord German Lloyd) You have early given me some hints and please will you do so and drop me line

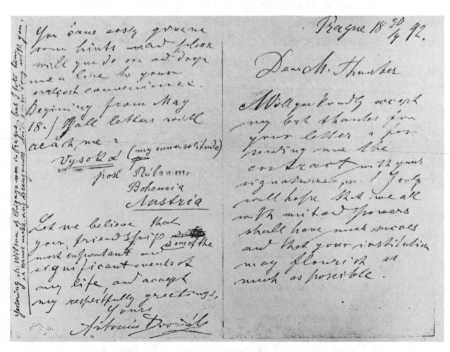

Dvořák's letter to Jeanette Thurber, April 30, 1892

to your earliest convenience.

Beginning from May 18./ all letters will reach me:

Vysoka (my summer solitude)
post Pribram
Bohemia
Austria

Let me believe that your friendship is one of the most important and significant events of my life, and accept my respectfully greetings.

Yours,   Antonín Dvořák.

(This in left margin):

Yesterday Mr. Wilson of Chicago was in Prague, but I told him we cannot make any arrangement with [*sic*] consulting with you.

Dvořák's letters are not very neat; he liked to enhance certain words by underlining them. Once in a while, he chose to use vertical lines to make the important paragraphs more significant. He would strike out words and add inscriptions, sometimes outside the margins of a letter, and usually a few words were not correctly spelled. However, the contents were more important for him than the letter's form. Music writing was his prime thing, not letter writing, and he always wrote this way.

A third letter to Mrs. Thurber was written on June 25, 1892. The Dvořáks' departure was coming near, and it was necessary to work out the final details of their trip. Dvořák had asked many questions, struck out words in the text, and being in a hurry to arrange everything necessary before their journey, did not care to rewrite his letters nicely again:

Vysoka 18 25/6 92

Dear Mad [*sic*] Thurber

Above all many thanks for your kindly letter which reached me quite safely at Vysoka and from which I was much rejoiced especially when I know something definite about our departure from Bremen which, as you say is fixed on the 17 of September but I am in a little doubt as to the tickets. Should I apply directly to Bremen or not?

Then I should like to know what is to be done to get good places in our cabins and whether necessary to be in right time in

Bremen?

I beg your pardon for asking you very much but I am very anxious to know definitely.

Just now I got a letter from Littleton of New York from which I see that you have the splendid idea. I should write a Columbus Cantata (or something like) which ought to be given at my first appearance in New York.

Repeating once more my thanks to you

I am sincerely yours   Antonín Dvořák

After he finished and reread this letter, he probably thought hard about the possibilities of composing and finishing a cantata, but meanwhile, he counted the weeks and days, and considered all the worries with their trip, tickets, and the children...and he decided to add a little postscript on a new page of a letter:

It is a great pity that I didn't know it some time ago, but now it is too late. In spite of this I will try to write a Te Deum for this occasion but even this I doubt I shall be able to get finished because the time is very short.

Besides of that I shall have some noveltys [*sic*] for the Americans—these are: "three ouvertures" [*sic*] Nature, Life and Love perhaps it would be right to bring them to a first hearing at one of my concerts in New York?

The items of information started to fall into a kind of relationship, and this gave me a good feeling that my work was progressing well. Here was a discussion of the same concert which had been colorfully described in the *New York Herald* when the Dvořák Overtures were first played. In another selection of these materials were Dvořák's letters written on odd dates. The collector who put most of them together probably found them in the hands of individuals in various places around the world.

The first letter was from Prague, written on August 18, 1878. Dvořák announces to some "Honorable Madam" that he is sending to her a "little present," his Trio in B-flat Major.

The second letter from February 23, 1883, was written in German, and was sent to a government councillor and musical critic, Dr. Eduard Hanslick.

Also the third letter which I found in that collection was in German, and was dated June 28, 1889. It was probably sent to the same recipient, Dr. Hanslick. Dvořák wrote that he was grateful for Hanslick's "esteemed congratulation on the highest award" (Dvořák was granted the Third Class Order of the Iron Crown).

The fourth item in that collection was a photograph of the Prague company I. Mulac, on Vodickova Street, no. 20. The composer wrote in German on the back side of it to some unknown recipient:

Dear Sir,

Only yesterday, I received your letter and the photograph, and it is my great pleasure to send it [the photo] back.

New York, January 15, 1895   Sincerely, Antonín Dvořák.

Beside it the composer sketched a few notes from the Largo of his Symphony *From the New World*.

For me, the discovery of new materials was an unexpected success. However, the best one of the collection items was a text never published before,

Last part of the contract for the composer's activities as Director of the National Conservatory of Music in New York City waiting here years to be discovered. There were still several more pages on my desk, eight of them written by some unknown person, each page 8" x 13-1/2", an unusual paper size. On the last page is a note written by Dvořák: "Prague 1892," and on the right-hand side is his energetic signature "Antonín Dvořák." He never forgot to put the correct marks above the "r" and the "a."

The document was a German version of the contract between Dvořák and Mrs. Thurber. In 1981, the American musicologist Merton Robert Aborn published his doctoral thesis, "The Influence of Dvořák's American Sojourn on the American Musical Culture." As the first American working on research about Dvořák, he quoted the English version of the contract. There was no mention about a German version in his work, and now, the real text of that version lay in front of me!

It seemed that the dark and uncomfortable room suddenly became cozy and bright. It would be hard to describe my pleasure completely. With unremitting attention, I began to read the very important details of the contract. After a brief look-through, I began to study every item. The contract was precise, no particular was omitted from the text, and the rights and duties of Dvořák, and of the National Conservatory were carefully spelled out. Eleven main points of the contract included everything important for both parties — financial stipulations, schedule, holidays, sick leave, even the rules for handling any dispute between the parties.

This was an outstanding day, one of the best I had in the United States. I had no idea that a similar discovery awaited me in New York's Greenwich Village, and that several weeks later I would find other important documents in Ames, Iowa.

My other search brought me to the City Museum of New York. At first glance, I did not care much for its Southern style, suitable enough for Georgia or Alabama but hardly acceptable for a villa built on the edge of Central Park. The building, standing on the intersection of Fifth Avenue and 103rd Street, was begun in 1923, and finished in 1932.

The exhibition there represented mostly the field of industrial art. Every room was furnished, and average paintings of the nineteenth century were hanging everywhere. Only one picture interested me, a copy of a portrait of Marie Filip, whose ancestors were Czech immigrants. Marie had rejected "the hand of George Washington, the father of his country." It is said that the original painting was kept in Van Courtlandt Manor, Westchester County, in the Colonial Dames Museum. I found here also a large collection of figurines, dressed in styles of the last centuries, showing tools, utensils, serving dishes, and all kinds of household objects. The mezzanine was used for the Fireman

Museum. The exposition included two wagons from the nineteenth century. The rooms in the last, fifth floor, recalled the quarters of the millionaire John D. Rockefeller, with study, bedroom, and dressing room. This exhibit of "The Life Styles of the Rich and Famous" never ceased to attract visitors.

The guardian was disappointed with my lack of interest, but I was looking for photographs showing the city at the end of the last century. Because I needed to know the face of New York City from 1892 through 1895, I placed an order with the attendant. I got the photos, and the city looked picturesque and interesting, nothing like a large European city of that day.

In the group of old photographs in front of me were pictures of horsecars on Lower Broadway (horse-transport systems were licensed only in 1885, but in fact the horsecars in New York City started up on November 14, 1832, the first street railway in the world), aged omnibuses filled the streets, and among them were gentlemen with black hats, and ladies wearing ornamented skirts with full bustles. There was a photograph from 1887, taken five years before Dvořák's arrival.

The horsecar system was the city's pride, and its last appearance in 1917 called for a very sentimental celebration. The "elevated railway," the aboveground "el," existed during Dvořák's time in New York City. It made use of small steam engines with the rails running over iron trestles, usually one or two floors above the street. Its indisputable advantage was its speed. Dvořák used it often, especially when he was in a hurry to get to the harbor; or during his family Sunday trips from First Avenue to Long Island. This system offered good sightseeing, but the dirt and noise accompanying it everywhere caused the "el" to gradually disappear from New York City streets, the last one closing in 1940.

I searched through the photos more than one hundred years old. In place of the six-floor Hotel Glenham, built in 1875, there is today a skyscraper. The eight-floor Hotel Plaza (built in 1890) on the corner of Central Park and Fifth Avenue was replaced by another Plaza Hotel, built in 1907. It was then considered to be the most luxurious hotel in the world. Of course, today the center of Manhattan, with newly risen skyscrapers, is absolutely different from that part of the city during Dvořák's time. However, I could see that even then it was huge in comparison with London, Vienna, or Prague. New York City, infused with a special confidence born of its magnificent, modern structures, must have influenced Dvořák strongly.

Something special, never heard in Dvořák's music before, appeared in his compositions. I came to America to look through archives, museums, and libraries, in hope that I would be able to discover something about that special musical quality, and what inspired it. There was no recipe for it. To my mind, it was like a mosaic made up of little stones. Its colorful design could not be completed until the very last piece was found. Could I find them all? They differed in kind, size, even in importance, and combined in the right pattern, they might explain this miraculous unison, described by Dvořák in his letter from April 1893, as an "influence of America."

Besides all the articles about the reception by his countrymen and by Americans in the New World, besides letters and the German contract with the conservatory, besides the harbor and Battery Park—what was I still missing?

As Kovarik recollected, after their discovery of a little aviary with about two hundred pigeons in a huge cage in Central Park, they had visited here weekly, at least, although they could not compare with his "pointers" and "fantails" back home in Vysoka. I would like to take Honza there to photograph the flock which had grown so much since Dvořák's days.

We first saw Central Park the second day after arriving in New York City on our informative drive around the city. We saw the Metropolitan Opera with Moore's sculpture in the middle of a little lake; we stopped shortly at the Lincoln Cultural Center, went through Broadway, to Rockefeller Center with the "New York Experience" show in the basement. As we descended, the eighteenth-century image of New York City took us into the past. We drove across part of Central Park to the nearby Metropolitan Museum, which, built in 1880, has over three million art works.

Today, we walked. It was a beautiful afternoon. The sky, after a morning cleaning was spotlessly blue and the trees were vigorously pumping green nourishment for leaves. With wide-open eyes we saw the lakes; five, six, seven gray squirrels; more lakes, more squirrels. Flocks of pigeons ignored the visitors and went about their business. This area had dozens of small hills, slopes, and boulders. The roads and sidewalks were asphalt-surfaced. The center of New York City was built on a huge rock outcropping, and the rock here is sticking up everywhere. The hundred-year-old trees create a perfect setting behind which the skyscrapers rise, as if on guard.

The park was busy, with women who brought children to play, girls who should be in school, an old man with his dog, joggers, kissing lovers, picnickers, bicyclists, people with dogs again, and so on. The area is a half-mile wide, and two-and-a-half miles long. Hidden by trees is the forgotten Egyptian obelisk from Heliopolis. Its sign says that it originated in the sixteenth century B.C., and was brought here under the auspices of Mr. William H. Vanderbilt on February 22, 1888. I recollected that members of the millionaire

Vanderbilt family were in their loge during Dvořák's first concert in New York City.

We found that the aviary described by Kovarik in his memoirs was located in a corner of the park, and had apparently been modernized into a little zoo since Dvořák's visits. How had it looked to him one hundred years ago? Just at the entrance to the zoo was a merry-go-round, combined with some kind of ancient clock and chimes, going around every hour. A bear was dancing, an elephant played an accordion, a kangaroo blew on a trumpet, a hippo played a violin, and a buffalo was blowing his double-trumpet to entertain the children and their escorts. The children's eyes were sparkling with joy, responding to every attraction of this charming afternoon — the colorful balloons, the cotton-candy delicacy sold nearby, the several frolicsome California sea lions playing ball in a nearby pool, zebra, antelope, orangutan and parrots — all of them in one delightful picture.

And there were the pigeons. Not in cages, as in Dvořák's time, but waddling around freely, fluttering among the visitors who had to be watchful so as not to step on them. These pigeons no longer seemed to have beauty or dignity in them. They had become commonplace after all these years, so that my story about their inspiring influence on the famous composer a hundred years ago sounded like a lie. The pigeons were everywhere. They begged for scraps at a nearby stand which sold snacks, coffee, soft drinks, and some kind of beer of peculiar taste.

Antonín Dvořák wrote home in the fall of 1894:

> It is 6 o'clock in the evening, and we just returned from Central Park. The weather was most beautiful, like in summer, and the afternoon went fast. Everything in the park was as always: even the terrible coffee has not improved. We went into a restaurant near where the pigeons were. The prices there were the same, too. Everything they sell is terribly expensive, so we spent a whole dollar.

Dvořák was quite attracted by this area, according to Otakar's memoirs:

> ...our Sunday afternoons were often dedicated to visits to Central Park, where large flocks of father's fine feathered friends received his continuous attention and admiration. They kept there Brazilian hummingbirds, vultures, pelicans, and many other kinds of birds. However, the pigeons were the most enjoyable attraction for father. He was always thinking of them, and recalling his flock back home: "What might my darling

pigeons be doing at Vysoka...?" At that moment, his face
would darken and his eyes fought to hide his tears....

Dvořák's second hobby—the engines—was not easy to check on. Because
only train passengers could enter the railway-station platform, Dvořák,
according to Kovarik, had to travel by elevated railway up to 155th Street to
see his engines.

Before we went to search for Dvořák's observation point above the railway, we went to the "Prague" restaurant for dinner. The dining room there
was decorated with emblems of the provinces of Czechoslovakia before the
Munich settlement in 1938: Bohemia, Moravia, Slovakia, Silesia, and Car-
pathian Ukraine. The menu was Bohemian-American, but the names of some
dishes were changed for easier pronunciation: "kenedeliky" for knedliky
(dumplings), for example. Hand-painted ceramic plates, photographs of
Bohemian and Slovak cities, landscapes, and castles were hanging on the restaurant walls. Only English was spoken.

The host offered us an imported pilsner. He also recommended that we
try a local brand; they were selling Michelob Light. In the last century a smart
businessman bought the brewing license from a little town in Bohemia,
Mecholupy, and changed the name of his product to the easier-sounding
"mikelop." A similar transaction brought to life Budweiser from Budweis, the
license for which was bought from the Southern Bohemian city, Budejovice.

After dinner, we drove to the very north corner of Manhattan. Approximately at 130th Street, the bay ends and flows into the Harlem River. Behind
it lies the Bronx with all its social problems.

The Island narrows quickly in this area, and when it reaches 155th Street,
its width is less than half. We stopped under a huge iron construction—the
remnants of the "el" railway. A high staircase brought us up to an asphalt
road, connecting the Bronx with Manhattan. We were in the Black area of
Harlem.

We asked a few people for directions, but they just shrugged their shoulders. Only the third pedestrian knew where we could find a railway:

"You have to go to the other side of the island, but..." she interrupted
her explanation with funny a look. Was there something we didn't know?

Somewhat puzzled and uneasy, she twisted her head, and left us without
any explanation. So down the stairs again, and to 155th Street, which brought
us to the large Holy Trinity Cemetery on the west side of Manhattan Island.
Behind it was a steep bank, and under it the railway. Just a narrow thicket

divided it from the Hudson River. We stood over the railing on Riverside Drive, and observed the view. A Circle Line recreational steamboat and a few freighters sailed the river. Instead of coaches drawn by horses, cars were whizzing along on the wide highway. Where was that elevated railway which Dvořák used to take to get here? Just beside the road, three pairs of embarrassed, rusty rails were running somewhere, one of them overgrown with bush, and two others covered with garbage, tins, a wrecked car, mattresses, all the refuse of a civilization.

From this hill Dvořák and his faithful Kovarik had waited for the moment when the engine would emerge from the distant tunnel, and they observed the express trains on their way to Boston or Chicago. It was the speed and rapid acceleration of the engines which fascinated Dvořák.

At closer look, I could see the decaying railway ties and the rotting stairs joining Riverside Drive with the railway. The walls were covered with graffiti having some mysterious symbolic meaning. All about us was Harlem with a population of a million Blacks. Dvořák felt very sympathetic toward them, and had seen the Black people as the musical hope of America. Was he wrong? Probably not, although their music took a different direction in the meantime, one that he could not have predicted.

The Hudson River is very wide here, and more steamships ploughed its surface, creating waves which splashed on the banks and quickly hurried back along the Holy Trinity Cemetery to touch another bank on the opposite side.

We entered the cemetery to see if they had used it as a burial place in Dvořák's time. What would Dvořák have found here if he had come for a visit? The first tomb marked the grave of Margaret Travers, born in Ireland, 1793, deceased 1889. Three years later James Kemp had arrived in America from Ireland, and was buried on March 31, 1886. Benjamin Foster, 1865; Hazard Field, 1883; and Clement G. Moore 1828, were there. How many miles away from home they had died! Almost every one of them came from another country, mostly from Ireland. Only for their children could America become a real homeland. A path between graves was the easiest access to the heights above the railway. It was here that Dvořák's pious soul, deeply touched, could meditate about the eternity of human life, far from busy Broadway and the creaking sounds of heavy anchors and chains in the harbor. All that must have influenced Dvořák, especially his music. Whenever he escaped Lower Manhattan with its American rhythm of life, he entered this unusual atmosphere.

After we left the cemetery and walked back to our car from the heights called Fort Washington, we noticed an unusual building—the Indian

Museum. It was a Museum of American Indian culture. We decided we must see it.

The building was large and spacious with numerous rooms. Names which I read as a boy in novels by Karl May began to look more real here: Shoshones, Bannocks, Comanches, Iroquois, Kiowas, and the others. There were beautifully painted masks and carved peace pipes. (How many times as a boy did I try to carve them of elderberry wood; and now I can see the originals used by real Indians). I admired numerous household items; ornaments made of colorful beads, chiefs' headpieces. We had to make them of colored goose feathers. The Indian clothing included coats, mostly of leather, shoes also of leather, dozens of moccasins, very worn, faded. Everything that could show the ingenuity of Indian craft and skill is here. A beautiful display of wooden shaman masks with hair, necklaces, jewelry, more cloth, decorated, painted shirts—this all reminds me of the faded photographs in the composer's house at Vysoka; old Big Moon was holding a similar headpiece on his lap.

There were records on sale at the museum and I bought a cover of big Indian women in their costumes. The songs from the Indian reservation at Warm Springs, Oregon, had very poetic symbolic names: "Song of the Burning Arrow," "Song of the Butterfly Dance," and "Song of the Peace-Pipe".

Our drive back through Harlem deprived me of the romantic fantasies I had created about that city. The streets were ordinary like some of the quarters in Prague, the four- and five-story houses were different only in that the inhabitants were Black. Harlem had been originally an independent township in the suburbs of New York City. It had its own churches, stores and theatres. Beginning at 110th Street, it had spread to 150th Street. Almost all the houses we can see there now were built in the eighteen-nineties. Land here was less expensive than in the middle of southern areas in Manhattan, and it attracted the less fortunate Blacks. They built their own world here. However, the city kept changing and after the subway took over Manhattan, Harlem lost its unique character. Today, it looks only ordinary, normal, and conventional.

I hoped to be better rewarded for my search by the record I had purchased in the museum that afternoon. Even that did not happen. The songs were monotonous, only the drums sounded different. Honza ridiculed my disappointment about it:

"And who can say that Indian motives can be heard in the Symphony *From the New World*?"

First of all, Hermann Kretzschmar, who wrote the *German Guide through the Concert Halls*, analyzed Dvořák's Symphony *From the New World*. When

Dvořák read Kretzschmar's book, he became angry. Later, at the beginning of 1900, when Oskar Nedbal conducted this Dvořák Symphony in Berlin, Nedbal asked for Dvořák's advice, and the composer sent him Kretzschmar's analysis with the following comment:

> …you should omit that nonsense that I used Indian and American motifs because it is a lie. I just wanted to express the spirit of these American national melodies! Otherwise, you can do as you wish, and what you think will be best. You already have memorized the tempos well, and this is the most important thing. The prelude should be done "slowly."

Dvořák's explanation of the subject is clear enough to us. Of course he had composed his Symphony in 1893, and wrote about it to Nedbal at the beginning of the twentieth century. The American premiere was in December 1893, and we have seen the reviews the American press carried. We also know what Dvořák said about his work and the origin of American music. Indian music occupied an eminent place in his head.

Our next trip would take us to East 17th Street where the Dvořáks lived during their years in America. We would look around, find the house and its surroundings; the Hotel Clarendon, the National Conservatory, and we would visit the area where James G. Huneker and "Old Borax" went that day.

I must say that the second or third day after our arrival, we tried to visit No. 327, but a voice on the intercom system said that we must have permission of the owner, Mr. Miller, so we arranged that. Our visit was scheduled for 10 A.M. the same day.

We left immediately after breakfast to have some time for looking around. We finally came to 18th Street, near enough for parking, and here we were. Honza was carrying cameras, and I had my thick burgundy notebook, in which I kept important notes. In one of Kovarik's recollections written in the nineteen-twenties, he said: "At the beginning, we used to visit the cafe 'Boulevard' on Eleventh Avenue and 10th Street,"

I also had the address of Hotel Clarendon on the corner of Fourth Avenue and East 18th Street. The Conservatory was at 126–128 East 17th Street.

Dvořák's son Otakar cites a letter he received from Dr. and Mrs. Smith of New York on October 2, 1941. Dr. Smith wrote:

> First, I would like to introduce myself. I am a medical doctor with a practice at no. 327 East 17th Street, in a house which my wife and I bought a few years ago.

In September 1941 on the occasion of the anniversary of
your father's birthday, at the insistence of the composer Burleigh, a very old black man today, and with the help of many
other admirers of your father—a commemorative plaque was
placed on our house. It shows a relief portrait of your father. I
do not exaggerate when I write that more than 2,000 people
participated in that celebration. 17th Street was overcrowded.
After the celebration ceremony was over, Mr Burleigh guided
the groups to the composer's apartment to show them the Master's study, your dining room, and the other rooms.

I was astonished to observe the behavior of those people—
above all, of the elders, probably the Master's contemporaries.
They were kissing the door knobs, crying, and recollecting
many things. It took some time before we were able to bring
another group in. I will never forget the day when those groups
of enthusiastic visitors and admirers toured Dvořák's formal
apartment from 11 A.M. until 7 P.M..

Because I received your address from Mr. Kovarik, I feel
that it is my responsibility to inform you about this event. In
this letter are included two large photographs of our today-so-
famous house, and only the time needed for making copies
made me delay my letter. I hope that you will be pleased to
receive all the materials.

Yours truly,   Dr. & Mrs. E. M. Smith

Let us start with the cafe first. We had to walk back a bit, but it was good
for us to learn about the neighborhood. The houses, most of them still original, were four stories high, and only around Fourth Avenue could we see
buildings much taller. When we found the corner where the Hotel Clarendon
accommodated the Dvořáks after their arrival in New York City, we found
instead a skyscraper of the publishing house ARCO, and no trace of the
Clarendon at all. The place was surrounded by structures of the newer New
York City, buildings of ten to fifteen floors. Fourth Avenue was wide and
modern with almost nothing left from the nineteenth century. We returned to
Second Avenue and 10th Street, the location of the cafe where Dvořák used to
read his National Newsletters.

The situation here looked better, even very good. At the intersection of
10th Street and Second Avenue were two cafes! The waiter in a cafe on the
left-hand corner was somewhat embarrassed at our question. He knew nothing about the Cafe Boulevard, so he asked his boss, who spoke Polish-
English, but he was helpless too. Even the oldest guests could remember

nothing. Only one of them recalled a dairy which had been here before the cafe was opened.

It was probably on the opposite corner, so we entered the second cafe, which offered an atmosphere of antiquity. The leather-upholstered booths created oases of tranquillity, and it was comfortable to rest there, have something to eat, and read the newspapers. I asked the owner my question, but again he could not tell me anything. His predecessor had told him nothing about the previous name of the business. Buildings in New York City can age very quickly, and so do memories of their inhabitants. The only thing we could be sure about was that Dvořák walked under the trees of this street. Perhaps the little church at the corner of the park could recall him better.

Before we visited the house, we still had time to walk down East 17th Street. Its style is not unified; the buildings of both the nineteenth and twentieth centuries were mixed up together. Once the houses here had steps down to the street. According to photographs from 1893, the house No. 327 had ten steps then but everything since the last century had been changed, and we could see that:

> No. 331 still had a staircase with an iron railing
> No. 329 had no staircase
> No. 327 Dvořáks,' had no staircase
> No. 325 had a staircase
> No. 323 had a staircase
> No. 321 had no staircase

These six houses surviving from the nineteenth century were an island representing the past. It is quite possible that "Dvořák's" house, with the commemorative tablet placed there in 1941, was one cause of their preservation.

Every house on the left-hand side of the street had been demolished to make way for the new Beth Israel Hospital. This massive white building was spread over a large area. On the right side of the street, behind No. 321, was a block belonging wholly to the hospital. It was joined to the main building by an overpass at the second story.

For my better remembrance of this place, I stopped on the corner of First Avenue and East 17th Street, and tried to imprint into my memory the few old houses on the right side; the renowned no. 327, and the huge hospital just across the street. Continuing to walk down 17th Street, we reached an intersection with Second Avenue, where the simple sign informed us that we had just entered Stuyvesant Square.

"That is the name of the last Dutch governor," recalled Honza. Indeed, he was right. Before our trip here, the governor's name meant for us only a cigarette brand. Now we saw Stuyvesant's statue in the nearby park. The plaque on it announced that the sculpture was of Peter Stuyvesant,* "Director-General of the Netherlands 1647–1664." The artist had replaced the governor's lost leg with the realistic shape of a wooden stump.

Behind the statue was the St. George Episcopal Church, built for the American congregation by the local millionaire J. P. Morgan. The description on the church wall said that Peter Stuyvesant dedicated this land, a part of his farm originally, for the construction of a simple little church. Only later did this ostentatious church replace it. The date above the entryway of the red-brick neighboring house with the white-framed windows shows the year of 1860.

New York City had not changed in this area too much. The large square looked the same as when the composer walked here a century earlier, hoping to get over his pre-concert nervousness. Only the sycamore trees were bigger and more majestic a century later.

On his way to the conservatory which was just around the corner, Dvořák must have walked along this park, too. But the conservatory? Was I wrong? I looked back in my notes—yes, the number of the conservatory was 126–128. We went back, checked the street, and found it was correct. The conservatory, which used to be here, was gone. A red house on the corner had the number 140; the neighboring house built of ochre bricks was No. 134, and the other almost identical house was numbered 132. Both houses stood on street level and had three stories. One of them advertised a sale of some obscure objects for "extrasensory perception." On a display in the window were a colored bust of an Egyptian Pharaoh, posters of dream- and fortune-tellers, spices, essences, oils, and astrological books. A purple oval sign alongside said that there was also a 17th Street art gallery, and another sign had only one word: "Tailor."

Another street number was on the house no. 130. It was a four-story house, and the conservatory was supposed to be just next to it but it was not. On the property of No. 128 and 126 was a high school bearing the name of the American writer, Washington Irving. His statue was a magnificent bust at the school entrance. Across the street was an ancient house and store where the Dvořáks used to have dinners and suppers. On another nearby corner house

---

*Peter Stuyvesant, 1592–1672, Dutch administrator in America. —Translator's note

was a memorial tablet for Washington Irving. No sign of the National Conservatory nor any mention about Dvořák anywhere.

Shortly before ten, we walked back from Irving High School past the store with the "ESP" items, past the little St. John Baptist Church, and on past the grocery store where Dvořák's wife, Anna, or maid, Barbora Klirova, had probably come to shop for family meals. This house, built in the style of the last century, looked as if it were trying to slow down time. Only the buildings of the hospital and school reminded us of our time, a hundred years later.

The house No. 327 was not too far from the style of the rest of this area. Except for the ground floor painted white, it was built of red bricks, and with the black window shutters, it carried a kind of distinguished dignity. The new style of architecture had done away with the stairs typical of the nineteenth-century house, stairs which led from the street directly to the mezzanine. The mezzanine had thus become the main floor, only three steps under the street.

The massive entrance door imitated the older style, and two lanterns of the same period hung above our heads. It was two after ten when the owner, Mr. Dick Miller, dressed in jeans and red pullover, opened the door. I guessed that he was a successful businessman, about fifty years old. He invited us upstairs because there was nothing special of interest to us on the mezzanine. The first surprise was waiting for us immediately after we entered the hall. Everything was modernized, and in the middle of the hall was a shiny, gold-colored winding staircase leading to the next floor.

Mr. Miller noticed our perplexed looks and started to explain about the changes he had made: "We have a kitchen facing the street, with a pantry adjoined. The winding staircase of course wasn't here. Now we have this floor joined with the upper floor, a very convenient arrangement for us, indeed."

I could understand the reasons for these alterations. The narrow staircase from entrance to upper floor was now used only by a tenant.

Mr. Miller pointed out the reception room in the direction of the garden.

The planning done by his interior designer was excellent. The interior showed well-thought-out ideas executed in every detail. The plan included a bright-colored fireplace built into the wall. While I was trying to make a mental sketch of this room, a voice coming from the hall welcomed us in. It belonged to a slim, smiling lady—our second surprise.

"This is Charlotte." Mr. Miller introduced to us a young woman in a flattering house gown. She had beautiful, long legs and perfectly made-up eyes. Instantly, she filled the apartment with the grace and charm of a woman perhaps not yet thirty.

Honza took pictures of the interior, and I made notes about everything in view. The door from the hall to the living room looked older, and the bronze forged knob must have been made in the last century, I supposed.

"Not at all," explained Mr. Miller. "This door is not the original one. The previous owner purchased it as an antique item. In Dvořák's time the door here must have been different."

What else could have survived here? My thoughts were chased away by another surprise, number three in the series. The well-known strains from the beginning of the Symphony *From the New World* filled the apartment with their noble, majestic sounds. Charlotte smiled: she had put the record on.

"Beautiful music," said Mr. Miller.

There was no doubt about it.

The winding staircase brought us to the upstairs hall. There was a modern study facing the street, with built-in closet, and walls decorated with contemporary, mostly abstract graphics. Everything was in bright, blinding white. Another room faced the garden. The bed, not yet made, stopped me on my way to the window, but Mr. Miller encouraged us to enjoy the interesting view below.

So we did not mind the untidiness of Charlotte's dresser with its numerous cosmetic containers, bottles, and jars; and indeed, the view was worth it. The music occupied the whole space, and thanks to speakers installed in each room, it followed us everywhere. Directly under the window was a yard paved with large stones and bricks. It was the place where the hired photographer had taken a picture of the Dvořák family.

Behind the yard and the garden were two- and three-story houses, with old iron stairs, of course. The peace and quiet existing on that side penetrated the house. One spacious elegant bedroom had been made from the two original ones. Here also, modern graphics gave the space a pleasing well-unified style.

My feelings were mixed. Should I be disappointed? There are no existing rules on how to modernize rooms in cases like this. Should the occupants live respectfully in the apartment as it was at the end of the last century? What should the proper answer be?

The second movement of the plaintive "Largo" was touching everybody's emotions. Charlotte had stopped her enchanting activities to sit down in the front room and listen. Mr. Miller exchanged a few words with Honza in a subdued voice, and I sank into a deep couch, closed my eyes, and meditated on this beautiful music which had originated right here.

The splendid music flowed through the house as it had a century ago, filling it entirely; then it escaped through the open windows, and conquered the entire world.

It was a moment that could happen only once in a lifetime.

Symphony *From the New World* ∽ A

L ET US NOW LOOK at the circumstances surrounding the Symphony
From the New World—the origin and unfolding of this remarkable
work.

Dvořák wrote to his friend in Olomouc, in January 1893:

> Presently I am working on a new Symphony (in E Minor). I
> feel that American soil has had a good influence on me, and per-
> haps, you will be able to hear this in the new Symphony.

Mrs. Jeanette Thurber wrote about it several years later:

> There is no doubt that Dvořák's most important achievement in
> America was his composition of the Symphony *From the New
> World*. This is one of the rare compositions which were inspired
> mostly by the environment. In Dvořák's work, here and there,
> are original interpretations of the spirit which he had discov-
> ered in Negro songs. As much as I could, I helped to supply
> him with the materials which were necessary for his work, as
> did his pupil Harry T. Burleigh, who is now the foremost com-
> poser of his race.
>
> Evaluating my thirty-five years of work as President of the

National Conservatory of America, I cannot see anything else that could make me prouder than my successful negotiation to bring Dr. Dvořák to our country. Actually, it gave me the privilege of opening the door for one of the world's most renowned symphonic masterworks, and also for his chamber music, of which some works are even better than those written before, in Europe. Who could forget the day when the Kneisel Quartet came to the Conservatory just for a chance of rehearsing in the composer's presence! The premiere of his Symphony *From the New World* proved to be a festive event of New York musical life. It was played by the New York Philharmonic conducted by Anton Seidl. The concert remains one of the most important events in the history of this assembly.

"Dvořák seemed to be quite happy in his new environment," continued Mrs. Thurber,

but being an ardent patriot, he was homesick most of the time. What Anton Seidl said about the Symphony may be true, that the strong pathos in its slow movement was inspired by the composer's nostalgia, by his longing for home. The composition of the Symphony was actually my idea. He had been feeling lonely, especially on foggy days while reading the sailing news in the *New York Herald*. At such a time, thoughts about his homeland could make him shed tears. Once, I tried to encourage him to write a symphony which would represent his experience and feelings in America, and he accepted my idea immediately.

In some quarters it is held that the slow movement of his American Symphony was inspired by Longfellow's "Hiawatha." Indeed, Dvořák had hoped to use this poem as a libretto for an opera he planned. He wrote me about it in one of his letters:

As you already know, I am a great admirer of Longfellow's 'Hiawatha.' This work attracts me so much that I can hardly resist composing an opera based on this story since I believe it would be well-suited for it.

Although I succeeded in getting him a permit from the publisher, and Miss Alice M. Longfellow allowed him to use the poem, Dvořák did not live long enough to fulfill his plan. However, it is possible that this work would not have achieved the same success as his Symphony. His operas, in spite of the fact that one can find so much beautiful music in them, have never become renowned outside Bohemia. That he was deeply involved in writing this "New World Opera" is obvious from a letter he wrote to me one day:

> I have an intense, persistent wish to have the libretto of "Hiawatha" at hand, and wonder where it is? If I cannot get it soon, much will be lost.

After our discussion about available librettists, I took him to see "Buffalo Bill's Indian Dance" which could be used as a ballet in his opera. It is a pity that this valuable opera project was never finished.

In 1919 Jeanette Thurber said clearly that she herself gave Dvořák the idea of writing the Symphony, and that he "accepted it immediately."

Of course, Mrs. Thurber forgot one thing: Dvořák's mind was filled with the need to write music, and into that mind poured everything that had happened to him in the previous three months. Under such pressure, he would never think of anything that Madam President of the Conservatory suggested. Her remark about his plan for the an opera based on *Hiawatha* is nonetheless interesting. The idea of setting Longfellow's poem to music pursued Dvořák as long as he lived in America.

In his interview with the *New York Herald* on December 15, 1893, shortly before the premiere of his famous Symphony, Dvořák said:

> The second movement is an adagio. But it is different from the classic works in this form. It is, in reality, a study or sketch for a longer work, either a cantata or opera which I purpose [*sic*] writing, and which will be based upon Longfellow's "Hiawatha." I have long had the idea of someday utilizing that poem. I first became acquainted with it about thirty years ago through the medium of a Bohemian translation. It appealed very strongly to my imagination, and the impression has only been strengthened by my residence here.
>
> The Scherzo of the symphony was suggested by the music at the feast in "Hiawatha" where the Indians dance, and is also an effort which I made in the imparting of local color of Indian character in music.

Dvořák's words testify that Longfellow's verses were deeply rooted in his soul for a long time. Jeanette Thurber, in promoting Dvořák's interest in Longfellow for her own benefit, had only reawakened his lasting interest.

Therefore she negotiated with the publisher and with Miss Longfellow, and struggled to get an appropriate libretto for the composer. However, the time was passing, and Dvořák wanted to begin, so he used some of his Hiawatha musical ideas in *From the New World*.

Arnold T. Schwab, in his book about Huneker (whose recollection about his trip with "Old Borax" through the East 17th Street area was previously described here), wrote about Dvořák:

> When Dvořák decided to compose a cantata based on Longfellow's poem about "Hiawatha," Huneker became his assistant and translator. He was to help Dvořák negotiate a deal with his friend Francis Neilson, the young English actor, dramatist and librettist. Neilson was supposed to write the needed libretto for Dvořák, but after a time of hesitation, he decided that Longfellow's poem was not a suitable theme, and the deal did not go through. Nevertheless, thanks to Huneker and Burleigh, Dvořák developed a profound interest in Negro spirituals, and included in his famous symphony a few of his sketches which were originally written for his cantata.

Dvořák talked about the origin of "Hiawatha" on December 15, 1893. He said that Longfellow (1807–1882) based his "Song of Hiawatha" on an old Indian myth about the Onondaga tribe and its mythical hero. He commanded magic and supernational powers that helped him set his tribe free from the evil sorcerer. After that, he taught his tribesmen the importance of love, goodness, work, and nurture. Finally, he gave them a degree of literacy. Because of his ability to see into the future, he knew that some day the white people would come and his tribe would perish. His prophecy came true, and when the whites invaded the country ruled by this wise leader, Hiawatha himself walked at the head of his people to welcome the intruders. Feeling that his role had been fulfilled, Hiawatha then left his tribe, never to return.

The story of this wise teacher of love and peace fascinated Dvořák tremendously. The poem was published in Czech in 1872, and the translation is a work of Josef Vaclav Sladek, who had previously lived in America for several years. Sladek's work shows his sensitivity to American legends and myths.

From the above information, we learn two things:

Conductor Seidl supposed that "the strong pathos of the slow movement in the Symphony *From the New World* was inspired by the composer's nostalgia, by his incessant longing for his homeland." This information agrees also with Mrs. Thurber's recollection.

However, Dvořák's explanation was slightly different. He said that this section is actually a study or sketch for his cantata or opera based on the poem written by Longfellow.

We would like to know the truth about all this, and not about the second movement only. Do we know for certain where and when the symphony originated?

Let us start with the problem number one—the question of the work's physical origin. The answer would seem to be simple, but there are contradictory opinions.

After the premiere of the symphony, a short article came out in the weekly magazine *Musical Courier*. It carried a major "discovery," namely, that the symphony had originated fourteen years ago in Europe, had been previously played in Hamburg! This news was based on the statement of a clarinetist in the New York Philharmonic who had supposedly played it there. We can say little about this rumor. The American press, always sensation-hungry, did not care to verify new facts, especially those which promised to attract public interest. We would pass over it in silence except for the fact that the magazine column "Musical News" was edited by Huneker. From the style of his memoirs about "Old Borax," we already know of his tendency to exaggerate. Nevertheless, it is hard to believe that he would dare to publish this news if it was entirely invented. In 1907, three years after Dvořák's death, *Pilsner Newsletters* published a passage from V. Drazan's memoirs concerning Dvořák's statement:

> It is always written that I gathered motives for my last symphony in America, and that it contains some Indian melodies. This is not true. Yes, I composed it there but the motives are my own, and a few of them were brought with me. The symphony is and always will remain "Bohemian" music.

In the course of time, what Dvořák had brought with him to America may be explained. However, it is a fact that various stories were going around about this matter, and they grew even more. In 1928, on March 17, Jaromir Weinberger wrote in the *Czech Newsletters* from New York:

> The Symphony *From the New World* is not only the most mature work of its composer, but also of the entire period since Beethoven. The motives and melodies have nothing in common with exoticism. Its syncopation is exclusively Slavonic, and the meditative chords at the beginning of the Largo have the complexity of Slavonic religious fervor. The

whole Scherzo is carried by the dance rhythms and meters typical of the colorful festivities of Slavonic tribes. The character of every beat and every note of the whole composition bears the seal of Dvořák's inspiration and creative method: the integrity of Beethoven's form with pure Slavic inspiration. Only the title of the work is outlandish and exotic. Otherwise, this work is a perfectly original symphony, incomparably Bohemian in substance.

If everything stated above is factual, musically and ideologically provable, it would be possible to deny the legend about the exoticism of the work not only by its spirit but also by knowledge of the circumstances under which the composition was created. Dvořák's idea to write *From the New World* came to his mind before his departure to the United States, and the whole Symphony had originated in Bohemia.

This statement of Weinberger represents one extreme. The other is that *From the New World* originated during Dvořák's vacation in Spillville, Iowa. This idea was broached in studies about Dvořák, first of all by William Arms Fisher, his former pupil in composition and orchestration. Fisher adapted the famous Largo theme from Dvořák's Symphony into a song which became popular around the world. When the record came out as the "Scottish Folk Song, 'Goin' Home'" in July of 1922, Fisher made a comment that it had originated in Spillville. He explained the circumstances in the following way:

In 1893, longing to hear his native tongue and with something akin to homesickness, he [Dvořák] spent the summer in Spillville, Iowa, a small community of Bohemians. Here as the outcome of his enthusiastic study of the folk music of the American Negro, he wrote the symphony *From the New World*, Opus 95; the String Quartet, Opus 96; and the String Quintet, Opus 97. In these significant works he did not incorporate Negro themes but invented his own after the Negro manner. He told me after his return that he had been reading Longfellow's *Hiawatha,* and that the wide-stretching prairies of the midwest had greatly impressed him.

Josef Jan Kovarik (in his article "About Dvořák's School of Composition in New York") briefly characterized eight of the composer's most important pupils. He wrote about one of them:

Fisher, William Arms, born 1861 in San Francisco, California, became renowned mainly because of his arrangement of the

Master's "Largo" from the Symphony *From the New World*. It was done for solo-voice baritone, with male choir, and he named the song "Going Home," writing a suitable text for it. The song helped make his name and, most of all, lots of money because many hundreds of thousands of copies of his arrangement were sold. Somewhere on the radio, we hear this beautiful song every day. In my opinion, Fisher should not have done it; he was not in need of this money. He was Chief-director of the Publishing House in Boston, Massachusetts, and probably earned a reasonable salary. He wrote about one hundred songs, some of which became widely known. I have no knowledge that he wrote any larger work.

Fisher was not the only one who testified that *From the New World* had been composed in Spillville. This rumor started before Fisher's tale spread, but the affirmation given by Dvořák's pupil carried much weight.

The *Cedar Rapids' Republican* carried an article written by Freeman R. Conway, headed, "About Old Spillville." The author was absolutely positive that it was right there, in Spillville, where the Symphony originated. This article was reprinted in the *Czecho-Slovakian Review,* and along with the writer's information, there was a photo of the house where the Dvořáks lived in the summer of 1893. Conway stated, "This is where Dvořák composed his Symphony *From the New World* and Humoresque."

This "once already pronounced truth" was spreading more and more; the Des Moines *Register Magazine* announced it as absolutely self-evident that the Symphony had originated in Spillville. The *Register* also published a photo of the composer and the house where the Symphony was written. Another picture shows "a bend of the beautiful Turkey River," where Dvořák used to walk, and where he supposedly sketched Humoresque. Therefore, "People from Spillville think of that place as sacred."

All this false news was disproved by Josef J. Kovarik in the sixth edition of his English serial in the magazine *Fiddlestrings,* in 1926:

> The first time I ever saw the name of my home town in print was just after Dr. Dvořák's return from his vacation there, when the *New York Herald* printed an account of his stay. Later it appeared in the programmes of the Philharmonic Society when Dvořák's "New World Symphony" was being performed, the same stating that the symphony was composed in Spillville, Iowa. Much as I would like to give my home town the credit, the fact nevertheless must be stated that the symphony, with the

Dvořák's letter to Kozanek about the composer's holiday he would take in Spillville in the summer of 1893. Dvořák used the official envelope of the Conservatory.

exception of a few finishing touches, was composed in New York City.

Kovarik also explained why and when Dvořák came to Spillville, and disputed what the writers said about his Iowa birthplace. They described it as a village where *From the New World* originated. He closed his argument with the following passage:

> After reading such lovely and well-written articles, it seems almost rude and cruel to say, that, Humoresque, like the New World Symphony was written in the year 1893 in altogether different environment—that is, in New York City—the exact spot being 327 East 17th Street—a considerable distance from the "Bend of the Beautiful Turkey River."

Kovarik's assertions are backed up by Dvořák's letters. The first mention about his new work was in a letter to his friend Geisler, on January 24, 1893, from which we have already quoted. The composer talked for the first time about the Symphony in E Minor. He named it the Symphony *From the New World* in the fall of 1893.

Dvořák's second remark about the new Symphony is in a letter to Dr. Emil Kozanek on April 12, 1893:

> Because there is not much work at school, I have enough time left to finish my new Symphony in E Minor. This work gives me great joy, and the composition is going to be absolutely different than my previous works. Well, everybody with a good rapport must feel the influence of America.

Dvořák's emphasis on the word "influence" gives us a hint that he was well aware of the new elements in his Symphony, and about what had influenced it.

Two days later, he wrote to Antonin Rus in Bohemia, and in his letter we can find the third mention of the Symphony *From the New World*:

> Because I am not too busy at school, I have enough time to work for myself. Right now, I am finishing the new Symphony in E Minor, and it pleases me well that my new work will be different from what I have written before. This time it will be more in an American style!!! My works are being performed frequently.

The fourth remark in Dvořák's correspondence is in his letter written in Spillville on August 17, 1893, to his friend Rus again. The composer describes his work, which he has just finished:

> I want you to know that I have written a new Symphony in E Minor, and also a new quartet and quintet for strings. I hope that all my compositions will come to light in this season.

Finally, the fifth mention about the composer's new work is in a letter to his friend Kozanek on September 15, 1893, the day before Dvořák and family returned to New York City. The vacation was over, and he gave this account of it:

> I certainly hope to return to Bohemia whether my contract is renewed or not I must see my home at all cost. I hear that the newspapers there wrote about me as if I were going to stay in America permanently! Oh, no! Never. Thank God, I am fine here and in good health, working hard. I can say that my new Symphony, the string quartet in F Major, and the quintet for strings (which I composed in Spillville), would never have been written as they are, if I had not seen America!

Very important sentences, indeed. Those five excerpts from Dvořák's correspondence stating that he did not work on the Symphony in Bohemia or in Spillville, but in New York City during the first semester, disprove the earlier rumors beyond all doubt.

The second important thing is that the composer knew about the tremendous environmental influence on his recent works; that without seeing America he could never have written these compositions in their present form.

It is time for a few words about this situation. Many researchers (after the premiere of *From the New World*) have asked how much "American music" can be found in the Symphony, or how much Dvořák remained Dvořák. Looking forward, we find that on the day after the premiere a critic from the *New York Herald* used a witty comparison:

> To sum up, the work is remarkably beautiful one. It may be Indian in spirit, but it is Bohemian in atmosphere. Dr. Dvořák can no more divert himself of his nationality than the leopard change his spots.

But what does "the American spirit" mean? Dr. Jaroslav Salaba-Vojan, an enthusiastic propagator of Czech music in America, wrote in the *Almanac of New York Newsletters* in 1939:

> Dvořák's works which he composed in the New World, here and there show traces of exoticism. This is especially true in the characteristic pentatonic scale of American Indian music. The five-tone Major scale; the soft Minor scale with flatted seventh, lacking its sixth step; delays and returns to the tonic note; rhythmical punctuation and syncopation; these features, always found in Negro spirituals, can occasionally be heard in Dvořák's works which he wrote in America.

Dvořák's researcher, Otakar Sourek, had a similar opinion:

> Most of the thematic ideas in these compositions are created with the characteristic musical elements common in negro spirituals, as well as in the songs of Indians, or in some songs written by Foster. Of course, the melodic line of the Major key is made from a five-tone-scale (pentatonic). It is in opposition to our seven-tone scale and omits each fourth and seventh tone. In the Minor scale, the lowered seventh tone can color the melody, giving it the character of soft and dreamy melancholy.

Because this is not a professional work of music theory, we will not look for more details about this problem. However, it is interesting to see what Dvořák said later in Chicago, when he was interviewed by the *Chicago Tribune* while visiting the city for the World Exhibition on August 13, 1893:

> Every nation has its own music—Italian, German, French, Bohemian, Russian, so why not American? The earnestness of this music depends on its characteristic features, on its color. I do not mean by this that we should gather plantation melodies—the Creole or Southern—and use them as themes. This is not in my plan. I study certain melodies until I can feel that their characteristic qualities have penetrated me enough to enable me to create a musical picture which will correspond with their features and have their characteristics.

On December 15, 1893, the day before the premiere of the Symphony *From the New World*, Dvořák had an interview with the *New York Herald*. Besides his remark that the second movement of the Symphony was a sketch for a cantata or opera about Hiawatha, Dvořák said:

Since I have been in this country, I have been deeply interested in the national music of the negroes and Indians. The character, the very nature of a race is contained in its national music. For that reason, my attention was at once turned in the direction of these native melodies.

We have already mentioned the Black musician, composer, and singer— Dvořák's pupil—Henry ("Harry") Thacker Burleigh. He belonged to the group of people who accomplished a lot for Dvořák's legacy in America. Milos Safranek, one of them, succeeded in 1941, during the war, in getting the commemorative plaque placed on the house on East 17th Street. He recalled his meeting with Burleigh:

> Burleigh succeeded in getting a stipend at the conservatory, and immediately after Dvořák's arrival, he established an animated, cordial, and permanent relationship with his teacher. Dvořák's influence on the work of this significant American composer was decisive. Burleigh introduced Dvořák to Negro spirituals, which he himself, while preserving their traditional melodies, had adapted and published. His most popular adaptation is known as "Deep River." Several witnesses recalled that Burleigh, while still a conservatory student, and definitely before the Symphony *From the New World* was written, used to sing Negro spirituals for Dvořák.

Milos Safranek continued:

> In our discussions with Kovarik during the seven years of our relationship in America, he agreed that Dvořák had the profoundest interest in the songs sung to him by Burleigh. I thought the same thing from my conversations with Burleigh and Kovarik in the memorable Dvořák apartment on 17th Street. We either sat in the first-floor-room, where Dvořák's piano used to be and where the Master composed his music, or in Kovarik's smaller room, nearby. I became involved in the spirited discussions about Dvořák among Burleigh, Kovarik and other Dvořák contemporaries. Both Kovarik and Burleigh left in this consecrated place a part of their lives and hearts. I learned that Burleigh visited Dvořák quite often, perhaps daily, and sometimes the composer took him to see a new engine or to watch the departure of a steamship from New York. Burleigh led me in Dvořák's traces along Union Square, and showed me the former sites of little pubs where Dvořák used to take him

for beer.

It is certain that Burleigh was able to awaken the composer's interest in the Negro songs which he sang to him. Among them was the famous "Swing Low, Sweet Chariot," about which—in connection with the Symphony *From the New World*—much controversial material exists. Burleigh was one of those people burning with the pure flame of conviction. This was most visible when, in a narrow circle of friends, he started to talk about Dvořák, and saluted him as the artist who was the first to understand the spirit of Negro songs. "Listen," Burleigh once said, "and you can hear how much poetry and original inner spirit is in our folklore! You can see then," he added with indignation, "what others have made of our songs, and worst of all, what jazz has made of them!"

The last sentence shows that as a composer Burleigh was a prisoner of the opinion of the older generation about jazz. We would be most interested to know what Burleigh had sung for Dvořák before the Symphony *From the New World.* Indeed, the four beats of the closing theme of the first movement of the symphony remind one of the song "Swing Low, Sweet Chariot," but unfortunately, we have no evidence about when Dvořák first heard this song.

Burleigh's memoirs were written several decades after Dvořák's sojourn in the USA, which does not preclude the possibility that Burleigh's information might be an idealization of the facts. However, we have Dvořák's words from the interview on December 15, 1893, that his "immediate attention was given to the native melodies." He gave most important information on August 13, 1893, when he said, "I study certain melodies until I can feel that their characteristic qualities have penetrated me...." It is this second citation which should be used in any consideration about the Symphony *From the New World*. Remember Dvořák's decisive words from his letter to Nedbal when he talked about the same problem.

Let us return to Kovarik's recollections. He not only rejected the possibility that *From the New World* had originated during Dvořák's summer holiday in Spillville; he also brought accurate data about the composer's work on the symphony.

Kovarik's writings could not be a better, more precise source. He conscientiously recorded:

On January 8, 1893, Master finished the instrumentation of *The American Flag* and asked me to copy his score. Two days later he started with a sketch of his great new work, which is to be called the "Symphony in E Minor," Number 8. He worked on a sketch of the first movement until the 21st, on the second movement until the 25th, and on the third movement until January 31st. A sketch of the last movement was postponed for a subsequent time. Master was occupied by the instrumentation of the first movement from February 9th to 28th. He finished the second movement on March 14th, and the third was done on April 10th. Meanwhile, between January 18th and February 17th, he adapted selections from *The American Flag* for the piano.

By the end of March, Master was sure that finishing the Symphony before May 15th (1893), (when he planned to return to Bohemia for the coming summer) was out of the question. He started to discuss it with his wife. What should he do? Postpone their trip until his work, which was of great importance to him, was finished, or have his four children brought to America? After long considerations, they decided to send for their children and spend their summer holiday in Spillville.

Now, when the Master could be sure that his work would not be interrupted, he was more relaxed. The sketch of the fourth movement was done on April 12th, and the whole work on the score was finished on May 24th (at 9 A.M.).

Meanwhile, the composer's children were getting ready for the trip to America. On May 23rd they left from Bremen by the ship *Havre* and by a special coincidence, they arrived at Southampton, England on the same day that Master finished his great work. So, we can see two notes, written at the end of the score: "At 9 A.M.," and beside it is written that "the children arrived at Southampton; the telegram came at 1:33 P.M."

Thus it was that the Symphony originated in New York, where it was also finished. Its specification *From the New World* was added to it by the Master only after his return from Spillville, which was shortly before he sent it to the New York Philharmonic.

These Kovarik recollections, called *Dvořák and Spillville*, offer us many priceless particulars about the origin of the Symphony *From the New World*. They were first printed in Czech in the 1920s in *The Nation*, later in the *Catholic Digest* and the 1934 *Almanac*.

Could they be checked somehow? Yes, indeed. The existing manuscript of Dvořák's score, with his many notes, offers material for verification. For

Manuscript of Dvořák's score

example, on the title page the composer wrote out a list of all his symphonies, for he wanted to determine the number for his Symphony in E Minor.

There is another resource used by musicologists studying the origin of this composition: the first printed copy of the Symphony in E minor, *From the new world* (as Dvořák himself wrote on the title page, using small letters *n* and *w*), was published as Opus 95 at the beginning of May 1894, by the famous Fritz Simrock Publishing House.

Now let us examine the main resources of information about the Symphony: one is this first edition of Dvořák's manuscript published by Simrock. Jarmil Burghauser, the researcher and composer, made an interesting discovery—the publisher did not use an original manuscript by Dvořák, but rather a copy made by Josef J. Kovarik in Spillville. The composer sent this copy and other orchestral materials to Simrock in Berlin.

Karin Stockl and Klaus Doge, who wrote a commentary and an analysis of the Symphony for the German publishers Goldmann and Schott, who collaborated on the pocket score edition, reported that none of this material survived World War II and probably was consumed by fire.

As for Kovarik's description and the orchestral materials, both can be considered as resources. In comparison with Dvořák's original score, Simrock's publication shows changes in many places (especially in dynamic markings) that must have been in Kovarik's copy or with the orchestra material sent to Berlin after the premiere.

Thanks to Kovarik's memoirs we know how the copy originated. We quote from his Czech recollection:

> In the afternoon, on the first day in Spillville, Master gave me the score of the Symphony to be copied during the holiday. As he handed it to me, he made one of his typical remarks:
>
>> You know what, Little Indian? The symphony has 128 pages. If you copy four pages a day, you can finish it in a month. This will shorten your vacation!
>
> Anxious Master always worried that I would not know what to do with my spare time, so he gave me enough work to keep me busy. I agreed, but remarked anyway: "O.K. Master, but only four pages a day, right?"

After Kovarik's description of their everyday life in Spillville, he continued with information about the origin of the symphony:

> During the time that I was copying the Symphony I had to show up every evening for Darda—which the Master would not give up even in Spillville—and also had to report to him each day's progress in rewriting his work. My report was usually a stereotyped: "Four pages."
>
> But one evening, probably because he was not in a good mood or more probably because I had beat him badly in Darda, he attacked me (verbally) after I reported my four pages, "Look, Indian, you're lazy! Only four pages, and every one almost empty!" I simply said: "Empty or full, it doesn't make any difference." If you knew the Master well, you were not afraid of his "blow-ups." They did not mean anything, and he forgot all about them in a short while.
>
> However, when I walked home that evening, Master's

remark, "You are lazy" was like a sting of my conscience. So I decided to work harder the next day. Writing diligently, I copied sixteen "full" pages. I knew in advance that it would be "wrong," and I was right. After my report of "sixteen pages," Master "flared up": "What? Sixteen pages? That's not possible, what a terrible lot of work! Are you trying to commit suicide? Why did you do it? You are supposed to be on vacation!"

So, four pages were too little, sixteen too much — I decided to copy just ten pages a day, and we had a short truce.

It was important to this phase of the work that Dvořák and Kovarik take their vacation together. In spite of the fact that Dvořák's manuscript was legible and clear, there were places where it was necessary to figure out the position of the notes on the staff when the composer had used an eraser for correction. When this happened, Kovarik could ask Dvořák about it, and as a result his copy would be clearer than the original.

Dvořák used ink to write the new work. Later, he made notes in pencil alongside the ink. According to Kovarik's recollections, Dvořák wrote these notes himself in the fall of 1893 during the orchestra rehearsal in New York City. They consisted mostly of indications of tempo and dynamic changes. Since Simrock's first draft shows all these additional directions, and yet some others, it indicates that they had been added to Kovarik's copy. It is of course possible that some of the inscriptions were the work of Anton Seidl.

In any case, it is true that as far as we know Dvořák did not either complain or agree. Nor did he ask in a letter for any corrections to be made in the next edition after he received a copy of his published score from Simrock.

There is a possibility of yet another reason. Brahms, in Vienna, was willing to proofread the score. This avoided the delay of having Simrock send corrections to America by mail. We recall that it was through Brahms' help that the *Moravian Duets* found their way into the world and we know that Dvořák trusted Brahms completely.

I already mentioned that Dvořák put a list of all his symphonies on the title page of his score because he wanted to figure out the number of the new "American Symphony," originally marked as "8." He later changed it to "7," but even this was crossed out. The reason was actually in his hesitation about whether he should count his earliest experiments, starting with *The Bells from Zlonice*. To be sure, he made the list in chronological order, and figured out that his *From the New World* would be his eighth. *The Bells from Zlonice* was not included. However, Simrock numbered only those Dvořák symphonies which were published by his company (he did not publish the first four), and therefore, *From the New World* was numbered as the fifth, but actually it was his ninth one.

The dates on which Dvořák started the individual movements of his Symphony, found in Kovarik's memoirs, are indeed precise. Five of Dvořák's notebooks are preserved—some of them are the sketchbooks and notebooks from his time spent in America. These help us to verify Kovarik's dates, and reconstruct Dvořák's entire creative process. In addition to the Symphony *From the New World*, we find in his books other fragments of work composed in America: the Quartet in F Major, Opus 96; the Quintet in E-flat Major, Opus 97—both composed in Spillville; a Sonatine for violin and piano in G Major, Opus 100; ten Biblical Songs, Opus 99; the Suite in A Major, Opus 98; and finally the Concerto for Violoncello, in B Minor, Opus 104. Back home in Bohemia he later added a few fragments and sketches. The operas *Cert a Kaca* (*The Devil and Kate*) and *Rusalka* (*The Water-Nymph*) are two of these.

The first of his American sketchbooks had a format of $9\frac{1}{2}$" x $8\frac{1}{2}$" (side flap), and had 40 pages with six staves each. Dvořák added another leaf of a smaller size, $8\frac{3}{4}$" x $3\frac{1}{2}$", eight staves each. On the envelope is an oblong label with the title "Sketches and Motifs." On the first page is written "1st morning, 18 19/12 92," and above it "Motifs, New York."* It appears that the first eleven pages represent a variety of Dvořák's musical ideas, some of which never found their way into the Symphony *From the New World*. For example, a motif on the fifth page has the title "March"; another, "Menuetto"; and the third motif, crossed out, carries Dvořák's explanation: "it reminds me of Jacobin." On the 42nd page is the composer's remark "Warlike, Martiale," and the headline is "Overture." From the twelfth page on, the first "integrated sketch" of the symphony appears, dated "New York, 18 10/1 93."

The second sketchbook has a format of $10\frac{1}{2}$" x $7\frac{1}{2}$"(side flap), each having 12 staves. Dvořák used this book, wrapped in a black, yellow-speckled jacket, with a label saying "New York 1893, Jottings. Notes./Chamber," fifty-three pages of various notes. In it we find a coherent sketch of the "Quartet in F Major" from Spillville, dated June 8, 1893, and a remark "On way from Chicago to Niagaver." He also has a sketch here for the "Song about Hiawatha," and includes other works written during his vacation in Bohemia during the summer of 1894.

---

*Dvorak habitually wrote dates with a large 18, followed by the numbers for day and month is a smaller hand, and the remainder of the year in a larger hand. See, e.g., the score pictured on p. 175 above.

The third sketchbook, same size as the second, is labeled "Musical Jot-tings—New York 1893/ 1894/ Notes./ Orchestra." The composer used seventy-eight pages, and the most interesting one has a theme for the "Finale" of the Symphony *From the New World* as well as a theme for the "Scherzo" of the "Quartet in F Major." We can also read his notes from December 31, 1893, which were used later as material for "Humoresque, No. 1."

The fourth sketchbook, of the same size again, was labeled "New York 1893/ Notes/ Jottings," and had 66 pages, The first twenty pages contain the reduced score of the cantata *The American Flag,* with a date of "New York 18 18/1 93," and which concludes with the note "Finished on February 17, 1893." The evidence shows that Dvořák wrote this work simultaneously with the sketch of the first three movements of the Symphony *From the New World.* There is also the Quintet in E-flat written in Spillville, showing a date of June 23, 1893, as the beginning of the composition. The work was finished on the 1st of August. Dvořák also kept here a sketch of a symphony which he never completed. It was inspired during his overseas trip to New York: The move-ments are: (1) Neptune, (2) Merry Movement, Dances and Festivity on the Ship, (3) Choral Song, (4) Storm and Rest—Happy Return to Land.

The fifth and last sketchbook is of a small size, 8" x 5½" (205 x 130 cm), side flap, with thirty-four pages used. On the back is an address, "A. Dvořák/ 128 East 17th Str./N.York." Besides the sketches for his planned "Song of Hia-watha," Dvořák had made here a sketch of his Violoncello Concerto in B Minor. Originally, the composer started on the first page in D Minor, with a footnote: "Concerto for Violoncello. New York, November 8, 1894."

We now return to the origin of the Symphony *From the New World.* In none of Dvořák's preserved letters from October 1892 through January 24, 1893, written home to friends, is there any word about his creative plans. The first hint appeared in his letter to Geisler in Olomouc, written on the 24th of January, which we have already cited.

We will never know the truth about what actually moved Dvořák to write it. Was it the influence of Mrs. Thurber (as she recollected later), or the immense musical feasibilities coming with it; or a sudden change of atmo-sphere; the new, special feeling in the air before Christmas, with remem-brances of his homeland?

We know for sure that in his American sketchbook, page twenty, January 10, is his decision that the first work he was going to write in the New World would be a symphony.

We can follow here the process and progress of Dvořák's work, and it was here that Kovarik found (perhaps only later) all the information and dates about the individual movements which he used in his recollections. The dating of the individual parts of the Symphony are well correlated, and the summary is as follows:

	Sketchbook Page	Sketch	Score
I.	movement 12 to 22	1/10 — 1/21	2/8 — 2/28
II.	movement 23 to 26	1/25	3/14
III.	movement 27 to 31	1/31	4/10
IV.	movement 31 to 39	5/12	5/24

Kovarik came up with the same dates. The only exception he listed showed February 9 for the instrumentation of the first movement. In Dvořák's records it is February 8. Kovarik also wrote that Dvořák finished a sketch of the fourth movement on April 12. This is not likely because, according to Kovarik, the composer was supposed to finish the orchestration of the third movement on April 10. Therefore, if we should trust him, the composer sketched the fourth movement in two or three days. If Kovarik is wrong, the correct date is May 12, recorded April 12. Obviously, we can see in the original manuscript that Kovarik made an error, because beside the last beat of the movement is the composer's handwritten note: "Fine 5/12/1893, New York, A. Dvořák."

All the dates here show that Dvořák had sketched the first three movements with obvious ease, and relatively fast. According to Kovarik, the composer started to sketch the fourth movement only after a pause. We do not know what he was really doing between January 31 and February 8, so we cannot say when he began the score of the whole work.

There are more opinions and theories as to why Dvořák came to a "standstill." Why did he pause in his work? It might be for various reasons not necessarily related to his musical activities. In the spring of 1893 he was responsible for a concert given by his students; and in the second half of May, an important Dvořák article was carried by the *New York Herald*. Perhaps he had to prepare for the interview.

I suppose that those who later heard the Symphony *From the New World*, researchers Stockl and Doge, came to the following conclusion:

> The manuscript, with the exception of a few parts, represents the final version of the score, not only in its thematic and melodic course, but most of all, in its harmonic characteristic.... It shows that Dvořák composed the sketch of the symphony from its first beat to its last, that he did not work on the various movements and individual sections simultaneously, and first of

all, that he had a relatively accurate idea of the structure of the first three movements.

The researchers continued:

> It is remarkable that in the sketch of the 9th Symphony are thematic sections which are usually written directly in their final sounding. However, more avenues were sketched for the transferral and developmental sections before the version of the score originated.... It is most obvious from the sketches, and from the finished work, too, that Dvořák started with melodic fundamentalism, that his melody is always a substance of movement and the main carrier of the musical expression. The harmony and accompaniment keep in the movement only their secondary roles: to emphasise the melody, without suppressing it. Only once a while, are they emphasized, showing their own independent quality.

We can add only that the patches, erasures, and improvements of the individual pages of manuscript (especially of its transferral sections) can show Dvořák's responsibility and artistic ambitions.

Regardless of how much talent he had and how gifted he was, the composer worked hard and ceaselessly for five months. Being under constant tension, he sought to express everything that had impressed him about this tremendous country.

Faithful to his old custom, he concluded the final page of the score manuscript with a date, and at this time, he added a note about his children's trip and he thanked God, who gave him — as Dvořák openly and simply believed — his whole musical genius.

Symphony *From the New World* ⤳ B

When I RETURNED THAT EVENING from a visit to the 17th Street house now owned by Dick and Charlotte Miller, my head was buzzing. I sat in the room we shared at the Czech Consulate amid the piles of books and clippings I had gathered for my Dvořák research, but my thoughts were still in the house where Dvořák had lived during his stay here. With eyes closed I pictured the changes that had taken place since those days—the winding staircase, the forged brass knob on the entrance door. I wondered if there was anything in the house that still linked us with the composer.

I was brought back to reality by the sounds of the television program *The Price is Right*, with its dynamic character so like that of America. That reminded me of what Colonel Higginson had said in 1892, when he spoke at the occasion honoring Dvořák: "If you choose the picked young men of each college class and send them out on railroads, art must wait." I realized that there were many differences between conditions in Europe and those in the United States, but I felt that there is something else in the American spirit that we Europeans lack.

Dvořák had something to say about this, I remembered, and began hunting through the stack of letters and articles on the desk. Ah, yes, I found the

182

letter he wrote on October 14, 1892, to his friend Dr. Bastar, who was associated with the local choir of the town where I was born, Jaromer:

> Life here is very different from ours in Europe. This beautiful, magnificent city is encircled with the forest-covered hills, and there is lots of water with many ships. Wonderful! We have the same things in our country, but there is a different feeling here.
>
> The Columbus ceremony (celebrating the 400th Anniversary of the discovery of America) ended yesterday, and it was indeed great! We have never seen anything like it. This was America's first opportunity to show its skill and ability. Imagine row after row of marching groups in the magnificent parade representing industry, trades, sports (our Bohemian Sokol marchers included) and the arts. Actually every branch of American life was there.
>
> The celebration lasted three days, morning, noon, and night nonstop, with thousands and thousands of people constantly moving and regrouping, enjoying the activities, especially the diversity of bands and music!
>
> You can imagine that there were accidents, too. Mishaps occurred ever so often. People were standing on roof-tops, some as high as eleven stories, observing the crowds. It was estimated that one million people from all corners of America participated in the celebration.

I thought about all this wealth of impressions permeating Dvořák's soul and needing some outlet. Surely much of it made its way into his Symphony *From the New World,* whether consciously or not. Add to that his growing homesickness, his desire to be in his beloved Bohemia once again.

This was attested to by his friend Anton Seidl and his employer Jeanette Thurber. They knew of his fascination with the mail ships in New York Harbor, and saw his mood change when one of the liners left for Europe.

When Dvořák felt his sadness he would take the "el" north to 155th Street and walk through the quiet cemetery filled with graves of emigrants who had exchanged their homeland for the promise of future happiness, if not for themselves, at least for their children. The path took him to a point from which he could observe the trains, a place which reminded him of the railway station in Prague. Back at his 17th Street house, he might listen to the Black student, Harry T. Burleigh singing Negro spirituals, those songs which so well expressed desire and longing.

My thoughts were broken by a question from my photographer, Honza. He asked about the influence of American Indian music on Dvořák's compositions. I answered that Dvořák once had attended Buffalo Bill's "Wild West Show" at Mrs. Thurber's invitation, and had witnessed Indian dances there, but he was probably already familiar with them from other sources. He did see Indians when he visited in Spillville, but his Symphony *From the New World* was already written by the time he went there.

Then I remembered something that Dvořák had written for the *Pilsen Review*. He was objecting to the suggestion that he had put Indian songs into his Symphony. He said: "This is not true. Although the 'Symphony' was composed in America, all the musical themes are my own, including some I brought with me."

What did he mean? Did he bring along sketches and melodic ideas? Not at all. We know well that his American Sketchbook No. 1 originated in New York in December 1892. So it had to be something else.

We watched television awhile, enjoying some ice cream dessert that Honza bought in d'Agostini's Variety Store on the way home. But the competition on the show was too slow, and we became tired of guessing the prices of goods, so we resumed our conversation about Dvořák and the American Indians.

I told Honza that I had found an interesting article in the August 6, 1879, *National Review of Prague* about a production of Indian songs and dances, presented on Great Venice Island the previous day. I further discovered that the whole Indian group visited Naprstek's Ethnographic Museum on August 8, and had signed their names in the guest book.

I wondered where Dvořák was on those days. We have some indications—for instance, a postcard written from Berlin to his friend Gobl in Sychrov mentioning his dealings with Simrock. He added that he would probably be back home on August 2. Gobl received another postcard from Dvořák on August 21 from Marienbad. I admitted to Honza that I could not prove Dvořák had seen the Indian program, but it seemed sure that he was traveling through Prague about the same time that the Indian group was performing there.

Honza seemed interested but said that it was just as possible that Dvořák had gone directly to the spa from Sychrov on the 17th or the 18th of August, after the Indians had gone. I had further proof, however, and said:

"Even if I can't prove that he attended the actual performance, he almost certainly read an interesting article about it written a short time later by his friend, V. J. Novotny. Mr. Novotny accompanied Dvořák on his second visit to England in September 1884 and had rewritten the libretto for Dvořák's comic opera, *The King and the Collier*. He was a man whom Dvořák trusted as a friend and a collaborator, so it was almost certain that he would have called Dvořák's attention to the following article that appeared in *Dalibor*:

> A few days ago, the Association of American Indians, consisting of nine men and two women belonging to Iroquois and Comanche tribes, gave a performance on Great Venice Island. This production of interesting scenes offered a very clear view of the life, habits and peculiarities of their fabled nations.
>
> Most interesting for us were the scenes interwoven with Indian tribal songs. Generally believed to be insignificant, they actually contain many original melodic and rhythmic elements. And even though the instrumental accompaniment consisted of one tambourine only [the writer of the article probably meant "Tom-tom," a drum], the effect of the music on the audience was very pleasant.

I did not read to Honza the details of single numbers in the production such as wedding ceremonies, election of a chief, bear dance, battle scene, a raid to kidnap a girl, and a funeral song for a fallen Indian warrior. The article ended with these words:

> As we can see from any of the examples here, the music of the American Indian tribes has an original and interesting character. Some of their melodies are indeed beautiful, others are tainted with civilization, but on the whole, we are certain that they will appeal to every musician interested in primitive music.

Mr. Novotny had even illustrated his article with musical sketches, among which was one motive, often repeated (the captured enemy tied to a pole) which reminds one of the themes in C-flat minor from Largo of the Symphony *From the New World*.

Honza very graciously said that I had done good work in figuring out all of this. But I replied that there was nothing to congratulate me for since I had not made these discoveries. That honor went to the musicologist, Dr. V. Sefl.

Prof. Antonin Sychra found in Mr. Novotny's musical sketches examples which were very close to the leading theme of the slow movement of Dvořák's Quartet in F Major. This was composed in the summer of 1893 in Spillville, Iowa.

We decided that the time had come for us to go to Spillville, but we did not know how we would get there.

I found further information about the Quartet in F Major from an article written in 1894 by the American critic, Henry Krehbiel. He stressed the relationship of Indian folk music with the main movement of the quartet. This completely convinced me that Dvořák had no need to write anything in his sketchbook about Indian music; he had kept everything in his memory; thus he truly brought some of his themes with him when he came to America.

The TV show finally ended. The winner got a car. It was time to go to bed.

"What are we doing tomorrow?" Honza asked.

"Tomorrow, I would like to see Carnegie Hall, and then the Department of Manuscripts at Columbia University. I hope there is a pleasant surprise waiting for me there."

The next day, on our way to Carnegie Hall, we stopped at a travel agency to book a flight to Buffalo in order to visit Niagara Falls. Since Dvořák had stopped there during his return trip to New York City in the autumn of 1893, we needed to go there, too. We decided that the cheapest and fastest was by air (it was 375 miles between Buffalo and New York City by bus). By taking an early plane, we could get a discount, then rent a car, or go by a minibus the 18 miles from the airport to the falls.

Having completed these arrangements, we went toward Carnegie Hall. Built by Andrew Carnegie in the middle of the last century, it is one of the oldest halls in New York City. The Symphony *From the New World* was premiered there in its 2,500-seat auditorium.

In addition to Carnegie Hall, New York City has the Metropolitan Opera, a modern building belonging to the complex called Lincoln Cultural Center, which includes the City Theatre for drama and other attractions.

Our way took us along the Central Park. Dozens of men and women of all ages were jogging on the narrow paths as if they belonged to a nation of runners. Two or three times we heard the insistent fire sirens and stopped with everybody else to watch the roaring, careening, super-modern fire trucks flash by with folding ladders on top. Honza was really fascinated by the men in their blue uniforms with bold yellow stripes. He liked to think it was all being staged for him to photograph.

Further on we met two street musicians, saxophone and drum. They had an open box in front of them for donations. Then we passed stands where you could buy warm, salted pretzels, hot dogs, oranges, or flowers. We passed silent demonstrators, men and women of some religious group, carrying signs saying: "Find Consolation in God." Other groups had antimilitary slogans. If you add to all this the constant stream of yellow taxis vying for space on the streets, you will see that New York City is a vibrant place.

Carnegie Hall is situated on the corner of 57th Street and Seventh Avenue. A strange, massive building built in a peculiar style of narrow ochre bricks, it has perhaps three stories. Most of the windows penetrating the vast walls are blind and only irregular-sized arches break the monotony of the construction. I could see the movie-theatre entrance from Seventh Avenue, but the main entrance to the concert hall is on 57th Street. Above it is a flat roof with the words, "Carnegie Hall." On top of it flutters an enormous blue pennant punctured with holes to keep it from fluttering too wildly in the wind. It proclaims "The 91st Season of Carnegie Hall."

There are three entrances into the building. Once inside, you are in a hall of marble, undoubtedly very white when built, but now darkened by age. Here numbers of booklets and bulletins about coming events are available for visitors to pick up. At the left is the box office; on the right, a bust of Andrew Carnegie, who was born in 1835 in Scotland, the son of a poor weaver. He rose through the ranks in America and became a successful, self-made man. He returned to his homeland in 1901 as a millionaire American steel king. He stated that "we have to investigate the causes of poverty and crime at their roots and not just be satisfied with trimming the branches." The rich people, according to him, should be founding universities, libraries, hospitals, laboratories, public parks, spas, and churches. Rather than a church, he himself built a concert hall.

Standing in the marble entrance hall of this building, I could see the Greek pillars separating the glass entrances into the front hall, which opened into the main auditorium. In 1893 Carnegie Hall was the center of the musical world, and it was here that Dvořák's Symphony *From the New World* was played on the 16th of December.

I wanted to examine the bust of Dvořák, but it was impossible. The walls were covered with posters for the next program and recent attractions: Bach's gigantic Mass in B Minor, called *Hohe Messe* (although he belonged to a Protestant church, his work was written especially for the Catholic ritual), Beethoven's *Mass,* Dvořák's *Requiem,* Mahler's Fifth Symphony and works by Gershwin and Verdi.

Some of the best performers in the music world were being featured: Marielle Mathieu was going to play two concerts there; the Boston Symphony Orchestra, the Israel Philharmonic, and the Dutch Philharmonic were scheduled to perform.

In front of my eyes was a list of names: Mozart, Schumann, Liszt, Brahms, Debussy, Mendelssohn, Sibelius, Shostakovich, Handel, Stravinsky, and Dvořák. There was a poster featuring the Symphony *From the New World.* The first performance had taken place five days before our arrival in America. The next one would be presented while we were in Spillville. In between they would be playing his *Carnival,* the Concerto for Violoncello, and the Seventh Symphony. It was heartwarming to know that so much of his music was being played here.

We left the Hall with our pockets full of information about the next concerts. We were tempted to visit the three-story Russian Tea Room in the neighborhood, but resisted the temptation because Honza needed to work on his photographs and I was looking forward to the manuscript department of Columbia University.

We stepped back into the roar of the city—the squeaking brakes, the beat of some Black jazz musicians, and even the clip-clop of horses of mounted policemen preparing for a demonstration. I had not expected horses on the streets of New York City.

I had to decide whether to walk through Central Park or take the subway. When I reached into my pocket for glasses, I found a five-dollar bill I had forgotten about. Someone had told me to put the money there in case I was mugged in Central Park. Instead of reaching into my trousers, I should point to the little pocket in my jacket. That sounded strange to me, but I did it. However, rather than tempt fate, I took the metro. It was half empty, with only a few blacks and senior citizens. Before we reached Columbia University, though, it was full of young people.

I found my destination on the little map near the ceiling of the car and learned that I should get off at the 116th Street station. The crowd of casually dressed students moved me along through a wide, richly decorated gate and alley lined with linden trees into a large parklike square filled with greenery. This was surrounded by buildings of the University.

Early morning showers had dissipated, and the fragrance of freshly mowed grass was overwhelming. I looked around and saw an antique building on the right with fourteen Doric columns. Could this be the rector's office? On the left was a library with ten columns and a dome similar to the Paris Pantheon. Although there was a large amount of space between the buildings, something about the red bricks in the facade reminded me of Jolly Old England. In the middle of the open space was a little, round, marble construction which turned out to be a sundial. When I went closer, I could read the Latin inscription: "Horam expecta, veniet," "Wait for the hour, it will come."

When I inquired about the manuscript department, I learned that both buildings were part of the library. In between the pillars, on the left, I could see the names of famous statesmen: Washington, Franklin, Adams. On the right were writers: Irving, Cooper, Emerson, Longfellow, Poe, Melville, Whitman, Twain....

I went through many halls, study rooms, and workshops, using lifts from one floor to another, before I located the right spot to ask for material about Anton Seidl. The library contains a mass of letters, memoranda, notes, musical manuscripts and news related to his life and musical activity.

Up to this time I knew only that Anton Seidl had conducted the New York Philharmonic Orchestra for the premiere of the Symphony *From the New World* and that he was deeply affected by the slow movement—the Largo. So I started at the beginning: he was born in 1850 in Hungary. From 1872 until 1878 he was a member of Wagner's household, first as his secretary, later as conductor of Wagner's theatre in Bayreuth.... After that he spent many years conducting and promoting Wagner's music not only in Europe but in America as well.

The collection originally contained Seidl's letters from Wagner, Wagner's wife Cosima, and their children since Anton was like a member of the family. At some point Wagner's letters were removed and put in a special section. Now Seidl's collection contains his correspondence with Grieg, Dvořák, R. Goldmark, Maud Powell, and many others. There are also arrangements of the works of famous composers such as Liszt, Haydn, Grieg, Schubert, Gottschalk, Weber, and Mascagni. I found it interesting that in such a list Dvořák's name did not appear even once. I wondered why. I was amazed to learn that I had access to material about Dvořák not yet published in Bohemia.

The librarian brought me four inventory numbers, namely two of Dvořák's visiting cards with handwritten messages on them, and two of his letters. The first letter was written during the early period of Dvořák's teaching at the New York National Conservatory of Music. He had asked Kovarik not to return home to Spillville, but to stay with the Dvořák family in New York City for the entire school year 1892–93. In addition, he had interceded for Kovarik with Mrs. Jeanette Thurber and had spoken in his interest with Seidl. The letter, written to Seidl, does not make plain what Kovarik wanted or needed. Here is the letter:

My Dear Conductor Seidl, New York, 20th Nov., 1892

I would like to thank you cordially in the matter of my friend, Mr. Kovarik. If it happens that I can repay you in similar circumstances, it will be my great pleasure to do so.

With special respect,
I remain your devoted

Antonín Dvořák

Next, I read another brief letter that Dvořák wrote to Seidl:

New York, April 29, 1894

My Highly Respected Friend,

I have a request to make. I hear that you and your orchestra have been engaged for the summer in Brighton Beach. My request is that you do not forget Mr. Kovarik. He will be staying with me, and it would be desirable for him to earn some money through your help. Thank you for considering my supplication. I remain your especially devoted

Antonín Dvořák

I do not know if the letter produced the desired result, but it does give us an insight into Dvořák's character.

The third piece of Dvořák memorabilia was one of his cards with this message handwritten on the back:

Most Respected Friend,

Would you kindly hear Chopin's "Concerto in E minor" played by our very talented student, Miss Visanska.

With Cordial regards Yours....

The last letter was not at all related to Dvořák's American experience, so I was finished. I wondered how to fit these bits of information into the overall picture. But first I wanted to look at other material relating to Dvořák in another part of the library.

I was especially interested in trying to find his instructions to Seidl about conducting the Symphony *From the New World*. Did such instructions exist? The uncertainty of not knowing exactly what was available made my search exciting.

I stumbled my way through the building again until I found a room containing old magazines. I was brought a number of back issues of the *Etude* to examine. In the table of contents of one dated 1931 I saw the title "How Dvořák Taught Composition" by Harry Peterson Hopkins. I remembered that I had seen a framed photograph of Hopkins on the wall at Vysoka, and Otakar Dvořák (the composer's son) had written that Hopkins had later gone into politics and had become a member of Roosevelt's cabinet. I was not absolutely sure that the two men named Hopkins were one and the same, but that did not concern me at the time. [x]

H. P. Hopkins wrote that he had wanted to become a composer and was studying quite satisfactorily in that field at an American conservatory until the following occurred:

> One night I heard Dvořák's Symphony in E minor, *From the New World* and was enchanted by its beauty, tonal color and marvellous fresh themes. I decided to find the composer of this Masterpiece and study with him even if I had to travel to the end of the earth.
>
> I did not have to go that far. In six months I found myself in the heart of Bohemia in the midst of new people, different living conditions and a tongue-twisting language. However, I was happy because I had located my teacher—a real genius. To find out if he would accept me as a student, I sent him some music I had written in America. He liked it and answered positively.
>
> Dvořák spoke English very well because he had spent several years in America; this led to our closer friendship. He liked to speak with me in English in front of his fellow countrymen and often asked me to accompany him on walks to cafes, orchards and to various meetings in picturesque old Prague while he talked and talked, non-stop.
>
> We agreed on daily lessons in his house; and they proved to be far from academic. He would sit down at the table to look at my work, light his cigar, become silent for awhile, then suddenly explode with invective, sharp sarcasm or ardent praise, whatever my composition deserved. We discussed the orchestration, he checked the counterpoint, and we talked about the desired effect. In addition, we played the most important themes on the piano and evaluated them.
>
> After about an hour of teaching, Dvořák was ready for a walk to some market place. He spoke English with me, then

---

*The man in Roosevelt's cabinet was Harry L. Hopkins, 1890–1946. —Translator's note would turn aside to chat with the natives in their language. He was a real Bohemian who liked to mingle with his countrymen.

His instructions were very important to me. During the lessons, I had often attempted to turn the discussion to the Symphony *From the New World*. But no matter how clever I tried to be, I never succeeded. He was really stubborn about it. However, one day, being in an excellent mood, he took me aside and said: "Do not be discouraged—just wait. When Tony is ready, he will tell you everything." Since one of the main reasons for my stay with him was to satisfy my curiosity about this masterpiece directly from the composer himself, I had no other choice but to wait. I also knew that the musical world would welcome this information.

Dvořák's appearance was that of a big man, well-built, noble looking, who carried himself proudly. Consequently he made a great deal of commotion when he walked through the streets. During one of these walks, because summer was near, he came up with the idea that I should accompany him to Vysoka, a small village in the hills a few miles from Prague.

It was his custom to spend each summer in this refuge. The only problem was that there was no other instrument available in this place, except a piano in his house. I could see that he liked my work, though, so partially for my convenience and partially for his, he invited me to stay with his family.

When we reached his summer house, he became excited. Every day then, we would walk in the woods. He always carried his manuscript with him wrapped in a scarf. His wife and children, who always accompanied us, were greatly amused at this; but he was deadly afraid of fire and did not consider it safe to leave his manuscript anywhere else.

During our strolls in the thick, pine forests, I got very valuable ideas from him. For example, Dvořák stated that a man does not have to struggle to become a great pianist or singer in order to be a good composer or conductor. This idea came to him when he was talking about the performance of his Symphony *From the New World* directed by Anton Seidl in New York City.

Dvořák never analyzed the structure of his own works. He let himself be carried through the writing of his work guided by his subconscious feelings for form and proportions. In this way, he was a "free-thinker" musically speaking.

One day, in a pleasant environment, he agreed to talk about the Symphony:

"I first started it in F Major," he said, deep in thought. "It was happy and merry and I had finished half of the first movement...."

He noticed my surprise and continued: "The second theme was originally like this:

however, it was too simple, so, I changed it like that:

"I always carry my notebook with me wherever I go. Although I had sketched the motives as I conceived them in America, I decided it would be better to put them in a minor key, so now the symphony is in E minor."

He added that the symphonic conception of those themes had helped him to build the work as it is. He said that many composers try to bring us cute, tuneful melodies but only a few have been able to raise their work to the symphonic level.

When I praised his orchestration, he was confused. "Little emphasis should be given to orchestration," he said. "My main focus is on the music itself. Every concertmaster can do the orchestration as well as I can."

Some human weaknesses drew attention away from Dvořák's winning geniality. He was afraid of storms. When he saw dark clouds swirling, he really became frantic because storms in hilly country can be very violent.

The summer went fast. My daily contact with Doctor gave me the chance to see his family at close range. Just after breakfast, Dvořák began composing in his study, shielded from visitors by

Mrs. Dvořák.

The study was a pleasant place shaded by fruit trees. On the walls and around the room were treasured mementoes—a precious German pipe from Brahms, a silver teakettle from Tschaikovsky; an autographed photo of Saint-Saens, and several fancy batons of ivory from various musical organizations. The atmosphere was conducive for work.

Almost every composer follows a plan in his composition:

First, he makes a sketch of a melody or passage, writing it down, sometimes with the aid of a piano. Second, he harmonizes the melody in treble and bass. Finally, the idea is elaborated into its intended form; as a hymn, a song or an orchestral piece.

Dvořák followed this method in the last two stages, but, for the first, used a sketch from his sketchbook. This he kept with him at all times, writing musical ideas in it at any time or place. I often observed him doing this. He was especially adept at writing for instruments, knowing precisely what each one could do. His music for horn, for example, always sounded like horn music. Sometimes, while helping him transcribe instrumental parts, I would mistakenly copy a trumpet passage for horn; this would make him angry. He rejected the idea of safely supplementing certain passages with soft strings, preferring the distinct tonal color of the solo instrument. Among composers, few used instruments with such effect and authority. Dvořák's reputation as an orchestrator stands firm even today when writing for instruments has changed so radically.

I was quite satisfied with Hopkins' recollections. They helped me to flesh out the picture of Dvořák despite some minor inaccuracies.

Later, I went strolling downtown along Broadway amid the neon lights which advertised products, movies, and sex shows. It was a canyon of skyscrapers sunk in bright lights. I walked over to Fifth Avenue, a morse code of flickering, flashing lights and sounds. I gazed at Rockefeller Center, observing the nightlife, where crowds of skaters whirled around the larger-than-life statue of Prometheus. The sky had become cloud-covered, but flashes of lightning still illuminated the romantic scene. The president had just completed an address to the nation's top industrialists at a hotel a few blocks away. I watched the police horses being taken away in vans. It was indeed a city of contradictions, and there seemed to be no sign yet of settling down for the night.

I came to the New York City Public Library's main building with its two wise-looking lions guarding the pillar entrance. There were pairs of young lovers on the steps, as well as several student groups passionately arguing while an old woman distributed religious pamphlets. Some Black youngsters were humming a song, and I was reminded of the next day's work.

The next morning the Consulate driver offered to take me to the archives, and on the way we talked about hockey and tennis. As we cruised down Broadway, it looked quite different in the morning light, almost shabby, as if suffering from a hangover from last night's spree.

I felt at home as I entered the branch library on 43rd Street. I recognized the Black clerk from whom I had bought the Xerox tokens on my first visit. When he saw me, he grinned and tried to pronounce "Dvořák."

I searched through the spring issues of the *New York Herald* for 1893. During this time Dvořák was working on his Symphony *From the New World* in the 17th Street house, but I could find nothing about this in the papers; he was probably not talking about it to anyone. Finally, in the Friday paper of March 31, 1893, I came upon an article entitled "Music Laureates Receive Prizes." There was nothing in it about Dvořák's new creation; a series of subheads proclaimed:

> American Composers Honored with Money Rewards by The National Conservatory. — Dr. Antonin Dvorak Conducts — Symphony, Piano Concerto, String Suite and Cantata the Successful Works Heard. — With Seidl's Orchestra.

The whole article was written in typical American style — sometimes exaggerated, sometimes with open irony. However, most important for our research was that the whole affair was arranged to celebrate Dvořák's arrival in the United States. Its intent was to honor him and arouse interest in the propagation of the new American music. Mrs. Thurber obviously knew how to handle the publicity angles. The article stated:

> The National Conservatory of Music by way of marking the accession of Dr. Antonin Dvorak to its ranks, announced last autumn that it would award six prizes for musical composition as follows: — For the best grand or comic opera, $1,000; for the best libretto for an opera, $500; for the best symphony, $500; for the best oratorio, $500; for the best suite or cantata, $300; for the best piano or violin concerto, $200. The composition

was restricted to composers born in this country and not more than thirty-five years of age.

At the Madison Square Garden Concert Hall last night, Dr. Dvorak awarded four of the prizes, those for a symphony, a suite, a cantata and a piano concerto. The other awards will not be made until later. The jury upon whose judgment the awards were made last night was composed of Dr. Dvorak, Mr. Asger Hamerik, of Baltimore; Mr. Rafael Joseffy; Prof. John K. Payne of Boston; and Mr. Xaver Scharwenka.

The successful competitors were Henry Schonfeld of Chicago, Ill., for the symphony; Joshua Phippen of Boston, Mass., for the piano concerto; Frederik Field Bullard also of Boston, for an orchestral suite; Horatio W. Parker, of New York, for a cantata. Masters Schoenfeld, Bullard and Parker conducted their own works, and Mr. Phippen played his piano concerto, Dr. Dvorak conducting the orchestra accompaniment.

The conservatory gave the successful young composers every advantage in the performance of their works that they could have desired. An excellent orchestra, composed of Herr Seidl's men, was employed, and in the cantata a well-drilled chorus from the conservatory took part.

The large audience present last night heard some very good music as a result of the conservatory's public spirit, and was liberal with its applause. The concert began with the symphony by Mr. Schoenfeld, who is a Milwaukee man by birth, but settled in Chicago in 1879, after studying in Europe with Reinecke, Cyrill and Lassen. Several of his compositions have been played under Mr. Thomas' direction. The present symphony, which he [calls] the "Rural" is in four movements and contained the most interesting music heard last night."

Analysis of the several works followed, and the article ended with these words:

At the close of the concert Dr. Dvorak presented the successful composers with their prizes and said a few kindly words of congratulation.

The date of the concert at the end of March was well timed. The strenuous preparations for it were the director's responsibility. At that time, certain voices in New York City's musical society had started to question Dvořák's efficiency. Only a few closely related people could have known that he was writing a symphony, and his head was filled with ideas for the new work.

Mrs. Jeanette Thurber answered the critics clearly:

> The benefit of Dvorak's presence is greater than I expected. Everybody should know that a man gifted with a creative spirit is usually a very impractical person. This, however, is not the case with Dr. Dvorak. He entered into his duties at the conservatory fully and with enthusiasm. He is the Director, not in name only, but by virtue of what he does. I never dared expect that he could carry on the heavy load of work which this position demands, and with such energy.

Mrs. Thurber did everything possible to ensure the success of her Conservatory. She saw to it that people talked about the musical competition and kept the name of Dvořák in the public eye. She probably had also arranged to have a lead article on Negro songs appear in the Sunday issue of the *New York Herald* on May 21, 1893. She must have anticipated that Dvořák was finishing his new symphony. The composer had likely said to her something similar to what he was writing to friends back in Bohemia.

In these letters, he said that his new work "will differ very considerably from my others. Well, that's the influence of America."

We know that the Symphony *From the New World* was finished on the 24th of May and if the preparation of the *Herald* article took a week to ten days, it must have dated back to the period when Dvořák was finishing the last movement. He was aware of what he had created, and knew what he had used for inspiration. Therefore, the article entitled "Real Value of Negro Melodies" had a significance beyond just reporting the news. The subheads of the article revealed yet more:

> Dr. Dvorak Finds in Them the Basis for an American School of Music—RICH IN UNDEVELOPED THEMES—American Composer Urged to Study Plantation Songs and Build upon Them—USES OF NEGRO MINSTRELSY—Colored Students to Be Admitted to the National Conservatory—Prizes to Encourage Americans.

> It was Rubinstein who bitterly said that the world would make no more progress in music until the controlling influence of Wagner, Berlioz and Liszt had passed away. Right on the heels of this anathema Dr. Antonin Dvorak, the foremost figure among living composers came to America, the acknowledged leader of the dramatic school and the chosen target for the arrows of the lyrical school.

The great Bohemian composer has just ended his first season of musical exploration in New York and his opinion ought to stir the heart of every American who loves music.

"I am now satisfied," he said to me, "that the future music of this country must be founded upon what are called the negro melodies. This must be the real foundation of any serious and original school of composition to be developed in the United States. When I first came here last year I was impressed with this idea and it has developed into a settled conviction. These beautiful and varied themes are the product of the soil. They are American. I would like to trace out the individual authorship of the negro melodies for it would throw a great deal of light upon the question I am most deeply interested in at present.

"These are the folk songs of America and your composers must turn to them. All of the great musicians have borrowed from the songs of the common people. Beethoven's most charming scherzo is based upon what might now be considered a skilfully handled negro melody. I have myself gone to the simple, half-forgotten tunes of the Bohemian peasants for hints in my most serious work. Only in this way can a musician express the true sentiment of his people. He gets into touch with the common humanity of his country."

Dvořák went on to speak about the possibilities inherent in Negro melodies:

"In the negro melodies of America, I discover all that is needed for a great and noble school of music. They are pathetic, tender, passionate, melancholy, solemn, religious, bold, merry, gay or what you will. It is music that suits itself to any mood or any purpose. There is nothing in the whole range of composition that cannot be supplied with themes from this source. The American musician understands these tunes, and they move sentiment in him. They appeal to his imagination because of their associations.

"When I was in England one of the ablest musical critics in London complained to me that there was no distinctively English school of music, nothing that appealed particularly to the British mind and heart. I replied to him that the composers of England had turned their backs upon the fine melodies of Ireland and Scotland instead of making them the essence of an English school. It is a great pity that English musicians have not profited out of this rich store. Somehow the old Irish and Scotch ballads have not seized upon or appealed to them.

"I hope it will not be so in this country and I intend to do all in my power to call attention to this splendid treasure of melody which you have.

"Among my pupils in the National Conservatory of Music I have discovered strong talents. There is one young man upon whom I am building strong expectations. His compositions are based upon negro melodies, and I have encouraged him in this direction. The other members of the composition class seem to think that it is not in good taste to get ideas from the old plantation songs, but they are wrong, and I have tried to impress upon their minds the fact that the greatest composers have not considered it beneath their dignity to go to the humble folk songs for motifs.

"I did not come to America to interpret Beethoven or Wagner for the public. That is not my work and I would not waste any time on it. I came to discover what young Americans had in them and to help them to express it. When the negro minstrels are here again I intend to take my young composers with me and have them comment on the melodies."

And saying so Dvořák sat down at his piano and ran his fingers lightly over the keys. It was his favorite pupil's adaptation of a Southern melody.

Here then, is a programme of musical growth, laid down by the most competent mind that had yet studied the American field — a plan made without hesitation or reservation. It is a result of an almost microscopic examination and comes from a man who is always in earnest.

The article continues and announces that the National Conservatory plans to open its doors to colored students. As evidence of this need, a letter was quoted, written in Richmond, Virginia, in May of 1893 by the Black singer Fanny Payne Walker. In the letter she entreated Mrs. Thurber to open her kind heart and accept her in the National Conservatory as a pupil.

The writer of the article adds,

Two colored pupils of the Conservatory are to be made teachers for their own race in addition to the rest of the faculty—Harry Burleigh of Erie, N.Y., and Paul Holm from Poughkeepsie.

The article concluded:

Convinced by the success of the last year's competition in composition that, through a yearly award of prizes for the best work, American composers and librettists will be encouraged and stimulated to higher efforts the Conservatory announces that for the second annual concourse the subjects of prizes and general conditions shall be as follows:

Subjects and Prizes

For the best grand or comic opera (opéra comique) in one act ... $1,000

For the best libretto for a grand or comic opera (opera comique) ... $300

For the best symphony ... $300

For the best overture and cantata ... $200

For the best string quartet ... $100

Another interesting feature of the competition in composition was that the competition for opera and comic opera "is open to all regardless of age; competitors for the remaining prizes should not be above forty years of age."

Looking back on it now, a century later, one cannot deny that Jeanette Thurber was ahead of her time. Her efforts to promote equality of Black musicians with white in the 1890s gave opportunity for study to every talented student, regardless of color. This deserves great respect. We do not know how much of this was Dvořák's work, or to what degree the idea of composition contests came from Mrs. Thurber, but the fact is that it was Dvořák, the world-famed composer, who stressed the necessity of studying Negro melodies, or those songs which bore that name. It seems that he talked with Mrs. Thurber about this idea, drawing her attention to it, and the enterprising and democratic lady acted accordingly. She encouraged Dvořák to write the article just mentioned, and arranged with the editorial offices of the *Herald*'s European branch to send it to several European celebrities. Her purpose was to start a discussion of Dvořák's ideas, but the move also served to promote her National Conservatory and its famous Director, Antonín Dvořák. Let us, however, return to the idea of using "Negro melodies" as a foundation of a new American school of musical composition.

Dvořák wrote to the editor of the *Herald* on May 25, 1893. As printed in the paper on May 28, the letter bore this title: "Antonín Dvořák on Negro Melodies."

The composer brought to the interview more details and went deeper into his theory. Nevertheless, there is an error in his personal dates (Dvořák speaks about his first teacher—we know that it was Liehman—and says that they traveled together and made money for their livelihood). There is also the overall, slightly exaggerated tone of the "letter" (for example, in the first sentence he refers to a writer whose article "struck a note that should be sounded throughout America"), which does not sound like Dvořák. It is obvious that Dvořák's original text was edited by someone on the *Herald*. The article goes on to say:

> I was deeply interested in the article in last Sunday's *Herald,* for the writer struck a note that should be sounded throughout America. It is my opinion that I find a sure foundation in the negro melodies for a new national school of music, and my observations have already convinced me that the young musicians of this country need only intelligent direction, serious application and a reasonable amount of public support and applause to create a new musical school in America. This is not a sudden discovery on my part. The light has gradually dawned on me.
>
> The new American school of music must strike its roots deeply into its own soil. There is no longer any reason why young Americans who have talent should go to Europe for their education. It is a waste of money and puts off the coming day when the Western world will be in music, as in many other things, independent of other lands. In the National Conservatory of Music, founded and presided over by Mrs. Jeanette M. Thurber, is provided as good a school as can be found elsewhere. The masters are competent in the highest sense and the spirit of the institution is absolutely catholic. A fresh proof of the breadth of purpose involved in this conservatory is the fact that it has been opened without limit or reservation to the negro race.
>
> I find good talents here and am convinced that when the youth of the country realizes that it is better now to stay at home than to go abroad, we shall discover genius, for many who have talent but cannot undertake a foreign residence will be encouraged to pursue their studies here. It is to the poor that I turn for musical greatness. The poor work hard; they study seriously. Rich people are apt to apply themselves lightly to music, and to abandon the painful toil to which every strong musician must submit without complaint and without rest.

Poverty is no barrier to one endowed by nature with musical talent. It is a spur. It keeps the mind loyal to the end. It stimulates the student to great efforts.

If in my own career I have achieved a measure of success and reward, it is to some extent due to the fact that I was the son of poor parents and was reared in an atmosphere of struggle and endeavor. Broadly speaking, the Bohemians are a nation of peasants. My first musical education I got from my schoolmaster, a man of good ability and much earnestness. He taught me to play the violin. Afterward I travelled with him and we made our living together. Then I spent two years at the organ school in Prague. From that time on I had to study for myself. It is impossible for me to speak without emotion of the strains and sorrows that came upon me in the long and bitter years that followed. Looking back at that time, I can hardly understand how I endured the privations and labor of my youth.

Could I have had in my earlier days the advantages, freely offered in such a school as the National Conservatory of Music, I might have been spared many of my hardest trials and have accomplished much more. Not that I was unable to produce music, but that I had not technique enough to express all that was in me. I had ideas but I could not utter them perfectly.

There is a great opportunity for musicians in America and it will be increased when grand opera sung in English is more firmly established with public or private assistance. At the present time this country also needs the materials for orchestral work.

I do not agree with those who say that the air here is not good for vocalists. The American voice has a character of its own. It is quite different from the European voice, just as the English voice is different from the German and Italian. Singers, like Lloyd and Mc Guckin, have an entirely different vocal quality from that of German singers and members of the Latin race. The American voice is unlike anything else, quite unlike the English voice. I do not speak of method or style, but of natural quality, the timbre of the voice. I have noticed this difference ever since I have been in New York City. The American voice is good; it pleases me very much.

Those who think that music is not talent in the American will discover their error before long. I only complain that the American musician is not serious enough in applying himself to the work that he must do before he is qualified to enter upon a public career. I have always to remind my most promising pupils of the necessity of work. Work! work! work! to the very end.

This country is full of melody, original, sympathetic, and varying in mood, color and character to suit every phase of composition. It is a rich field. America can have great and noble music of her own, growing out of the very soil and partaking of its nature—the natural voice of a free and vigorous race.

This proves to me that there is such a thing as nationality in music in the sense that it may take on the character of its locality. It now rests with the young musicians of this country and with the patrons of music to say how soon the American national school of music is to be developed. A good beginning has been made in New York. Honor to those who will help to increase and broaden the work.

Antonín Dvořák

I read the article at least three times. It is a pity that we do not know the original text in Czech used for the English translation. I agree that the basic points in the article (and there are many) must have been stated accurately by the composer himself, as we see them in the article. No editor or translator would change these.

When he stated that Negro melodies could provide a sure foundation for a "new national school of music," he was convinced of that fact. He also could characterize the "poor" and the "rich" as he did because his feelings arose from his own experience. His reminder, "work! work! work! to the very end," is true Dvořák. This was the credo he lived by, and he was always convinced that without work, no matter how great the talent, not much could be accomplished.

Dvořák's opinions about the Negro melodies were potentially explosive. Jeanette Thurber had a well-developed sense of timing, and thanks to her, the *New York Herald* of May 28, 1893, brought out an article entitled: "Dvořák's Theory of Negro Music." The inevitable subheads stated:

> Interviews with Composers in Europe on the Feasibility of the Idea—RUBINSTEIN INCLINED TO DOUBT—He Thinks the Plan Possible, but Fantastic, as America Follows in Europe's Lead—BELIEVE IT DESERVES TRIAL—Others Say It Can Never Become Classic—Views of Musicians in Berlin and Vienna.

The European edition of the *Herald* printed an account by its correspondent:

Berlin, May 27, 1893.

I was lucky enough to find Anton Rubinstein on a flying visit.

The great composer was in a simply-furnished room of a leading hotel. He dislikes luxury.

Difficult to Prove

He stopped writing music to read the extract about Dvorak's
theory of negro music which was cabled to the European Edition of the *Herald*. He threw his long locks back over his massive forehead with a habitual gesture and said:

"I remember reading in a book which made the Hungarians angry that the Hungarian music was that of the gypsies.
Dvořák's theory is very difficult to prove. At the same time it is
quite possible. American musicians have not worked in the line
of negro melodies, but entirely in the European style. If there is
a great literature of negro melodies, Dvorak's idea is possible,
but I think it fantastic. In South America such an idea might
take, but in the North European music is too far advanced."

A New School Possible

After reading the extract in the European edition of the *Herald*,
Rubinstein added: "The ideas of giving negroes free musical
education is interesting. If properly educated they may develop
a new school. However, we can say nothing at present. In
twenty-five or thirty years we shall see perhaps whether the
negroes are capable of developing talent and founding a new
musical school."

A Unique Idea

Dr. Liebling, director of the new Conservatory of Music in Berlin, said: "Negro melodies are quite a unique idea. It deserves a
trial. We find national melodies at the base of the music of some
of the greatest composers. My opinion is that in twenty or
thirty years America will be the first musical country, for the
American student today is by far the most diligent and in opera
is well to the fore. America's musical progress is amazing."

May Be a Good Idea

Joachim, the eminent virtuoso said: "It is a difficult matter to
settle. A book could be written on the subject. It may be a good
idea to merge the negro melodies into an ideal form. Then they
would give a tint to American national music."

Joachim continued: "It is quite true that in the music of Grieg, Haydn, Schubert and others, national melodies are strongly blended and give tone. But don't let too much stress be laid upon particular melodies. Otherwise, they become monotonous. Let melodies be used to give local color. I am pleased to hear that the United States are taking such an interest in music."

Worth Trying
Arthur Bird, who resides in Berlin, said: "I have often spoken, especially with Morris Bagley, of the foundation of an American school of music. We spoke of Indian music, but never of negro melodies. I think the idea worth trying.

"We Americans at present are somewhere and nowhere in the field of music, but we are going to come out well ahead with men like McDowell [*sic*] and Strong. My ideal of the American school is a mixture of French and German. The French are far ahead of the Germans. As for negro melodies, their feature is that of simple and sad. They are musical, but their simplicity would make a difficulty in larger works. The question is, Wouldn't they lose in being made instrumental?"

What Musicians in Vienna Have to Say of the Plan
The *Herald* European edition publishes today the following from the correspondent:

Vienna, May 27, 1893.

I saw Anton Bruckner, Eusebius Mandyczewski and Hans Richter in relation to Dvorak's idea. Bruckner said: "The basic of all music must be classical works. Negro melodies could never found the groundwork of a school of music."

Mandyczewski expressed similar views, thinking his compatriot Dvorak was greatly influenced by his surroundings.

Richter Doubts
Professor Richter, who is the leader of the Imperial Court Opera, could not realize the possibility of the future school of music emanating from a race playing by ear. The "Hungarian Gypsies," he said, "All play by ear—men, women, and children; yet a real musician among them is an exception."

Much discussion was going on in Europe and in America. Dvořák had just finished a new symphony, Opus 95, and was probably secretly smiling at the stir he had made. Was he ever aware of how unconventional his idea was?

Not overburdened with American tradition and prejudice, he preached his ideas to his students. That fact must have been irritating for the respectable professors of European music. Some were angered to the point of open antagonism. What a statement!

"Study the negro folk music! Penetrate its spirit, harmony and melodic structure!"

Dvořák's Black student, Will Marion Cook (who earlier stayed in Berlin for several years to study with Dvořák's friend, the violin virtuoso, Josef Joachim), listened with almost religious fervor to Dvořák, who unafraid, proclaimed such peculiar ideas. A couple of years later, Cook wrote the first Black musical played on Broadway, *Clorindas,* or *The Origin of the Cakewalk*. Dvořák's other student, Maurice Arnold Stratthote, composed the *Plantation Dances* as well as a symphony and violin sonata, all inspired by the Negro folk music.

The most famous of Dvořák's students was Rubin Goldmark (born in New York, 1872; died 1936). In addition to the overture *Hiawatha,* he wrote the *Negro Rhapsody*. The review of its Boston premiere was written by James G. Huneker, who praised the color in Rubin Goldmark's composition: "It is filled with life, and because of this, there is also a variety of rhythms." (Other observations in the review are interesting because they indicate Huneker's fear that Dvořák's influences might prove dangerous for Goldmark.)

Later on, Henry Thacker Burleigh studied with Rubin Goldmark. He was the same student who, as a very young conservatory pupil, used to sing Negro spirituals for Dvořák. There was also George Gershwin, who had fallen in love with music while listening to Dvořák's Humoresque.

It never occurred to me, when I was so captivated by Gershwin's *Rhapsody in Blue,* that many suggestions and theories had been passed on by Dvořák to Rubin Goldmark and were now incorporated into the music of our generation.

Even Dvořák could not foresee, as he praised his Black student Will Marion Cook, that this young fellow (after a racially motivated disagreement with the management of the Boston Philharmonic) would form his own orchestra in 1919, and tour with it throughout Europe. He brought with him elements of protojazz: ragtime and blues. At the same time, Cook's orchestration was astonishing, and his own unique arrangement of Dvořák's Humoresque was also a surprise.

No, Dvořák had never foreseen such a thing, for the pathways of the future are unpredictable. Had this great composer been able to see the many consequences of his teaching, he would probably have only shaken his head, and listened in silence. But now it was the spring of 1893, and Europe was discussing these ideas, as was America.

Negro melodies? Oh, no! Who had ever heard of such an idea? And what was Dvořák thinking about at this time? He had probably completely forgotten about the controversy, for he had put down the last notes of his Symphony *From the New World*, and added his laconic and happy remark: "Finis! Praise God! Finished on May 24, 1893 at 9 A.M. The children have arrived at Southampton (the wire came at 1:33 P.M. with this good news)! Antonín Dvořák."

Going to Spillville ∽ A

F OR A LONG TIME THERE WAS only one explanation for Dvořák's
decision to stay in America during the summer of 1893. It was set down
faithfully by Otakar Sourek in his biography. We will see later, however, that
the situation was not that simple:

> After the first few months of Dvořák's teaching in New York,
> Mrs. Thurber and some of his students tried to persuade him
> that he should not miss the opportunity of seeing the beauty of
> America's inland regions. They described the land in all its vari-
> ety; Dvořák did not doubt them, for his thoughts had been
> influenced by his preoccupation with Longfellow's "Song of
> Hiawatha." Just then Dvořák could not seriously entertain any
> thoughts of making such a trip.

We see in Sourek's account that, in spite of their attempts to get Dvořák
to visit America's hinterlands, he had not taken the project seriously. However, about the middle of February 1893, he surprised his wife and children
with the news that they were not going home that summer but that the other
four children would be coming to America. The family would spend their
summer holiday in Spillville, Iowa. Kovarik covers this material in two versions, English and Czech, several years later. We will quote here from both
versions, and later will formulate our own ideas as to what really happened.
In his Czech memoirs (from the 1920s), Josef J. Kovarik states:

208

One evening, the Master asked me to tell him something about my birthplace, Spillville. I talked about it the whole evening, and the next as well. When I continued on the third evening, he asked me to draw a sketch of Spillville, and my narration continued until the Master became so familiar with the town that it seemed that he knew the occupants of each house, and had lived there for years.

Then Kovarik noted that Dvořák had finished the orchestration of his composition, *The American Flag,* and on January 10, he began work on the Symphony in E Minor. He calculated times when Dvořák worked on the sketches of the several movements (this passage is quoted above on page 180). Kovarik concluded:

During the month of January, the Master met Mr. E. Rosewater of Omaha, the owner of a local influential magazine, *The Omaha Bee.* He was a native of Bukovany, Bohemia. Mr. Rosewater invited Dvořák to visit Omaha. The Master did not promise him for sure; he just said quite casually: "If it suits me, I will come." The Master was urged from many sides to stay in America during the summer so that he could learn more about the New World, and see the various places that were recommended to him. Nevertheless, the Master always answered that in the summer he intended to be in Bohemia.

At the end of March, the Master began to see clearly that it would be absolutely impossible to finish his symphony before May 15, the date when he planned to leave for Bohemia. He started to consult with his spouse as to what they should do. Should they travel to Bohemia some time later after he finished his work? Or should he have his four children sent to America? After a long consideration, it was decided to finish his composition without interruption. The sketch of the fourth movement was finished on April 12, and he finished the score of the whole composition on May 24, at 9 A.M.

Kovarik's English version from 1926 has to be understood in a broader framework since some details are lacking. Let us check it and compare:

Because Dr. Dvořák did not care to go out for the evening, we spent time playing cards. He often called me funny names as we played. After the game, we talked about his hobby—ships—and then the conversation turned to the days spent in Vysoka (Dvořák's country home in Bohemia). It happened that during one such conversation he asked me about Spillville. I described it to him as well as I could, mentioning that it was a little Bohemian settlement where everybody speaks Czech, even those of German, Swiss or Norwegian origin. When I finished, his only reaction was: "Hmm!"

The next day he inquired about Spillville again. I had to draw him a plan of the settlement, and supply the names of the owner of every house in the village. Then he queried me as to woods, creeks, birds, and so forth that were there. He gradually learned the name of each owner of a household in my home town, and was able to correct quickly my accidental mistakes. After endless repetition of the same names, I made mistakes easily.

Next there follows the passage about Eduard Rosewater, who during his January trip to New York City, invited Dvořák to visit the World Exposition which was to take place in Chicago during the summer. Rosewater invited Dvořák to go from there to Omaha as his guest.

At the end of March, some of Dr. Dvořák's students asked him about his plans for the summer, and suggested that he should stay in America and spend his holiday in the Adirondack Mountains, the forests of Maine, the Catskills, or at the beach. And it was then when he said, "I am going to Spillville, Iowa!" When they inquired about Spillville, he answered, "I'm not sure, but according to what I can learn about it, I think I will like it!"

After he arrived home that evening, he informed Mrs. Dvořák, "The deal is settled. The children will come here, and we will all go to Spillville for the summer." Then he turned to me and said, "Yes, all of us are going to Spillville, but I warn you if I don't like it there, you will get it!"

Truthful to his word, next day he bought the steamship tickets for the four children, his sister-in-law and the maid, and on May 23rd the group left Bremen on a North German Lloyd steamer. They arrived in New York on May 31, and several days later the whole group of eleven members left New York and took the Pennsylvania Railroad train for Spillville.

Now we know both versions of Kovarik's memoirs. When read carefully, they actually agree on three points: (a) in the evenings, Kovarik had to talk about his birthplace, and Dvořák's interest in it grew gradually; (b) in january, 1893, the Czech-American, Mr. Rosewater from Omaha, came to New York City and offered the composer a place for the summer in his home;

(c) by the end of March, Dvořák decided not to go to Bohemia for the summer, but to Spillville.

Kovarik gives different reasons for Dvořák's decision in each of the versions of the story. The Czech version explains that the end of March saw Dvořák short of time to finish the Symphony *From the New World* and for creative reasons he had to stay in America. In the English version, this event is formulated differently. The students of the Conservatory suggested that Dvořák should stay in this country and visit several areas during the summer. But at this moment Dvořák announced his plan to visit Spillville.

Kovarik was well aware that he might disappoint his American readers if he gave them the real reason for the composer's choice. For Kovarik, the Spillville native, it seemed to be more attractive to say that Dvořák finally obeyed his American students and stayed in the United States. After all, the composer had chosen the place which Kovarik himself had offered. (Indeed, Kovarik had already done some advance planning in this matter, for in the review *Fiddlestrings* he appears in a promotion which praised the strings made by the same firm that published Kovarik's article in English about Dvořák.)

The main problem, then, is to find the truth of Dvořák's decision to spend the summer of 1893 in America. It was not an insignificant problem because we know that as a result of the visit to Spillville, two compositions were written which today are considered among the best in chamber music literature.

To better understand the situation, it is necessary to search through family correspondence, not too much of which survives. On November 29, 1892, Josefina wrote, "Rezi mentioned that you ask in your letter if Grandma would have the strength to bring the children to you."

This indicates that, already in November 1892, Dvořák must have been thinking of the possibility of sending for the other children. From this Josefina suspected that Dvořák most probably would emigrate. Her suspicions later proved false.

In her letter of January 2, 1893, Josefina noted:

> Mother does not feel that she would like to come because of the difficulty with the English (language), but most of all, she is afraid of the sea. Fanda also hesitates to take the trip to America; so, it must be Rezi who will come.

Josefina's letter concludes with these words: "[A]s you have already read in a letter written at mother's request, she is afraid of travel and cannot overcome her anxieties. Therefore, she decided not to come and will send Rezi instead. She will bring you the children."

The situation was obvious, perhaps not in the middle of March but certainly in November when this matter began to be discussed. At the beginning of January, or even by the end of December, the decision was made. The rest of Dvořák's children who were living with Grandma in Prague, all four of them, would go next summer with their aunt Rezi to America. It is interesting that Dvořák kept family discussions about it secret. Nobody in New York City, even Kovarik who was "almost a member of the family," was informed that the children would come and who would accompany them.

Six or seven important weeks had passed, and during that time the decision was suddenly changed. Josefina wrote on February 21, 1893:

> What kind of decision did you make about the children? What are you going to do? Rezi wrote something about it. They supposed that your decision about her and the children going to America was firm. However, she said you are changing your mind again, and you may come to pick them up yourselves. Therefore, there will be no travel for her.

Consider this; Josefina writes on February 21, in answer to the New York City situation as of the first of February. It took at least ten to twelve days for a letter to come across the ocean. For example, if Dvořák's letter was mailed on February 1, Rezi would get it around February 12. She then could inform Josefina in Vienna about the new developments. Josefina, in turn, could write Dvořák on February 21 asking why the plans had been changed.

Well, why not change plans? Dvořák managed to sketch three movements of his new symphony between the January 10 and 31, and his work was progressing well. The notes were pouring out onto the music paper, and his head was overflowing with ideas for elaborating some of the melodies he was always writing in his sketchbook. By the end of January, he could see that he would be able to finish the symphony on time. Therefore he could go in May to Bohemia. So he wrote to his sister-in-law, Rezi, that her trip would not be necessary.

Nevertheless, it took him a long time to think through the problem of completing the fourth movement. He knew that it should be the culmination of the symphony, and he felt he should build on what he had done in the first three movements. Days went by, then weeks, and finally on February 8, he was ready to begin the instrumentation of the first three movements. It became increasingly clear that the schedule he had set for himself in January was impossible. He would not be able to finish the symphony before their trip to Bohemia, and he had better have his children brought to him rather than go back to get them.

In a letter to Marie Bohdanecka in Cimelice (she was the daughter of Dvořák's friend Rus) written February 20, Dvořák explained:

> We wanted to come to Bohemia this year, but we have just decided against it. My sister-in-law, Mrs. Koutecka, will bring the rest of our children to America in May. Another family, the Weinfurts from Pilsen, will travel to New York also, and they will take our party with them. It will certainly help our sister-in-law during the trip which, with the children will be quite tiresome.
>
> During my four-month vacation, I would like to get better acquainted with America, so we plan to visit the parents of Mr. Kovarik who came to see you in Pisek once. He is staying with us now. I found him a good job here. We have to travel to his home town, which is quite far from New York—it is 1300 miles to the State of Iowa—and on the way we will go through Chicago. We would like to see the World Exposition there. After that, we will travel to the little village of Mr. Kovarik, who is the local teacher. The entire town is a Czech settlement with its own school and church. Everything is Czech. The priest, father Bily, came from Trebon, and I hear that he looks forward to our visit with great pleasure. He has two pairs of horses ("ponies" actually) and will take us for rides. It would be fun for the children and for me, too. This little Czech village will be my American substitute for Bohemia. You must know that I would prefer to visit you in Bohemia but it might be impossible this year. I remember my dear homeland every day, but what can I do? Once I agree to stay in America, I must make the best of it.

This letter is the first concrete news of Dvořák's decision to someone other than his immediate family. Although he did not name the village, it is clear that he meant Spillville.

In a letter from approximately March 22, 1893 (delivered on April 3, and carrying no date), the composer wrote something similar to his caretaker, Hodik. In this letter he named the village but was wrong as to the distance.

> We will spend our summer very far from here, with the parents of Mr. Kovarik, in Spillville. It is about 1,000 miles from New York, but to make up for that, I'm hoping it will be something

like Vysoka. It is a very nice village, entirely Bohemian—
schools, church, everything Czech.

Then he repeated what he had written earlier to Bohdanecka.

Josefina, of course, did not know the reasons for her brother-in-law's hesitation. In addition to that, she had been in Vienna since autumn and out of
touch with Rezi. For that reason, she had no idea that finishing the symphony was essential to Dvořák's professional life. It was this problem which
made her next two letters sound so uncertain. In her letter of March 7, 1893,
Josefina said:

> Dear Anton!
>
> It seems to me that you were hurt by my well-meant advice, and
> I am sorry for that. Although you are homesick for Vysoka and
> Prague, Anna, I suppose, had reasons for wisely dissuading you
> from your trip. Now you probably are worrying about it. I can
> understand your confusion well, but I think that such a refuge
> out in the country might be quite interesting, and it would be
> nice to see other parts of America, too. At least, you will be able
> to learn more about how people live there.

In another part of her letter she wrote about her illness, and then she
addressed Otilka:

> Watch for snakes and other reptiles while walking in the forest;
> be careful, for Heaven's sake! You also wrote that you visited
> some mountains where your Madam Thurber owns a villa but I
> have forgotten the name of the place. Kovarik had mentioned
> that colds and fevers were common in that part of Iowa and
> that he had suffered from such attacks in the past. Are they still
> living there, or have his parents moved?

It is hard to say what the truth was about the cold-and-fever scare in
Iowa. Did Josefina exaggerate the fact? There is no letter or document available to confirm her worries. Maybe Dvořák's desire to visit a Bohemian environment was so strong that he unconsciously "forgot" Kovarik's story about
the colds and fevers.

Almost three weeks later—when Josefina sent them another letter on
March 26—she still did not know that the definite decision had been made a
long time ago in America. She would be pleased to welcome Anton and his
family at home soon in Bohemia. She wrote that she was still ill and planning
to go to a spa or to visit Switzerland:

...therefore I do not know if I will be able to see you immediately after your arrival in Bohemia. We will probably meet in Vienna. I look forward with pleasure to seeing you all. It was wise of you to sign another contract with America; it will be beneficial for your income, and help you to strengthen your popularity in America. Now, after two full seasons there, you can see better the values of your art, and you will begin to flourish. But all that could vanish over the horizon, and you would be forgotten in a couple of years if you do not stay. You should make for yourself a good name, find there a publisher and get rich. In four years you might really be satisfied. It would be nonsense not to stay longer.

Josefina Kounic did not change a bit. In her letters, she was smart, open, realistic, and even teasing once in a while. When she learned at the beginning of April that the Dvořáks were staying in America, she mentioned that Otilka should get treatment for her illness in some "sea spa" or at least in Willspill.

[I]t is supposed to be a little spa, very cheap and beautiful, only three hours from Chicago. Would that not be more sensible? You would be close to the Exposition and would possibly meet some of your acquaintances from Bohemia while visiting the fair. Moreover, it would not be necessary to make the hard trip of 300 miles further to Spillville. At the same time you will enjoy the summer and see a lot.... However, this is my own idea only, and maybe you prefer absolute solitude. I think that it is up to us to use every opportunity when abroad to learn more about the world and its wonders.

Then she informed them about the preparations for the trip at home, and that the maid Fanda at the very last moment refused to go. In her letter of April 27, Josefina wrote: "Dear Anton!...concerning the preparations, the children are ready to go, and only Reza still has some clothes to finish. Now come the worries with baggage." The following news in Josefina's letter is more interesting:

You probably know how much demand there is for Smetana's operas in Vienna. It would be advisable for you to have on hand something new you can offer them after Smetana's repertoire is exhausted. Or you can revise something you have already written; "Jacobin," etc. There is still time for this and it should be done because the third act of that opera is still impossible....

Goodbye from your Josefina

It is obvious that these remarks of Josefina Kounicova came from her wide knowledge of the social-political events. For example, she characterized Prime Minister Taaffe with an anecdote. She learned much about politics thanks to the senatorial rank of her husband, but she was also knowledgeable about other aspects of life. In her previous letter, she praised "Dear Anton" for signing a profitable contract, and because she well knew the value of a good reputation in art and society, she advised him on opera matters, too. Her words could sometimes be unpleasantly direct as we read in her letter of the 18th of June, 1893, when she criticized Spillville and advised him to go to a better place, and not only because of a cold and fever outbreak. You can feel new, bitter disappointment in another part of her letter because they did not take her advice. She wished them a good time in that village which "might" substitute for Vysoka.... She always signed her letters "Yours, Josefina," to show her closeness, and Dvořák was well aware of her feelings.

While they were packing in Bohemia, the composer was working in New York City on the final movement of what was to be his most celebrated symphony. In moments of rest, he wrote letters to friends in his homeland to inform them about his decision to spend the summer in the New World. Besides the letters to Marie Bohdanecka and to his housekeeper Jan Hodik, he remembered Emil Kozanek with this letter:

> New York, Wednesday morning, 7 A.M., April 12, 1893
>
> My dear friend Doctor Kozanek!
>
> For your convenience I must tell you that Thanks be to God; I am healthy as a fish and merry (in spite of a few little problems) as well. The things which irritate me are the street knaves and policemen, and also the drunk Irishwomen in the streets, but one can get used to it and forget almost everything.

Dvořák talked then about the musical news, what was on a certain program, and what the reviews said about it afterward. He confessed that the critics were

> partially against me, but the rest of them ... are writing righteously about me, and sometimes quite enthusiastically. I would like to have even more enemies, as I had in Vienna, with the well-known exception of Dr. Hanslick. I have a good nature, can tolerate a lot, and on top of that, forgiving gives me pleasure. Concerning all this, you do not have to worry, I am sitting pretty, and even with those little complaints, as I said, I like it here.

My wish to return to Bohemia cannot be fulfilled this year; we have decided to head the other way.

He did not explain what his reasons were for staying. Why should he write about his creative problems at all? Just the opposite, he occasionally boasted, "Because I do not have too much work at school, I have enough time left for my own work. Right now, I am finishing my new 'Sinfonia' in E minor. It gives me great pleasure."

He gave lots of details about the children's trip across the ocean, and then revealed that the whole family was going to Spillville. Some of this information was repeated in his letters to Bohdanecka and Hodik:

> The children and my sister-in-law, Mrs. Koutecka, are coming here. They leave Prague on May 23, and depart from Bremen on the steamer *Havel*. God willing I will see the faces of my beloved and long-missing children on May 31! Shortly after that, we will travel to Chicago to see the Exhibition, and from there, we will go to our "summer-Vysoka," the little village of "Spillville," in the State of Iowa. Everything there is Czech — teacher, priest, everything. I will be among my countrymen, and am looking forward to it with great pleasure.
>
> Mr. Kovarik, a teacher who came from Pisek (Bohemia) twenty-six years ago, and Father Bily from Budejovice district, (Bohemia), who, I suppose, is a very active fellow, will be most probably my closest companions, and we will be together most of the time. I will have pigeons there, and will play "Darda," as well. What a pleasure! Father Bily has two pairs of "ponies" and will take us to Protivin, a town close to Spillville. In America, you can find the names of cities, towns and villages of all the nations in the world!!
>
> The State of Iowa where we are to go is 1,300 miles from New York, but such a distance is insignificant here. We will be there in 36 hours by the express train, and it is further away than it is from you to London!!! We also will stop in Buffalo (the name of an animal — the bison), the city near Niagara — and we will go to see the magnificent falls. The thought of all this gives us an indescribable joy!

In the last known letter before his journey across America — which was quite a distance, indeed, — Dvořák wrote to his friend Anton Rus. Rus was the father-in-law of Mr. Bohdanecky, the director of the Schwarzenbergs' estates. (In the postscript is the composer's request that the gardener from Cimelice should tend to the trees in Vysoka garden.)

Dvořák repeated in the letter all the previous information with one more new detail. He said that the ship *Havel* was nicer and faster than the *Saale* which brought them to America. In another sentence, portraying himself as an experienced traveler (a little boasting again), he said, "These distances are insignificant for us here. Even the journey across the ocean seems not much longer now, than was my first trip to London nine years ago! One gets used to everything."

Perhaps his thinking was influenced by the American spirit, the distances, the local atmosphere and opinions, all of which were very different from the stagnation of the bureaucratic Austro-Hungarian Empire. This idea that he would take a trip with wife and children which was longer than the distance from Prague to London certainly put him in that special mood.

It was sufficient to look at the map: Traveling from New York City to Philadelphia, through Pittsburgh, and further west to Canton, they finally reached Chicago, situated on fabulous Lake Michigan. Then further again across the plains and over the magnificent Mississippi River they come to Calmar, the last station. How many North American states will they see! New Jersey, Pennsylvania, Ohio, Indiana, Illinois, Wisconsin, and Iowa, and on the way back, they will pass through Michigan, New York, and Canada, as well. To the Europeans every name calls up a fantastic picture of the marvelous distances of this continent.

I wondered what Dvořák felt in his soul. He loved Vysoka and the Bohemian forests, but most of all he needed to bring over his children whom he loved immensely, even more because their first three children had died.

Dvořák's nervousness gradually grew, but he continued writing every idea down in this sketchbook he carried with him all the time. The nervous restlessness and tenderness for his family was indicated in those sketchbook notes. A telegram from Southhampton to New York City from May 24, announcing the safe arrival of his children, filled him with such joy that he inscribed it on his score of the Symphony *From the New World*.

Now only a few more days before the ship would leave England for the New World.... The weeks of tension and indecision as to whether they should go to Bohemia for the summer or stay in America were gone for good.

Finally it was Wednesday, May 31, 1893. Several years later Dvořák's son Otakar remembered the event:

> As if it were today, I can clearly see my father waiting for his children in Hoboken Harbor, waving his hand and welcoming

us while we were still on board. Even more joyful was our meeting after we left the ship. All ten of us: father, mother, six children, aunt and maid Barushka* got into a tram which took us to the corner of First Avenue and 16th Street. It was just a few steps to the 17th Street house where our family lived. Very quickly both stories of the house at No. 327 were filled with our voices.

I remember the name of the owner of the house — Mrs. Drew, the widow of a businessman. She had a daughter Cily, just a little older than my oldest sister Otilka, and they became good friends. Otilka and our brother Tonik learned from her a successful amount of English and soon could converse.

From that time on, our father felt more at home here and his worrisome urge to go back to Bohemia, which earlier had bothered him terribly, now diminished rapidly.

Kovarik's writing holds quite accurate evidence about further occurrences, written again in several versions:

On Saturday, June 3, 1893, just three days after the children arrived in America, our journey to Spillville, Iowa began. Master's longing for country life was so strong that he became deaf to my suggestion that we wait a little for the children to get more rest after the long ocean voyage. Because I was in charge of our travel, I decided to take a route through Pennsylvania and the Allegheny Mountains, and to return from Spillville via Niagara Falls. I hoped that this was the best route for learning about America. Master absolutely agreed with my plan, and so we left home at eight in the morning so as to pass through the Allegheny Mountains in the daytime.

(Printed in the Czech journal *Venkov* (*Country*) in 1929. Kovarik had sent his recollection in a letter to Otakar Sourek.)

The 1926 English version in the magazine *Fiddlestrings* was shorter. The Czech version in the Czech-American press cited only the name of Mrs. Koutecka; the maid was called only "companion." Kovarik characterized Dvořák as being "unspeakably happy to have his family together after nine

---

*Translator's note: Otakar made a mistake in name. Barushka (Barbora) Klirova came to America with the Dvořáks in the autumn of 1894 when they returned to New York City from their Bohemian holiday. At this time, it must have been another maid, because we know from Josefina's letter that their maid Fanda, who had served the Dvořáks in Prague for several years, canceled her trip at the very last moment.

months of separation; and happy, too, that he will soon find himself in the country."

Jan Lowenbach wrote in Kovarik's biography that they had left New Jersey "with provisions for three days."

Kovarik explained it in a letter published in *Venkov:*

> Our caravan was a troop of eleven people — Master with his wife, Mrs. Koutecka, six children, a maid (who came with Mrs. Koutecka from Bohemia), and myself. The trip from New York to Spillville (roughly 1320 miles — about 2,112 kilometres) took us through Philadelphia, Harrisburg, the Allegheny Mountains to Pittsburgh, then to Chicago and from there we travelled to Spillville. Master was very interested in our journey, and I had to explain every detail. Everything went right, the train was on time, and although the Master had been more and more captivated by the sights, I had a feeling that something would happen soon that would give him cause to swear.
>
> I was right, indeed. The thunderstorm came earlier than I had expected. However, it was not too bad after all, and everything ended well.
>
> Master's wife made thorough preparation for the trip — she roasted chickens, and God knows what else she took with us. Our provisions would be good enough for a trip to the North Pole and back. Nevertheless, after a good meal one gets thirsty, and after the well-satisfied Master finished his meal, he said that it was time for a glass of beer.
>
> An excellent idea, indeed, but where to get it? First of all, our train was stopping only every second or third hour, and besides, even if Prohibition did not exist yet in America, there was no distribution of beer through the train as was customary in Europe. My suggestion to try in the dining compartment failed, too. We were told that it was a state law in Pennsylvania — which we just were passing through, against serving any alcoholic drinks on the train. We would have to wait until we crossed the borders to another state where we could get whatever we wished.
>
> Good! But it was still at least eight hours to the border. While the conductor was explaining the problem to us, Master stayed quiet. However, the moment we returned to our car, he became abrupt with me:
>
> "So, this is America, the land of freedom! Free country! And one cannot get his glass of beer here! You should see how

one travels in Russia. The train there moves for half an hour, then stops for an hour, and you can comfortably eat and drink!"

I do not know anything about traveling in Russia, but I suspected that Master was exaggerating. I objected to his allegations by saying that if we were to travel in such comfort as they do in Russia, we would arrive in Spillville when our holiday was over. Luckily, mountains started to appear on the distant horizon, and Master, charmed by the beauty of the landscape, forgot about the beer.

In between Harrisburg and Pittsburgh (approximately 250 miles) we entered the Allegheny Mountains. The route was beautiful and interesting. The scenery changed unceasingly; it was hard to judge which part was most enticing. No wonder that our Master, with his immense love of nature and endless astonishment for everything so beautiful, had forgotten all his previous problems, even his hunger!

His enthusiasm kept him happy until we arrived in Pittsburgh. There his thirst protested again. Because the train was stopping here for twenty minutes, I offered to get him some beer. I bought three large bottles in the nearest inn and satisfied, walked back to the station. I could imagine the Master's joy when he saw his desired beverage, but I was wrong!

I found that the train had been moved to another rail line now, and because about five more minutes were left, I waited on the platform until the signal for departure was given.

The situation in our car was terrible! Never before had I seen Master in such an "amiable" mood. He was running back and forth like an angry lion, and as soon as he saw me coming, he shouted:

"You, go away! I don't want to see you, you Indian!" (He called me Indian because of my American origin.)

I was terribly disappointed by his unfriendly welcome after I brought his beer, and had no idea what the reason was for his anger. Nevertheless, I hoped that he would restrain his temper better when I told him about the beer. No way; as soon as I started my explanation, Master began to swear again:

"I told you already, go away!... and throw your beer out, I do not want it!"

It was easy to say, but it was not easy to get rid of something you had just acquired with such great difficulty. And after all—it was very hot and the thirst was terrible.

According to Master's command, I stole away. It was easy for me because the American train cars are big—maybe for eighty people—and there were no other travellers except us. We had plenty of room just for ourselves. I put the beer bottles in an ice-box and tried to find the Master's wife. I hoped that she would explain what made our Master so irritated. She told me that the moment the train was switched to another track, Master thought that we had started for Chicago, and you, with all travel tickets in your pocket, were missing. It really made him angry.

Meanwhile, Master was sitting alone in another compartment and quietly smoking his long pipe, signifying that the storm would end soon.

We decided to punish him a bit. After awhile the beer was cold enough and we started to drink it with loud appreciation for its excellent taste. The bottle was soon empty.

The moment came when Master could not resist any more and, afraid that it was the only bottle I had bought, objected vehemently. As usual, I was a light[en]ing conductor again:

"You are a lousy Indian! You had a beer, but not for me. Of course you know very well how thirsty I am!"

"Well," I answered undisturbed, "you told me before to throw the bottle out. Why should I? We were thirsty, too, so we drank."

"You drank it, good," continued Master with something like regret, "but you could have offered a little to me, too. You know pretty well that I do not mean to do harm to you."

"Never mind, Master, there are two more bottles left," and I went to get them.

I could not hear Master's reaction over the loud noise of the train. I did hear him call me "Indian" again; however, this time it sounded different in some way—more tender....

By eleven A.M. on Sunday we were in Chicago where my brother was waiting for us. We took a break for ten hours, touring the city in the afternoon, and at nine in the evening we continued on to Spillville. On Monday morning at eight we came to McGregor, Iowa. Before we started for Calmar, our last station (the train did not go all [the] way to Spillville), we had breakfast, and observed the rolling waters of the Mississippi River. Master was in an excellent mood, interested in everything, and most of all pleased that in two hours we could finally leave the train, and enjoy the countryside.

In Calmar we were greeted by my father, by Father Tomas Bily from Spillville and by Father Frantisek Vrba from Protivin

[Iowa]. I cannot remember the place in Bohemia from which he came. Shortly after their welcome Master and his group boarded a coach and set out for the last five miles to our destination, Spillville.

After Master's decision to spend his vacation in Spillville, I wrote to my father asking him to find a house for rent. There was none, so father made a deal with Mr. Schmidt, a German who had an eight-room apartment for rent. Father also helped furnish it, so everything was ready for our arrival except a piano.

Kovarik did not come to Spillville with the main group. He had to stay behind and supervise the baggage, which made him about an hour late. He remembers later:

> It was then, on the farm-wagon loaded with trunks, that a terrible idea came to me; what if Dvořák did not like it in Spillville?
>
> Finally I arrived home, too, and saw Dr. Dvořák standing with my mother and father in front of our house, smoking his long pipe contentedly, having eaten a good meal. The look of pleasure on his face assured me that there was really nothing to fear.

In his Czech memoirs written for the Bohemian-American press, Kovarik returned to the final miles of his travel, and tried to correct some of his statements. He repeated his worries that Dvořák might not like Spillville enough. His sense of responsibility had remained uppermost in his mind, and whenever he thought back, the same question came to mind again with equal intensity:

> I did not know how favorably Master was impressed with Spillville after his first look. During our trip I was busy and responsible for everything,* and it happened also in Calmar that I had to care for much baggage that we brought with us. Only after everything was loaded did my uncle Frantisek Bily, who willingly helped us to bring the baggage to Spillville, take me to my home town. High noon and heavy load made our travelling slow, almost endless. I had plenty of time to think over the whole matter of the trip, and suddenly the question about Master's satisfaction with Spillville hit me. It did not come to my mind before on the train. I confided my worries to

---

*Kovarik's biographer Lowenbach wrote that "he always stood in the front of the train car, counting the members of his party, and only then, as the eleventh himself, did he sit on the train."

my uncle, and he immediately dispelled them when he said calmly: "Why should he not like Spillville? We all like it there, he will like it too, do not wrack your brains needlessly." It helped to calm me, and about two in the afternoon we finally came to Spillville. It was only after we unloaded the baggage in the apartment ready for Master, that I could go home.

We lived in a schoolhouse then, and near my home, I saw Master standing alone in the front of the building—the rest of our group were probably still sitting at the table—smoking his pipe and smiling. When he noticed me, he shouted: "Welcome to Spillville!" And I knew that I had won, and my worries were unfounded.

Absolutely unfounded, as the following weeks proved, indeed.

Going to Spillville ∽ B

"WE ARE LANDING," I CRIED uselessly. Everybody knew that. It would be difficult for me to describe Chicago's O'Hare airport, one of the busiest airports in the world, transporting nearly forty-four million travelers a year. The perplexity of the halls, corridors, restaurants, bars, large open spaces, and the many, many buildings joined by over- and underpasses and roads is characteristic for this human anthill—the surest place to get lost.

"Get the baggage first," suggested Honza.

Until now I had no idea how we could manage our first steps in that Babylon.

"The gods liked you, Miroslav," my old friend, an experienced writer, said when he listened to my adventures back in Prague. "You should be grateful."

I am grateful now, but I did not think about the gods at all when they tried to help us. I had never met Mr. Roger Dvorak who was to take care of us. However, he met us at the airport. He came with his girlfriend Draga, and in a while, we were sitting comfortably in his car driving toward the city.

My curiosity to see Chicago was tremendous. It is said to be a center for Czech emigrants, and sometime earlier, the Czech colony here had a population of about one hundred thousand. Therefore, in 1893, during the World Exposition, among the sporting events and multicultural exhibits of the many nations, there was a "Czech Day" representing the Bohemian and Slovakian Society in America. The producers of the event invited Dvořák to Chi-

225

cago and he, with special permission of Mrs. Thurber, conducted a concert of works composed solely by Czechs.

I was aware that the majority of Czechs live in the suburb of Berwyn. There is also a main street named after the late Chicago mayor, Anton Joseph Cermak.

Our host, Roger Dvorak, lived in Elmhurst, about eighteen miles from Lake Michigan and from the center of the city. He was a lab technician in a hospital close to the downtown area, and sometimes was able to take us with him on his way to work. Otherwise, he suggested that we take a train. If you take an express, there are only two stations between Elmhurst and Chicago — the passenger train stops more often. Chicago is a huge city and very different from New York City. It has more factories and business, and the many sectors of the city are spread along Lake Michigan as far as one can see.

Roger looked to be around thirty-five, and he was single. He spoke a very soft Czech, which he learned as a child from his grandmother during vacations in Prague. Later on, he depended more on textbooks. His ancestors came from Treboradice, probably from the same family branch as the family of Antonín Dvořák. Antonín's family had moved later to Nelahozeves, but Roger Dvorak's ancestors stayed in Treboradice. Was his name just a coincidence?

After we made ourselves at home with Roger, his friend Draga invited us to dinner in an old club in the center of the city. Its patriotic atmosphere of the 1920s reminded me of some American movies I had seen a long time ago in Bohemia. During the meal I talked about our stay in New York City and my research in the libraries and archives.

"Chicago also has a large collection in the Newberry Library and in the University Archives," remarked Draga. "They might have a section with Bohemian materials — and do not forget to look for documents owned by the Czechoslovak Society of America."

Roger spoke eagerly about other Chicago attractions. Since 1974, Chicago has had the highest skyscraper in the world, the Sears Tower. The city, extending along the lake, is twenty-eight miles long, twenty-two miles wide and has many institutes of science and arts, galleries, shopping centers, and numerous famous memorials. It is quite possible that Chicago also has the largest Czech cemetery in the world.

I needed to know if they could locate the old Lakota Hotel, which accommodated the Dvořáks in 1893 during the World Exposition. In some of the local archives there might be detailed descriptions of the "Czech Day" during the festival.

Our discussion changed to another subject important for us: how do we get to Spillville? It was a big problem for us. It was more than three hundred miles away, and I hoped that we could take a Greyhound bus which had connecting lines to all corners of the United States.

After dinner we said farewell to Draga, who lived in a beautiful skyscraper situated directly on the lakeshore, and returned to Roger's home in Elmhurst.

It was time to get to work, and we were using every minute in Chicago for our research. Usually we took a train to the center or went by car with Roger. It did not surprise me when we found that the Lakota Hotel was no longer standing. The building, built a long time ago on the corner of 23rd Street and Michigan Avenue near the lake, was torn down after the war because its old structure could not function in our modern times.

The next Saturday evening the Czech community surprised me with an unexpected celebration of my birthday in the Old Prague Restaurant, where Roger took us for supper. I could not believe my eyes; how could they know about my birthday? Later I learned that some members of the Society, curious to know more about me, had found some information in one of the American encyclopedias and thus discovered my birthday. At the same time, the *Chicago Tribune* carried an article about our research concerning Dvořák with some details of my career as a writer.

I could not thank my countrymen in Chicago enough for their attention and for the typical bounty of their Czech hospitality, accompanied by music and the singing of touching Bohemian national songs.

It was a very friendly evening, indeed. Besides being entertained, we were offered a ride to Spillville by Mrs. Lilian Picha, a member of the Society. She was willing to stay with us and take us back to Chicago after we finished our research on Dvořák's remarkable holiday.

Mrs. Picha was an employee of the Czech Insurance Company and was able to get a week's leave from her work. She introduced me to another lady, her friend, Mrs. Marie Hosek, who would be our "navigator."

Pleasantly surprised, I did not know how to thank them, but immediately started to plan our tour.

On Monday morning, we said farewell to Roger and set out on our adventure, the journey across the Mississippi. Mrs. Picha got the address of a Czech couple from Spillville: Mr. and Mrs. Fric Kala, who would be glad to give us guidance during our stay in Spillville.

Soon we left Chicago and drove fast to our destination. Mrs. Picha's car was a comfortable eight-cylinder Ford. Lilian was behind the steering wheel,

Marie, with her auto map, beside her, and Honza with me in the back. We could watch the last silhouette of Chicago diminishing slowly in the haze.

The landscape looked ordinary. Many advertising signs, small scattered towns and areas with their gasoline stations lined the highway. We crossed the Fox River, which was as dull as the whole gigantic plain around us.

It took some time before our conversation became more open, and we talked about our families, homes, friends, and so forth. By that time, heading west, we had bypassed Rockford. The landscape closer to the Mississippi River was fresher and more colorful with every mile. We reached the town of Galena, and I could feel a breath of history permeating the place. It is the birthplace of General Grant, the victor in the Civil War between the American North and South.

After a few miles, we were at the river—the great Mississippi. How many songs are sung about her, how many stories written? Because as a boy I loved its heroes, Tom Sawyer and Huckleberry Finn, I tried to find Hannibal on the map, where the novel was set.

"We have to cross the river farther north, at Dubuque," said Lilian.

I was waiting for the moment when I could see the mammoth iron bridge, and begged Lilian to slow down, because the railing blocked my view of the powerful, overwhelming current. How I wished I could stop time. This moment will never come again. The river was wide, very wide, flanked by woods. It flowed murky and fast, giving life and taking it away.

Dubuque, originally a French station, has as interesting a history as most western cities. The river gave it birth but the city returned nothing. Not even a little scenic overlook, a stopping place for observation.

However, we kept searching while traveling along the river toward Guttenberg and found a little observation platform there very high above the surface of the rolling waters. The magnificent river, the queen of all streams, flowed majestically between her banks, creating green islands, nurturing emerald trees and meadows. A century ago, Dvořák crossed the river at McGregor by train. The river had not changed since the moment he had admired her stunning energy and regal power.

Meanwhile, Lilian and Marie talked with a young boy, a snake hunter. He showed us a basket full of writhing poisonous reptiles. I felt safer back in the car.

After a break for sandwiches and drinks, we still had almost one hundred miles to go to Spillville, but for an American driver it was only a small distance.

"We'll be there before evening," Lilian assured us.

We sang and talked, and I remembered the Czech journalist who, years ago, had found some clippings about Dvořák in the Historical Institute in Des Moines, the capital of Iowa. The moment we crossed the Mississippi River, we passed the eastern border of the state. The country was still hilly, mostly pastures and some fields; nothing showed us that we had entered the most efficient agricultural area of the United States. Only an hour later the landscape quietly leveled, the curved highway marched straight ahead to the west, and the railway, parallel with our road, followed along. The same rails had brought eleven members of Dvořák's group to Iowa almost a century ago.

The railway track, carefully embedded in pinkish gravel, still followed us to Ossian. The road sign pointed to the world-renowned cathedral a few miles on the left. We did not stop, however; Spillville was waiting and we were only seven miles from Calmar. The rolling land became hilly again, and I could see a close resemblance with the country around Pribram in Bohemia where Dvořák's beloved Vysoka lies.

The tracks ended in Calmar. The station looked a little shabby, as if it could easily remember the end of the last century. It was here that the Dvořáks left the train, awaited by Kovarik's father, also by other welcoming Bohemians with their coaches, who took the famous guests to Spillville.

After we took a few pictures of the place, the waterworks, railway station, and the Red West Bar just across the street, we resumed our trip. Four more miles to go, the sign at the intersection said, and I had a nervous feeling. Only two more miles then, the farm with a blue roof on the right, a creek, patches of woods, and slopes made way for a valley, the first houses and farm buildings, and the road sign that said, "Home Cooking—Czech Inn." We were in Spillville.

Finally, and very slowly, we crossed the bridge over the Turkey River. The only street took us through the village to the post office. It had a sign ornamented with roses and hearts. Farther back was a little hill with the church of St. Wenceslaus surrounded by its cemetery which breathed with the pleasant smell of tall spruces. We needed to find the Kalas and so we drove to a neightbohood of nicely kept homes with fresh, green, immaculate lawns and colorful flowerbeds.

Our ladies went inside the Kalas house. Suddenly the sound of evening bells floated over the village, down the hill, and up the opposite side of the valley, finally dying away in a profound silence. Not quite a total silence, for birds answered the call, trilling into the evening air.

Honza rushed to the car and got his tape recorder to capture the precious sounds of our first concert in Spillville.

American Vacation ⤳ A

K OVARIK'S FEAR THAT Dvořák might not like his hometown, Spillville, vanished in a few hours on the first day.

Dvořák's soul longed for a good rest in the simple, unpretentious environment which he found in Spillville. No sea spa or mountain hotel, nothing that Mrs. Thurber and his students at the Conservatory had suggested that he look for, could have suited him more. In his subconscious, or perhaps consciously, too, he desired to meet the ordinary people and chat with them on the village green about the harvest, as in Vysoka. All of this he had long missed in New York City. Kovarik remembered:

> My mother, always the first in the family to get up early, was shocked to see the Master in front of the schoolhouse at five the next morning shuffling from one foot to [the] other. She got scared supposing that something terrible must have happened to the Dvořáks during the night. Not knowing that Master always got up early, she ran outside asking him what was wrong. Master answered kindly:
>
> "Nothing happened but actually quite a lot did. Imagine, when I walked in the woods along the creek, I heard the birds singing for the first time in six months! But birds here are different from what we have in Bohemia; they are more colorful and sing differently, too! Now, I'm going back to the house and have breakfast, but I will come back here again...." (Reported by *Venkov*, 1929)

Josef Kovarik remembered in his recollection from 1950 that Dvořák then said, "But your birds sing differently than ours."

> The reporter asked me:
> "What did Dvořák actually mean, Mr. Kovarik?"
> "What else than that the bird melodies sound different here than in Bohemia. And he was right. After all, this is another continent and Dvořák sensed that. When I came back to Spillville several years later, my wife, returning from a walk in the woods, sang to me a melody she had just heard and which moved her very much. Would you believe that it was a melody with a trill that Dvořák had used in one of his quartets? I suppose it was the one called 'Spillville.' He was in perfect harmony with nature and lived it with his whole heart!"

Kovarik continued in the journal *Venkov:*

> Dvořák left for breakfast, but soon was back. We, the idlers, were just getting up and he had already inquired about a mass, saying that he would like to play the organ. It started at seven, and meanwhile the rest of Dvořák's family arrived and together we went to church. Master at the organ played an old Czech religious song, "God Before Thy Majesty," and we started to join him in singing. Only the old ladies in the church watched him, wondering what had happened? It was very unusual for them that their "silent mass" was suddenly changed by the organ and singing. After that, Master sat at the organ every day, except for days he went to Chicago, Omaha or St. Paul. The old women got used to it and soon sang along. This pleased him immensely. Once in a while, one of the old parishioners was encouraged to talk to him. They called him "Master from Dvořáks" and liked to show him their appreciation: "We had a good time singing together today!... And which one are you going to play for us tomorrow?"

Those morning activities were refreshing for Dvořák. It reminded him of the old days when, as a young musician, he made some extra money playing in St. Vojtech's church in Prague; and in Zlonice when he was playing with his teacher, Liehmann, and then in Czech Kamenice later still.

After this vacation, Dvořák never forgot the organ and the singing in Spillville. He took a postcard from there on his Bohemian holiday in 1894. The picture on the left showed the school where the Kovariks lived, and on the hill was St. Wenceslaus church, surrounded with trees just recently

Spillville, Iowa, with Saint Wenceslaus Church on the hill. The school where Kovarik's father used to teach is on the left.

planted, a few tall poplars towering above. On the back side he wrote this dedication:

> To my friend, Dr. Kozanek.
>
> Church and School in the Czech settlement of Spillville, State of Iowa in America.
>   In this church I liked to play the organ often—which the grandmothers there especially enjoyed. The hearing of our beautiful, religious songs again "God Before Thy Majesty" and "A Thousand Times We Greet Thee" after so many years, gave them great pleasure.
>
> Prague, June 6, 1894   Antonín Dvořák

Those moments were very precious for Dvořák and the people of Spillville. Which of them could have guessed whom the young Kovarik would bring home with him after five years, following his departure to "Golden Prague," where he had gone to seek his fame in art?

The composer's son Otakar remembered their vacation of 1893 years later:

> On the Pacific train, our father was fascinated by the outstanding speed and moved by the sight of a new, never before seen

country with its cities, endless prairies and the vast, extensive land.... When we went to Spillville, he found there everything he really loved; good Czech folks, the church organ, Turkey River for his frequent, enjoyable strolls and the birds, which he had missed for a long time, singing everywhere. Even the pigeons, his old love, were there. In a short time the local people became as dear to him as the folks in Vysoka. He really loved them... and the people in Spillville, in return for his fondness and understanding, surrounded him with their respect and love.

Spillville became a tranquil oasis for Dvořák as J. Kovarik said in his recollection from 1929:

[Master] got up at four and went for a walk along the creek or river. After his stroll he worked, and at seven he was seated at the organ in church. When the mass ended, he had a short chat with parishioners and went home to continue his work, after which he took another walk. Usually he strolled alone — the nervous spells which bothered him in Prague were gone — and often nobody knew where he had gone.

Frequently he went with Father Bily, who had a pair of ponies, to visit Father Vrba in Protivin or to Fort Atkinson to see Father Kromolis. Most of the time he called on the old Czech settlers — above all on the elderly Jan Bily who came from Sepekov, Frantisek Klimes from the Bernartice area, and with my grandpa, T. Kovarik from Vsetec.

In the magazine *Narod* (*Nation*) Kovarik formulated it differently:

There was no day that he did not visit some of those three seniors, and often he invited them personally for an afternoon meeting, which usually lasted until dusk.

He let them chatter about their bitter and difficult beginnings in America. The old men described their life as they worked on the railway — about 40 miles from Spillville, a trip they had to make on foot — while their wives and children toiled on farms. All this interested Master very much. It was entirely new for him and it was no wonder that his questions were endless.

Although there had been many crucial moments in Dvořák's life, he understood that conditions here had been infinitely worse, and the good roof above the heads of those folks was their much-deserved reward for their

Photograph of Dvorak sold by the Bily Clock Museum in Spillville, taken perhaps by a local photographer during the summer of 1893.

strenuous work. One more thing was becoming clearer to Dvořák during their chats at dusk; the price that his countrymen had to pay for American freedom and equality. It came as quite a surprise to him when he came to New York City and then to Boston and met these immigrants. He pondered that if the people from Spillville had to walk forty miles from home to work, returning on Sundays, they certainly were not in the mood for Bach or Beethoven.

Kovarik continued:

> Master almost never spoke about music during his visit in Spillville, and I can say that this was one of the reasons why he liked to stay there and was so happy. I can remember well that Master disliked it when visitors to Vysoka intruded, especially when they asked him about his work. Such problems were not confined to Spillville.

On only a few occasions did the opposite happen as Kovarik described in 1950:

> Nobody in Spillville troubled Dvořák by talking about music. However, he did not mind when some of the old settlers occasionally asked him about it.
>
> "Mr. Dvořák, how do you write that music of yours? Can you hear it? And how do you know that it is right this way?"
>
> "Hm, it's like this...." Dvořák paused while thinking. "Do you know what? I will tell you about it some other time!"

In Hopkins' recollection (beginning on page 191) we saw already Dvořák's reluctance to talk about his work. He disliked doing that in Prague and in Spillville, too. However, it is quite possible that he could not really explain the basic principles — the conception of ideas or the formation of motifs in the very pristine moment of inspiration. With the knowledge we have previously gained about his creative methods, we can say that Dvořák needed most of all a peaceful atmosphere.

When he came to America, he did not open his sketchbook for nearly three months because he was too much preoccupied by outside events. Only when things got settled and the emotion of being in a new environment began to subside, did he start to sketch the motives which had been growing in his mind. First he stored them randomly, the way they came to him, and did not consider what he would do with them later.

There was enough peace for him in Spillville, but one problem remained unsolved. There was no piano he could use. Kovarik remembered (in the Magazine *Narod* [*Nation*] and in other publications):

> In the rented apartment Master was lacking a piano so much needed for his work. In all Spillville there was only one piano at that time. It was in the school—an old, obsolete, quadrangular instrument, with yellowish keyboard. When Master saw it, he touched a few keys and said, "A nice little piano; I could use it." My father objected: "An old wreck," but Master commented immediately: "Oh no, if I could always have such a piano!"— and added that it needed only a little tuning and that the "Little Indian" (Little Indian again!) "will fix it up and tune it and then we will move it to our place!"
>
> The outlook for a pleasant vacation became better and better with every moment. Master lived in the upper floor of the house owned by Jakub Schmidt, the hardware store proprietor, formerly the tin-smith. When the piano was ready, they moved it to the apartment. Master was just then working on his new composition, but before he had the instrument, he used a harmonium (reed-organ) he had discovered earlier just across the street at father's cousin, the saddler. Dvořák surprised my relatives quite often as he entered to try a few chords and hurried home again. This was how the String Quartet in F Major, Opus 96 originated.
>
> Master started with a sketch of that chamber music on the third day after his arrival in Spillville, June 8. On June 10, in an amazingly short time, the whole sketch was finished. Interesting is his note on the last page of the sketch: "Thanks be to God. Finished on the 10th of June, 1893—Spillville. I am satisfied. It was done quickly!"

Kovarik's account continues:

> The score of the first movement was composed between the 12th and 15th of June—the second movement between 15th and 17th, the third from 18th to 20th, and the last movement between 20th and 23rd June.

The exact testimony in Kovarik's recollection is invaluable. It shows that Dvořák could create easily and with pleasure when the conditions for his work were good. This inspiring joy was evident in most of his works.

If Kovarik in 1950 had characterized the atmosphere in Spillville as "a blessed summer," a similar evaluation came from the composer's son, Otakar:

> I remember how much my father enjoyed his strolls on the banks of the nearby Turkey River. He liked to listen undisturbed to the gentle, natural sounds in the woods and usually took my brother Tony or me, sometimes both of us, with him. Once, I and my friend Frantik Kapler (I still keep in touch with him by letters) both equipped with simple fishing rods, set out for a trip to the spot called River Side Park. We took my father, too, and intended to leave him somewhere with his thoughts, and do some fishing. However, father's ideas advanced faster than our preparations of fishing tackle on the bank. After a while he returned to us and ordered: "Hello boys, pack your stuff and let's go home!"
>
> I expressed surprise that his cherished walk in the beloved site was over so early. However, he came back with quite a laconic answer: "I have scribbled notes over both my cuffs already and there is no blank space to continue."
>
> At that time father was writing his Quartet in F Major, Op. 96. He began on the 12th of June and in four days was finished. Almost infinite are my memories of the origin of this chamber music which I always liked the most. Indeed, the motives of that quartet were inspired in the vicinity of the Turkey River when I had to give up my catch I had longed for the whole summer, only because my father's cuffs were all covered with notes. He himself had brought home from the river the complete structure of the first movement, but I had returned empty handed. Therefore his assertion on the last page of this quartet besides the usual note: "Thanks be to God. Finished on 16th June, 1893," extended in a comment unusual for father: "I am satisfied" and also: "It was done quickly." Soon after that, father started with the composition of another chamber work, the Quintet in E Flat Major.

Such was the recollection of the composer's son Otakar. As we see, it differs from Kovarik's story. When Otakar wrote about the origin of the composition between June 12 and 16 (he certainly meant the sketch), Kovarik introduced June 8 and 10 as the dates for the sketch, and June 12 to 23 for the finished score. Who is right?

Otakar Dvořák was too young then (eight and a half) to remember exactly what had happened. Dvořák's assistant and copyist, Kovarik, had an even closer access to everything and had also participated actively in the premiere of the composition. He wrote (again in the magazine *Narod*):

> At the same time that Master finished the score for the quartet, I was done with my copy of the symphony score (*From the New World*). How glad I was that I had everything done, but my joy did not last too long. Master brought me the score of a quartet and asked me to copy out the parts because he was expecting us to play it. The parts were copied and, indeed, we performed it. Master played first violin, my father second, sister Cecilie and later brother Jan, who came home for vacation, played viola and I played violoncello. After that we played the Quartet every day, usually in the afternoon. I do not know what evaluation our ensemble would get from a competent critic, but Master praised us, saying, "the Quartet improves day by day...."

Another story about the study of the new Dvořák Quartet was documented by Kovarík. He wrote that when they came to the third movement where

> the first violin should play in a higher position, Master stopped, spluttering, "Phooey! That damn bird!" Everybody looked at him with astonishment; what had happened? But Master, calm enough again, explained: "Indeed, the poor bird cannot be held responsible for the fact that I forgot how to play the higher positions!" And he revealed later to us that the first morning when he walked in the woods, he noticed a little bird and followed it for an hour. It was all red with black wings and sang continuously.

John Clapham, the Dvořák scholar from England, tried years ago to decipher the secrets of the little red bird. He found that, according to W. E. Ricker (from the Fisheries Research Board), the state of Iowa is the habitat of the scarlet tanager. When the BBC editor Eric Simms loaned him records with the songs of various birds, Clapham verified that the scarlet tanager

> has a song similar to Dvořák's interpretation. The only difference was that instead of Dvořák's four melodies he found five. It is possible that Dvořák missed some of the bird's song, because its singing is quite fast and comes from the very tops of the trees. Therefore Dvořák could easily overlook a few details of the color. The existence of certain melodic variations is also quite possible. The nomadic thrush sings in a similar way, only

a little slower, and is, too, somewhat red. In contrast to it is the Virginia cardinal, which looks similar but sings differently.

Let us go back to Kovarik's recollections from 1950:

> We started to play with vigor and up to tempo. It was not easy but finally we succeeded. For the string Quintet we called my brother from Chicago to join us. We all felt how splendid it was that we could play Dvořák's new chamber music, and it was very good for him, too, to hear what he had just written. In spite of some difficulties, my whole family was very pleased with our achievement. The entire house resounded with Dvořák's music.

Now, let us take up another of Dvořák's works written in Spillville, the Quintet. Kovarik narrated (in the magazine *Narod*):

> When Master finished his Quartet, it did not take him long to begin a new sketch, just three days later, on June 26. Again it was chamber music, the Quintet in E Flat Major, Opus 97—this time with two violas. Master had worked on the score of its first movement from the 1st to the 11th of July. He made a sketch for the second movement on the 12th, and worked on the score until the 20th of July. The sketch of the third movement was done on the 21st, a score on the 27th. The sketch of the last movement was completed on the 29th of July, and the whole work was finished on August 1st. On the same day he brought me his scores, asking me to copy out the parts. "Since we have two violists in Spillville now, both should play!" Nevertheless, it had to be postponed for a while because of his trip to Chicago.

In addition to the use of Indian motifs which we will investigate later, we should call attention to the fact that Dvořák took more time and used a different method for writing his Quintet. He did not sketch the whole composition first, then develop it in a score later, as he had in his work on the Symphony *From the New World* and on the Quartet in F Major. Here he worked simultaneously. He sketched the second movement of the Quintet on July 12 and immediately after, from July 13 to 20, he worked on the score. Also, the third movement was sketched in one day (July 21) and without a stop, he proceeded to score it.

Another point is interesting. Among Dvořák's American sketches from 1892 to 1895 are motifs which he used years later, namely in his Opera *Rusalka*

(*Water Nymph*), similarly in his "summer" Quintet from Spillville, we find application of certain sketches from the previous period in New York which he had recorded earlier, on December 19, 1892. A most intriguing fact is that he did not intend to use the sketches in a Quintet but was saving them for a new American anthem. When he first heard "My Country 'tis of Thee" during a concert in New York City, he recognized that the melody was based on the old anthem of England, "God Save the King," and decided to use the words of the American anthem, setting them to a new melody.

It was just an idea inspired by the composer's patriotic mood during a touching moment, but it is interesting that Dvořák did not forget about it. He wrote on October 13, 1893, to his publisher Simrock in Berlin describing his Quintet in E Flat Major. He explained that the theme and variations in the third movement contain "the melody of a not yet published song on an English text, which I hope to publish as an independent composition and therefore retain my copyright."

He did not explain that the melody would be set to the new national anthem of America as he still probably thought in the autumn of 1893, but he mentioned to Simrock that he should not be surprised to hear the variation movement of the Quintet as a song "for baritone, choir, and orchestra."

The issue of Indian motifs in Dvořák's work was already mentioned in the composer's biography written by Sourek in 1930 (as in his previous works) when he stated that the expressive elements of national songs are strikingly displayed in the Quintet. Some elements, wrote Sourek, "were supposedly found by Dvořák during the musical exhibitions of the Indians."

Because Otakar Sourek had actually cited Kovarik's remembrances it would be interesting to see what is found in Kovarik's writing. In a text published in the journal *Venkov* (*Country*), written originally for Sourek, he said:

> In about the middle of July a salesman of Indian herbal medicinal products came to Spillville accompanied by two Indians of the Iroquois tribe. One Indian was about 70 years old, the other fellow a little younger. Before they began with a sale of miraculous products, they gave us a performance. Accompanied by a drum, they sang several Indian songs and danced. Master became so much interested in their show that while those redskins stayed in Spillville, he came to see them every evening.

Kovarik wrote the same story once more but in greater detail for the magazine *Narod* published by Czech-Americans:

> Around June 15th we were relieved from playing "Darda"
> because a little group distributing Indian herbal medicinal
> products appeared in Spillville. In the band were two Indians —
> an old man about 65 and his nephew — from the Iroquois tribe.
> Before those charlatans started to praise their miraculous medi-
> cations which supposedly spontaneously cure every illness, they
> gave a little performance of Indian songs and dances accompa-
> nied by a little drum. Master was very interested in seeing the
> genuine Indians, especially to hear their songs. For fourteen
> days while the group remained in Spillville, Master and I spent
> every evening there. Immediately after they left, we started up
> with "Darda" again.

All Dvořák scholars the world over, familiar with Kovarik's words as interpreted by Sourek, have used this incident. We have no reason to doubt it though, except that in his second (American) version Kovarik gave another date for the Indians' visit, one month earlier!

When we compare the memories of Dvořák's son Otakar* the situation becomes more complicated. He brought some entirely new information and writing about the founding of Spillville and about its inhabitants. He said:

> The population was entirely Czech and it was a rarity to hear
> English spoken there. However, Iroquois Indians lived there,
> too, about 30 of them. They were civilized and, speaking
> frankly, I can say that they practised lay medicine and called
> themselves "medicine men." Their chief, Big Moon, had a wife
> Large Had (misspelled for "Head"); the name of the vice-chief
> was John Fox. My father and we children received from them
> many good suggestions for our life-style.
>
> Once, our father asked the chief to perform some songs
> and dances, and when his wish was satisfied, we children were
> invited to see their exhibition, too. Many local people came,
> and everybody enjoyed the program so much that it had to be
> repeated. For my father, their songs and also the musical instru-
> ments were most interesting. As a token of their esteem, they
> gave him their photographs which are still kept in a commemo-
> rative room of our estate in Vysoka.

It is hard to say who was right. According to Kovarik, two Indians and a salesman of herbal medicines came to the village, and in his more extended

---

*Translator's Note: The English translation of Otakar Dvořák's manuscript was published as *Dvořák, My Father* by the Czech Historical Research Center, Spillville, Iowa, in 1993.

Big Moon in Spillville, Iowa

memoirs Kovarik talked about the "small band" of Indians which had appeared there around the 15th of June and stayed for fourteen days. Their performance of songs and dances was supposed to attract customers.

Large Head in Spillville, Iowa

According to Otakar Dvořák, thirty Indians lived there permanently, and it is quite possible that their songs and dances performed for Dvořák's sake influenced the composer's work immediately after his arrival in Spillville, before June 8. Three pictures of them exist in Vysoka, each one marked by a strip of paper glued to the bottom, showing their names—Big Moon, Large Had (Head), and John Fox. We cannot know the exact truth of the matter.

Even if we consider the fact that Otakar was still a child and Kovarik's recollections could be more accurate, on the other hand we must remember that Kovarik did not know about the photographs that Dvořák brought home with him, which makes it obvious that the composer must have had some closer contact with the Indian group.

John Clapham, the author of a book and various articles about the composer, wrote in one of them, under the title "Dvořák, Iroquois and Kickapoos":

> If Dvořák had heard American Indian songs during his first winter in New York, it would be very likely that it was music of the Iroquois, a majority of whose tribes are in that area. Although their songs happen to show a great sense of rhythm, many of them are beyond the scope of a regular metric scheme, and could be compared with some of the songs from Slovakia.
>
> The melodies of these songs just approximate definite pitches, giving no feeling of a fixed melodic structure as we would expect from any civilized music.

Clapham, analyzing the Iroquois music, actually argued with Dvořák's statement carried by the *New York Herald* on December 15, 1893. (Clapham used Dec. 14, however, he gave the correct date in several other articles and in his book *Antonín Dvořák: Musician and Craftsman.**

On Friday, December 15, 1893, the *New York Herald* carried the article "Dvořák on His New Work" with the subtitle "An Interesting Talk about *From the New World* Symphony, to be Produced for the First Time To-Day."

The editorial introduction explained that the composer studied the national music of this continent very thoroughly, especially the music of the Indians and Blacks: "He has made a serious study of the national music of this continent as exemplified in the native melodies of the negro and Indian races."

Dvořák said in his interview, "I therefore carefully studied a certain number of Indian melodies which a friend gave me and became thoroughly imbued with their characteristics—with their spirit, in fact...."

---

*Prof. Antonin Sychra also cited an incorrect date when he said that the interview with Dvořák was conducted on December 12. Those mistakes were caused by copying and recopying the citations—by one author from another—and nobody had ever verified the statements and dates of the *New York Herald* articles mentioned on this page.

However, Clapham did not agree with this statement and wrote:

> After studying and hearing about 200 Iroquois songs, I must deny any resemblance of the spirit in Iroquois music with the Symphony *From the New World*. It is almost doubtful that Dvořák had the opportunity to learn anything about the real American Indian music during the first month in New York. There are no proofs that he visited any of the Iroquois reservations in New York State because he would certainly have mentioned the experience in some of his letters.
>
> He might have heard something in New York City which he had taken for Indian music, but it must have been performed in a misrepresented form. If this indeed happened, it could explain Dvořák's statement that he had used certain elements of Indian music in the themes of his Symphony.
>
> Although there is no existing evidence of any resemblance between the Iroquois music and Dvořák's Symphony, the melody for English horn in the Largo section reminds one strongly of Negro spirituals, and we can find hints of the Negro song "Swing Low, Sweet Chariot" in a segment in G Major of the first movement. It is well known that Dvořák was attracted strongly to the songs of American Negroes.

When we compare Clapham's explanation with the words of Dvořák, we may have questions. Did the composer give any hints about his study of Iroquois music at all? He did not mention the friend's name, and we cannot say whom he meant. Perhaps it was Novotny.

Furthermore, we have no idea what part of the Indian songs he had studied. The melodies of Negro songs were sent to him by Hill Mildred (they were found in Dvořák's property after his death) and also by Henry Krehbiel (sent after the premiere of the Symphony *From the New World*). We can also see some association with Dvořák's interest in Indian songs in a letter from John Comfort Fillmore written in Chicago on August 11, 1893. However, at that time the Symphony and also the Quartet and Quintet were finished.

Dvořák spoke about Indian music in general when Clapham analyzed Kovarik's statements about the Indians in Spillville, who according to Kovarik, should belong to the Iroquois nation. Kovarik testified that there are no Iroquois melodies in the Symphony *From the New World*. Evidently, this must be the truth. The Iroquois music started to interest the general public from the moment Dvořák arrived in Spillville, where he possibly heard it. In his passage about the complexity of this difficult problem, Clapham cited another version of Kovarik's recollection ("we were told they are Kickapoos from the Iroquois tribe") and continued:

> As most laymen, Kovarik could make a mistake when he spoke about things he knew only a little about. The Iroquois are not a tribe, but a Tribal Confederation of Five Nations and also a very important language group. Kickapoos are not Iroquois, but only a small tribe belonging to the very extensive Algonquin language group with territory spread from the East Canadian coast to the Rocky Mountains....
>
> The census in 1890 showed that there were 237 Kickapoo Indians in the reservation in the State of Kansas, and also 325 Kickapoos lived on one of the Oklahoma reservations. They were called 'Mexican,' because when they moved from Mexico, they returned to the United States and were the only Kickapoos registered in the USA. Unfortunately the Kickapoos are an insignificant tribe and there is nothing known about their culture.
>
> Generally there is an obvious likeness between them and the Fox tribe. Both tribes are supposed to be the most conservative of all the Indians. It is an interesting fact that after the French massacre in 1728, only about 50 or 60 Foxes succeeded in escaping, but already by the next year, thanks to the release of some captives, and to some Indian tribes who had captured or adopted some of the Foxes, they grew to 250 again. Those events must have caused profound changes in the tribal culture. Yet despite what we know about the Fox culture, their music remains unknown to us.

His words are really interesting because among the photographs that Dvořák brought from Spillville to remember meetings with Indians, one is described as the picture of "Fox." Might this indicate that the Indian belonged to the Fox tribe? In this case, the music played and sung by the Indian group in Spillville during Dvořák's visit could have some relation with the original melodies of that tribe. It is unnecessary to analyze the details of his observation. In conclusion Clapham says:

> It is obvious that the music of American Indians did not affect Dvořák's music nearly so strongly as the Negro spirituals. Indian music offered him very little because of its primitive character. Here and there we can find some indications of such an influence, but only with careful consideration can we try to

confirm that the flatted seventh, the pentatonic keys, dotted rhythms and persistent tones of the basic motive had infiltrated Dvořák's music as the result of the influence of Indian music. We can find all these things in Dvořák's work from his pre-American period, too. His themes are constantly carried by dotted rhythms, as in the finale of the String Quintet in E-flat Major, and in the Sonatine. All these features were already evident in the third movement of Dvořák's Piano Quartet in E-flat Major which he had written three years before he went to New York. As for his pentatonic keys and the flatted seventh in Minor keys, it seems to be reasonable to suppose that Dvořák used them in his American compositions more often because he really loved the Negro spirituals very much, and less frequently utilized them as a result of his brief interest in Indian music.

Is Clapham right? It is true that Dvořák's familiarity with Negro folklore was greater than his familiarity with Indian tradition. Nevertheless, the composer did not make any difference between the two, to be exact. He did not stress either one as to its significance and influence on his music. For example, in his discussion of December 15, 1893, he said, "Since I have been in this country, I have been profoundly interested in the national music of Negro and Indian races."

However, many scholars are skeptical about this statement, the foremost being Krehbiel. It is true that in his work about Dvořák's Quartet in F Major from 1894, he spoke about a certain similarity with an Indian song, but two years later, in his longer study he wrote openly, "As far as Indian music goes, I do not believe that the Doctor [Dvořák] heard or even saw one of the songs of our kinsmen."

It was this conclusive statement that was more or less identical to the judgment of J. Clapham, written more than half a century later.

The university professor of aesthetics, Antonin Sychra, also contributed to the discussion with his own opinion about the influence of Indian folklore on Dvořák. He concluded that the composer

> did not know the traditions of Indian folklore thoroughly... but it is impossible to pass judgment based on two exceptions only:
>
> (1) it is impossible to say that the composer never heard or saw Indian music;
>
> (2) any connection of Dvořák's music with the Indians' music cannot be observed in Indian collections and books only. It will

be necessary to search in other areas, in the scope of city folk-lore.

As we will see later, Sychra's last sentence was important. He brought up interesting material related to point (1), namely the fact that in the Quartet from Spillville, "the concluding theme of the first movement—its basic intonation and thematic 'head'—reminds us apparently of a Kwakiutl Indian song from British Columbia."

Everybody can object that Dvořák could not have known a song of a small tribe of Kwakiutl from British Columbia. The song, however, was published in an edition by Alice C. Fletcher, called *Indian Story and Song from North America*! The book was reprinted in 1900, seven years after the origin of the Quartet. Of course, more important would be that the first edition came from the Peabody Museum at Harvard University under the title *The Songs of Omaha Indians*.

Krehbiel wrote about Dvořák's Quartet in 1894, "[I]t might be no coincidence that Fletcher's edition from the Peabody Museum reminds us much of Dvořák's work."

Looking ahead, we find that the American researcher Alice C. Fletcher was occupied with evidence of Indian songs she had published in several volumes—and nobody can frankly say if Dvořák had any opportunity to see the results of her collection, printed in several issues since 1893. Dvořák did not care to use folk songs literally. He was linking his work to the folklore tradition and wished only to capture "the basic principles of expressive intonation and create his own melodic invention. Not even the citation [of the Negro spiritual] 'Swing Low, Sweet Chariot' [in the Symphony *From the New World*] is used there more literally."

Sychra emphasized, too, that Dvořák strived for

> accuracy in representation of the melodic, expressive wave in Indian song. Even the songs of the Iroquois, according to Clapham, contain "constantly descending tendencies which gradually level off but occasionally ascend sharply to reach higher tones and descend gradually again."

Dvořák used the same method with the melodic waves in his sketch of "Cibokav's Song for Minnehaha," written on page 24 of the sketchbook containing his Concerto for Violoncello. Although this sketchbook belongs to a later period of Dvořák's life in America, we can find in it his earlier sketches for his conception of "Hiawatha," written in 1893. Here again can be seen the influences of Indian songs on his ideas. (In sketchbook no. 2, there is a theme with Dvořák's remark "Hiawatha—childish," which he used later as the basis for his fourth Humoresque for piano.) We can conclude that Dvořák was indeed concerned with Indian folklore, and the knowledge he gained from his study was used in a creative way in his compositions.

Sychra's second point expressing his reluctance reminds us that not only should the Indian songs collected up to that time be studied, but that we must know more about so-called "city folklore" and its echoes in Dvořák's creative work.

In his book *The American Songbag,* published in New York City in 1927, Carl Sandburg said:

> Earlier than 1880 patent medicine men and their wagons were travelling. Kickapoo Indian Sagwa as a spring tonic and Kickapoo Snake Oil for rheumatism and neuralgia were bespoken and proclaimed by dancing and shouting Indians. The Wizard Oil remedies had their merits sung by slick-tongued comedians with banjos. Flaring gasoline lamps lighted their faces as the throngs surged about listening to the promises made to the sick, lame and sore. Harry E. Randall of San Diego, California, heard the Wizard Oil mountebanks in Illinois in the late 1870's. [The song, "Wizard Oil" can be found in *The American Songbag,* on pages 52 and 53].

What did Kovarik write about this? He said that the medicine show sales-man was a "quack" who praised his "miraculous medical products which would benefit human health." It could not be a performance of some reli-gious ritual with drums because such a ceremony was carefully guarded by the Indians from the non-Indian audience, and therefore this affair had to be just a clever business strategy. Most probably

> they were not the real Kickapoo Indians, but the name "Kick-apoo" was only a trade mark for their products. It is not just a coincidence when the rhythmical and tonal likeness with the motives of the song "Wizard Oil" is found in the Scherzo theme of the Quintet in E-flat Major.

Therefore, when this problem was discussed years later, Kovarik, who had heard that particular melody during the performance in Spillville, recalled and transcribed it.

We must understand that when Dvořák talked about the songs of Indians and Negroes, we cannot be absolutely sure that he always spoke about "real folk music." After all, these folk songs sung during the railway strike in 1893 came from the plantations, and from everywhere the Blacks have worked, and their Negro singers and composers expressed whatever was close to their hearts.

When Dvořák declared that "no subject should be too low for a musician because 'the voice of the people' must be heard everywhere," he confirmed the statement by his creative work.

For example, in his American sketchbook no. 2, under the title "Orchestra," is his comment: "Night. New Year's Eve, New York, 1893–94," and on the fourth and fifth staves is a song with the remark, "people singing in the streets."

And what is most interesting, the basic theme of that song appeared later and almost without change in his Humoresque no. 6!

To return to Spillville, Dvořák enjoyed life there tremendously and was happy to be there with his family. He wrote about it in several letters. He wrote to Hodik, Dr. Tragy at the Conservatory in Prague, and friends Geisler, Kozanek, and Rus. All the letters painted a picture of great satisfaction. We feel it immediately when we read his first letter addressed to Hodik in Vysoka:

> Thanks be to God, I am here. We all are healthy and we like the place. There are Czech farmers scattered around the countryside, mostly in the woods, living about an hour from one another. The population is very scarce, but once they get a start, they do well. However, everybody here says that if you have even a small livelihood in Bohemia, do not come here! As we say: anywhere is good but home is best!
>
> Opportunity is changing here, too. The land is getting expensive, and new emigrants must move farther west. The land available out there is still free or very cheap.
>
> Our Father Bily has nice ponies and takes me and the children for a ride every day, and we have lots of fun. The State of Iowa has passed a restriction on brewing and selling beer, but the innkeepers sell it anyway. When officials get the word about it, they have to pay a penalty of up to 1,000 zlatys.
>
> The Americans are strange people. One can hardly believe it, but they want to drink their beer in spite of what the law says...in spite of the Prohibition they legislated themselves. This is better in our country, of course.
>
> If you have such hot weather in Bohemia as we are having here, you must be thirsty—I am sending you five dollars (you can exchange it for 11 zlatys, 50 groschen in Pribram). One

dollar is worth 2 zlatys and 30 groschen at least, so drink to my health. Invite Fencel and uncle Prokop also, and be very merry. Give a part of the money to Lojzka, too, for her anniversary. About 9 zlatys, and the rest is for beer.

Other Dvořák letters from Spillville were brimming with satisfaction. He wrote to the vicar Geisler:

We like it here very much and, praise God, I work diligently and am healthy and happy. Just now I am going to church where I play the organ. One Czech farmer is getting married and so I want to celebrate, too.... (Dated: "Spillville on 11th July, 1893, Winneshiek Co., Iowa, U. S. of America.")

The most important letter, summarizing his visit, was written one day before their departure from Spillville — September 15 — to Dr. Kozanek in answer to his letter of August 26:

The three months spent in Spillville will become a dear, life-long memory for all of us. We liked it here and were really happy in spite of the extreme heat which did not let up for three full months. However, we had something else here. We could live among our Czech countrymen, and this pleased us very much. Otherwise, we would not have come here at all.

Spillville is an entire Czech settlement founded by some Bavarian German named Spielman, who christened the place "Spillville." He died three years ago, and every morning, on my way to church, my route takes me past his grave, and strange thoughts always fill my mind at the sight of it as of the graves of many other Czech countrymen who sleep their last sleep here. These people came to this place about forty years ago, mostly from around Pisek, Tabor and Budejovice. All the poorest of the poor, and after great hardship and struggle they prospered and live very well now. I liked to go among the people and they, too, are very fond of me, and especially the old women and men are pleased when I play to them in church their favorite Czech hymns "God Before Thy Majesty" and "A Thousand Times We Greet Thee."

I became a close friend of our Father Bily, and so did our children. Together we rode to visit the Czech farmers, some-times up to nine miles away from Spillville. It is very strange here, a few people for lots of empty land everywhere. Some-times one farmer lives four miles from the next, especially on the prairies, which I call 'Sahara.' You can see nothing but vast acres of fields and meadows. You do not meet people (everybody rides here) and you are glad to see the meadows and woods full of countless cattle, grazing in pasture, summer and winter long. The men must milk them in the woods or out on the meadows, as they follow the herds. And so everything here is "wild," sometimes almost sad. One can easily become discouraged, but eventually one gets used to it. I could go on and on, and you would learn the strangest things about America....

It is understandable that Dvořák could not write those sentences in the first weeks after his arrival in New York City. He needed time to comprehend and understand all sides of life in this country. In the conclusion to his letter he wrote:

...therefore I am hoping to come home for a while whether my contract here is renewed or not. I must see my Bohemia at any price. I hear that the newspapers in our country have written about me as if I am planning to stay in America for good! Oh, no! Never. I live here pretty well, thank God, and am healthy. I work hard, knowing that my new Sinfonia, the String Quartet in F Major and the new Quintet (all composed here, in Spillville) could never have been written as they were, had I not seen America!

However, the homeland was important to him. He must have discovered Erben's book of poems *Kytice* (*Bouquet of Folk Tales*) with poetry of the Bohemian countryside containing vivid descriptions of folk customs. These enveloped him with their fragrance again. The paradox was that the Bohemian theme for his proposed composition using Erben's words had inspired him right here, in the middle of Iowa, the heart of the United States of America, in a village roughly 1,320 miles from New York City. There, in the evenings, he enjoyed the songs of Indian salesmen who praised their healing oils and medicines; and in the mornings, he listened to the trills of the scarlet tanager along the splendors of the Turkey River.

He concluded his letter with a few more sentences:

Now, I feel enthusiastic and inspired enough to be ready for my future composition "Zahor's Couch"! If I can do it as well as Erben wrote his poem, it will be all right! Hurrah! Nazdar! [Czech greeting] Kissing you and always yours....

Spillville, not aware of its role, had fulfilled an important task.

American Vacation ᗡ B

THE EVENING BELL CEASED ringing, the birds retired to their nests and blissful peace flooded the small plateau around the Spillville church. An older, husky man appeared and, with a pronounced accent, introduced himself in distinctive, clear Czech: "I'm Fric Kala. My father was a playmate of Dvořák's son, Otakar. The whole Dvořák family was here, but it was years ago, you know?"

"Yes, Mr. Kala, I know," I answered him with growing curiosity as to what else he could tell us along those lines.

After that short introduction, we began to plan our researches in the Spillville area. There was no motel in the village where we could sleep, though we might rent rooms in a nearby town, Decorah. It would be more cheerful for us there, as Mr. Kala said: "Because here, as you say at home, every evening they roll up the sidewalks."

Hence, we drove to Calmar and from there followed the road to Decorah, founded years ago by the Norwegians. The local motel had several vacant rooms, and after we got settled and ate supper, we went to the bright lights of the downtown area. Our guides, Lilian and Marie, took us bowling, a game I had never played before. Unfortunately, all the lanes were busy until ten, so our ladies suggested that we leave it for another time.

After we said good night in the motel lobby, deciding to meet next morning for breakfast at eight, we found our room comfortable, and I opened the notes I had brought with me from Vysoka. This reminded me of

254

the moment I had discovered a red file labeled "Czech Settlements in America" on the shelf above Dvořák's desk (4th edition, published by Josef Pastor, Hamburg, 1888).

My hostess and I searched for some information about the Spillville area in Winneshiek County and found that 333 Czech families lived there, and prior to Dvořák's visit there were

> 38 Czech families living in Calmar
> 46 in Conover
> 180 in Fort Atkinson
> 10 in Ridgeway
> and 59 Spillville.

All total, 333 Bohemian families were living in Winneshiek County, Iowa, in 1888. I was surprised to learn how many families had lived in Fort Atkinson, probably for the protection of the fort, which was still important at that time. The low population of Spillville astonished me, too; however, I could not find anything about neighboring Protivin because it belonged in another county.

The first settler came to the banks of the Turkey River in the middle of the nineteenthth century. His name was Charles Korek and the year was 1849. Josef Spielman from Bavaria appeared here a year later, and after him came Riehle and Herzog. The most practical of them proved to be Spielman. On the creek which flows into the Turkey River, he built a log cabin with a sawmill. Although his work was destroyed in 1853 by a flood, he rebuilt his enterprise the next summer.

At that time the first families of settlers from Bohemia arrived: Martin Bouska, Frank Payer, Wenzel Mikesh, Andrew Kubesh, and John Novak. Despite the fact that five homesteaders from Switzerland immigrated here too, the Czechs soon became the majority. An official map of the settlement carried the date of April 15, 1860. One month later, on May 16 (possibly even May 11), the foundation stone for a church dedicated to the patron of Bohemia, St. Wenceslaus, was laid with the help of the population. This demonstrated that the Czechs had most of the votes. The first church mass was served on September 28, 1861 — St. Wenceslaus Day in Bohemia — and years later, both chapels on the sides and a tower were added. In 1870, they built the Czech school, the educational and musical center for the community. The first teacher was J. J. Kovarik, father of Josef Kovarik, Dvořák's secretary. In 1876, the settlers purchased a new organ for their church, the first in the whole county. Years later, in the summer of 1893, Antonín Dvořák played that organ every day. According to the later census of 1970, the population of Spillville was 370 and 82 percent of the population were of Bohemian origin.

Next morning we returned to Spillville. Its name was originally spelled "Spilville," with three l's only, but later was Americanized to Spillville. The settlement is situated in rolling country with sporadic, leafy groves or plots of shrubs. Scattered farms are found marked with two or three aged spruce trees or pines in front of the house and a herd of cattle grazing freely in the pasture. It was the same picture as in Dvořák's days—the farmhouses built of white painted wood, some of bricks, adjoined with barns and shops—reaching as far as the blue line of the distant horizon. When we came to a small quarry, the valley was wider and the forest in the background eased the monotony of the landscape. Spillville was waiting for us.

"Where should I stop?" Lilian asked me.

"At Dvořák's museum, or as they call it, the Clock Museum."

I discovered the site on a prospect from Spillville amongst the materials I collected for my trip in Bohemia. Supposedly, people from all over the United States visit this place.

There was only one straight, paved street in Spillville, bordered by family houses and gardens on both sides. We approached a tiny square with the veterans' monument standing in the middle of a green patch of lawn. It was also the intersection with roads running to the mill and the school. In between, on a hill, stood St. Wenceslaus church.

On the main street was the post office and a red, two-story building with six windows upstairs, four downstairs, and the entrance in the middle. On each side was a sign, one in English, another in Czech, saying that "Antonín Dvořák, the great composer, lived here in the summer of 1893." Another sign nearby advertised the "House of Handcrafted Bily Clocks," the work of two brothers from Spillville, and above it all was a large blue sign: "Bily Clocks."

The wooden clocks were a great American curiosity, and indeed, who would think about handcrafting clocks of wood in those busy days? Only those two "fools" from this village busied themselves painstakingly with their unusual hobby for years. We bought tickets and were almost stupefied by what we saw! Not Dvořák, but only clocks, clocks were everywhere. All carved of wood, some two yards high—charming, naive art of two brothers who for almost half a century, from 1915, had been sculpting them in every free moment of their lives.

They created images of typical American activities and scenes: an Indian family; a train from the beginning of this century; grazing deer; an airplane; a stable with man and horse; folk musicians and a clock honoring Lindbergh; a clock with the blacksmith and his workshop; clocks; clocks; and finally one dedicated to Dvořák. A face, portraying the composer with the first bars of his famous "Humoresque" were carved on the surface of a huge violin. Clocks were ticking, striking, playing all the time. For more effect, the cashier lady set the chimes up for us, and pointing to the opposite clock, she explained that the Bily brothers were offered one million dollars for that work. They rejected the tempting proposition with a smile and went on with their carving.

"Oh yes! You see it, hey?" Kala called to us from the entry. Another gray-haired man, roundly built and good-natured, came with Fric and introduced himself as Postmaster Balik. Both wanted to help us.

"Do you need us?" they asked, hesitantly.

"Of course." I accepted their offer, a little amused. "Sure we need you."

They took us upstairs where Dvořák's room was located as was the well-known harmonium. In the hall was a collection of old farm tools; an assortment of old coins and bills kept in a glass case; Indian flint stones, embroideries, peace pipes, and ornamented leather moccasins; also a Wehrmacht hat, German bayonet, and belt— the gifts of Louis Benda who probably brought everything from Europe after the Second World War. The whole collection was guarded by a group of ludicrous plaster dogs.

"You see, everything here was willed to the museum by the deceased folks of Spillville," explained Kala proudly.

"I see, I see," I answered him.

From that hall we entered a small vestibule with four doors leading into various rooms. In the first one we found several phonographs with the huge, old-fashioned horns, an old sewing machine, and a model of a ship. In the corner room was a glass showcase full of sea animals and exotic creatures— starfish, lizards, shells. The walls were decorated with embroideries, old irons, and coffee grinders, everything brought formerly from Bohemia. At the window were two sewing machines and a wooden cradle with a painted clock above it. A small spinning wheel was placed at the entry. Similar donations were stored in another corner room. Its walls were covered with many faded prints of the national heroes and other motifs from the Old Country.

The last room was once occupied by Dvořák. However, next to the mementoes of the composer, there was a huge, untidy Bily Brothers bookcase, covering the largest wall in the room. On the opposite side stood another big cupboard full of religious relics, some of them preserved since 1859, and even 1798, donated by the deceased Mrs. Kubish and Mr. Frank Kapler. What memories must be attached to all of those objects!

The third wall was dedicated to Dvořák. On a shelf of a cupboard full of photographs, I recognized a letter written by the composer to Hodik in January of 1895, and another letter from Dvořák's son Otakar. Among the photographs of the composer I saw one which was taken in the USA. I was most interested to learn where it was shot, and Kala supposed that the only person who would know about it would be Margareta, but she no longer was alive. Margareta had become very interested in the events of Dvořák's visit, and got in touch with Mrs. Kovarik and her husband, who had brought the composer to Spillville. The American photo was probably taken by Charles Andera, the owner of the local photo-art shop.

Because I became curious about the letters left by Margareta, both my guides left us to see how many could be found. Another remarkable piece in the Dvořák museum was an old harmonium. According to Kovarik, Dvořák used it before their piano had been fixed. Dvořák often ran to the household of a cousin of Kovarik's father, the saddler, and tried new tunes he had just written, leaving hastily afterward to continue work. Now the same harmonium, with the music book opened to the page where his Humoresque No. 7 begins, was the central item of the memorable Dvořák collection.

We started with a search of the property, Honza taking pictures and Marie and Lilian helping me carry the documentary materials to an adjoining room. We chose it for its space and used every available spot to spread out our stuff. I was diligently checking every package, every sheet of paper. No inventory had been made, and I had to look at every individual book and paper that might be associated in some way with Dvořák's visit.

In addition to the "Century Calendar," I found the atlas of the local county with a plan of Spillville from 1905, twelve years after the composer's departure from the village. Cards were also there announcing the death of some of Dvořák's children, later—Magda Santrucek died on March 25, 1952; Engineer Antonín Dvořák died on June 10, 1956 and finally Otakar, who died on September 15, 1961.

Quite interesting was a citation from the book by Dr. Lowenbach: "However much Dvořák enjoyed his Spillville holiday, he left at once after his daughter fell in love with a local lad. He resolutely disapproved of this affair."

I could not believe my eyes. Which of Dvořák's daughters was it? And who was the boy? Magda was still too young in those days; it could only be Otilka. We will see!

Another document was bound in an old marbled cover and labeled "Record of Registered Letters Received and Delivered." The first postmaster in Spillville was J. J. Haug, whose office was later taken over by the local teacher, J. J. Kovarik Sr.

Inside were the official records, provided with a title: "Record of registered Matter received and delivered at Spillville Post Office by J. J. Kovarik, Postmaster." I found several records of mail received by Dvořák:

> June 20, from New York, small package, receiver's signature:
> A. Dvořák
> July 7, from New York, letter received by A. Dvořák
> August 11, from New York, letter received by A. Dvořák
> August 19, from New York, letter addressed to Mrs. Drew (the
> owner of Dvořák's apartment in New York: Kovarik's
> record was perhaps wrong and she might actually be the
> sender)
> September 7, from New York, letter received by A. Dvořák

They left for New York nine days after Dvořák wrote his last letter addressed to Kromeriz (Bohemia) and dated September 15, carrying the message, "…for tomorrow morning, on Saturday, we are going through Chicago [to New York City]."

Amongst my briefcase notes was Dvořák's letter to his friend Rus written in Spillville on August 17. The composer wrote, "About the 17th of September we will leave here for New York City and will stop for a few days in Chicago."

When I thought about the exact date of a departure given by Dvořák in the middle of August, I became suspicious of the previous citation that their return was expedited by Dvořák's disapproval of the love affair of his daughter. Maybe the folks here "heard lots that ain't so"?

Other materials from Spillville were sometimes quite moving. I read how the countrymen recalled Bohemia, and then I found the clippings of an article about Dvořák from the county paper *Decorah Public Opinion*. It ran for several columns under the title "Dvořák's Visit to Spillville" and was written by the Reverend Father W. A. Dostal from Fort Atkinson, at that time an Iowa settlement with a large Bohemian population.

The Editor's Note stated that the *Iowa Catholic Historical Revue* had published a very interesting article by Reverend W. A. Dostal, the Catholic priest at St. John of Nepomuk's church. Because of the "author's artistic appreciation of the theme he writes about," they reprinted it for their readers, too.

The actual article was preceded by the editor's note that

> there are two things which make this an especially timely article
> for this issue. The first is that this year is the fortieth anniversary

of Dvořák's coming to Iowa. The second is that but a short time ago, Dvořák's "New World Symphony" was heard, not only by the 23,000 who packed the Chicago Stadium while they attended the impressive funeral of an unschooled Bohemian immigrant boy who had risen to greatness among our nation's martyrs, but by many millions who listened to its strains as they were wafted through the ether and the radio.

The article concerned the magnificent funeral held in 1933 for the late Chicago mayor, Anton Josef Cermak, whose significance we have already mentioned. I agree that some information given by Reverend Dostal was new and interesting. His introduction was also most attractive:

> Since my boyhood days I wanted to write about Dvořák and his visit to Spillville. When a young lad I lived for awhile with my brother, Father Josef, who was at that time Pastor of Spillville. He was a fine violinist and my sister, who was our housekeeper, was an accomplished pianist and an organist at St. Wenceslaus. Many times I have enjoyed a concert of Dvořák's compositions, my brother playing the violin and my sister playing the piano. It must have been here that I have heard the beautiful Humoresque for the first time. "Do you like it?" my brother asked me. "It is Dvořák's Humoresque. Come with me and I will show you the exact spot where he composed it." We went out for a walk and came to the sacred spot. And believe it or not, I could almost heart [*sic*] the first strain of the lovely melody, echoed in the bubbling stream below us. I expressed my thoughts to my brother, and he said: "You are correct, Now let's go hunting and find the spot where the Largo was written." He hummed the melancholy tune of the famous Largo and I said to him: "This must be out in the prairies, away from the people and from everything else…" So you see why I like Dvořák, his Humoresque, his New World Symphony with its haunting Largo melody.

Then Dostal's article went on to describe chronologically the life of Dvořák. He talked about Dvořák's life in America and tried to describe in a lyrical impression a typical day in Spillville, as it was when Dvořák arrived.

He wrote that "the carpenter, cobbler, blacksmith, and saloon keeper, each followed his dutiful way…. Only a few knew that a new family had arrived, and only those concerned with their coming knew who they were."

Unheralded and almost unnoticed was the arrival of genius. Antonín Dvořák, with his wife, five children [Dostal made a mistake, six was the correct number], his sister-in-law and maid arrived and adopted at once the routine of the European village in an American setting. The villagers with a casual and unconscious disregard of his superior gift accepted him as one of them. To them he was a compatriot interested in the same traditions and familiar with the same customs. The fact that he was Bohemian was all the passport he needed for admittance to the inner recesses of their confidence and affection.

Then Dostal told of Dvořák's first experience in Spillville—when, by getting up so early, he shocked Mrs. Kovarik—and about some of the "troubles and bits of discomfort" he met. Not even the maid he brought with him, who had to polish the shoes and brush the clothes for the whole family every morning, was able to satisfy all his demands. Indeed, she could not bake bread and thus they occasionally had to call Mrs Benda, still living in Spillville (in Father Dostal's days), to try it. Mrs. Benda did what she could, not always being able to give it the same texture and taste as did the bakers in Bohemia.

All the members of the family were fastidious about the condition of their clothing. Mrs. Benda, who also served in the capacity of their laundress, has told time and again with what painstaking effort she rubbed and starched, bleached and ironed....

Often, while she did the washing in the rear of the house, Dvořák visited with her cobbler-husband in the front part of it. What they found in common she does not know. To her Dvořák was just another neighbor, kind and simple, for whom she did laundry for four dollars a week....

As the days came and went, as summer wore on into fall, the Largo from the New World Symphony was born.

This last remark gave me a good hint of the author's intention. The wish often becomes the father of the idea, as we say, and this was exactly the case of Father Dostal. His article continued:

By day he often sat for hours in his or a neighbor's back yard watching and listening. Oddly, pigeons absorbed much of his attention. He seemed to analyze their every mood. Might it be that in their affectionate capers and coos he found some solace for his home-longing?

As he watched the last of them retire into some hayloft, he would rise abruptly, —as he did frequently even in midst of a conversation, —and stride in almost any direction. Times without number he tramped through a cornfield, looking neither right nor left, intent upon capturing the rhythm of the swish of the stiff cornstalks as a gentle breeze sent a moaning, longing song through them, or using it only as a short cut to something he heard in the woods on the other side of it.

In another part of his article Dostal described an area adjoining the bend of the Turkey River. He said that

no greater cathedral could he have found for his form of worship.... The road twists and rises a bit as it approaches the quiet stream, and unexpectedly reaches the turn where the Humoresque is reputed to have been written.

One could not doubt that

there the sparkling, lilting, elusive bit of immortal melody was born. Even if Dvořák did not write it in that secluded corner, it is certain the emotional mind could nowhere find a more perfect setting for its conception.

Even if Spillville cannot definitely claim to be the birthplace of Humoresque, it hopefully boasts a much great [*sic*] honor. It is thought that here the Largo from the New World Symphony took its final shape, —exactly where no one knows, since Dvořák always sought inspiration in solitude.

Indeed, the same idea (that the composer created at least a part of his most famous symphony in Spillville) has been discussed already. How did Reverend Dostal undertake to verify his hypothesis? He wrote:

There are three men that can speak with authority on this subject. First of these is Prof. J. J. Kovarik [Sr.] of New Prague, Minn., an intimate friend of the composer, a musician of note. His home was in Spillville at the time of Dvořák's visit. Next to him is his son Joseph [Jan] of New York, a violin virtuoso, who was influential in bringing Dvořák to Spillville. The third one is William Arms Fisher of Boston, former student of Dvořák and a great admirer of his music.

Then Dostal cited a letter from J. J. Kovarik Sr. to his friend Martin Soukup:

As to Dr. Dvořák's works composed in Spillville, Iowa, I cannot give you much information as he did not speak much about himself or his compositions.... On Sundays he always played the organ in the church. Of the compositions we use [*sic*] to sing he liked F. Z. Skuhersky's Mass the best.

Judging from many inquiries which I received, it seems the Iowa people would like very much to hear that the Symphony *From the New World* Op. 95 was composed in Spillville, Iowa. I myself, as a former citizen of Spillville would like it very much, because it would make the old, dear place historical in the annals of Music. But alas! the wish is not not [*sic*] always the fact! When Dvořák came to Spillville, the Symphony was already in Score (Partitur)....

Prof. Kovarik's letter is more or less discouraging to those who believed that the entire Symphony *From the New World* was written in Spillville. It is certain, however, that some parts of the Symphony were written or at least revised in Spillville. Mr. Fisher seems to prove it in the following letter:

My Dear Father Dostal:

I regret that absence from my office has greatly delayed reply to your inquiry regarding Dvořák's New World Symphony. I was a pupil of Dvořák at the time he wrote the New World Symphony, as well as his Quartet Op. 96 and Quintet Op. 97. The printed statement that precedes the copy of 'Goin' Home' I am sending you under separate cover is the best statement that I can give you.

That he penned every note of these works during the Summer he spent in Spillville, Iowa, I do not know. His preliminary sketches were doubtless made before the Summer began, for he was a very fecund writer. Musical ideas poured from his mind like a torrent down on scraps of paper in rapid loose notation that no one but himself could decipher.

How far he had carried his work on the symphony before going to Spillville I have no way of

knowing. It is possible as Prof. Kovarik states that
he had sketched out the symphony fully before
going to Iowa but I have always understood that
the final construction of it, and the scoring of it,
was done in Spillville, and that when he came back
to New York in September it was practically completed for the task of copying the parts for a symphony orchestra is a big one and involved weeks of
time.

Dostal extended the article with a footnote which included a full "declaration" sent to him by composer Fisher. Fisher's words were related to his
own arrangement of Dvořák's Largo published under the title "Going
Home." Despite the care he took in writing to Dostal, his explanation of the
Symphony's origin is found in a preface to the publication of his song based
on the Largo, and presents a clear statement that the symphony *From the New
World* had originated in Spillville.

I kept Dostal's article and tried to determine the truth of it. In Dvořák's
American sketchbook is the composer's handwritten note that he finished the
score on May 24, 1893 — but who can guarantee that during his summer vacation, while Kovarik was working on copying the composition, Dvořák did
not make any further changes? Indeed, Kovarik made such a remark in his
English version of his memoirs: "More or less, I have to assert that the Symphony — with the exception of a few last finishing touches — was composed in
New York City."

What did Kovarik understand as "a few last finishing touches"? In the
nineteen fifties, he recalled his work on copying the score:

> I noticed that trombones were no longer used in the finale, yet
> they had been used along with the other instruments up to that
> time. It was logical to me to expect them in the finale of the
> whole work. Surprised, I went to Master for advice.
>
> "Nonsense," he said, "bring me the score!" He looked at it
> thoroughly and agreed at once: "You are right, I have omitted
> them. And do you know why? At that time I had just received a
> wire that our children had landed safely in Southampton and
> were on their way to New York. I felt such relief and joy that I
> entirely forgot about the trombones."

So we know that trombones were missing and were added to the score in
Spillville. What else had he changed? Perhaps he made changes even in the
Largo, influenced by the magical setting of the environment?

When I went through the other papers, I found three more typed pages with only a few words handwritten in the margin. The text alternated from Czech to German, and the initials "L. Z." of the author suggested composer Lorando-Zelenka, who lived in America but had studied in Prague. His notes could be preparations for an article or lecture, and on the second page was an especially interesting paragraph:

> The question of whether Dvořák did make further additions or changes in the original composition of the Largo during his visit in Spillville could be answered from my own experience in assisting Dvořák, and with the following words: "Im zweiten Satze entstanden Änderungen nach der Rückkehr von Spillville."
>
> The Largo was influenced by Spillville and its surroundings. If Master did not make any changes there, he perhaps had been sketching and contemplating some modifications. He was too busy to elaborate on any such changes while working on the Quartet and Quintet, travelling to Chicago, Omaha, St. Paul and exploring the countryside around Spillville.... I am sure that Dvořák made his changes himself. He would not permit Kovarik to do it for him as he never let me touch his score when he was working on his symphonic poem "Little Dove." First of all I had to copy the whole composition, and then he started with the changes. The alterations were glued directly onto my duplicate, which I did not rewrite after.

I do not know where Lorando-Zelenka found his German citation that some changes in the Largo originated after Dvořák's return from Spillville. It is hard to say if he was right or not.

After an hour the postmaster returned, his face glowing, and handed me another file containing more of the yellowish pages.

Anxious to see what was inside, I opened the package and found a whole collection of new materials. The first letter I read was in English and dated "New Prague, Minn., January 31, 1933" and signed by Anna M. Kovarik. Evidently, Anna was a sister of Josef J. Kovarik and had been previously approached by Miss Margareta Balik from Elgin, Minnesota. Anna wrote back to her:

> Dear Miss Balik:
>
> Your letter, addressed originally to my father, reached him but he is not able to answer you himself because of his sickness.

Hence, I decided to do it for him. My father is very old, 82 now, and his memory, as you would expect in his age, is not precise any more. He cannot exactly remember the various episodes of Dvořák's visit to Spillville.... If you would write to my brother, he perhaps could give you further information on the subject because he used to be on the most familiar terms with Master. Whenever you come to the New Prague area, we would be glad to have you for a visit.

"Quite interesting, isn't it?" asked Kala with pride.

"Here is another letter that could be even more important to you," remarked the postmaster.

Unable to wait, I reached for the document and looked for the signature. The letter was written in New York City by Josef J. Kovarik and dated April 17, 1933. It suggested that Margaret Balik had turned to him immediately after she received the answer from his sister Anna. Kovarik's English letter to her was handwritten and answered in general her eight interesting questions.

I wondered why two Czechs would write each other in English, and Maria Hosek explained to me with a sigh:

"What else do you expect? The environment plays the most important role in human life and when you change it, it is just a question of time as to how long you can keep your nationality. Our children were brought up in America and feel at home here. In Chicago some parents are sending their children to Czech schools, but the majority adapt to the American way of life."

I understood the pressures on immigrants to learn to speak English, at least at jobs, and because further discussion about that subject could not bring us any solution, I proceeded to investigate Kovarik's letter. He wrote:

Dear Miss Balik:

Excuse please my belated answer to your letter from March 20th. I was very busy at that time but I am not going to waste further time with my explanation, and will answer your questions related to Dr. Dvořák, as well as I can.

1. "Was Dvořák dissatisfied in New York, or just only homesick?"

Dvořák was not dissatisfied in New York; just a bit homesick, especially the first and third years of his stay in America, for he brought only two of his six children with him the first year, and the third year he brought only one of his boys with him for he did not want to keep the other children away from school. The second year of his stay in America, when he had all of his children with him, he regarded, as he had on several occasions expressed himself, as one of the happiest years of his life — and that was the year when he spent his summer in Spillville.

2. "Was it at your mention of Spillville that he first heard of it?"
Yes. It all came about thus. One evening…

and Kovarik repeated to her what he had written in his recollections previously.

3. "What did the people of Spillville think of him when he came? Did they appreciate the genius in him?"
Well, I have never spoken with any of the residents of Spillville about Dvořák. All I can say, as far as I have observed, that they regarded him as a great man (which he really and truly was), and were at first a bit shy or rather backwards towards him, but after he had stopped them on the street and started a conversation, inquiring as to what part of Czechoslovakia they came from, about farming, crops, cattle, etc., he was simply their man; there was no conceit in the man whatsoever, and thus made friends easily.

4. "What was there about Spillville that he enjoyed especially?"
First of all, Dvořák, an ardent admirer of nature, greatly admired Spillville's beautiful location and the beauty of the surrounding country—a thing that many of Spillville residents fail to notice—its customs—the old customs the older residents brought with them from Bohemia, which they retained and adhered to since childhood—for very frequently he expressed himself with these words "just like at home in Bohemia." Every morning he would attend church, for he was a devoted Catholic, would preside at the organ and played—"Boze, pred tvou velebnosti" ("Holy God, We Bow Before Thee")—and the heartier the congregation would respond in singing the happier he felt. Then every afternoon he would meet a few of the older settlers and made them relate to him their early beginnings and experiences. Further he greatly enjoyed his little trips to the nearby villages of Protivin, Fort Atkinson, Decorah, Calmar, and later as far as Omaha and St. Paul, but he was always happy to be back at Spillville.

5. "Can you recall any impressions that Dvořák related after his return to NY?"

Dvořák wrote from Spillville to his friends—"Spillville is a beautiful place, and I feel perfectly happy here, and the people are fond of us." But by far more important is, that upon his return to New York, he missed Spillville, talked nothing but Spillville and said that "Spillville is an ideal place and I would like to spend the rest of my days there!" And the fact is, he intended to buy a place and live there—only things turned out differently, and his wishes never realized—but that would be a long story. But I may add that, had his wishes or rather dreams realized, he surely would have lived a happy life for a number of years more than he did, and would have enriched the musical world with many great works. For as my friend Mr. Sourek told me, that Dvořák about a year before his death, while talking about Spillville, remarked, "That was an ideal spot, that was when I felt happy, and I should have stayed there."

6. "Was he inclined to be morbid and temperamental?"

No, I would not say he was morbid, [but] short, ...temperamental, and irritable, especially in the interims between works—that is after finishing one, and before another was started,—it was then that he was hard to please, hard to handle, irritable, impatient—otherwise, when he was occupied with his work, he was very available and the kindest and most good hearted man I ever knew.

7. "What in so far as you know, did he compose in Spillville?"

During his stay in Spillville Dvořák composed a Quartette in F major, opus 97 [*sic;* Kovarik's mistake for 96] for strings, and a String Quintette in E flat major opus 97—and further made a few sketches—among them the famous Humoresque, but that, however, was finished in New York. And this I ought to know for sure, or rather certainly, for I copied all the works he composed in America.

8. "Did he have any unusual habits and peculiarities?"

No—unless you would deem it a peculiarity if a man goes to bed or rather retires at 10 o'clock at the latest—that is, speaking of regular habits—once in a long while he got to bed a little later and getting up at 4 A.M. Taking a stroll in the woods, as in Spillville, or at Vysoka, his little country home in Bohemia, watch the sunrise, etc. then sit down to work and finish from 10 to 20 pages of a musical score, before the rest of the family gets down for breakfast? I will add though, that he smoked, and enjoyed his glass or two of beer with his meal—but that I would never call a peculiarity—as so many now do that—even ladies these days.

I believe that I have been able to answer roughly all your questions, but if you still have anything else you wish to know, do not hesitate to write.

Concerning my writing a book about Dvořák, I have not started yet, but I keep thinking about it. If I only had more time! However, that should not stop you from asking more questions....

With my best wishes I remain

sincerely yours, Josef J. Kovarik

I wondered if this document had ever been printed somewhere before, maybe just in some local periodical of a little town like Elgin, Minnesota. The answers to questions 1 and 2 correspond with Kovarik's other recollections. The third answer tried to characterize some of Dvořák's qualities ("there was no conceit in the man whatsoever"—I remember Marie Cervinkova-Riegrova wrote about him similarly in her diary) and extends our conventional knowledge about the Spillville summer. Truly interesting is the mention in Kovarik's fifth answer of a secret which most probably will never be explained. I refer to his words: "but that would be a long story"—I wonder what he meant by that? In the Prague Museum of Czech Music there is a letter written to Dvořák by Kovarik's father, the teacher and postmaster in Spillville, with the date of December 21, 1894:

Dear Doctor:

I am still waiting for any news from you, and also from our Josef, who did not send a word yet. Almost nothing here is changed. Your old acquaintances, Humpal, Bily, Hrnecek and Grandpa—all are still alive, going to church for mass and chattering on the way home.... Remember us on Christmas Eve. According to the good Bohemian custom we are still celebrating that event. Christmas Eve can enchant us still with its inexhaustible poetry—which unfortunately the Americans do not care for. We fast in the promise of seeing the golden piglet— only a sip of caraway brandy in the morning helps us through that hardship and it can sharpen our imagination and assist us to see the promised appearance. "Oh, Christmas Eve, the magical night of wonders" was described for us in the beautiful

Bohemian poem by Karel Jaromir Erben. If you just happened
to be here on that wonderful day and on Christmas Day, too,
you would sing with us the old Czech Christmas carols after
mass!... J. J. Kovarik

The interesting fact about this letter was that an additional text under the
signature had been torn off! What did he write that had to be deleted? Kovarik did not do it for sure because he would not dare to send a letter to the
famous composer with a torn-off section missing at the bottom of the page.
Most probably Dvořák did it himself (or another member of his family); but
why? What had Kovarik, the old postmaster, written and who could have
wanted it suppressed? Was it related to Kovarik's sigh, "but that would be a
long story"?

I asked Mr. Balik: "What do you think about the rumor about Dvořák's
daughter?"

He looked puzzled: "I do not know what you mean. People can say
things that are not necessarily true."

After reading the rest of the questions, I have to admit that the inconclu-
sive answer to the fifth one perplexed me even more. There was a clear evidence of Dvořák's attitude in his letter to Kozanek when he rejected all the
speculations of Bohemian newspapers that he might stay in America, with the
simple assurance: "No, never!" It is possible that after a few years back in
Bohemia, after different and difficult tasks and disappointments with his
operas, a new desire awakened in Dvořák to recapture an already-idealized
summer of 1893 in Spillville.

The seventh answer was also special. It is known that Dvořák made
sketches for his Humoresques earlier, but it is a fact, that the most famous of
them was composed during his vacation in Vysoka, in the autumn of 1894,
when he stopped there briefly from America for a short visit. He took back
with him to New York the completed Humoresque. However, we just
learned from Kovarik's letter that Dvořák had finished it in New York "for
sure, no doubt about it, because I copied all his works composed in America."

After we grew tired, Kala invited us to his home for lunch. On our way
we stopped in a little gift shop downstairs. The shop displayed a great variety
of souvenirs: cups, plates, tags, all labeled "Bily Clocks"; slides; cards with
Charles Andera's photograph of Antonín Dvořák; and among others the
T-shirts with an English text, "Kiss me ♥ I'm Czech".

Fric remarked: "How smart!" and tried to hasten us along. To my astonishment he promised me another bundle of letters he had found; an even
more extensive collection than I received from Balik. I wanted to see it right

away and find out who wrote the letters and to whom they were sent, but Fric put me off until after the meal. His wife would be angry if she had to wait for us with the food.

The Kalas served us venison sausage and the American national dessert, apple pie. "If you don't get apple pie, you are not in America!" they laughed.

Fric was telling us a story about his father's job in a Chicago meat-curing plant, and how they had to move away from the city when his dad began to cough up blood. After they came to Spillville, he started a butcher trade, and later, he bought a farm. Fric did not care to work in any of his father's businesses and instead delivered oil to farmers, from which work he had recently retired.

"I am 71 and now have plenty of time for other activities," he said, "If you'd only stay here longer, we could catch some turtles. Did you ever catch one?"

Perplexed, I had to explain that I never had, since we have no turtles in the Krivoklat forest where I usually stay in my summerhouse.

"Oh, you could learn it fast. Now, in the early spring, they are still hidden, but later, you just find a nice creek, tie a piece of fish or chicken to a string. The turtle bites, and you have a catch. You better watch your fingers though. They like to bite them off. Then I keep the turtles in fresh, running water for two weeks. I lock them in a cage to prevent them from getting muddy until the water purifies them. When I kill the turtle, I put the meat in a freezer which makes it yellowish and very tender. It is best to hang the shell on a tree in the garden for birds. They get the leftovers; sometimes even squirrels come, and I get them, too. They taste better than pork."

We went to see the half-nibbled shells in Kala's garden and also the spots for picking mushrooms in the woods. Fric's parents used to dry them and send them to the Chicago market, trying to improve their economic level. The family also cut ice in the Turkey River, and sold it to breweries and butter producers in Protivin.

Directly underneath Kala's garden flowed the Turkey River, and he showed us with pride three ponds on his property that provided him with fish. For trout he had to go to Czech Creek, which was on our way to Protivin, where we were heading the next morning.

"But you promised me some letters," I reminded Fric again.

"Yes, the letters, indeed," he agreed.

Our visit with the Kalas was interesting and delightful. We ate again after the stroll and enjoyed a bowl of pickled mushrooms and oatmeal pancakes. Then we sampled tasty nuts and talked about Czechoslovakia and the

USA. Our chat was accompanied by the merry jingling of chimes hanging at the main door. The sound was pleasing—I truly liked it.

In the evening, in our motel room, I could no longer wait to open the large parcel I had finally received from Kala to study. First, I read a letter from Otakar Dvořák, who remembered the summer he spent with his parents in Spillville:

> Now I am able to shoot even a deer. I learned it from Prof. Kovarik when he showed me how to shoot a fish in the river current. It was not an easy job to shoot a fish in the water. You have to contend with the light refraction, which can improve your skill tremendously." (March 5, 1947).

> I am adding one more enclosure to my message. It is a letter my father wrote from New York to his housekeeper Hodik in Vysoka. As you can read there, Hodik was taking care of father's darling pigeons during his absence. It is hard for me to give this letter up, but I am glad to do it for Spillville, the place I adore so much that when my time comes, I would like to die there. However, I am pleased to send it to you with no regrets or rewards expected, please. (June 19, 1947)

> Spillville in America came to have as great a significance for my father as did Vysoka in Bohemia. He always spoke about it with such love that his affection must have been transferred to me, too. (June 25, 1947)

> Do you still remember Frank Kapler who lived in Spillville when we went there? We still write each other, and he just informed me that many of his old acquaintances in Spillville have died. For example, Mrs. Benda who took care of our laundry. (March 15, 1955)

The many letters, dozens of which could bring to life the old times again, included affairs we already know or have a faint idea about. Here, these were described again. Reading them, I thought about people's destiny, their characters, what can bring them together, and what separates them. I studied the documents until late that night for I wanted to keep my promise to take the bundle back the next morning. This I did.

Our group met in the parsonage of St. Wenceslaus church and were welcomed by the local priest, Father Benda. In Dvořák's opera *Jacobin* there is a teacher-musician called Benda, too, but almost nothing of that prudent, enthusiastic figure from the opera libretto reminded me of the modern man in the sport jacket that represented the local clergy. I tried to find a history of the village or parish, or any document related to Antonín Dvořák. I looked for any association with Father Bily, who gave him frequent rides around the Spillville area, reminding the composer of the Bohemian landscape. I hoped that Father Bily's estate might include a diary that he may have kept, but nobody remembered any item of that kind. Nevertheless, it might still be hidden somewhere, and maybe fifty years later, when somebody else tries to find more facts about Dvořák's visit, it will be discovered after all. Father Benda gave us only two thin booklets. One of them was the *History of St. Wenceslaus Parish,* published in 1935 for the 75th Anniversary of its foundation. The information in it was concerned mostly with the priesthood and parishioners, with many photographs included, but no word about Dvořák.

The second booklet was published for a hundred-year anniversary and consisted of similar material, extended only to 1960. Again no mention about the composer's activities in the church and community.

"Does nobody here care anymore that he used to play the organ for your parish?" I wondered.

Father Benda assured me that they do remember. How could they not? Only they did not see any reason to mention it in their publications. He took me inside the church to examine the organ.

The interior was cold, very cold, and severe. The plans for renovation were designed by a modern architect who removed the neo-Gothic pulpit and altar from the nave, and with it almost everything that Dvořák could possibly have seen from his seat at the organ during the service. The whole area was transformed into some inexpressive, contemporary style. The segmented ceiling was leveled, religious pictures taken away, the ornaments on the purple walls erased, and only the simple crucifixion scenes were left. The stained-glass windows only reflected the light, giving color and brightness to the cold temperance of the unadorned space. Each window carried the name of its donor: Mikes, Kovar, Novak, Tupy, and others, and while I was ascending the stairs to the choir, I pondered on what Dvořák would think of the drastic changes in his favorite church. However, another surprise was waiting for me upstairs. I found an old organ but it was all repainted in white with pink panels. Its seventeen green-painted pipes looked at me as if disgraced. Only a small, old wooden section around the keyboard still had its original, deep brown color.

"Do you want to play?" Father Benda encouraged me, not understanding the true reason for my emotion.

Because I have never learned to play, I just touched the pedals, caressed the wood, reading the English text on a metal placard which said, "This organ was installed in 1876, used by Ant. Dvořák in 1893, restored in memory of Josef, John, Marie, and Katerina Bima in 1975."

I tried to remember Bima's name, but the only name beginning with "B" which came to my mind was Benda, the name of the washerwoman who complained often of her difficult task when she had to wash Dvořák's shirts and clean the cuffs, completely scribbled over with the dots and lines of his music. If she could only know their value today, instead of washing she probably would have ripped off the sleeves and replaced each shirt with a brand new pair.

With special respect, we gingerly touched the keyboard, which years ago had been expertly touched by the fingers of the great Master. Father Benda hesitantly heard our request and finally put the light on and opened the music book.

Slowly and with apparent uncertainty, he started to play and sing in his tired and quavering voice, an old Czech hymn, "Let Our Song Soar to Heaven," whose original words he could no longer pronounce or understand. My imagination took me to the beautiful baroque churches all over Bohemia, far away across the sea. The thought that a similar sensation might have moved Dvořák's heart when he sat here at the organ a century ago, awoke my feelings.

Honza's job was to take several pictures of the interior and we asked Father's permission to climb the tower and look over the area from above. It was impossible for Honza to get his photographic equipment upstairs, and after we carefully climbed a ladder, we stumbled over many planks scattered in all directions on the upper platform and heavily soiled with pigeon droppings. We found only a wee, glass window, barely allowing us a miniature view of the village and surrounding fields. Finally, we satisfied our curiosity and without any problems, descended the tower and met our waiting companions at the main door.

Around the church was a cemetery with the graves arranged in European style. The rectangular mounds were filled with soil and flowers were planted in immaculate patterns. Only a few plots were covered with heavy slabs of marble. The graves from the last century were marked with a simple, sparsely decorated cast-iron cross, or only an angular stone with names and dates. The same degree of distinction marked the grave of the founder of the Spillville settlement: "Josef Spielman — geb. den 21. Juni 1801, gest. den 19. Feb. 1888 im Alten von 86 jahr 7 mo. 25 tag."

We read the names, dates—how many times had Dvořák stopped here on his way to church, as he once described in a letter to his friend Kozanek? What kind of ideas might have filled his head then?

"Do any Indians live in Spillville?" I asked Father, thinking of their burial somewhere nearby . My question astonished everybody in the group, so I had to explain my interest:

"Dvořák's son Otakar remembered that at the time of their visit, about thirty Indians used to live in the village. However, I see only Czech names on the monuments, some spelled in English, but no Indian name."

Father admitted that he never had heard about any Indians who lived here, and suggested that we inquire about it in Protivin, where we were just going anyway.

At the road outside Spillville stood a large, white sign:

VITAME VAS
WELCOME TO SPILLVILLE
ONE OF THE OLDEST INCORPORATED CZECH
VILLAGES IN AMERICA

The unusual text was decorated with ornaments showing flowers, hearts, bells, and leaves, as you would find in South Moravia, one of the Czechoslovakian regions.

Kala took us through the hilly, picturesque country with its fertile, brownish soil. The landscape was occasionally scattered with small, leafy woods and in a short time we came to Czech Creek, as was promised earlier. The stream was not controlled and in most places it looked more like a shallow river bordered by trees. It flowed fast through meadows with grazing cattle. Fishermen were casting for fish, mostly trout, under the railway bridge.

The creek accompanied us all the way to Protivin. The brewery there makes a good beer, sold in cans and decorated with Czech symbols. Kala promised to give me one as a present to take home with me for a souvenir. Protivin is a nice settlement, bigger than Spillville. In his writings Kovarik spoke about Reverend Father Vrba from Protivin, but nobody could remember if he left any notes about Dvořák's visits.

Everything in Protivin was bigger than in Spillville. Before they built their church, however, they had to travel regularly for services to Spillville. The settlers here, too, worked from dawn to sunset, and their living standard gradually improved quite noticeably. In 1912 they built a club house and in 1927 the secondary school, which they called the "Rudolphinum."

Looking for the oldest living inhabitants, we found Mr. Karel Chyle. He was born in 1893, the year that Dvořák used to visit Father Bily in Protivin on his regular rides around the country.

The old man could remember what his parents told him about Mr. Kovarik, the teacher; that the composer came to Spillville with his whole family for a summer holiday; that he scribbled on his cuffs with notes, and liked to walk along the Turkey River and Czech Creek. Unfortunately, that was all he could recall.

In the evening again, I tried to evaluate the research I had done today, and my experiences in Protivin. The pastor of a local church was very skeptical when I asked him for diaries, letters, or any other possible materials. Indeed, none was known to exist. But any priest in the whole county would help us with anything we needed for progress in our search. Nothing was found in Protivin, nor in Calmar or Fort Atkinson. Only the letter from Kovarik to Margareta Balik was valuable.

Nevertheless, it touched on the problem of Dvořák's sudden decision to leave Spillville, a problem which remains unexplained. This question seems to be related to a forbidden love of Otilka for some local lad. However, the date of their departure had been planned by Dvořák a month earlier but the complication with Otilka's affair could not be dismissed entirely. Maybe the bottom part of the letter which was torn off by somebody in the family had its own special significance.

Maybe we could learn more from the oldest folks in Spillville. One of them was Mrs. Kerry Sobolik, whom Fric Kala had suggested earlier. But she was in the Decorah hospital with a broken leg. The visiting hours there were from 6:30 till 8:30 every evening, so we went to Decorah, found the hospital, and with the help of a nurse, we found the patient's floor and room.

After the introduction, Mrs. Sobolik allowed us to use our tape recorder, and I proceeded with my first question:

"At what time did your parents come to Spillville?"

"In 1876," she answered and went on to say that she was born in America, in 1895. Her mother told her that the village she came from was located somewhere near an intersection with the sign marked "Kingdom of Bohemia." It must have been close to Vienna because her father used to work in that city before her parents moved to America.

"Why did they choose Spillville?" I asked her.

She explained that her mother's cousin already lived there, and they moved in with him. The father worked first as a farmhand and after he learned to build the stone foundations, he worked on a railway and as a farm-hand.

"Did you know the Kovariks? He used to be the postmaster and a teacher, too?"

She knew both Kovarik families, and Schmidt's, too. Schmidt, the tin-smith, rented the second floor of his house to Dvořák. He bought his estate previously from a man called Thaler, she heard. Mr. Schmidt had several children, and the family lived in that house for many years.

"Did you ever hear anything about Dvořák's visit to Spillville?" I continued.

"People repeat the same story about it all the time: that he liked to play our church organ, and the old women in the village enjoyed singing the old Bohemian songs with him. He also liked his walk in the woods, with all the birds singing around."

Mrs. Sobolik spoke a broken Czech. Though she tried to recall the mother tongue of both her parents, her Czech was heavily accented and frequently mixed with English.

"They also say that he used those birdsongs in his symphonies. Is that the truth?" Mrs. Sobolik wanted to know.

To my further questions about the mysterious red-feathered bird, she answered only with a smile:

"It must be a cardinal, a beautiful red bird. It sings very nicely, too." Then she remembered again: "I heard that Dvořák came alone first, but sent for his wife and children later and all of them stayed in the 'tin-smith house.'"

New recollections were coming to Mrs. Sobolik's mind and she became quite excited when I asked her about the rumor spread about Otilka's love affair. She tried to tell me what she had not discussed with anybody for years:

"It might be the truth. It is said that when the Indians gave some kind of performance here and Dvořák found out about his daughter's love affair, he packed immediately and the family left with him right away, too."

"Did she fall in love with one of the Indians?" I wondered.

"Oh, yes, she was supposed to have, and there was another story yet. It says that Otilka loved one of Kovarik's boys. And this last rumor I had always heard from my parents, but nothing about the Indian."

"And what else did you hear, Mrs. Sobolik?" I tried to elicit more information from her.

"That Mr. Dvořák liked beer," she continued, "and the children used to bring it to him in a pitcher from the nearby inn. At that time there were three breweries in Spillville, for a population of one hundred, as far as I can recall."

"Don't you know about any letters?" I tried again.

"Oh, yes! Dvořák's son Otakar often wrote to the son of our Fric Kala. And how is Otakar now?"

I explained to her that he had died more than twenty years ago, and the old woman was surprised. She also expressed her regret that she could not be at home and show us many articles she had clipped from the newspapers. She promised to send me copies of her material if Lilian would help her.

We talked for a time about the old days and about her illness, and left the hospital quite late. One more thing I was to see the next day was the fabulous Turkey River.

We left for our last trip in the morning and it was still very cold that early. Our American trip took place in the spring, yet Dvořák's holiday was in the humid, hot months of summer. We left our car in a parking lot near the river which flowed about a hundred feet away. It was also untamed and its banks created a romantic refuge with overgrown trees and shrubs reminding us of a primeval forest. The branches were touching the ground and sweeping the surface of the water, and the old, decayed trunks had fallen in the river or were leaning over it. Broken tree trunks rotted in the deep water.

I believe that nothing had changed here since 1893. The opposite bank was covered with a wild, untouched forest, full of birds. None of them reminded me of the scarlet tanager, or of the cardinal. Who knows what sort of bird Dvořák saw then? I pushed through a thicket and ended up trapped in muddy sediment under the bank. The bleached trunks, immobilized by time and water, stood lifeless. Only the Turkey River ran and ran to join the Mississippi, Queen of Rivers.

I wondered if turkeys had ever lived around the river to give it its name. The conditions looked quite favorable for such birds in the midst of all this untamed beauty. A century ago this pristine setting had enchanted the heart of Dvořák. Somewhere here he had walked, and according to the testimony of neighbors, scribbled notes on his cuffs to record the birdcalls heard with such delight. On some other spot, little Otakar and his pal were fishing, very happy to escape the vigilant eyes of father. Meanwhile, Dvořák, immersed in the sounds of nature, felt himself one with the musical harmony of the universe.

Everybody in our group was strolling here and there. We had agreed to meet in half an hour at the monument. Dvořák's memorial consisted of a white base, with titles of some of his works engraved in the stone surface, and on it was set a large boulder, bearing a metal commemorative plaque.

Monument to Dvořák, in Spillville.

Once, a Czech critic of Dvořák's work declared that Dvořák stood in the way of musical progress like a boulder which should be removed. The rival was wrong. Although Dvořák was indeed a giant, his work has not been an obstacle for any gifted musician of the new era. It needs to be understood within the context of his time and his great accomplishment.

The English text engraved on the tablet expressed simply that which was hard for people in Spillville to say when he still lived there:

IN COMMEMORATION OF THE VISIT
OF
ANTONIN DVORAK
RENOWNED COMPOSER
TO
SPILLVILLE IN 1893
THIS TABLET IS ERECTED BY
HIS FRIENDS
AND
THE IOWA CONSERVATION ASSOCIATION
1925

The monument was unveiled thirty years after Dvořák's departure from America.

The Turkey River flowed on toward her destination, turning many corners, resounding with the harmonious songs of birds. When we were departing from Spillville, a few friends—Kala, his brother, Balik, and others came to say farewell. Fric, very moved, tried to break the mood of sadness and remarked kindly:

"I hear that you liked the chimes hanging in my house. My brother made them. Once they were made by the Indians. They made the little bells out of clay, baked them, and hung them side by side. Moved by the wind, they rang beautifully. Czechs have minds that are always open. Now we use aluminum pipes instead of the ceramic bells of the Indians. They are tuned to sound like the divine music of the angels."

With a wide and sincere smile, Fric handed me a set of chimes:

"They will tinkle and jingle for you at home in Bohemia and remind you of Spillville, the faraway village beyond the Mississippi River. Maybe you will remember us and the time we searched together for all those papers about Dvořák."

After my return from America, we hung the chimes on a wooden pillar in front of our summerhouse in the Krivoklat Forest, and we gave them the lovely name of "Spilvilek" (Little Spillville).

Life in Chicago ∽ A

AS TIME PASSED IT SEEMED to everyone that nothing could disturb the peaceful summer in Spillville. However, something developed which had that result.

On the Fourth of July three board members of the Bohemian Society in Chicago visited Dr. Dvořák in Spillville and invited him to participate in Bohemian Day, scheduled at the Chicago World Exposition for the 12th of August. The three associates were Mr. Josef Vilim, the famous violinist and a graduate of the Conservatory in Prague, Mr. Kralovec, and Rev. Vanek. Master hesitated at first, trying to explain that he must first obtain permission from Mrs. Thurber. His reluctance was easily overcome, however. This is how one of the group described it:

> Our delegation came well armed with the permit from Mrs. Thurber, which we received prior to our visit with the Master. Therefore, he could find no reason to refuse, and accepted our invitation.
>
> Because a prominent violinist came with us to negotiate, Master did not miss the opportunity to replace his own voice in the quartet by Mr. Vilim which enabled him to listen to his brand new work. That same evening, the visitors left for Chicago.

The newspaper articles praised the future Exposition as the world's largest: "The space prepared for the Columbian Exposition could harbor quite comfortably all three former world exhibitions; the Parisian, Philadelphian and even that of Vienna, at the same time!"

America wanted to prove its strength. The idea was first considered in the summer of 1889, and a World Exposition was planned to honor the 400th anniversary of the discovery of America by Columbus. There was competition between New York City, Washington, Saint Louis, and Chicago. Chicago won because the Chicagoans signed a contract for five million dollars, and on top of that the city added another five million. The total capital of ten million dollars had discouraged the competitors.

The exhibition opened on the May 1, 1893, and closed in the fall, on October 26. Over 21 million visitors came to see it. The grounds were spread over 586 acres of Jackson Park, seven miles southeast of the city hall. Because the park was not able to find places for all the buildings planned for the show, additional acreage in Midway Plaisance Park (80 acres) and Washington Park (371 acres) was added to the original area. Over one thousand acres were needed to provide space for all the attractions, an almost incomprehensible size for an Exposition at that time.

Kovarik remembered in 1950:

> No matter how much Dvořák disliked to interrupt his quiet days in Spillville, we had to make ready for Chicago where he had promised to conduct his works. He grumbled about it on the way there, and did not stop complaining even when the moving love and admiration of his fellow Bohemians surrounded him constantly in Chicago.

In 1900, the author Pavel Albieri wrote an essay, "The Bohemian Element in Chicago." He stated:

> Chicago is recognized not only as a metropolis where American-Bohemians succeed by their numbers, and by their intelligence and wealth; but at the same time it is the city with the second largest Bohemian population following Prague. It is said that Vienna is the "largest Bohemian city" with its Czech majority; and that more "Bohemians" live there than in the so-called "Mother of all the cities of Bohemia," Prague, which is also recognized as the "head of the kingdom."
>
> Nevertheless, we come to a conclusion which nobody can doubt, that Chicago greatly surpasses Imperial Vienna because we have more pure Bohemian associations and schools in Chi-

cago, to say nothing about the cathedrals and newspapers. The greatness and success of our ethnic life here cannot be compared with the weak activities of Vienna.

Indeed, the local Bohemians claimed their rights with the board of the World Exposition, and were given the go-ahead to arrange their own "Day" to celebrate their national character.

Because the two countries, Bohemia and Moravia, were not yet included as one independent European state, all products and artworks coming from them had to be exhibited in the Austrian Village at the Exposition. The famous Czech artists exhibited their works: V. Brozik with his historical pictures; Benes Knupfer with his paintings of the sea; paintings by Hanus Schwaiger and the sculptures of Josef Myslbek represented this talented nation. Next to the Czech artists from Europe was the exhibition of the American-Bohemian artists. It included the works of Frantisek Dvořák, the Korbel brothers, Karel Kresl, Josef Lindauer, V. J. Capek, Jan Ruzicka, and Frantisek Pfeffer. In addition to the exposition of Czech embroideries, there were the samples of hops, barley, malt, liquors, and mineral waters. You could see the typical Bohemian baby carriages, photos of the Ringhoffer factory and, best of all, of beautiful Prague. It was in part the achievements of these artists and craftsmen that made Bohemian Day a success. As for the number of visitors in one day, the event ranked fifth, and we should remember that the Exposition lasted for a half year. The largest number of visitors came here to see Independence Day with 283,000 people; then Illinois Day with 243,000; in third place was the British Day with 168,000; and after that came the German Day with 165,000 and the Bohemian Day with 151,971 visitors.

The success of the Bohemian Day was guaranteed largely by the presence of Antonín Dvořák, who conducted the principal concert for the celebration. Kovarik remembered:

> Master, accompanied by his wife and daughters Otilia and Anna, left Calmar on August 6th, at half past four in the afternoon and arrived at Chicago at eight the next morning. He was awaited by a deputation of Bohemians, who took him to the Lakota Hotel on Michigan Avenue where their rooms were already booked. After breakfast, a visitor came — Mr. Theodor Thomas, who was then the conductor of the Chicago Symphonic Orchestra and the great propagator of Dvořák's music in America.
>
> The meeting of both Masters was cordial. Mr. Thomas welcomed Dvořák to Chicago and was curious to know why he

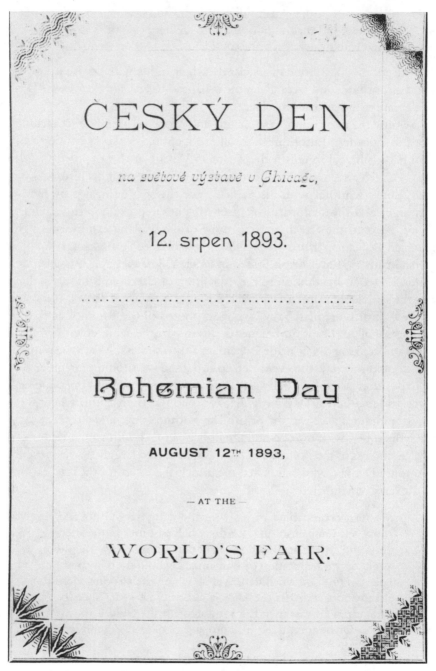

ČESKÝ DEN

na světové výstavě v Chicagu,

12. srpen 1893.

Bohemian Day

AUGUST 12TH 1893,

— AT THE —

WORLD'S FAIR.

Czech program for Bohemian Day during the World's Fair in Chicago.

had been silent for such a long time and had not published any new works. Master explained to him the trouble with his Berlin publisher Simrock, "who became furious when I offered my last symphony, in G Major, to the publisher Novello in London. Nevertheless, everything is going fine again, and many of my new things will be on the market soon!" And with the same assurance, Master informed Mr. Thomas that he had finished a new symphony before he left New York and had written a Quartet and a new Quintet in Spillville just prior to his trip to Chicago. He surprised him with a score of the new Quartet which he brought with him, and Mr. Thomas was really delighted by the good news. As a younger man, he had been a violist and had his own quartet. He was always an eager champion of chamber music and offered to give Master's work to a quartet if he wished, and said he could come to listen to them play it. Master was very pleased with Thomas' consideration.

It might be true that Dvořák took the score of his Quartet in F Major in his baggage because he hoped that Theodore Thomas would have it played. His hopes were fulfilled when his Quartet was played by a professional ensemble. He appreciated the performances in Spillville, too; however, he knew well that it deserved a perfect performance which would show off the best qualities of his work.

Who was Thomas? He came to America as a young boy. His father was a strolling musician and made his son perform throughout the South as the "youngest world-famous violin virtuoso, T. T." He used to paste up posters of the concerts around the little towns where they played. It is said that the young musician was often criticized by bigots and fanatics who called his performances "devilish."

Because little Theodore learned about the country from their low social level—from the very bottom, so to speak—his rapid ascent excited the admiration of many Americans. Dvořák knew also that Thomas was a good friend of the musically gifted Garrigue family who lived close to the Dvořáks in New York City.

In 1864, he was hired as a violist and later became chief conductor of the New York Philharmonic. In 1891 he left for his post in Chicago. As one of the greatest promoters of Dvořák's music, he had produced the composer's third *Slavonic Rhapsody* in 1880; later on, on the November 8, 1884, he programmed the *Scherzo Capriccioso* with the Brooklyn Philharmonic.

As a champion of Bohemian music, on the July 2, 1888, he conducted Smetana's Overture to the opera *Bartered Bride*. During his engagement in

Chicago, where he became one of the founders and the director of the Symphonic Orchestra, he performed in the winter of 1893–1894 two of Smetana's symphonic poems, *Vltava* (*Moldau*), and *Sarka* (the name of the mythical Bohemian Amazon).

Thomas loved Dvořák, and every year in his programs he included one of his works. Now he was able to greet the Master personally!

Kovarik remembered:

> At ten the next morning Mr. Thomas came, bringing with him the musicians of "Spiering's Quartet." They played the new Quartet for Master not only once but twice. They played it at least twice or three times more at another time.
>
> With them came a number of other visitors and press correspondents. Master did not appreciate the presence of the journalists at all. He said that they "distort" everything they touch; and whenever it was possible, he avoided them, saying that he was too busy.
>
> For a few days, until the 12th of August, the Master used to stroll about the city, visiting the exposition. In the evenings, he liked to visit the Austrian restaurant "At Midway," where he could get an excellent Austrian beer from "Pilsen" (Bohemia). The Master also liked a wonderful Turkish Brass Band which played there, conducted by Ziehrer.
>
> Master's first appearance in the Austrian restaurant caused a great turmoil amongst the musicians of the band. The bandmaster Ziehrer came to greet him, introducing himself—and they talked and talked. Shortly after his arrival, the band played one of the Master's *Slavonic Dances*. During the intermission, the members of the group also came to salute their admired composer. At that moment, Master could see that the whole band consisted of Czechs only. Henceforth, he liked to come here in the evenings, and had fun talking with the musicians. They did not discuss music, but Master asked every individual player where he came from and what it was like there and answered, "Indeed, I know it there very well." From that time on, he went there every evening.
>
> The 12th of August was near and it was the day when the Master was to be introduced to the Chicago public on Bohemian Day. The concert took place in Festival Hall, and was scheduled for the noon hour. Before that, perhaps until half-past eleven, Master watched the parade of the Bohemian Clubs marching through downtown Chicago, and suddenly remarked

with wonder: "Where did so many of my countrymen come from?"

Shortly after that he left for Festival Hall, but the parade throughout the city was either late or perhaps more people participated than was expected by the sergeant-of-arms—I do not know—but the parade did not enter the area of the Exposition before one P.M.

It must have been an unforgettable experience for the participants and the visitors, too. During Bohemian Day the American Czechs, without any religious, political, or social differences, joined together in demonstrations of their national strength. Originally, only the display of the Sokol organization was planned, but later the program was extended to other groups because more of "our dear brothers from our Bohemian homeland have arranged to come."

A contemporary and member of the Memorial of the National Union Sokol Society, Mr. Josef Cermak, wrote about it later·

The event was magnificent, and the program had the following schedule:

1/ Parade in the morning—Czech Clubs supposed to show the strength of the Bohemian element in Chicago;

2/ Czech concert in the great Festival Hall of the Exposition, before the noon hour;

3/ In the afternoon, the Exhibition of the Czech-American Sokol Organization, performed by the Ladies Organizations and by the children of the Bohemian Gymnastic Schools in Chicago.

Mr. Cermak recalled, too, that the violist, Professor Vilim, went to New York City, where he dealt privately with Mrs. Jeanette Thurber about Dvořák's participation in the music performance in Chicago. She agreed with one condition only; that the National Conservatory, as the employer of Dvořák, would be named in this program.

This condition was quite difficult for Vilim to satisfy because the conductor of the Thomas Orchestra—that is, Theodore Thomas—was not on good terms with Mrs. Thurber. At the beginning, it seemed that their plan for Dvořák's participation would suffer a disaster. Years earlier, Thomas used to be employed by of Mrs. Thurber as the conductor of her National Opera Company (which performed in English only) when her enterprise was lost to bankruptcy! Mrs. Thurber's permission for Dvořák's performance in Chicago proved that she, indeed, loved music more than her personal prestige. Dr. Dvořák could appear in Chicago after all.

Mr. Cermak continued:

> At that time, the Director of the Petrograd [St. Petersburg, Russia] Royal Opera, Professor Hlavac [a Czech], was visiting Chicago. He, too, was asked to conduct some of the compositions during the concert. As a good patriot, he promised to participate. One thing especially should be mentioned. The program committee for the Exhibition had no funds. Everything, transportation to the grounds and the long-distance trips—for example, to meet Dr. Dvořák, and to contact Mrs. Thurber in New York—was financed from the private funds of each individual member, with no guaranty that his or her expenses would ever be paid. When we promised to pay the orchestra $500, and invited the whole family of Dr. Dvořák to Chicago, we did not have one single dollar in our money-box! If the Bohemian Day had not been a success, or bad weather had come instead of sunshine, I do not know what the committee would have done. The majority of its members were not well off, but the debts had to be paid. Just thinking about the possible failures can still give me goose-flesh.
>
> Fortunately, everything ended well. The sky stayed blue from morning till night, and the visitors were moved by excitement and patriotic enthusiasm. At dawn, the Czech Chicago district of Plzen was very busy because the rows of individual parade units were put together in the adjoining streets. The groups of uniformed or civilian members of the individual clubs with many decorated floats, were finally ready to march through the city. The parade seemed to have no end.
>
> Dr. Dvořák was watching the festival from the pavilion of the former Jacob's Theatre (now the Bijou), and soon tears came to his eyes.

The whole event had to be deeply moving. The environment and the intense emotions gave one feelings of identity and unity with the crowds. The idea of a nation and national destiny was carried out in everything that was here. This made a definite difference from what one could feel in the privacy of his home, divided from this crowd by walls of isolation.

The Festival Hall was a huge concert auditorium with six thousand seats. Long before this moment, the preparation committee discussed what would happen if the space was not filled. After all, the people care very little for classical music.

Program of the concert in the Festival Hall, printed in Czech and in English.

The worries proved to be unnecessary, and soon the Hall became over-crowded. The atmosphere was unbelievable — never to be repeated by any Czech-American Society. The press wrote that at the moment when the overture of *The Bartered Bride* resounded through the hall, the audience listened first in silence up to the end, and then the outburst of increasing applause shook the very foundation of the building and the excitement of the audience was indescribable. Everybody in the hall felt that this unexpected success could add glory to the name of their homeland. It certainly has in this distant, foreign country. Everyone's eyes were flashing with great enthusiasm.

After this performance of the Overture, the lieutenant governor of Wisconsin, Mr. Karel Jonas, addressed the crowd with an English and Czech welcome, and his words intensified the excitement even more.

The American–Bohemian periodical *Amerikan* for 1894, also wrote about the occasion:

> Finally, Dr. Dvořák appeared in front of the ardent crowd and the applause seemed to be endless. From all sides came shouts of !Hurrah! and !Bravo! and applause came also from the musi-

cians. Our Master had to bow in all directions until the storm in the auditorium died out.

Josef J. Kovarik described those moments in a similar way. He remembered that the concert started at one P.M. and the first part of the program featured Dvořák's Symphony in G Major, Op. 88. Kovarik wrote:

> Master was introduced to the audience by Mr. Thomas who, unwilling to miss this special opportunity, brought Dr. Dvořák on the podium. When Mr. Thomas beckoned the crowd to stand, the "first on her feet" was the brilliant Chicagoan pianist, Fannie Bloomfield-Ziesler, and her gesture encouraged the rest of the somewhat indolent audience to give the Master his first standing ovation and stormy welcome.
>
> After the performance of his symphony was ended, Master was continually called back to the podium, until the applause finally ended. The same thing was repeated in the second part of the program, when three of his Slavonic Dances, Opus 72 (Numbers 6, 2, and 3) were played; and also after the closing Overture of Samberk's play *J. K. Tyl*. This work is known in America as *My Home*. The success of all the works was overwhelming, the ovations endless, and Master himself was happy.

Perhaps, at the moment when he was receiving such salutation and respect, and was being showered with flowers thrown to him from the balconies by beautiful ladies and girls, he finally was glad, not for his own sake but for the sake of the Czech national pride—that he had come. The morning parade of the more than twenty thousand participants, which lasted for several hours, showed him the strength of the Czech national movement. His achievement that afternoon brought to him a feeling of pure satisfaction.

Besides the compositions already named, other works of the Czech composers Bendl, Fibich (The Mourning March from the *Bride from Messina*), Napravnik, Hlavac, and again Dvořák, were played. The tickets cost 50 cents, one dollar for a box seat. After the concert, a big gymnastic exhibition was on for the whole afternoon, and this was not yet the end of that memorable day. Kovarik continued:

> The same evening, when Master showed up again at his favorite Austrian restaurant, another stormy welcome from Ziehrer's Band awaited him. All the members of the orchestra were present at the afternoon concert. This unexpected welcome made the master a little uneasy but his embarrassment was over-

come soon. It happened when a man came to Dvořák's table and introduced himself as the Rev. J. Rynda, Father from St. Paul. He was a Moravian, which meant a lot to Dvořák who especially liked the people from Moravia.

Both men soon became friendly, and during that evening, Rev. Rynda invited Master to St. Paul. Because the invitation came from the Moravian, Master could not resist and accepted his offer gladly. He was also happy that he would finally see Minnehaha Falls as he had desired for a long time.

The final meeting of the Chicagoan Bohemians with Dr. Dvořák was organized for the next evening in the Bohemian Club on 12th Street, and the next day the Master and family returned to Spillville.

It seemed that everything connected with the Chicago trip had already happened, but not really. The next day after the Bohemian Day, the performance of Waraus's comedy *King and Rustic* was given in the Haymarket Theatre in a production by Josef Smaha, the stage manager of the National Theatre in Prague. And the next week, on Sunday, Smaha again directed the production of Smetana's opera *The Bartered Bride*. Smaha's conducting was a great cultural success. The artistic delegation from Bohemia was accompanied by the writer Frantisek Herites, who furnished an interesting assessment of that cultural affair:

> The chief attention and interest in the auditorium were focused on Master Dvořák, his compositions, and his personality. At that time, his authority and popularity in America were so great that his presence alone at the Bohemian Day concert made it the foremost artistic event of the highest order.
>
> The result of this achievement not only fulfilled all expectations but the success of the music was truly prominent. The audience became moved and were delightfully entertained. The applause was so thunderous that no applause in Bohemia could surpass this American expression of peak satisfaction and pleasure. I was only afraid that this indescribable excitement could shatter the walls. Anglo-Americans are little inclined to become excited by the beauties of foreign arts. However, they were moved, too; and finally, when the event was over—especially after the end of the Slavonic Dances—the Anglo-Americans, too, stormed the Hall in their unbounded enthusiasm.
>
> I can still see Master Dvořák as clearly as if it were yesterday. The man who always disliked getting compliments bowed

and bowed, holding a huge bouquet of roses as red as fire; bowing lower and lower to hide the fact that he was crying. His tears of profound emotion and patriotic feeling were falling into the soft American roses in crystal drops, pure as the morning dew.

It was, indeed, a glorious day.

Life in Chicago ∽ B

A s I STROLLED ALONG the shores of Lake Michigan in 1982, I thought about time: how there is a time for everything we do in our life. How much time does it take for a day of great glory? Or for a whole epoch of acclaim?

The lake was poetic in its beauty, and for as far as I could see the water was an intense blue, resembling a picture by Spala, the famous Czech painter. From the shore I walked into the city, trying to find the areas that were once populated by the Czech immigrants. Yesterday evening, Roger took us to remote parts of the city that used to be the centers of Old Country life. We still found there some points of interest which symbolized the past. The churches mostly carried names in the Bohemian tradition; St.Wenceslaus, St. John of Nepomuk, and some schools in the old quarters were named after famous Bohemian personalities, one of them being Antonín Dvořák. A few monuments also recalled the illustrious past, but only by the names on them.

The Old Country life had died with the generations which were buried in the large cemetery on the north side of Chicago. Roger tried to find his way there, and it took us almost an hour to reach it. I was surprised when I learned that 94,035 Bohemian immigrants are buried there. It must be the largest Czech burial place in the world. How many of the deceased listened to Dvořák's concert? How many of them found their happiness in this promised land of America?

293

The cemetery was founded in 1877, which means that it already existed when Dvořák visited the city. However, its size at that time must have been much smaller. I read the names on the monuments, some unknown, some forgotten, some remembered and respected still today.

There was a tomb of the late Chicago mayor of Czech origin, Anton J. Cermak. It was he who, with his own body, protected President Roosevelt during an assassination attempt in 1933 and died. His words "I am glad it was me instead of you," carried by the American press, are engraved on his monument. President Roosevelt came personally to honor him during his funeral.

We found other important monuments and memorials connected with the history of our little country in the middle of Europe. The tombstones and the little shrines reminded us of events one hundred years ago, the memory of which was engraved in the weather-beaten stones.

Tomorrow would be my day for research in the library and archives. I hoped to find something new and interesting there.

The Newberry Library got its name from the Chicago businessman and public activist, Walter Loomis Newberry. Prior to his death in 1868, he had established a trust for the library that he wanted built. With its 1,300,000 books, 5 million manuscripts and documents, and many cultural activities, it became one of the foremost libraries in America.

The entrance to the library creates a special atmosphere, characteristic of temples from the early Gothic period in Europe. Because the United States lacks the grand features of the older European styles, it seems driven by a perpetual need to create its own copies.

The staircase, halls, study rooms, everything was built in an old English style, similar to that of the Central City Library on Fifth Avenue in New York City.

I wondered if I could find any document there which referred to Dvořák. In a moment, the library clerk brought me what I asked for.

I could not believe my eyes! In a file I found a translation — from German to English — of a letter from Brahms to Theodor Thomas, from August 1892. In his letter, Brahms refused Thomas' offer to come to Chicago and participate in the musical program scheduled for the World Exposition. Brahms' dispatch was delivered on the September 9, which date indicates that preparations for the Exposition began quite early.

The translation was actually a translator's draft written in pencil. On the other page followed a translation of a different letter done by the same hand. The signature at the end was Dvořák's.

The original letter was fastened to the draft and carried the official letter-head of The National Conservatory of Music of America.

Another document showed Dvořák's typical handwriting—scattered and running quickly over the page. Because the conductor was German, Dvořák used this language for his message, too:

Dear Mr. Thomas:

I beg your pardon for my delayed answer because I was very busy with my concert and also with my apartment for a week and could not find time to answer your kind letter.

But let's get to the point!

I would be pleased to conduct one of my works in Chicago. However, I cannot make such a decision alone, without acknowledging Mrs. Jeanette Thurber, or more correctly said, without her permission. [The last word of the sentence was not completely finished.] Therefore, I would be glad if you can wait until the secretary of the Conservatory, Mr. Staton, will answer you himself.

After that, I will be able to make a decision.

Regardless of the outcome, would you please accept my most cordial thanks for everything that you have done for me and my art in this beautiful country.

Your truly devoted, Antonín Dvořák

Of course, he marked his signature with the accent over "a" and a hook for "r" as always.

The letter is concerned with a condition in the contract with the Conservatory given him by Mrs. Thurber. It stated that he must not conduct anywhere without her permission.

In the materials was another letter from him written to Thomas, dated April 14, 1893. The letterhead on the official paper of the Conservatory showed a graphic design combining an image of a lyre with a sunrise. To the former address of the Conservatory with No. 128 was added a new No. 126. Mrs. Thurber rented, or bought, another house next to her Institute when she needed another extension of her Conservatory. The letter was written in English:

18 14/4 93

Mr. Theodor Thomas

Dear Sir

I got just a Chicago paper from my friend Henry Schonefeld from which I learn that the performance of my "Requiem" has just passed. You have taken much pain and trouble in preparing and performing my work, and therefore I feel it my duty to extend to you my heartful thanks.

Believe me

respectfully yours   Antonín Dvořák

His letter agrees with our previous information that in April Dvořák was supposed to conduct Thomas' Orchestra. This assembly of ninety musicians also included a choir of 400 singers. However, the composer refused Thomas' offer because he was just then occupied in working on his Symphony *From the New World*. Nevertheless, according to Otakar Sourek, Dvořák's *Requiem* was performed in the Apollo Music Club in Chicago, on April 17 and 18; but in the Dvořák letter in front of me was a date, the 14th of April, and the composer is saying that he had just learned about it from the press.

In the collection of Dvořák's materials were a few other interesting things: various letterheads, and correspondence paper with the reproduction of Dvořák's portrait signed by the composer in the upper left corner. In the upper corner on the right was only "Chicago, Dec. 14th, 94." In the center was a calligraphic address not written by his hand:

Mr. Theodor Thomas,
Auditorium, Chicago

The rest is cut off, showing merely two loops which remained from the letters on the first line. This letter or message was written in English, and it would probably be impossible to identify its author. The date is close to the day when the composer's stay in America ended. It was December of 1894, and Dvořák was writing his concerto for violoncello. There is no hint to explain the purpose of this letter from the composer.

Another letter has no date and was written in German on the official paper of the Conservatory, probably after this Institution owned both houses, nos. 126 and 128. The handwritten date "1893" was inscribed by pencil by the same person who had also translated both previous letters from Brahms and Dvořák. The letter says:

Most respected Mr. Thomas:

I am taking the liberty of addressing you with my request, which I hope will not be rejected.

A young musician, 23 years old, born in America in the State of Iowa; graduate of the Conservatory in Prague, and very good violinist, whom I can highly recommend to you—(Josef Kovarik), intends to compete for the prize which was assigned by the Musical Committee under your directorship.

Because there is the condition that only applicants which you have carefully selected can take the examination, I would like to ask you to consider this young, talented man whom I know very well, and recommend him to the respected Committee.

With cordial greetings from your most devoted

Antonín Dvořák

Another energetic signature with the typical display of both marks over the letters; again his careful consideration for Kovarik's welfare as we have already noticed in the materials in Seidel's property preserved by Columbia University.

Amongst the documents in the Newberry Library was Dvořák's card which was probably included with the property of Thomas—as were all other materials in the file.

It shows Dvořák's name and address, and his short, handwritten note in German: "…sends the best greetings to Mr. Theodor Thomas (Chicago) and asks him for his kind support of Mr. Zamecnik and his future as a composer. Prague, July 17, 1897."

The last letter of the composer made me wonder:

New York, Saturday morning, April 14, 1894

Dear sister and brother-in-law:

Your sorrowful news about the death of our dear father and Grandpa makes us very sad, and everybody in our family have been grieving and crying bitterly for him. Thanks to God, I was prepared for such news earlier, and there was no day or night when I did not remember my father. I was just praying for the opportunity to see him once more before we return home for good. Unfortunately, this was not my fate!

Let God grant him eternal peace! In two months, in May,

we will return to Prague, and certainly come for a visit. I thank
you for everything you did for my dear father!

I would be pleased if you could preserve some of the keep-
sakes for me so that I can remember my father and mother, too.
Most of all I would appreciate the old clock, chest, and the picture of Saint Mary which I remember well from my childhood.
And also those zithers which I would like to have, too. I beg
you to keep everything for me with care.

It is seven in the morning, and all of us are in a hurry to get
to church where the Requiem for my father will be sung.

It will be the Czech mass in the Czech church because we
want our children also, to be able to say their prayer for dear
Grandpa.

We will leave New York on the 19th of May and with God's
help, on the 28th or 29th of May, at half past two in the afternoon, we would be in Kralupy. I hope that we might see you
there, too.

Goodbye Yours,   Antonín Dvořák

When I come to Velvary, I will give my personal thanks to the
Deacon, the choir, and to the Honorable Mr. Janda.

I have no idea how the Newberry Library came into possession of this
letter. It must have previously belonged to somebody in the Dvořák family, I
suppose.

The contents might be classified as one of the important documents char-
acterizing Dvořák's soul, his relation with his father, and with his homeland.
Janda was a member of Parliament representing Velvary County. He was also
a mayor of the nearby Budohostice. In the spring of 1894, Dvořák was working on his *Biblical Songs* and perhaps knew from previous letters from home
that the health of his father (living at that time with his daughter in Velvary)
was getting worse. Besides that news, he also learned that his admirer, the
prominent conductor Hans von Bulow, and also another friend, the composer Tschaikovsky, had died. Originally, as we see from several themes in his
sketchbook dated between the March 2 and 4, he was considering writing
another symphony. However, he felt now that his emotions could be
expressed better in some more intimate work. From these feelings came the
ten *Biblical Songs* for solo voice, accompanied by piano. Because Dvořák
knew perfectly *David's Book of Psalms,* he was able to personally select the text
which could voice the state of his soul and depict his relation with God. He

finished the last song on March 26, and only two days later, on March 28, his father died.

After I put this important letter back in the file, I looked for more materials, especially articles in the press.

In an addition to the daily *Chicago Tribune,* there was a section called the "Columbian Souvenir Map of Chicago and the World's Fair." It shows the exhibition ground situated on the shore of Lake Michigan, south of the downtown area. According to the map, buildings of the University of Chicago were already there.

In the University archives I found an extensive section on Bohemian immigrants and settlers. I learned that the exhibition grounds were connected to the city by the elevated railway, the "el," and by funicular railway, electric tramway, railroad, and also by a small steamboat.

The list carried names of the 71 hotels in Chicago. However, I could not find the name of the Hotel Lakota where the preparation committee housed the Dvořáks. This hotel was probably not in the higher rank of those listed in this handbook.

The owner of that enterprise was Czech, and it might be the reason why Dvořák's rooms were booked there.

I read a list of the countries officially registered for the Exposition: France, Germany, Great Britain, Norway, Sweden, Spain, Haiti, Venezuela, New South Wales, Ceylon, Turkey. The list continued, showing also the index of buildings with several thousand exhibition areas; the American Indian Village, Chinese Theatre and Village, Villages from Dahomey, Germany, Ireland, Lapland; also the Cafe from Vienna (which Dvořák frequented according to Kovarik); the Indian and the Japanese Bazaars; models of the Blue Grotto on Capri, and of the Eiffel Tower; Hagenbeck's Animal Show; the Austrian Village, and many others.

I began to understand that "village" was the term for a pavilion with a certain sort of exhibit; and that dozens of them were there. Just in the Midway Plaisance, for example, there were forty exposition centers, each one unique. Next to the panorama of the Bernese Alps, one could see a model of St. Peter's Cathedral in the Vatican, or that recent hit, the Electric Scenic Theatre, and many other attractions.

I cannot forget Dvořák's words written on a card from the Exposition to his friend Dr. Kozanek:

Postcard from the World's Fair, sent from Dvořák to Dr. Kozanek

The Lakota Hotel, Chicago, August 11, 1893.

Dear friend:

My first greetings from the Exposition, which is magnificent!

Back in Spillville again, the composer described his impressions of Chicago to his friend Antonin Rus, on the 17th of August:

> On this day there was a great procession of all American Czechs at the Exposition where a big concert was held and a large Sokol (gymnastic) display. There were about thirty thousand Czechs in the procession marching through the Chicago streets to the grounds. The afternoon concert was in the huge Festival Hall (orchestra 114 performers) and I conducted my compositions, and Mr. Hlavac, from Russia, directed the works of other Bohemian composers. The orchestra and its performance were majestic, and so was the enthusiasm of the audience. All American papers wrote about it with a real excitement. Ergo, you are going to read about it in your newspapers, too. The Exposition was really huge, and it would be impossible to describe it all. One has to see it with his own eyes, and not only once, but again and again. However, you can never remember everything, because so many attractions were there, and everything so big—created in a real American style....

I have almost forgotten that the delegation from Bohemia arrived safely in Chicago, and I saw Mr. Herites with his family marching in the parade. I also met Mr. Smaha, and spent with him a nice evening. I do not know many other Czechs who have come (except Mr. Urbanek), and it would be, indeed, difficult to meet with them all in such a big city.

The press carried only superlatives describing the Bohemian Day, and foremost, the musical contributions of Dvořák. Many articles recounting the event can be found in the archives of the library; for example, the *Chicago Times* wrote that "[t]he applause given to Dvořák during his introduction was stunning, and when he finished conducting his works, the auditorium was flooded with flowers, filling the air with a refreshing fragrance."

The *Chicago Tribune* described the occasion thus:

> When Dvořák appeared on the podium, he was greeted with thunderous applause, and he had to wait for another two minutes at the podium, holding his conductor's baton and expressing thanks to the eager crowd. Even the musicians put their instruments away, and joined the applauding audience.

Because the Bohemian Day was on the schedule one week prior to the Austrian Day, the majority of Czech immigrants boycotted the Austrian event. This intensified the special, social character of their demonstration. In the library of the Ethnographic Museum in Berwyn (a Chicago suburb), I discovered a book with the title *The History of the Bohemians in Chicago*. There was a comment about Bohemian Day:

> For the first time in the history of Chicago's Bohemians they were successful at introducing themselves to the American public and to the world representatives present at the Exposition. They proved clearly that the names, "Austria" and "Austrian" represent only the geographic state, and not the "national totality." Because the Austrian government wanted to limit Czech participation in the Exposition, the "Bohemian Day" could be evaluated as a great national accomplishment.

The success of this manifestation was very much supported by Dvořák's own contribution to the event. He always, and everywhere—including New York City—presented himself as a Bohemian composer, proclaiming proudly his Bohemian origin. His statements thus take on important political and cultural significance. Therefore, his very presence in the demonstration against Vienna surpassed even his conductor's performance. On this occasion the edi-

The Chicago

854.   **SUNDAY MORNING, AUGUST 13, 18**

made of flowers, and the girls in the gallery poured upon him a shower of cut flowers.

Then the orator of the day, Charles Jonas, lieutenant governor of Wisconsin, was introduced. Applause was frequent and hearty, especially when, at the end of his remarks in English, he expressed himself in the Bohemian tongue.

Gov. Jonas' Speech.

Following is Mr. Jonas' speech in substance:

"FELLOW CITIZENS AND FRIENDS: Chicago is at the present day the great meeting place of nations, a veritable rendezvous of mankind. This is a most remarkable distinction for a city not quite sixty years old. Universal expositions have been held in cities like London, Paris, and Vienna, mentioned in the annals of history fifteen and even twenty centuries ago, but a universal exposition in a city which sixty years ago had no existence—that looks at the first glance like a wild dream, like a fable of the Arabian nights. And yet it is a grand reality.

"A gentleman perfectly competent to judge has repeatedly called Chicago a cosmopolitan city. I refer to the honorable mayor of the world's fair city, Carter H. Harrison. Mayor Harrison is right, as he always is. Chicago is a cosmopolitan city, and hence it is emphatically an American city, because America is a cosmopolitan nation. Every nationality of the old world, every race of mankind is represented in the population of Chicago, which today numbers 1,500,000, which at the close of the present century will outnumber the population of any other city in the western hemisphere, and which in the course of the next century will outstrip the population of any other city in the world. Chicago probably contains more Germans than any European city excepting Berlin and Vienna and Mayor Harrison has more Bohemian constituents than the mayor of any city in Bohemia and Moravia with the sole exception of the capital city of Prague. Why, my friends, even the corporation counsel of Chicago, Adolph Kraus, is a Bohemian, and a right royal corporation counsel he is, and I suspect there is some Bohemian blood in the veins of Mayor Harrison.

"I will state a fact not generally known in this country—general expositions of industry are of Bohemian origin. It was in the year 1791 when an exposition of arts and industry was held in the city of Prague in honor of the coronation of Emperor Leopold as king of Bohemia. It was the first exposition of that character recorded in all history, and two years ago the centennial of that event was celebrated by a grand and successful exposition of industry at the Bohemian capital.

"The name of Bohemia has been struck by fate from the list of independent states. She does not appear in the galaxy of independent nations represented on these grounds by the creations of their industry and their genius. The Bohemian flag in red and white which for centuries waved over hosts marching to victory in defense of justice and liberty is...

Fellow citizens, we have in our midst on this memorable day a large delegation of our Bohemian brethren from abroad. They come direct from that ancient kingdom of Bohemia, whose people are now waging a constitutional struggle for their historical and natural right of home rule, in which struggle they are bound to be sooner or later victorious. They have traveled a distance of 5,000 miles over land and sea, to be with us on the present occasion, and to see this universal exposition, created in its gigantic proportions mainly through the pluck and enterprise of the youthful city of Chicago under the auspices of our national government. I am sure that upon their return to their distant homes they will speak of this achievement in terms of the highest admiration. They have also come to see the land of the free—an immense republic stretching from ocean to ocean, a great nation enjoying the blessings of liberty and peace under a federal system wisely confiding the central government to its proper sphere and insuring perfect self-government to every state, a great nation secure in its rights at home, and respected and feared abroad, though almost without a standing army. They find here a nation of 65,000,000 composed of all the different elements and nationalities of the old world, living together in harmony and peace, enjoying perfect equality of rights, rejoicing in a common citizenship, and proud of their allegiance to the constitu-

DR. DVOŘÁK LEADS THE ORCHESTRA.

tion and flag of the United States. My friends, what a grand lesson for our thoughtful visitors! What a noble example for the people and the rulers of all foreign nations! This lesson of a free democratic and prosperous nation will certainly be appreciated by...

The Chicago *Sun* brought out a long article illustrated with a sketch of Dvořák conducting the Bohemian Day concert.

torial office of the *Chicago Tribune* asked him for a comment. The composer's comment was similar to his previous statement given to the *New York Herald* in May, which created such a turmoil among European musicians.

The more recent article was carried on the 13th of August, 1893:

> Every nation has its own music. We know music which is Italian, German, French, Bohemian and Russian; and why not American? The seriousness of music is related to its characteristic features and color. I do not mean that one should use melodies from the plantation, from the creoles, and those from the South—and elaborate them in the compositions; this is not my plan. However, I study these melodies until I begin to feel that their characteristic features have penetrated me so deeply that I am able to create music with the native features and character. A Symphony is a less suitable medium for such native inspiration, because its form cannot easily express the qualities and colors typical of a nation. There is no freedom in this direction. The most suitable medium for such expression would be the opera. It permits more technical freedom. My method or plan is simple; however, its fulfilment is quite subtle and difficult. It demands detailed and conscientious study, and a firm mastery over the essence and vitality of a given subject. I have just finished a quintet for strings which I wrote in Spillville. It will have its premiere next winter in New York. I think that it will show the real American spirit which I try to employ in my work. My new symphony has the same features, especially when it portrays the characteristic features of the American way of life.
>
> Recently, I have been teaching seven pupils in New York, and will have more next year. I always select the most progressive students of composition, which means that only those who are absolutely competent in harmony, form and instrumentation would be in my class. The most promising and talented of these pupils is a young Westerner, Maurice Arnold Strathotte, from St. Louis. There will be a production of his suite "Creole Dances," this winter. His work consists of materials which he elaborated according to my ideas.

Next day Roger took me to Lake Michigan, near the grounds of the World Exposition, to the campus of the University of Chicago.

I was interested in the Department of Slavic studies which has a section on Czech literature. It surprised me when I found a complete collection, divided by specialties (literature, history), all in alphabetical order and according to editions. There were many important works of Czech literature, representing famous writers, poets, scholars, and scientists—the oldest documents dating from 1775. Hundreds and hundreds of books and magazines, well organized, were right there before my eyes! Amazed, I looked over that treasure. It was systematically displayed in tidy rows on the shelves, and it did not surprise me any more when amongst all those unexpected riches I found my own works, too.

My search in the ethnic branch of the library turned up *The Catholic,* a Czech-American publication from 1934. It was published in Chicago and contained an article entitled "Dvořák and Spillville," written by Josef J. Kovarik. On one of the front pages of the *Amerikan* are five photographs, one of them a picture of Dvořák with his dedication "In remembrance of 'Bohemian Day' during the World Exposition in Chicago, on the August 12, 1893." I found several old country Bohemian magazines and documents from that period, but nothing important for my research. Only one detail, a little poster with a photograph from the premiere of Dvořák's opera *Water Nymph* in Chicago on the March 10, 1935, many years after Dvořák's death, supplemented my previous discoveries.

The only project left for my research in Chicago was a visit to Mrs. Jirak. She was the widow of the Bohemian composer, K. B. Jirak, the author of a study about Dvořák, not yet published in Bohemia.

The composer Jirak taught in the United States after the Second World War, as a Conservatory professor. It was Otakar Sourek who gave him the impetus to write his interesting study "Antonín Dvořák, and To-day's America."

We had afternoon coffee together, and the old lady talked about the past. Her husband had gone to Spillville for the first time in 1947. He found there some of Dvořák's contemporaries who could still remember his visit. He talked with a very weak old man and with an active lady of seventy years. Her name was Mrs. Benda, and she recalled everything about the Dvořáks as if it were yesterday. She used to serve them, washing their clothes and baking bread for them.

"Here is my husband's research study," said Mrs. Jirak, and I read inside the manuscript:

> Then, I visited Spillville with my wife two more times, in 1950 and in 1952. We always looked for that kind old lady who seemed to us weaker and more aged every year. Her life was

never very good, and she probably lived alone at the end of her days. She could describe very vividly what life in Spillville was like. When Dvořák stayed there, nobody in the village could speak English because they did not need to. In case someone of a different nationality moved to Spillville, for example the Irish, he had to learn Czech. Otherwise he could not make a living. And the same situation was everywhere in the rest of the neighborhood. The farmers, scattered around in their fields, were also Czechs, and the nearby town had a Czech name, Protivin....

"I remember, too," continued Mrs. Jirak,

> that we once walked in the cemetery and stopped at the St. Wenceslaus church, when I said to my husband, "Look, Karel, there is your Grandma sitting in a pew," a woman whom I had known only from photographs. We accompanied her outside, and she was witty and pleasant, and we asked her how she was, and she answered "that the winter was a thief," a remark which Karel appreciated a lot. We drove away, and my husband blew his horn, asking two Black men to move out of the way. They shouted back to him in Czech: "You, dummy!" So, he asked them if they were Czechs, and they answered, "No, we're Moravians!"

Our cups were empty, and Mrs. Jirak handed me the original text of the extended study written by her husband. When I saw this work, full of corrections and handwritten marks so dear to her, I refused to take it with me. We agreed that I would, instead, make a photocopy of the manuscript which I could keep. I thanked her and we said farewell.

Back at Roger's, I scarcely could wait to learn what Mr. Jirak wrote about Dvořák from his experience. I read quickly, and saw how hard he tried to find his own answer to the important question, "What influence did America have on Dvořák, and how has his music influenced the music of America?"

He wrote that

> this question was usually explained in a superficial way. It is said that Dvořák elaborated American motives (of Negroes and Indians) in those works which he created in America, and that he showed American composers which direction they should go in writing American music. This affirmation usually culminates with the statement that he was the founder of a self-reliant American school of composition.

Jirak continued in his explanation of the problem that "if we for example talk about the creation of a genuine 'American' school of music, we have to find the real meaning of that concept first."

Then he cited the New York City composer, pianist, and conductor Leonard Bernstein, and I felt that I needed more time and peace to analyze Jirak's study for my own purposes. I was curious to learn more about his study. Jirak's wife told me that her husband wrote it in 1950, and that he loved Dvořák very much.

When Jirak finished his own Symphony No. 6 in the United States, he could hardly wait to have it premiered in Bohemia. However, he died two weeks before this event was accomplished, in February 1972. Mrs. Jirak went to Prague anyway, but only to take his ashes there.

"He wanted to be buried at home," Mrs. Jirak added thoughtfully, "even if he remarked sometimes with a smile that the world surely looks different from the other side of that big pond."

Perhaps Dvořák knew that as well.

Pilgrimage ∽ A

T HE EXPOSITION WAS DAZZLING and Dvořák's mind was filled with many new impressions. However, he anticipated the pleasure of the peaceful environment in Spillville, too.

Before he left the Turkey River area for Chicago, he wrote a letter to his publisher Simrock on the July 28, 1893. He told him that he most probably would not make the four-hand arrangement of his "Dumky" for the piano. He explained that it would be too difficult, and most probably impossible, and therefore he preferred not to do it. He perhaps thought about it for some time during his trip to Chicago, and felt that he did not much care for the rearrangement at all. Or maybe he did not want to do such a favor for Simrock at the very beginning of their renewed relationship (which had been severed in the autumn of 1890 because of an argument over the payment for the Symphony in G Major). Now, in the second half of August, after his return from Chicago, Dvořák began thinking about the problem, which in his opinion was unsolvable.

We know about this from Kovarik's writing:

> After our return from Chicago, we played the Quintet, but Master had not yet begun yet any new composition. During the spring and summer, he had been coming to an agreement with his publisher Simrock from Berlin about his works. Because he knew that Simrock would require an arrangement of his trio *Dumky* for piano four hands, he started working on it on the

22nd of August, and finished it on the 1st of October, in New
York.

From the 2nd to the 3rd of September, Master, his wife and
I, had a visit with Mr. E. Rosewater in Omaha. When we
arrived, Master announced to his host: "Here I am, and in a few
hours, not later than tomorrow morning, I must leave for
another destination." However, Mr. Rosewater objected that
this would not be possible because he planed to show him
Omaha now that he was finally here, and that more preparations were made to celebrate his visit. Hence, Master could see
that "a few hours" would be longer than he had thought.

In the afternoon, they showed Master the city and nearby
areas including the big foundry. That same evening, Havlicek's
Bohemian Band serenaded him. After that, the host called them
inside. They were offered refreshment, and were able to have a
word with Master. It was here that he learned about two former
inhabitants from Vysoka now living in the city. He inquired
immediately where to find them, and went to see his fellow-citizens next morning. Both remembered Master from Vysoka and
his unexpected visit pleased them tremendously.

On the afternoon program was the visit to Mr. Rosewater's
printing company, and after that there was a banquet prepared
by the Omaha citizens in Master's honor. Later, the American
band came and serenaded him. At ten P.M. the Dvořáks left for
St. Paul, and Minneapolis.

Next day, the *Omaha Bee* carried the full account of the important visit,
but in spite of the friendliness of this late summer episode in Omaha, it did
not contribute significantly to Dvořák's work.

The composer mentioned his trip in four of his letters to Bohemia, and
wrote about it later to his friend Rus, from New York City:

> As you know from my letter sent to you from Spillville, we have
> spent our summer in that distant corner of America where time
> always passed swiftly. Our children are now homesick for their
> beloved Spillville, and remember often the beautiful summer
> we had. On the 12th of August, I participated in the "Bohemian
> Day," in Chicago (281 miles from here), and on the 1st of Sep-
> tember, my wife, Mr. Kovarik and I, made a trip to Omaha in
> the State of Nebraska.
>
> In Omaha lives Mr. Rosewater (from Bukovany) — but I
> think that I wrote about him before. He is quite a rich man who

publishes the a newspaper, the *Bee*, and is also a Republican with great political influence. I went there because of his invitation prior to my vacation in Spillville. Omaha (1,500 miles from New York) is a beautiful city (30 years old), situated on the Missouri River with nice surroundings. Approximately eight thousand Bohemians live there, and among them two of my fellow-citizens from Vysoka, whom I also met. They were pleased that I called on them, and both could still remember me from Vysoka; their names are Rozmajzl and Sadil and the last of them was our maid's lover. She used to serve us and lives now in the "Sheep-Fold."

The welcome given to Dvořák in Omaha was proof of his popularity with the American public. He soon became the center of interest, and his unostentatious behavior was admired everywhere. Fame could not change him, and no trace of snobbery was in his character. He had a few good friends to whom he liked to write often — and it did not make any difference to him if they were educated, or only simple folk — his housekeeper for instance. The content of his letters did not change with the status of the addressee.

It was already dark when the Dvořáks and Kovarik left their friends in Omaha by train for St. Paul. Kovarik continued in his memoirs:

> At eight in the morning, on the 4th of September, we arrived in St. Paul where we were awaited by Reverend Rynda who took us to his parsonage. Immediately after breakfast, Master started to talk about the waterfalls, urging us to go there right away because he had no time and must leave soon. However, Father Rynda was thinking about all the other plans he had made for Dvořák, and turned a deaf ear. He tried to change the subject, telling lovely, funny Moravian stories to amuse his guests. In the middle of all this, a delegation of Bohemians came, inviting Dvořák for an evening celebration prepared in his honor. It was hard to refuse.
>
> Master admired the afternoon tour enormously. They drove through the city to the Mississippi River, and then they came to the Minnehaha Falls. This sight, no matter how small, excited Master by its beauty and charm. "How enchanting!" shouted Dvořák, and there was no way to make him leave; he spent a whole hour there, listening and watching. The evening was cordial and three thousand visitors came to the celebration to greet the Master.
>
> No matter how strenuously Father Rynda tried to keep Dr.

Dvořák there, we left the next morning at eight, on the 5th of September. Master could not wait to be back in Spillville again. The moment the coach stopped there, he ran to see his neighbor, Grandpa Bily, crying: "How glad I am to be with you again!'

In his later memoirs, Kovařik remembered Dvořák's aggravation during the trip to Chicago, and continued now in his description of their latest trip:

> Master quite enjoyed our trip to Minnesota. Since he had read Longfellow's poetry last winter, and had become enchanted by its cadences and began to think that the poem "Hiawatha" would make a good theme for an opera libretto. While he observed the glittering rapids at the Minnehaha Falls, a melody came to his head, and he called to me: "Hurry up, give me paper and pencil!" I had a pencil but no paper, so he sketched the melody on a starched cuff of his shirt. This melody appeared later in the second movement of his "Sonatine, Opus 100," which he wrote for his children to play. Kreisler rewrote it afterward, and named it "The Indian Cry'.

Dvořák reported his enchantment with the Minnehaha Falls to his friends. He described it to Geisler:

> I had a wonderful time there. We travelled on the Mississippi River up to the waterfall called "Minnehaha'. It is the place which Longfellow's beautiful poem made famous.

In a similar vein, he wrote to his friend Rus: "And now about the Mississippi River which we sailed on up to a little valley with the Minnehaha Falls. It is hard to explain how wonderful it was."

Master also wrote about his trip to Dr. Kozanek:

> Omaha is 400 miles distant from here [Spillville]. Guess with whom we visited! Father Rynda, whom I met in Chicago during the "Bohemian Day'—and do you know where he lives? In the State of Minnesota, in the city of St. Paul, about 400 miles from Nebraska. He is a Moravian from Kojetin, and has been in his parish for eight years. We were his guests in the parsonage, and stayed with him for two days.
>
> From there we returned to Spillville, a trip of 300 miles. Father Rynda is an amiable man and an excellent priest. He plans to visit his mother in Kojetin next year. We might travel together, because I too hope that I can visit Bohemia. Whether

my contract will be prolonged or not—I have to see my Bohemia again—at any price.

However, Dvořák was quite glad to be back in Spillville, his refuge and oasis for his summer holiday. Kovarik remembered:

> After our return from St. Paul, Dvořák did not work with all his strength; he used the few days left for visiting friends in Protivin and Fort Atkinson. He walked long distances and visited spots which he liked the most—to tell them farewell –perhaps knowing that he would never see them again. On the 16th of September, he went back to New York.
>
> Master was very happy in Spillville, as he said later many times. He remembered it in New York every day, and after that in Bohemia. He liked to recall his visit to Spillville and talked about it with pleasure. It was a blessed summer. Dvořák was happy and at peace. He lived there as if it was just another corner of his homeland, and in addition had the feeling that it were a free country.

There were no details of their return to New York City in Kovarik's memoirs, which is interesting. There is a possibility that his silence about it was related to the incident that happened during the last days of their holiday. The composer wrote something about this in his letter to Rus:

> …and finally, on the 17th of September we went back through Chicago again, Niagara Falls, Buffalo to New York City. It took us three wearisome days, and we all returned happily home. It is really great to see Niagara Falls; one cannot imagine really how fascinating it is. It is fantastic!!!
>
> As you can see, we have already visited quite a big part of the world; however, the most beautiful for me of all would be to meet you in that world of ours again, and talk with you no end.

Dvořák's longing for his homeland became more urgent now, and the longer he stayed, the stronger it grew. However, with Dvořák, this was quite normal.

Now his whole family was back in New York City, welcomed by the lovely weather of September, and it would be difficult to get any true account of the last days before Dvořák's departure from Spillville. Since he knew four weeks ahead of time that they would return in the middle of September, one cannot believe that his departure was caused by the love affair of his daughter with some local lad. On the other hand, the citizens of Spillville knew their story, too. The young couple often walked along the Turkey River in the dusk, and people are inclined to speculate.

It was also not normal for Kovarik to summarize their three days of traveling in one sentence only: "On the 16th of September we went back to New York City."

According to Sourek, Kovarik remembered Dvořák's excitement at seeing Niagara Falls, recalling Master's words: "Good Lord, this will be a Symphony in B minor."

It is hard to say why he had never written it. We know from his notes (without indication of date, place, or reason for sketching) that he had used one of the motifs from there later, in his Humoresque, No. 8.

However, his visit to Spillville was over, and the whole group—the composer and wife, six children, sister-in-law Rezi, Kovarik, and maid—returned to New York City, and normal life resumed. The sister-in-law left for her homeland on the 3rd of October, and we can read her colorful description of her visit in a letter from the 25th of February of the following year, to Dvořák's friend Gobl:

> In spite of his excellent position and substantial salary, he is very homesick. Dvořák and Otilia, both of them, are missing their homeland. When I was leaving New York, everybody went with me to the harbor, and Dvořák began to cry and told me: "If I could, I would go with you; even if I had only a tiny place between the decks to share." Also little Zici remembered her home, threatening that she would stay with her grandma and aunt if the family ever went to America again. She packs her toys every evening, asking if the ship for home was already there.

The letter of Tereza Koutecka brought interesting testimony about the summer of 1893. She described her trip to America in May, and their vacation in Spillville,

> where they stayed for several months. Meanwhile, I went to Chicago and stayed there for three weeks, visiting thoroughly the Exhibition grounds and the city with its surroundings, too. In a few days after my return to Spillville, Dvořák, together with my sister Anna, Otilia and Andula went to Chicago, where he, as you already know, conducted a concert in the Festival Hall for the "Bohemian Day" during the fair. Dvořák's concert

was the last of the Exhibition, and it must be God's will that the last part of the program was Dvořák's overture "My Home?," which he composed for the play *J. K. Tyl*. After his return from Chicago, Dvořák, my sister and Kovarik, made the tour West. To be sure, everywhere he went, he was welcomed with honor, and received excellent hospitality.

Koutecka continued in her description:

> By the 13th of September [she used a wrong date, because Dvořák wrote that they would be in Chicago on the 16th of September; and Kovarik used the same date], we all were on our way to New York. First we had to stop in Chicago where we visited the Exposition and the city again. After two days, we continued to Niagara Falls where we could take a short rest. It was a great pity that we stayed there one day only; it was just good enough for us to see the falls, some related islands, and the city briefly from the coach. We did not have time for sight-seeing the country which is so enchanting and must be one of the most beautiful corners in the world. One could not help thinking, "How beautiful it would be to live and even to die here." I think that I will forget almost everything that I have seen during my visit, except the Niagara Falls.
>
> From there, we went to Buffalo, and after a few hours again, we left for New York. Several days later, I went home.

The letter of Terezia Koutecka has an interesting story. It was addressed to Dvořák's friend Gobl. The composer had sent several letters to him before, but never got an answer. A year later, Dvořák asked his daughter Otilka to write to her "dear godfather," too, because he was himself embarrassed to write him again without any answer.

Otilka's letter bore the date of December 9, 1893. She wrote: "My father is giving up his hope that you will ever answer his previous letters and asked me to write you instead. He thinks that I might be luckier than he was."

It could not be just a coincidence because the letter from Otilka was not answered either. Dvořák asked his sister-in-law, Terezia Koutecka, to write to Gobl, too. We do not know what had severed the relationship between the two friends, but almost a year later, in the winter of 1894, Gobl wrote for the first time. Dvořák was glad about it, and answered him on the 27th of February.

Sourek explained that letters were sometimes lost on their way, but it is quite possible that this incident had another cause. After all, the other correspondence of Dvořák with his relatives and friends—Rus, Geisler, Kozanek, president Hlavka, director Tragy, housekeeper Hodik, Mrs. Bohdanecka and the composer's father, Frantisek Dvořák—was delivered on a regular basis. In sixteen months, the composer wrote about 27 letters, and all of them were delivered safely to Bohemia, except the letters addressed to Gobl. Possibly, they were lost somewhere, and therefore Gobl was not able to answer.

While we are discussing the mystery of the lost letters, we should mention Dvořák's correspondence with his family, too.

According to an inventory of the Antonín Dvořák Foundation, which was completed by employees of the Museum of Czech Music in 1981, the following letters of Dvořák, written to his family, are preserved in the Museum collection:

> 1892 ... none
> 1893 ... one (from February)
> 1894 ... seven (plus one inscription in Otakar's letter)
> 1895 ... three (plus three additional notes in Anna's letter)
> and one letter without a date.

Antonín Dvořák wrote home quite often, most probably because he was homesick. There should be dozens of his letters somewhere; are they kept in some private collections? What has happened to them?

The state archives have no letters written by Dvořák to his brother-in-law, Count Kounic, nor to the count's wife, the composer's sister-in-law, Josefina. Do they still exist?

Mrs. Koutecka then went back to Bohemia, and the children, whom she brought with her, stayed in New York City. Dvořák decided that the whole family would go to Bohemia in the spring next year, after school was over. He wrote to Hodik, on the 1st of November, 1893:

> Today is All Saints Day at home. Unfortunately nobody here knows it. For them it is just an ordinary weekday. That shows you how things are here! I was glad to receive your last letter with the information that everybody is healthy and happy and that you have survived that hot summer. The fruit must be in abundance in our garden this season, I hope you make lots of money by selling it.
>
> When you write about the drought, you should tell me about the trees, too. How much did they grow, most of all the little spruce trees on the back; and the fruit trees, how are they? I would like to know everything about our garden, and how it

looks. Write me about it, and very soon. And what about my pigeons? Do you feed them enough? If necessary, ask Grandma, she will give you more money. If the young doves are nice let them fly out to grow strong. I would like to get some yellow striped ones — or a pretty pouter or fantail.

We have occasional frosts here, but never too cold. Today we have nice warm weather. Hopefully, it will last until the end of the month. Our children are going to school and work very hard there. Tonik already speaks English, and is doing well in classes; Marenka and Otakar, too. Otta and Anna have their private teacher at home and also make good progress. Otta will write to Mrs. Koutecka today, and his letter to Prague will be in English.

Give my regards to Fencl and Kolar, to the Kovars, and to all our friends. Goodbye. Yours, A. Dvořák

The composer had never considered himself above the other people. He was really a special kind of human being, and this kind of fairness was always typical for Dvořák. After the summer holiday, he was in excellent health. However, in spite of his fitness, he could not become absorbed in any major work. Later on, he began to write a simple Sonatine for the piano and violin, which Opus was marked by the distinguished number "100." He had dedicated it to his children, Otilka and Tonik, and therefore the composition was written "in an easy style," as Otilka described it to Gobl.

A new school year at the Conservatory had begun, and his mind had to be shifted to practical, everyday work. However, in spite of these daily activities and his recreational walks in Stuyvesant Park on the way to school, and even despite his work on the Sonatine, Dvořák's mind was involved in a more important task. The production of his Symphony *From the New World* was under way. At that time, the work was still without a name. It was just labeled "Symphony in E-minor." Perhaps waiting for the premiere made him, in fact, a little nervous.

It was an interesting period in the composer's life. Once he had given his score to Seidl, he talked about it with him only occasionally.

In the letter from the 27th of February, 1894, he talked about the Symphony *From the New World,* about the Quartet and Quintet from Spillville, and stated: "I can dare to judge these three works of mine as being my best and most original compositions."

The critics were of the same opinion and one of the papers, the *New York Herald,* wrote: "Why didn't Dvořák come here earlier? In truth, nobody in America can write such music."

In the fall of 1893, a new person important for Dvořák's future appeared on the scene—Anton Seidl. During my research in New York City, and also before, I was always looking for any news, any little scraps of information, anything that could help make the man who became the first conductor of the Symphony *From the New World* clearer to me. Antonín Dvořák later characterized him to his students in Prague:

> He was an extremely talented musician, one with vast experiences. He often liked to talk about the time when he worked as secretary to Richard Wagner. He never tried composing music, but he was an excellent musician and brilliant conductor. Of course, he had his caprices, too. He was wild, rebellious and godless; and when he spoke, it could sometimes be quite shocking. Otherwise, he was well educated, and I was always pleased to discuss with him whatever interested us both. We spent much time together, and I still do not know what I would have done without that man in America. I would probably have been bored to death.

In his position as conductor of the New York Philharmonic, Seidl had a wide-ranging influence, and in that way, he became quite indispensable to Dvořák. They met twice a week, and Josef J. Kovarik wrote about it in his letter to Otakar Sourek:

> In the afternoon, Master visited the Fleishmann Cafe on the corner of Broadway and 10th Street. He came there for meetings with Anton Seidl, who was then the conductor of the New York Philharmonic, and at the same time, the conductor of the German (mostly Wagner's) operas at the Metropolitan Opera. Seidl was an excellent conductor, especially of Wagner's works (with whom he had been associated until now). Master liked to ask him about Wagner's methods of working and similar questions. Their interesting discussions easily turned into debates, often becoming quite sharp. However, all their arguments were finally settled. Both of them would think a lot about their controversies at home, and when they met next time, one of them would gallantly admit that he was "a little bit" wrong and everything would be fine again.
>
> One day, Master proclaimed that *Tannhäuser* was the best

opera Wagner ever wrote—which statement Seidl did not agree with at all. He could not be persuaded, and a long, earnest debate began. Naturally, such a serious problem could not be resolved the same day.

However, the next day, Seidl began with this explanation: "So, I thought about our discussion yesterday for the whole evening, I was analyzing the problem from every side, and have to admit that you were right. From an operatic standpoint, *Tannhäuser* is the best. However, do you know *Siegfried*?" When Master said that he had heard this work only once, Seidl promised to get him a ticket for the next performance of the opera under his conductor's baton at the Metropolitan.

When the tickets came, they were for seats in the Diamond Horseshoe, one of the most prominent areas of the Metropolitan. Its occupants were supposed to come at the very last moment, or better, when everything had already started. It was expected that they should wear the latest fashion in formal apparel, and expensive jewelry.

Nonetheless, Master came in his slightly dark suit, and I? No matter how much I had tried to select the darkest suit from my scanty wardrobe, it was still too light for the fashionable occasion of that evening.

Wherever Master had to go, he always hurried wanting to be prompt. At this time he was especially prompt. The usher looked at us with amusement—it was probably our improper outfits, or he was not used to ushering the holders of these box seats half an hour early. Because the nearest parterre was still empty, Master pulled out his watch and said: "I think we are little early." So we observed the parterre being slowly filled by the audience, which made our waiting shorter. Suddenly, we heard the voices from the next box to us, and when Master saw his neighbors wearing expensive formal outfits, he quickly moved his seat back. I found his action proper and did it, too.

So there we sat, each in a rear corner, waiting until the lights went down. Finally, the opera started! However, the conversation around us did not stop, and Master tried to "signal" the talkers with his special look, but it was absolutely hopeless. So he paid no attention to it after all, and in spite of the tumult coming from nearby, he listened attentively. However, we went home after the first act. The usher could not believe his eyes— he probably thought: "Funny patrons, others are just coming, and these two are already going home!"

When Seidl next met Master, he asked for his opinion about *Siegfried.* Master did not hesitate, and replied boldly that he left after the first act! He rated the act which he had heard, and said that the production was excellent; however, the fixed rhythm, continuously repeated, made him tired!

Kovarik wrote in this passage about the Fleishmann Cafe; but the composer's son Otakar remembered it differently:

After our return from Spillville, the world-famous conductor, Anton Seidl, asserted his right to conduct the Symphony and to become the first conductor of this work in history. My father complied with his wish willingly, and they began to study the work. At that time, their meetings were usually at the cafe "Central," on Madison Square, and they talked exclusively about the Symphony. My father liked to take me with him. Their conversation was in German, which I could not understand. I was not able to follow their discussion at all, and therefore, I rather looked at the pictures in the magazines available there.

On the first floor of that building was a store selling toys. Father and I came there often, admiring the models of overseas ships. We liked them best, not paying much attention to the rest of the beautiful toys. It was my desire to own one, and I could well imagine what pleasure it would give me to see it in Vysoka floating on the pond which was called "Korycky," situated in the meadows nearby. Once, being encouraged by this idea, I inquired about the price of the model which carried the magnificent name *Majestic* on its bow. It cost 45 dollars. When we stood in the front of that store again, admiring the ship, Seidl touched father's shoulder and asked, this time in English so I could understand:

"What are you looking for?" I told him eagerly that the favorite object in the window was the ship called the *Majestic;* but that it was too expensive, and father would never buy it for me. I think that my father did not mind the dollars as much as the size of the model. The colossus included a boiler, two propellers, and measured seven feet lengthwise. How could we transport it to Bohemia? Nevertheless, Seidl saw it differently:

"Never mind, wait to see how things will go with Father's new symphony, and remind me then."

We can smile at this story as it was experienced by the child. According to Otakar, the future of the ship *Majestic* was dependent upon the reputation of his famous father.

We can learn more on the subject of Dvořák's prestige from the rest of Otakar's memoirs:

> At that time, my father's popularity was reaching a peak, and of course, typically for America, various companies were after him to use the name of "Dvořák" for their products. Soon the store windows and show cases of the largest shopping centers were filled with this merchandise — canes, ties, shirts, an endless variety of products which carried the name "Dvořák".

Jeanette Thurber also appreciated this development. She knew well that Dvořák's presence in America, which was exclusively her doing, became the peak achievement of her entire life. Dvořák's creative energy was at its utmost height, and his responsibility toward his creative work was tremendous. He had been polishing each composition, being seldom satisfied with his first idea; he elaborated the themes, combining them reciprocally. In spite of his genius, creativity was for him a puzzling task which he had to accomplish, and at the same time he liked the excitement of the challenge greatly.

The West German authors, Stockl and Doge, analyzed the Symphony and showed how Dvořák changed and reworked his compositions. For example, take the second movement, the famous Largo. Its introductory chords were actually redone. We do not know exactly when that happened. In another version of his memoirs, Kovarik wrote that after his return from Spillville, Dvořák worked on the Symphony again. He described it in these words: "Master...was making various improvements and changes — most of all in the second movement. He had not changed anything in the third and fourth movements, and was occupied with his revision for a whole week."

This could mean that the Spillville holiday had its influence on the final version of the Largo, indeed. Stockl and Doge concluded this passage with their observation:

> Certain sections were pasted over and erased, and some other improvements on the original pages of his work show that many changes in the Ninth Symphony were made during the last stages of its development, before the final harmonization was completed, and the composition as a whole was finished.

The question is, What was meant by the "last stages of development?" How much time did they estimate he needed to accomplish his work?

Kovarik talked about a time period of one week. This might involve only the changes made in the second movement, which were done after the holidays. Was the composer making the changes, erasing and pasting, somewhere else? It is hard to say when and where it was redone.

Kovarik continued in the same account:

> Once in the cafe, Seidl mentioned that he had heard about some new symphony which Master was supposed to have written, and asked permission to produce it at one of the earliest concerts of the New York Philharmonic. Master thought about it awhile, and before they departed, he agreed with Seidl's proposal. This was in the middle of November, 1893. The next day, Seidl announced to Master that the Symphony would be produced around the 15th of December, and asked him to send the score as soon as possible. That same evening, before I left to deliver the score, Master expanded the name of the Symphony in E-minor extending the title with the addition "From the New World."

Was this just Dvořák's spur-of-the-moment idea without real reason? Not at all. When he wrote to the publisher Simrock, on March 5, 1894, he also asked him vehemently to use this extended title in its entirety. If Kovarik had thought this notion to be one of Dvořák's innocent games, we will soon see from other sources that his ideas about the composer's deed were incorrect. Dvořák's demand written to Simrock signaled that the composer knew well why he should use this title.

Kovarik wrote about it to Sourek:

> When I brought the Symphony to Seidl, he asked me to play it for him, I excused myself, informing him that I was not a pianist, which was true. I was very curious to learn what Seidl's judgment about the Symphony would be because Seidl was one of those skeptical musicians who doubted Dvořák's idea that American music can and has to be built on the characteristic features of Negro and Indian melodies. He wrote an essay about it in the monthly North American Review. I did not show this essay to Master before I had delivered the Symphony to Seidl. When he read it, he said: "So, Seidlicek [nick-name for Seidl] doubts it, too? Well, we will have to wait and see what he will say later."

Their meeting next day was quite funny. The gentlemen talked about everything but the Symphony. I was sitting there on tenterhooks! At five, the painful waiting ended. Before they left, Seidl called me aside and told me that he was going to examine the score the whole evening, and added: "Wissen Sie, die Sinfonie ist lauter Indianermusik!" On the way home, when I was telling Master about Seidl's remark, he said smiling: "So, Seidl has changed his mind? He will not be the last one!"

The title of the Symphony *From the New World* provoked then, and still does — at least in America — many disputes and much furor. There were many who said, and are still saying that the disputed title should be understood as designating the work as an American Symphony, and that Master gave it an American stamp. This is a mistake. The additional part of the title, produced in the very last moment, was only one of Master's "innocent jests." The title means nothing more than "Impressions and Greetings From the New World," as he once described it.

So, when the premiere of the symphony was finally over, and Master could read the various opinions given by the editors and critics concerning the title *From the New World*, he laughed and said: "It seems to me that I messed up their thinking a bit" and added, "However, everybody back home will understand immediately what I had in mind."

Dvořák's ideas were intimately linked with his homeland, and this remark proved true. At that time, in his letter from November 16, 1893, he wrote to Dr. Tragy:

> There is something else in my heart that I want to tell you. I have been asked to extend my contract here for one or two more years, and I would like to ask your advice about what to do. It would suit the situation in my family because I would be able to make enough money that I should not worry about my livelihood as long I live.
>
> You surely know that my love for my country is above everything, and that I always will offer my services where they will be needed. After my return home, I will always work for the welfare and development of our national art. I would like to accomplish this, and with God's help, I will finish all my tasks which I have begun, and about which I always dreamed.
>
> Therefore, I beg you, respectable Doctor and friend, to trust me if I should stay here a year or two longer for the benefit of my family. You can be sure that I will heed your call immedi-

ately, and will be willing to return to my homeland if needed. I beg you to answer me as soon as possible, or better, write me immediately, because I need to give my decision to Mrs. Thurber (our President).

With my profound respect, Yours, Antonín Dvořák

P.S. My new symphony in E-minor will be produced on the 15th of December, and on the 16th again. The conductor is the famous pupil of Wagner, Anton Seidl, the Director of the Philharmonic Society of New York.

In a similar way, Dvořák confided his problem openly to Antonin Rus. He wrote him shortly before the premiere of the Symphony *From the New World*, on the 12th of December, 1893:

Our life here is always quite monotonous. We go nowhere, and I have to sit at school, and then just a few steps home, sitting some more and smoking, or sometimes working. The children can bother sometimes, too—and this is all that we can do here. Although theatres are here, too, there is nothing for us to see— mostly just the clamor and comedy that they like best here. Also there is the Grand Opera—everything from Europe, of course, with an extremely expensive budget that can swallow lots of millions. But Americans are rich, and want to pay only for what they really like.

I have not yet been to the Opera, and am not sure if I want to go. The miserable opera theatre cannot excite me any more, and until it changes for the better, I do not want to know anything about it. I am sorry now that I had sacrificed so much work and time to my operas in the past. However, I should not be lamenting only, and better tell you about something more pleasing.

For the next Friday and Saturday, the Philharmonic Society in New York prepares the first production of my Symphony in E-minor. The papers write that this event is awaited with great expectation.

The American public at large was really excited about this event, and the changes this new Symphony *From the New World* would bring to American culture.

Pilgrimage ⌇ B

Located several miles from Manhattan, Newark airport was the launching point for our flight to Buffalo. New York City was still sleepy with streets half empty and unusually peaceful as we drove to catch our morning plane.

This flight, which we planned to take before our big trip to Chicago and Spillville, was one hour long. We had breakfast at the Buffalo airport, rented a car for the day, and drove to Niagara Falls. Everything went according to our plan, and soon we were only twenty miles from the fulfillment of my boyish dream to see the famous waterfalls. Dvořák here, on his way back to New York City, admired and enjoyed this miracle of nature tremendously, and inspired by its great majesty, he wished to compose a new symphony, in B-flat, on a powerful theme he had heard above the whirlpool.

The highway took us along the Niagara River which spans the 35-mile distance between Lake Erie and Lake Ontario. Across the river from Buffalo is Fort Erie, the fortress named after the lake. The lake waters flow into the river, shallow and wide there, running faster and faster as they come closer to the falls. On the other side is Canada. Only the river separates the two countries, and to me both sides looked the same—the same houses and trees on each side of the current.

Finally we came to Niagara City; the hotels, restaurants, police, the waterworks, motels, services, shops, everything is designed for the tourists. The original town is located farther above the edge of the waterfalls.

Attracted by the sight of that roaring phenomenon, we parked our Fiat and hurried to join the crowds at the terraces viewing the falls. The seagulls circled elegantly around our heads, and the sounds of thunder came from the abyss beneath us. The water was dashed against the rocks on the bottom of the foamy river, clouding the air with fog. Millions of miniature drops flew against my face and glasses, temporarily blinding me.

A stunning experience, indeed. The river is about three-quarters of a mile wide, and the waterfall on the Canadian side must be half a mile across and almost 50 yards high. The American side is less formidable. From the airplane, the waterfalls must look like a horseshoe with a little nail on one side, Goat Island.

While Honza was taking pictures, I studied the map. Looking at it, I tried to guess the exact spot which had contributed so greatly to Dvořák's overwhelming experience and inspired him with new ideas a century ago.

Traveling from Chicago, through Jackson and Detroit to New York City, the Dvořáks' train had crossed the Canadian border to Ontario. The trip took them through the Province along Lake Erie to Niagara City in the United States. Dvořák was quite excited by the exceptional grandeur of the scene. At that time Niagara Falls was one of the wonders of the world. However, the observation towers on both sides—American and Canadian—were not built then, and the Dvořáks could not take a lift up to the top and see the falls from a height, as we did.

After seeing the falls, we continued our drive along the river up to Lake Ontario. On the cliff above the water towered a fortress similar to bastions of the seventeenth and eighteenth centuries. The Niagara River here seemed more docile and placid, and the beautiful lake of heavenly blue color was marbled with thousands of white ice floes. Playful waves embraced the water's surface, and I became so impressed by the sight that I promised myself I would write about it sometime.

On the way back to the falls, Honza, skeptical as usual, dampened my enthusiasm: "So, we didn't find anything about Dvořák at the Falls, I guess!"

He was probably right. The commercialized setting could no longer remind us of Dvořák's visit. Perhaps the poetic changeability of the Falls, with seagulls entering and reappearing from the foggy cloud above the whirlpool, and a rainbow arching above it, had been enough to inspire him. Perhaps Dvořák's pious mind was concentrated on God, the Creator. The excitement may have brought melodies to his mind which could have been woven into a symphony, but alas, we can only imagine what he really experienced.

Back in New York City, Dvořák felt the pressure of everyday responsibilities, and felt also that finishing touches must be given to the Symphony *From the New World*. His soul, however, still vibrated with the emotions which he had brought with him from the endless, ripening fields around Spillville. Maybe even some Indian music from the medicine-man show still remained in his head. In the past, Indians used to live around Niagara, too, but now only the figure of a paddling Indian on the relief decorating the entrance of the hydro-electric plant reminded one of their existence. This was the first hydroelectric plant in the world, and was built according to the ideas of Nikola Tesla.

Although our trip to Niagara had been short, our impressions were unforgettable. Several days later, before our departure from Spillville, while we were walking on the village green, along the Turkey River, I thought of the Niagara and the Indians again. Dvořák certainly had found some traces of the surviving Indian tribes during his trip to the waterfalls, and maybe they had lived right here on this end of the Iowa settlement, too.

At the end of our visit to Spillville, my guides Lilian and Marie asked if I was satisfied with my findings there. I tried to assure them that everything was very good, just what I needed. However, Lilian did not feel that way and was afraid that I had not found enough materials. She surprised me with their offer to take me to Des Moines.

I could not believe what I had just heard. Lilian must have read my thoughts. But she laughed and explained that she had remembered what I was talking about when we crossed the Mississippi River on our way to Spillville. She recalled my wish to visit the Historic Museum in the capital city of the State of Iowa. It was true; I had expressed such a wish.

"Look, I'm doing it for Dvořák's sake," Lilian assured me, since she was determined to go there. "You fought to make this trip in Czechoslovakia, and actually planned it from the ground up. Now you must finish what you started."

So we went to Des Moines. What would happen there? I did not know, but I was willing to take a chance.

The hilly landscape with pastures, woods, and creeks escorted us up to Fort Atkinson. The entire scene changed there and extensive fields awaited us as we turned southwest. We passed Jackson, Lawder, and New Hampton, to prairies with black, fertile soil—the real Iowa.

"Des Moines is about three hundred miles away, and we can be there in a short time," Lilian informed us.

The highway was straight, and the farm country on the map looked like a chessboard. Its order was disturbed only by the big rivers; the Mississippi River on the East, and the Missouri River on the West, with the state of Iowa in between. No European-style villages along the road, just little towns and lonely farms spread over the vast land. Des Moines was settled in the middle of the plains.

The city was founded in the first half of the nineteenth century, and is still young. Its urban design shows regularity of streets lined with magnificent buildings, and winding through it is the river which gave it its name. Having an important railroad intersection helped the city to grow quickly. At the time of Dvořák's visit, fifteen periodicals, fifteen churches and eight bridges were there. It is the home of a university and of many factories and places of business. The most important point of the city for my research was the state library!

We rented rooms in the Plaza Motel located on the outskirts of the city, and since our guides insisted again on bowling after supper, we had to join them. While we were waiting for our game, Honza and I had a few chances to try our bowling skill, but it was hopeless. We decided to leave it for the ladies, and we talked about the research we planned for the next day.

Iowa is the state in which Dvořák spent the summer of 1893 — a blessed summer for him, and for his music, too. As I had already learned, history is a very important subject to the American people. They like the past, and therefore I hoped that their respect for and emphasis on history had not let them forget about Dvořák and his visit to their state. I expected to find some new materials for my research there.

Next afternoon, we went to the State Historical Memorial and Art Building where I asked for materials concerning Dvořák, who had visited Iowa for three months in the summer of 1893. As always, my anxiety was tremendous because I had to wait. I could easily write an essay about impatience and eagerness. Suddenly, the clerk returned, asked me to sign the receipt, and handed me an extensive file.

The file contained materials of different sorts; clippings, newspaper articles from papers and journals of different kinds, all dealing with Dvořák. I read every word in the documents, but found no letters. Only one English memoir which somebody had typed was included. The handwritten note said that the author was Josef J. Kovarik, "the pupil and secretary of A. Dvořák."

Among the articles was one which was written in Czech under the pen name Musicus and was quite interesting. It was published in *Hlas* (*Voice*) in June of 1933, bearing the title "What Antonín Dvořák Composed in Spillville, and What He Didn't," with the subtitle, "On the 40th Anniversary of His Vacation in the Bohemian Settlement in Spillville, Iowa."

The same journal revealed some other interesting articles. For example, on the September 26 (perhaps 1933) there was one called "Commemorative Celebration of Dr. Antonín Dvořák in Spillville." This article, reprinted from a Cedar Rapids, Iowa, newspaper, described an Antonín Dvořák ceremony in Spillville at his commemorative monument there.

From the periodical *Music* (volume 4, 1893), published in Chicago, there was an extended review of Dvořák's *Requiem*. I found also a few smaller clippings. For example, the short article "Symphony Not Made in Iowa" cited Kovarik's opinion, written for Mrs. L. B. Schmidt; the paper *The Tribune Capital* announced on the November 15, 1929 that Highway 52 from Calmar to Conover, Spillville, Protivin, and Cresco, Iowa, continuing to Preston in the state of Minnesota, was given the name "Antonín Dvořák," in honor of the composer. Another clipping was a poem, honoring Dvořák, by Joe Flynn. Unfortunately, there was no information on the publisher or date.

The next clipping was an even more mysterious one, without any bibliographic date, and only the heading: "On Capitol Hill—Senate Ratifies Following Regulation…" and its seventh point said: "A New Ratification—the Approval of Dvořák's Largo as the Official Music of Iowa." The document showed the year 1951, nothing else.

This action by the Senate puzzled me a lot. What did the term official music really mean? Where was the link between Dvořák's Largo from the Symphony *From the New World* and the ratification? No explanation was readily available.*

There was also an English booklet, *Dvořák's Visit to Spillville*. It was the work of W. A. Dostal, the priest at St. John of Nepomuk Church in Fort Atkinson, which I had found in its Czech version elsewhere.

Another newspaper clipping, from the Des Moines *Register,* was an article about somebody called Alois Kovarik, now 78. As a little boy, he accompanied Dvořák for early morning fishing. He became a professor of physics at Yale University, and in 1959, after he had retired, was living in Spillville.

The Chicago *Times* of August 12, 1893, carried information about Bohemian Day during the World Exposition. More articles, notes, and even an idealized sketch of Dvořák's portrait were included in the materials.

---

*Additional notes include new documents about this event which were sent to us from the Iowa State Senate. —Translator's note

Among them were a few articles written by Mrs. L. B. Schmidt—the same lady to whom Kovarik had sent a letter saying that the Symphony *From the New World* was not composed in Iowa. She must have been profoundly interested in Dvořák's music, and I wanted to know who this lady really was.

Everybody in our company was anxiously following my work, and Lilian offered to search for the mysterious lady. This I welcomed.

Among the other materials was a document written by Dvořák's pupil, Harry Rowe Shelley. He remembered:

> To become a successful student in Dvořák's class, you had to have a thorough knowledge of the basics, which he himself did not teach. Dvořák's job was to point out to the student all the good and bad sides of the work which he had brought that day. They discussed the natural interrelations between the keys of the contrasting themes and the orchestral color which was most favorable for the contents. He stressed that music should never be written at random for an instrument, but rather for the instrument most appropriate for the musical expression according to the demands of the composition. He insisted on regular work and urged the students to present at least three new sections of a large composition each week. He used to say: "If you cannot do this, you are not a composer."
>
> He reserved for himself the right either to teach the student or discharge him for lack of talent in composition, saying: "This will hurt you just once but save you lots of pain later. Good-bye!"
>
> He passionately disliked charlatans. For example, when the student used material from another composer, or used ideas faintly reminiscent of some other composer's music, he was angrily rebuked with the sharp remark: "Perhaps—but it is not from you!" He began to realize that American students work differently from those he had known in Bohemia and lack respect for the entire musical art which he valued to its highest degree. He loathed the popular songs of the so-called Viennese schraml, calling it the cafe style.
>
> He used to cite the ideas Hanslick had given in his review of the *Slavonic Dances,* when he wrote that the first one is the most musical, the second most nationalistic, and the third is the most beautiful.
>
> Twenty minutes after he finished writing the theme of the Largo in his Symphony *From the New World,* he sang it with fervor, his eyes dilated, the veins in his neck flooded with pulsing

blood. When he played it for somebody, his body would begin to tremble and he would ask: "Isn't it beautiful music?" Seidl was responsible for Dvořák calling this movement "Largo," and not "Larghetto" as he originally named it. Seidl was always pleased to conduct the Symphony. It was the last work he conducted in his career; however, he often criticized its name: "This is not a good title for it—From the New World! It means tremendous longing and homesickness."

Dvořák spent New York afternoons in the Viennese cafe with one or two of his friends, talking about music, sipping coffee, or occasionally beer, always contributing some clear idea about the musical problem under discussion. Once, he showed them a letter from Simrock. The publisher wrote that Brahms had just told him how much he appreciated the music of Dvořák and that Brahms, too, really wished to know how to write music that held so much sunshine.

Dvořák made one of his pupils work on solving the thematic problems of an overture for forty weeks, giving him three lessons a week. This student wrote thousands of measures after which Master evaluated his work thus: "Well, now you have it in good shape, and finally you know the ways in which composers have worked from Haydn down to me. If you ever try to be a copy of somebody else, you will become a bad musician. Work now in your own way."

Often pupils asked Dvořák why he did not like certain parts of their composition—parts which they personally appreciated and were quite proud of. His answer was clear: "I don't know; simply—I don't!" His judgment was meant for the pupil's future musical development, and perhaps he did not have time to work out the musical "mathematics" without having the appropriate academic equipment available.

He disliked the fugal style, and proclaimed: "Yes, this is a good theme but why should one annoy the listener by telling him the same thing over and over? It might be offensive."

He recommended that students compose a quarter of an hour in the morning, sketching out the themes and material for further work, saying: "If you would be a composer, write your ideas down when they are fresh in the morning."

He was a great man, and he became one of those immortal composers whose music has become the divine inheritance of the whole world.

It was interesting testimony and in detail, too. The author Harry Rowe Shelley was one of Dvořák's famous pupils, and he ought to know the details. For example, when Dvořák sang the Largo, and Seidl made his comments, Shelley heard them firsthand.

In 1941, Josef J. Kovarik wrote about Shelley in the article "About Dvořák's School of Composition in New York City":

> born in 1858 in New Haven, in the State of Connecticut, he became the organist of various Protestant churches, mostly in Brooklyn. His larger works include two operas and two symphonies, an orchestral suite, a violin concerto, the *Santa Claus Overture* and a few cantatas.

Besides these documents, there was other testimony given by Camille W. Zeckwer, who was also Dvořák's pupil. Josef J. Kovarik characterized him in his article, too. He wrote:

> …an excellent pianist and violinist (he studied violin with Florian Zajic in Hamburg), born in Philadelphia, Pennsylvania, in 1875, and died there in 1924. Master liked him very much, and appreciated his great talent. Zeckwer wrote several valuable works of which the most famous are: Suite for Violin and Piano, two violin Sonatas with piano, and a Piano Trio.

A variety of other compositions cited by Kovarik followed: "…an opera and a serenade, *Mélancolique* for the violoncello." Zeckwer described in his slightly sarcastic memoirs the following circumstances:

> My contact with Dvořák was the high point in my life. In spite of the twenty-five years which have passed since I was privileged to study with that fantastic man, the memories of that precious time of my youth are still fresh and alive.

Zeckwer recollected the time when, as a lad, he wrote his four-movement sonata for piano and, "armed with my composition, I went to New York to meet Dvořák personally."

He continued:

> The old man was sitting at a table in the far corner of the room. He blinked at me as if I'd been some tax-collector, or an insurance agent, and without any response to my greetings, he ordered me to play my sonata. At that moment, I lost the rest of my nerve and managed to play only with a great effort. I tried to steady myself, counting out beats carefully and thinking of

how much longer I could play before breaking down completely. To my surprise, I finished the first movement uninterrupted.

With enormous relief, and growing confidence, I followed the composer's command to continue. Before I finished the whole sonata, the ridicule on his face changed to an expression of satisfaction. The real kindness of this man came through when he offered me a scholarship. He even talked me into moving to New York so that I could study with him daily.

My dear father was waiting for me downstairs. He had tried several times to make contact with Dvořák before, but never succeeded in meeting him. The despot was quite unattainable, except when things went as he willed.

After I was registered, I was immediately assigned to write a trio for violin and violoncello. This work included nine different modulations in the first movement, following those of Beethoven's piano sonatas. My assignment was so detailed that I had to adjust my themes to the perfect modulations and beats of Beethoven's work. My first concept of the slow movement was formulated in a similar way to the Adagio of his Sonata *Pathétique*. Only then, as the space of my imagination grew larger and freer, was I allowed to proceed with my work on the original slow movement. A painstaking study of Schumann gave me the basics for the *Scherzo*.

Obviously, the original scores of these great Masters were the textbooks Dvořák used in his classes. He loathed pedagogical treatises. Most of all, he loved Schubert. He looked up to him as if he were a prophet, and often said paradoxically that the music of the future could be found only by looking back, into the past—actually, to Schubert—by trying the expansion of his musical ideas into the modern melodic forms.

"Schubert," he used to say, "yes, Schubert, this was very long ago—long ago, indeed—but not for me!"

One of Dvořák's likeable vanities was reading reviews of his own symphonies. When he found that somebody had compared him with Beethoven, he chuckled impishly. Of course, these comparisons were based on symphonies written prior to *From the New World*. This new work signalled a higher level in his development as a composer.

However, we could observe almost no sign of this kindly, naive side of his character during his classes. I have often seen him tweaking the nose of some unfortunate student, pulling him across the classroom, a form of punishment that apparently gave him closer anatomical contact with the culprit than the time-honored pulling of the ear lobes.

Fortunately, I always escaped this special pedagogical method. I was none of those spoiled brats, not at all! However, I can only guess at how many times he threw my innocent manuscript on the floor, savagely crushing it under his heel. He underlined this theatrical performance by grunting like a wild boar. Presently his safety valve would allow his anger to dissipate and then, almost kindly and tenderly, he would lift my offensive manuscript off the floor and make some remarks about a few bars which by some miracle had escaped the destructive power of his heels.

When he finished composing his Symphony *From the New World,* he played it for me in its entirety, and he also took me with him for the first rehearsals by Seidl.

One morning, he said to me: "Oh, my dear Philadelphia" (the name he gave me), I don't have time for your lesson today. However, you might go with me; Seidl is going to rehearse my overtures today (*In Nature's Realm, Othello, Carnival*). He took me by the arm and led me inside the hall, where I had to sit beside him as his enthusiastic audience.

It was said at the conservatory one day that Dvořák was sick. That morning I had come early from Philadelphia, and his absence disappointed me bitterly. Suspicious of Dvořák's sudden sickness, I took the trouble to find him at his home. When I knocked timidly at his door, there was no answer, so I entered anyway. His only sickness was "composition fever." The room was littered with the leftovers of unfinished meals, and it seemed to me that he had barricaded himself in for at least several days. My interruption could absolutely not be ignored, and my ingenious excuses reached his ears. Initially, he agreed to go through a few bars of my work, and then he kept me with him for several hours.

I continued to invite him to visit me in Philadelphia. Finally he agreed, but at the moment he was to board the train, he ran off without an explanation! Later, I learned that he was afraid it would be impossible for him to go to mass at six o'clock next morning, which was his invariable custom.

As I already said, the instructions of my Master were entirely based on the legacy of Beethoven, Schubert, Brahms and Wagner. However, the dominant influence on my creative work came only from the inspirational resources of his individuality. Those two years of my study with him (1894–1895) were my great privilege, and were the important impulse given to my nineteen- and-twenty-year-old youth. At the same time, however, I was too young and immature to do justice to this great opportunity in my life. I could not yet absorb everything that came with it. There is no right formula for combining the enthusiasm of twenty years with the wide horizons one has in his forties.

My father wrote to Dvořák to get permission for me to stay with him after he returned to Prague, but he never received an answer. I always missed his presence; and everywhere I went abroad during my European studies, I felt that something was lacking. After him, none of my teachers could give me such inspiration. Dvořák to me was like my second father—good, kind, godlike, with great admiration for everything beautiful in art and life. He could be as unpretentious as a child, but he trusted his own opinions. He often gave proof of his inviolable conscience and his profound authority.

As a special paradox in his life, there is the fact that, though Dvořák composed his best works in this country, his life in New York was immensely unhappy. He said to me: "Do you know, my dear Philadelphia, that I now make fifteen thousand dollars a year? But fifteen years ago, when I was hungry, I was much happier."

At the time, half of Dvořák's children were in Prague, and his wife, who stayed with him in America, could not understand our country at all. Her constant complaining must have increased his longing for his homeland even more.

In spite of this, as I already said, Dvořák found great inspiration here and profoundly believed that the new musical school in America would originate from Indian and Negro melodies. However, themes used in his work were slightly colored with a Bohemian flavor—not that which is found in New York, but with the true inner spirit of his native Bohemia.

These statements ring true but perhaps instead of "slightly colored" one should say slightly saturated, or permeated. However consciously Zeckwer may have been looking for the example which might lead him to overstate his case (which is quite typical of American memoirs), his recollections show respect and the ability to make penetrating observation. In his conclusion, when he cited Dvořák's sigh about happiness, the significance of the author's statement extended far beyond the level of the story itself.

I can remember the question one had to ask himself at the Chicago cemetery, "What is happiness, really?" I do not know if there is any answer to it.

Honza showed me more clippings. God knows how they got here, and who collected them. One came from the *Ames Daily Tribune,* dated the 3rd of October, 1925. It carried a detailed account of the unveiling ceremony of Dvořák's commemorative monument in Spillville. The speech was given by Mrs. L. B. Schmidt again.

Another clipping was from November 19, 1893. The *New York Herald* carried in its distinctive style an extended interview with the composer. As far as I can determine, the article has never been printed in its entirety in Europe. It has many interesting passages about the first information of the coming premiere of Dvořák's new symphony. The date suggests that at the time of the interview, the title of the symphony was not yet known.

The article was illustrated with a drawing of "Dvořák in Spillville."

The sketch shows the composer at the organ surrounded by Spillville women standing amongst the pews. This picture of the St. Wenceslaus church is a composite, showing part of the downstairs nave on the same floor

DVORAK AT SPILLVILLE.

Sketch of "Dvorak in Spillville" in the *New York Herald,* November 19, 1893 as the choir loft. The artist had never seen this church before, and could not know about his mistake. His picture, however, had possibly another purpose than to provide an exact description of the scene. Perhaps he wanted to deepen the interest of American society in the life of the famous composer, and show him as he played for country folks in the simple church. On the other hand, perhaps he meant to lend importance to the interview.

In the article, Dvořák enumerated the activities of the conservatory during the past year and spoke about the compositions of his students, written under his leadership. The major part of the interview was given over to a discussion of religious music. Dvořák recalled his activities in the Spillville church the previous summer, admitting that he was "moved to tears" by the reaction of the settlers toward his work.

The interview concluded very simply and adequately: "And so his work goes on."

I stretched a bit, but before I could rest, Lilian appeared in the library door, bringing good news: "Mrs. Schmidt was the wife of a professor at the Iowa State University, in Ames."

"Now I know why her article was carried by the Ames paper," I thought aloud.

"What article?"

"Here it is," and I showed her the article from October 3, 1925, containing Mrs. Schmidt's address given in Spillville. Lilian read the long headline:

"Thousands Attend Dedication of Dvořák Memorial at Spillville Monday; Ames Woman Is Speaker."

In the first paragraph was written that

> Before an audience estimated at more than 3000, Iowa's memorial to the visit of Antonín Dvořák, Bohemian composer, was dedicated Monday, Sept. 28, at Spillville, where the famous musician lived during one summer 32 years ago. Mrs. Louis B. Schmidt, chairman of the historic spots committee of the Iowa Conservation association, delivered the dedicatory address. As she finished, Humoresque was played by George Kovarik, nephew of Prof J. J. Kovarik, Dvořák's most intimate friend and pupil in Prague, and the memorial was unveiled.

Lilian could not believe that the ceremony was held on a Monday. After a while it came to me:

"That day was September 28, Saint Wenceslaus' Day in Bohemia, the Patron's Day of the Spillville church."

In the address, Mrs. L. B. Schmidt said:

> Friends!
> We have gathered here today to commemorate an event in the cultural history of our state. This is the first memorial erected to honor a musician within the borders of our state. This event is one of more than state wide interest. It is one of national and international interest for the name of Dr. Antonín Dvořák is known throughout the entire world.

Mrs. Schmidt described every detail of her club's achievement. Her words indicated that she was the representative of the Iowa Federation of Music clubs, which would explain her own interest in music. She continued:

> Five years of investigation has given me the absolute belief that Dvořák found the inspiration for Humoresque in these woods and hills.... Much, too much, has been written and said about the "New World Symphony" having been composed in this entirety here. Investigation shows that this story is without foundation. Evidence shows that only minor changes were made here and the orchestrations completed.

To support her statement, she cited the letter written to her by Josef J. Kovarik, which I had found in Spillville. Only a few of that letter's details need be recalled: Dvořák did not have the means to buy the scores of old masters, did not possess the necessary four cents to enable him to hear the performance of *Der Freischutz,* did not have the use of a piano for lack of funds to rent one, and waited years for recognition.

Considering the Symphony *From the New World,* Kovarik wrote to Mrs. Schmidt:

> Now, Spillville, [Iowa] is generally regarded as the place where this work originated—but erroneously. The best way to put it would be thus: born in New York baptized in Spillville, and confirmed in New York—that is, written in New York, some changes in the score in Spillville, and its first performance in New York.

"Well said," Lilian remarked.

In another letter to Mrs. Schmidt from Kovarik there was one more mention of the Symphony:

> Dvořák worked (in Spillville) on the score of the Symphony *From the New World,* made a few changes in the Largo and in

the finale of the last movement. Then he began another work in the domain of chamber music; this time, the Quintet in E Flat Major for strings, with added viola. This work, even if not frequently performed, according to my opinion, excels over his Quartet in F Major. The third movement, a theme with variations, is one of the best movements ever written. At first, this theme had been considered by Dvořák for the melody of our new (American) anthem.

"I did not know that," Lilian admitted.

The conclusion of L. B. Schmidt's address was very poetic. She said:

> [Y]ou can never separate Dvořák's visit from Iowa. He was here—here under these trees. Here he wandered along the banks of this stream. He was often physically and in a sense mentally lost in these woods—for when the song of a wild bird drew his attention he forgot all but the power and beauty of that bird's song. Dr. Dvořák was here on the streets of this village with his songs, his art—and today the memory of him lingers here.
>
> Antonín Dvorak, the winds
> In the prairie grasses sigh no more,
> The wild bird's notes are hushed,
> Your heart has ceased to beat.
> But memory blesses us this day
> And in the years that are to come
> Of winter's snow and summer's sun
> Your name will live. Amen.

Marie Hosek, the gray-haired woman whose grandchildren know only a few Bohemian words, secretly dried her tears. Lilian Picha cleared her throat, and afraid that she would spoil that precious moment, whispered to me:

"Miroslav, I know now where you would like to go."

Did I understand? Yes, she had said that we were going to Ames. Perhaps some other property of Mrs. Schmidt, who had liked Dvořák so much, could be found. Maybe our pilgrimage would finally lead us to some special, unexpected point. So the same day, we went to Ames and visited the campus of Iowa State University.

Victory ∽ A

F RIDAY CAME LIKE MILLIONS of ordinary Fridays since the beginning of time. People went on with their lives, not knowing that somewhere something important had just happened, something quite extraordinary.

It was December 15, 1893, in New York City. For several weeks concertgoers had lived with special expectations. They knew that Dvořák's new composition had been rehearsed by Anton Seidl and the Philharmonic. They knew also that Dvořák's theory of Indian and Negro music could become the foundation for the new American music.

On the day of the public rehearsal in an overfilled hall, December 15, 1893, the *New York Herald* carried an expressive article under the title "Dvořák on His New Work."

The subheads specified: "An Interesting Talk about *From the New World* Symphony, to Be Produced for the First Time To-Day."

How many interviews had been carried by the press concerning Dvořák's activities in America? Some of them were not serious, written for stimulation and excitement only; others gave quite explicit accounts of the composer's opinions. In an article published December 15, Dvořák talked about his Symphony and the intentional experiments in his work. Here is the introduction to the interview with the composer's comment:

Dr. Antonín Dvořák, the Bohemian composer and director of
the National Conservatory of Music, has been in this country a
little over a year. America has strongly affected his sensitive
imagination. He has made a serious study of the national music
of this continent as exemplified in the native melodies of the
Negro and Indian races. What the effect of this study has been,
the New York public will have an opportunity of hearing this
afternoon. Then will be played at Carnegie Music Hall, the first
fruits of his musical genius in this country. It is a long symphony for full orchestra, is called *From the New World,* and will
receive its first performance in public at the Philharmonic concert to-day.

Chattily at his residence, No. 327 East Nineteenth [*sic*]
street, last evening, Dr. Dvořák gave a few details regarding this
his latest composition. "Since I have been in this country I have
been deeply interested in the national music of the Negroes and
the Indians. The character, the very nature of a race is contained
in its national music. For that reason my attention was at once
turned in the direction of these native melodies. I found that
the music of the two races bore a remarkable similarity to the
national music of Scotland. In both there is a peculiar scale,
caused by the absence of the fourth and seventh, or leading
tone. In both the minor scale has the seventh invariably a minor
seventh, the fourth is included and the sixth is omitted."

The Scotch Scale

"Now the Scotch scale, if I may so call it, has been used to
impart a certain color to musical composition. I need only
instance Mendelssohn's *Hebrides* overture. This device is a
common one. In fact, the scale in question is only a certain form
of the ancient ecclesiastical modes. These modes have been
employed time and time again. For example, Felicien David in
his symphonic ode *Le Desert,* Verdi in *Aida*. I have myself used
one of them in my D minor symphony.

"Now, I found that the music of the Negroes and of the
Indians was practically identical. I therefore carefully studied a
certain number of Indian melodies which a friend gave me and
became thoroughly imbued with their characteristics — with
their spirit, in fact.

"It is this spirit which I have tried to reproduce in my new
symphony. I have not actually used any of the melodies. I have
simply written original themes embodying the peculiarities of

the Indian music, and using these themes as subjects, have developed them with all the resources of modern rhythms, harmony, counterpoint and orchestration.

"The symphony is in E minor. It is written upon the classical model and it is in four movements. It opens with a short introduction, an adagio, of about thirty bars in length. This leads directly into the allegro, which embodies the principles which I have already worked out in my Slavonic dances, that is, to preserve, to translate into music, the spirit of a race as distinct in its national melodies or folk songs.

"The second movement is an adagio. But it is different to [*sic*] the classic works in this form. It is in reality, a study, or sketch for a longer work, either a cantata or opera which I purpose writing, and which will be based upon Longfellow's *Hiawatha*. I have long had the idea of some day utilizing that poem. I first became acquainted with it about thirty years ago through the medium of Bohemian translation. It appealed very strongly to my imagination at that time, and the impression has only been strengthened by my residence here.

"The scherzo of the symphony was suggested by the scene at the feast in *Hiawatha* where the Indians dance, and is also an effort which I made in the direction of imparting the local color of Indian character in music."

The Final Movement

"The last movement is an allegro con feroco [*sic*]. All the previous themes reappear and are treated in a variety of ways. The instruments required are only those of what we call the 'Beethoven orchestra,' consisting of strings, four horns, three trombones, two trumpets, two flutes, two oboes, two clarinets, two bassoons and tympani. There is no harp and I did not find it necessary to add any novel instrument in order to get the effect I wanted.

"I have indeed been busy since I came to this country. I have finished a couple of compositions in chamber music, which will be played by the Kneisel String Quartet, of Boston, next January, in Music Hall. They are both written upon the same lines as this symphony and both breathe the same Indian spirit. One is a string quartet in F Major and the other a quintet in E-flat for two violins, two violas and violoncello."

It is possible that some of these articles were written by the editor of the *New York Herald;* however, the content and the facts are undoubtedly Dvořák's. One word quoted wrong would easily change the whole sentence. For example, when he said: "I found that the music of the two races [Indians and Negroes] bore a remarkable similarity to the national music of Scotland."

We can only guess as to when the Friday rehearsal of the Symphony started. In spite of rain, a waiting line for tickets had formed at noon. Dvořák was not present that afternoon, and later, Kovarik wrote the following about the concert in one of his letters to Sourek:

> The first production of the Symphony was in Carnegie Hall on Friday, December 16th, 1893. The concerts on Friday afternoon are called "public rehearsals"; and because Master was absent at the first production, I went to hear it myself. Master and his family were present at the concert on Saturday evening.

The *New York Herald* editor described the famous Friday afternoon in an extended article, carried on Saturday, December 16, 1893, under the title: "Dr. Dvořák's Great Symphony."

The subheads described the occasion in an impressive way:

> *From the New World* Heard for the First Time at the Philharmonic Rehearsal — ABOUT THE SALIENT BEAUTIES — First Movement the Most Tragic, Second the Most Beautiful,

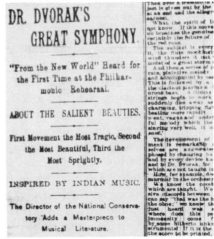

The *New York Herald* of December 16, 1893, devoted most of its pages to the premier of the Symphony *From the New World,* including a portrait of Dvořák.

Third the Most Sprightly—INSPIRED BY INDIAN MUSIC
—The Director of the National Conservatory Adds a Masterpiece to Musical Literature.

Dr. Antonín Dvořák, the famous Bohemian composer and
director of the National Conservatory of Music, dowered
American art with a great work yesterday, when his new symphony in E minor, *From the New World,* was played at the
second Philharmonic rehearsal in Carnegie Music Hall.

The day was an important one in the musical history of
America. It witnessed the first public performance of a noble
composition.

It saw a large audience of usually tranquil Americans
enthusiastic to the point of frenzy over a musical work and
applauding like the most excitable "Italianissimi" in the world.

The work was one of heroic porportions [*sic*]. And it was
one cast in the art form which such poet-musicians as
Beethoven, Schubert, Schumann, Mendelssohn, Brahms and
many another "glorious one of the earth" has enriched with the
most precious outwellings of his musical imagination.

And this new symphony by Dr. Antonín Dvořák is worthy
to rank with the best creations of those musicians whom I have
just mentioned.

Small wonder that the listeners were enthusiastic. The
work appealed to their sense of the aesthetically beautiful by its
wealth of tender, pathetic, fiery melody; by its rich harmonic
clothing; by its delicate, sonorous, gorgeous, ever varying
instrumentation.

And it appealed to the patriotic side of them.

For had not Dr. Dvořák been inspired by the impressions
which this country had made upon him? Had he not translated
these impressions into sounds, into music? Had they not been
assured by the composer himself that the work was written
under the direct influence of a serious study of the national
music of the North American Indians? Therefore were they not
justified in regarding this composition, the first fruits of
Dr. Dvořák's musical genius since his residence in the country,
as a distinctly American work of art?

Thus there was every reason for enthusiasm.

Even the orchestra seemed to be transformed by the singu-
lar beauty of the symphony. Certainly the members put ever so
much better work into it than they had previously exhibited in

the preceding part of the programme. Even Mr. Seidl seemed to lose somewhat of his usual impassive air of calm authority, (as) he with quick, nervous gestures he communicated his wishes to the Philharmonic Orchestra.

It was essentially a ladies' day. The Philharmonic rehearsals always are. But yesterday, in particular, Carnegie Music Hall seemed to contain nothing but the members of the fairer sex.

The downpour of rain could not keep them away. At half-past one there were small groups of enthusiastic admirers of the Philharmonic, of music of Dr. Dvořák, of Marteau scattered about the great hall, chatting merrily, and to tell the truth, rather noisily, about a variety of matters—principally private, though that by no means caused them to moderate their voices.

Outside there was a long line of tardy ticket purchasers. Each individual in the row, which stretched down the steps and along Fifty-seventh street, impatiently tried to push forward his immediate predecessor. The ushers were like the people spoken of by the prophet who would "rush to and fro." And heartily tired of it all they looked long before the flutes gave the first notes of the *Midsummer Night's Dream* overture.

No one seemed quite at ease during the earlier part of the concert. There was an air of excitement pervading everyone. People read and reread the analytical notes accompanying the programme. I am sure that the lady next to me must have known by heart that "Dr. Dvořák made a study of Indian and Negro melodies and found them possessed of characteristics peculiarly their own." That "he identified himself with their spirit, made their essential contents, not their formal, external traits, his own," and that he had striven "to reproduce in the present symphony the fundamental characteristics of the melo-dies which he had found here by means of the specifically musi-cal resources which his inspiration furnished."

At any rate, she studied the remarks with an intensity that was rather awe inspiring.

In the following part of the article, the author carried his detailed analysis of the four movements of the composition, and was quite excited by his impressions. He concluded:

To sum up, the work is a remarkably beautiful one. It may be Indian in spirit, but it is Bohemian in atmosphere. Dr. Dvořák can no more divest himself of his nationality than the leopard change his spots.

That it is musicianly goes without saying. Nothing but superlative terms can describe the orchestration. The workmanship throughout is excellent.

And above all the spontaneity of the composition strikes one. Nowhere does it "smell of the lamp!" Dr. Dvořák evidently finds America congenial to his nature, for the work is the outcome of happy surroundings, or else music is the most deceptive of arts. It is sad, but it is the sadness of the Slavonic temperament which even in the happiest moments of life tinges everything with a gentle hue of quiet, tender melancholy.

The performance was excellent. Individually and collectively the orchestra did good work in the symphony.

The article is almost at an end. Some of the editor's remarks showed his sensitivity. For example, when he talked about leopard's spots or "Bohemian …atmosphere." He was less understanding, however, when he wrote that "Dvořák evidently finds America congenial to his nature, for the work is the outcome of happy surroundings."

First of all, Dvořák's character was not of an American type; he was different. Of course, immediately after this ingenious composer had arrived in this new continent, he was shocked, overfilled, and satiated by his impressions, which were good but also bad. Therefore his Symphony *From the New World* is a sum and expression of his life experiences, new to him, and of course, important to his perception.

In the conclusion of the article the editor offered "Some Musical Opinions":

When I saw Herr Seidl after the concert, he was delighted with the success of the new symphony. "I think," said he, "it will serve to inspire the younger American musicians to work in the lines laid down so successfully by Dr. Dvořák and which point in the direction of the establishment of a truly national school of musical composition."

"I like this symphony, I think it is a great work. I have discovered new beauties in it at every rehearsal. But from the very first I have been deeply impressed by the Adagio. It is so sad. It sounds to me so suggestive of the loneliness of the immense prairie; of the Far West. And it is pathetic with the pathos of homesickness."

Mr. Walter Damrosch said: "It is a most beautiful composition. I am not exaggerating in saying that the second movement, the adagio, is exquisite. It is a most welcome and valuable addition to the literature of the highest class of music—that for the orchestra. As to whether it is American or not I cannot say. To me it suggests nothing American. It is Dr. Dvořák. His genius has evolved the work and you can see him in every bit of the work."

Mr. Victor Herbert was enthusiastic in his praises of the new work. He, too, thought he preferred the Adagio. I asked him if he thought it would have any influence upon future compositions in this country. With a laugh he said, "Yes, if the composers are Dr. Dvořáks."

Mr. Richard Arnold, the concertmeister of the Philharmonic Orchestra, was equally strong in his expressions of admiration for the work. As to it forming a school, he did not think such a thing possible. Dr. Dvořák wrote the symphony in such a manner because he felt it in that way.

Dr. Dvořák was not present at the concert, as he had given his tickets to someone who was very desirous of hearing the work.

When I asked him which movement of the symphony he liked best. "Why, look you," he said, "I like all my children. An Adagio always appeals straight to the heart—if it is good. For this reason Richter says, Beethoven was the only musician who possessed the power of writing a grand second movement."

"As to which movement I prefer! Well, I will tell you a little anecdote. When Louis Elhert, the musical critic from Wiesbaden, first came across my Slavonic Rhapsodies, he wrote to me and said,'The first, in D Major, is most beautiful, the second in G minor, is the greatest, and the third, in A-flat Major, is the most national.' But he would not tell me which he liked the best. I am like Elhert."

People were leaving the hall, and the editor tried to get the names of the "most prominent visitors" (Mrs. F. Frances Hyde, Mrs. Samuel Thorne, Mrs. J. D. Rockefeller, and dozens of other well-known names were published in his article). Carnegie Hall was waiting for the celebrated premiere of the Symphony, which would be played under its roof the next day.

Nobody can tell us how Antonín Dvořák spent the afternoon and evening of December 15. His mind was probably wandering around the music hall, but the social ethic specified that the author should appear at the premiere. He was forced to wait for Kovarik's return and for his comments, and then quickly go to bed and sleep. Tomorrow would be an important day.

Saturday, December 16 came. The devoted Josef J. Kovarik has described what happened before the premiere, who visited them, and what the Dvořáks talked about.

Indeed, what else could they have talked about? The preparations for the evening concert had probably begun in the afternoon; the question of who would be sitting with Dvořák had been decided a long time ago. Only their plans for the evening awaited realization. Besides the composer, his wife Anna and daughter Otilia were going, and in another part of the city, Mrs. Jeanette Thurber, pianist Miss Adela Margulies, and two of Dvořák's students, Maurice Arnold Strathotte and Harry Worthington, all were getting ready, too.

Darkness comes early at this time of year. Finally, the coach arrived in 17th Street, at Dvořák's residence. It was too dark to wave from the window so they said quick good-byes in the entry hall. Everybody was getting nervous. In front of Carnegie Hall there was a long line waiting for any unsold tickets that might be available. Public interest in the event was increased to the maximum.

The *New York Herald* carried the detailed description of the famous evening the next day, Sunday, December 17, 1893. Two extended articles with headlines proclaimed:

Dvořák Hears His Symphony

Director of the National Conservatory of Music at the Second Performance—Played to a Vast Audience—House and Orchestra Enthusiastically Applaud the Famous Bohemian Composer—Score and Interpretation;

and

Dvořák's Symphony a Historic Event

First Rude Draft of the Original—Thought Appeared in the Herald—Eve of a New Musical Epoch—Much Credit Is Due to the Persistent Labors of Mrs. Jeanette Thurber—Critics Suffer a Defeat.

These indicate the festive air of that outstanding evening.

This was how the first of the articles characterized the high emotions of the event: "Radiant with happiness Dr. Antonín Dvořák listened to the second concert of the Philharmonic Society in Carnegie Music Hall last evening."

MR. SEIDL LEADING THE NEW DVORAK SYMPHONY.

This sketch in the *New York Herald,* December 16, 1893, accompanied the first review of the Symphony *From the New World* review.

The article continued:

> The famous Bohemian composer is indeed difficult to please if he was not gratified with the enthusiasm created in the immense audience by his new Fifth Symphony in E minor, *From the New World.*
>
> He received a genuine ovation after the second movement—the larghetto. The applause swelled to a perfect tumult. Every face was turned in the direction in which Anton Seidl was looking. Every neck was craned so that it might be discovered to whom he was motioning so energetically. Whoever it was, he seemed modestly to wish to remain at the back of the box on the second tier.
>
> At last a broad shouldered individual of medium height, and as straight as one of the pines in the forests of which his music whispered so eloquently, is descried by the eager watchers. A murmur sweeps through the hall. "Dvořák! Dvořák!" is the word that passes from mouth to mouth.
>
> And while he is bowing we have time to see what manner of man is this musician, this tone poet, who can grip the hearts

of a big audience and create every thought of beauty that the most sensitive imagination can conceive.

He is dark. Dark hair, scanty upon the top. A dark, short beard, fast becoming grey. Dark eyes, wide open with a cheerful steady look in them—a look which from time to time changes into a far away regard that has somewhat of pathos in it. The face is honest, kindly and with a general expression of a perfectly guileless nature.

The Man of the Hour. This is the man whom the audience is so rapturously applauding. It is his brain, his imagination which has called out of the vague unknown the work to which we have just been listening. It is upon this sensitive nature that the scenery of the New World has graven so deep an impression. And this man, so quiet, so dignified, so grave, is the first musician who has transformed into a wonderful thing of beauty the naive musical utterances of the red man and the untutored Negro.

With hands trembling with emotion Dr. Dvořák waves an acknowledgement of his indebtedness to Anton Seidl, to the orchestra, to the audience, and then disappears into the background while the remainder of the work goes on.

A second hearing only serves to deepen the impression created by the first audition on Friday afternoon.

The work is a great one. It is unique in certain respects. Rarely has a work of such grandiose proportions contained such an endless stream of melody.

The editor spoke again about the Negro and Indian melodies, about missing scale tones, and continued:

Following the principles which Brahms, Liszt, Schubert and even Haydn have followed in certain of their compositions, Dr. Dvořák made the spirit of this savage music his own. He became saturated with its peculiarities, with its rhythms, with its suggested harmonies.

Then he wrote this symphony upon the lines which he had already followed in his Slavonic Rhapsodies. He created original themes which partook of the characteristics which he had discovered in the native music. These themes he employed as the subjects, the backbone of his composition, developing, harmonizing and accompanying them in every manner which musical science and modern theories of harmony could suggest.

A Great Work of Art. The result is a great work of art. From the first note to the last there is not a wearisome passage. Effects of the most novel character are being continually unfolded to the listener. Piquant rhythms and combinations of rhythms strike the ear in every part of the work. The harmony is simple and yet it is full of fresh combinations which arrest the attention in many instances.

And the instrumentation! It is simply gorgeous. Such sonorous employment of the brass, such delicate combinations of the wood wind, such ever varying nuances and degrees of tone in the violins! A most happy effect is the repetition of the cor anglais solo in the larghetto by a single violin. The melody is broken in a reflective, hesitating manner. It recommences; again it remains unfinished, and then with all the violins, the pathetic subject closes the movement, leaving an indescribable feeling of sadness.

He is fond of the oboe in his orchestration, and the flute also sings some of the most lovely passages. That is an exquisite moment in the scherzo where the wood wind gives out a simple melody accompanied by interrupted trills in the strings.

This sense of rhythm is developed to the highest point. The subjects themselves are cast in novel rhythmical forms. The last movement is characterized at certain places by a barbarous swing which hints very strongly at the wild mirth of a savage race.

The way the themes are employed and developed is also strikingly original. They are metamorphosed by every imaginable means. The first subject runs through the entire work. It is heard in reminiscent sort of a sway at the end of the adagio. The cellos suggest it in the scherzo. In the last movement it is pealed forth with all the savage energy of the brass.

The subjects are heard augmented, diminished, contracted, changed in every way.

In short, it is a fine work and the greatest contribution to the literature of symphonic music which we have seen for some time.

The performance under Anton Seidl was a most poetical one. At its close the composer was loudly called for. Again and again he bowed his acknowledgements, and again and again the applause burst forth.

Even after he had left his box and was walking in the corridor, the applause continued. And finally he returned to the gallery railing, and then what a reception he received! The musicians led by Mr. Seidl applauded until the place rang again.

Dr. Dvořák occupied a box with Mrs. Jeanette M. Thurber, the founder of the National Conservatory of America, of which he is the director, and Miss Adela Margulies, the pianist; in the same box were Mrs. Dvořák, his daughter Otilia, Mr. Maurice Arnold Strathotte and Mr. Harry Worthington Loomis, two of his composition pupils.

The Sunday edition of the *New York Herald* carried this article in the first section of the paper; however, the second article, under the title "Dvořák's Symphony a Historic Event," was printed in the third section again. In the middle of a page was a facsimile of the sheet

on which Dr. Dvořák jotted down his first idea when he resolved to write a symphony suggested by the melodies of America and prove his claim that Negro melodies and other native themes offered a sure foundation for a distinctly national school of the Western World.

The title page of the New World Symphony's score, printed in the *New York Herald*.

We know that the circumstances were slightly different. First came the Symphony, and then, in the second half of May 1893, Dvořák published the theory which caused such a tumult. So it is apparent that his theory preceded the production of the Symphony, but not so the origin of the composition.

We can understand the *Herald*'s intention to prove their connection with Dvořák when they published the first page of his manuscript which they most probably got from Mrs. Thurber. In fact, the discussion about the Indian and Negro melodies was printed in this paper, too. We can speculate about their aim in planting this idea in the public mind. They wanted to create a rumor that the previous discussion in the *New York Herald* was the impetus for Dvořák to write the symphony. The first statement at the beginning of the article makes it clear:

> Through the courtesy of Dr. Antonín Dvořák there is reproduced on this page in his own handwriting his original idea for the great symphony which he wrote in consequence of the famous controversy aroused by a series of articles in the *Herald*.
>
> The notes are given just as the distinguished composer dashed them off when he made his mind up to write a symphony founded upon the suggestion of American Negro and Indian melodies, and so prove that the thematic material for a national school of composition already abounded in North America.
>
> The production of this majestic work on Friday and Saturday is an historic event, and it is singularly appropriate that the first rude draft of Dr. Dvořák's original thought should appear in the *Herald*. The influence of such a composition, written under such conditions and in such a spirit, can scarcely be overestimated.
>
> This inauguration of a new epoch in American music is the outcome of Mrs. Jeanette Thurber's labors as president of the National Conservatory of Music. In spite of all obstacles, and in spite of criticism and apathy, this brave and intelligent American woman has steadily pressed toward the goal she set out to reach—a native school of music. At last the light is dawning, and the foremost living composer has set an example to American musicians.

Then came a brief description of the negotiation between Jeanette Thurber and Dvořák, which resulted in the composer's arrival in America, and his job to

lay the foundation for a national school of composition. When
he arrived in New York he began to study native music. The
Negro melodies aroused his enthusiasm. But for a long time he
said nothing about an idea that was slowly taking shape in his
mind. There is no more impressionable man in the world than
Dvořák. His moods vary with the hours. He is as sensitive as a
child. His imagination will take fire instantly. He absorbs color,
form, sentiment, everything from his surroundings.

The last description of Dvořák's character is penetrating and truthful.
The article continued with the opinions about Indian and Negro music that
he had expressed in the famous series in the *Herald* the previous May:

> [The composer] gets into touch with the common humanity of
> the country. In the Negro melodies of America I discover all
> that is needed for a great and noble school of music. They are
> pathetic, tender, passionate, melancholy, solemn, religious,
> bold, merry, gay, gracious, or what you will. It is music that
> suits itself to any mood or any purpose. There is nothing in the
> whole range of composition that cannot find a thematic source
> here.

The *Herald*'s explanation carried more details:

> Hardly had this appeared in the *Herald* when the so-called
> musical critics of the country wagged their heads and said that
> Dvořák was all wrong. The composer answered his critics by
> printing a signed article in the *Herald* reiterating his views in
> still stronger language. The controversy raged far and wide.
> Composers were interviewed in all parts of Europe by the *Her-*
> *ald*. The views of Rubinstein, Reyer, Joachim, Liebling, Bruck-
> ner, Mandyczewski, Richter and many other distinguished
> musicians were cabled to America. The weight of opinion was
> against the Bohemian composer.

According to the editorial office of the *Herald*, "Dvořák prepared for a
summer of hard work, and bravely announced through the *Herald* that he
would write a symphony based upon American Negro and Indian melodies
to prove that his position was sound and sincere."

However, when we see the date of the article, the 28th of May, 1893, with
the title "Antonín Dvořák on Negro Melodies," which theory had been
refused by the majority of the European musicians, we have to remember that
the score of the Symphony was finished four days earlier, on the 24th. The
article concluded:

The great composition which has just been produced is the result. A very remarkable thing about the advent of this symphony is the conspiracy of silence among the newspaper critics as to the credit due to Mrs. Thurber and the National Conservatory of Music. Even the Symphony Society, which was permitted to use the symphony without cost, failed to acknowledge its indebtedness on the programme.

Such problems come often when some great work originates. People like to argue as to whose was the impulse which initiated the accomplishment. But, indeed, nobody asks who gave this impulse to Beethoven when he wrote his famous Ninth Symphony. However, it is understandable that Mrs. Thurber could feel bitter when every bit of the applause went to Dvořák, and only a few remembered who brought him here and gave him his chance.

Dvořák described the response to his work in a letter to Simrock:

The success of the Symphony was tremendous; the papers write that no composer has ever had such a success. I was sitting in a box; the hall was filled with the best New York audience. The people clapped so much that I had to thank them from the box like a king! alla Mascagni in Vienna (don't laugh). You know how glad I am if I can avoid such ovations, but there was no getting out of it, and I had to show myself willy-nilly. Seidl said that he will send you a wire about the success. There will be two other productions of my work in Boston, on the 23rd and 30th of December.... I am happy....

These last two words expressed Dvořák's feelings completely. Dvořák's son Otakar remembered:

The success was so great that father had—about twenty times—to thank them for the unique reception. The next day, on the title page of the *New York Herald* there was an article carrying the news about the production of the Symphony in E minor, and about my father's victory. At the next occasion of our visit to Cafe Central, I reminded my father of the promise made to me by Seidl, which he silently acknowledged. Because Seidl had at that time shared in the payment of the toy ship, I have my own remembrance of the first production of the Symphony. Josef Kovarik, who was a collector of criticisms and articles about my father, suggested that I should buy some elegant album and start to collect the signatures of famous men. Later,

when I asked Seidl to write a note for me in my album, he
inscribed a motif of the Symphony *From the New World,* and
under it followed his dedication: "To the Captain of the Majestic."

Dvořák's last work, and also the last symphony he composed, took the
musical world by storm. Otakar wrote about it later: "He recognized his
artistic victory, a triumph which never before had been given to any Bohemian composer for his creative work."

His statement was true.

Victory ⌒ B

W HERE IS AMES?" asked Honza, and I showed him a point on the
    map north of Des Moines.

In a short while we left the city center and drove through an immense
expanse of farmland. In about an hour, the skyline of Ames—the modern
buildings, the playgrounds and parks, the residential areas, decorated by
flower gardens and lawns—appeared in front of our eyes.

Ames is the seat of Iowa State University and has a population of fifty
thousand, half of which are students. The university includes six schools, and
was founded in 1858. The city of Ames has grown to an important center in
the past sixty years.

I tried to decide on the best place for us to start; perhaps in some institute or the university library. I knew from the previous search that
Mrs. L. B. Schmidt, the author of several articles about Dvořák, who had
given the address during the unveiling ceremony in Spillville in 1923, had
lived in Ames. Her husband worked here as a university professor and if she
was at least twenty-five in 1925, she would probably not be alive today. Was it
reasonable for me to travel such a distance to visit a lady who most probably
was no longer living?

However, I began to think about the circumstances of her Dvořák
research. She had cited a letter from Kovarik, which could mean that she was
in touch with Dvořák's former secretary. In her speech she mentioned William Arms Fisher, Dvořák's former conservatory student. It would be most

355

important for us to find what remained of her property. This might be quite possible, because her husband had a prominent position in Ames.

"We have to look for some local archive." I explained to Lilian, "What we're looking for could be at the university.

We inquired of a group of nearby students for directions to the university campus. We passed the stadium, the student residence halls and several institutes, and finally came to the main library with an archive on the ground floor. The willing archive clerk looked quite puzzled when he saw our order.

"Isn't it rather late to search for these things?" he wondered. "Maybe there will be nothing of Mrs. Schmidt's property left. Then what?"

We filled out an application anyhow, and said we would be back in an hour. Meanwhile, each of us would find some interesting area of the library and wait.

I have always liked to look for information about places I visit, and I soon learned that the library has about 1,150,000 books, 16,000 magazines and newspapers, and 750,000 microfilms. And where had the name of the city come from? Oakes Ames had represented Massachusetts in the U.S. House of Representatives. His financial interests included construction of the nearby Missouri railway. He donated a bell to the local newly built church, and took an active part in the building of this city. For that reason the settlers gave it his name.

There were several articles about Dvořák on microfilms. The premiere of his Symphony *From the New World* came in December 1893. And look here! On Sunday, December 17, 1893, the *New York Times* carried an article under the title "Dr. Dvořák's Latest Work," and as usual, the subheads proclaimed:

> His Fifth Symphony Produced by the Philharmonic—*From the New World* a Study in National Music—How a Famous Composer Has Utilized the Material Found in America—A Vigorous and Beautiful Work Founded on Characteristic Themes—A Lesson for the American Composer.

The introduction, carried by this foremost American paper, was written in a witty spirit:

> The attempt to describe a new musical composition may not be quite so futile as an effort to photograph the perfume of a flower, yet it is an experiment of a similar nature. Only an imperfect and perhaps misleading idea of the character of so complex a work of art as a symphony can be conveyed through the medium of cold type; yet when there is no other way, even that must be tried. Accepting, then, the doubtful premise that

music can be treated intelligently in words, no one need look for a more fruitful topic at present than the new symphony made known by the Philharmonic Society at Music Hall on Friday afternoon and repeated last night, to the evident delight of a large audience. This music is entitled *Z novecho sveta,* [*sic*] which is being translated *From the New World.* It is dated 1893, and is Op. 95 of Antonín Dvořák, the famous Bohemian master, now a resident of this city.

Following was an excellent review, with an evaluation of the positive qualities of Dvořák's work. The author talked about the composer in superlatives only, and his summary concluded with a confident statement: "it is a great symphony and must take its place among the finest works in this form produced since the death of Beethoven."

His final sentences expressed his feelings on national identity:

> Dr. Dvořák has penetrated the spirit of this music, and with themes suitable for symphonic treatment, he has written a beautiful symphony, which throbs with American feeling, which voices the melancholy of our Western wastes, and predicts their final subjection to the tremendous activity of the most energetic of all peoples. We Americans should thank and honor the Bohemian master who has shown us how to build our national school of music.

What was Dvořák's reaction to the review? We read it in his letter to Simrock, when he wrote: "I am happy!"

I still had time to look for other materials, and found a review, carried by the *Evening Post* in New York City on Monday, December 18, 1893, entitled "Music and Drama," with the subhead, "A Notable Concert."

It said:

> Although the Philharmonic Society has been in existence more than half a century, it is doubtful if it ever gave a more important or more enjoyable concert than that of Saturday last, doubtful if a larger or more enthusiastic audience was ever assembled to hear it play, doubtful if the orchestra itself ever played with more finish and animation than it did on this occasion...as late as eight o'clock there was a string of ticket buyers extending across Music Hall and out into the street. And there was reason for this state of affairs, in the promise of a new American symphony by the greatest living orchestral composer.

The review considered other aspects of Dvořák's activities in America:

> When Mrs. Jeanette M. Thurber had the happy thought of
> engaging this eminent Bohemian master as director of our
> National Conservatory a little over a year ago, we took occasion
> to say: "It will be interesting to observe what effect, if any,
> American life will have on Dr. Dvořák's future compositions.
> He has already expressed his desire to write an opera on an
> American subject.... It would be odd if this Bohemian com-
> poser, with his great faculty of assimilation, should succeed in
> writing the first really American opera. The American compos-
> ers should bestir themselves."
>
> The American composers did not bestir themselves; they
> appear to suffer, most of them, with megalomania, and only a
> few have even taken advantage of the rare opportunity afforded
> last year at the Conservatory of studying the art of composition
> under the greatest living master of orchestral coloring and
> form. But Dr. Dvořák did bestir himself; he has written not an
> opera, as at first he intended, but a symphony, and in view of
> the splendid results no one can regret the change of plan,
> which, it is to be hoped, means only a postponement. The sym-
> phony is entitled *From the New World,* is its author's fifth work
> of that class, and was composed last spring in New York. No
> one who has heard it once, could deny that it is the greatest
> symphonic work ever composed in this country.

The editor continued with a description of the circumstances in which
the work had originated:

> He might have followed the example of Brahms in his *Academic
> Overture,* in which German student songs are used as thematic
> material; or that of Liszt, who welded Hungarian melodies into
> his rhapsodies; or else he might have travelled west, allowing
> our incomparable scenic wonders—the Grand Canyon of the
> Colorado, the Yosemite, the Alaska fjords, the Yellowstone gey-
> sers, the limitless prairies, or Niagara Falls to inspire in him
> grand musical thoughts.
>
> He followed neither of these plans in the present sym-
> phony. It was written before he had seen the West... he simply
> sought to assimilate certain rhythmic and melodic traits of folk
> song, reproducing them in his own ideas. In other words, his
> genius has simply distilled perfumes which recall the fragrance

of the wild blossoms in the Bohemian forest. This is what he
has attempted to do for this country.

The analysis of Dvořák's composition was similar to observations carried
by the other press. He concluded:

> [T]here is not a dull moment, not a bar of padding, in the
> whole symphony, it is every inch a Dvořák.... It is by their slow
> movements that great geniuses are stamped as such. By this test
> Dr. Dvořák is one of the greatest of musical creators...as for the
> instrumentation, we can only say that if Schubert had heard
> Wagner he would have probably orchestrated as Dvořák
> does.... A masterwork has been added to symphonic literature,
> and the Philharmonic audience was not slow in noting the
> fact....

It was time for me to return to the archive. The clerk welcomed me with
a smile, and handed to me an extended file:

"I cannot believe that we have really found some items of Mrs. Schmidt
here. As far as I know, nobody has ever studied this file before."

I believed everything he said, and anxiously opened the file, trying to
control my excitement by rebuking myself: "Miroslav, better calm down!"
First, I had to separate all of the material already known; for example, the
material about Dvořák's visit in Spillville; and several articles which we had
found in Des Moines. What was left? A ten-page essay with a photograph of
the Dvořák memorial, published by Grace Boston in the *Iowa Magazine* in
1925 under the title "Dvořák Wrote the Humoresque on His Cuffs." The file
contained three more letters; one was sent to Lauraine Mead by Dvořák's
pupil William Arms Fisher; the second was written by Rozalie Bin, who was
owner of the house in Spillville where the Dvořáks rented their accommodation for a holiday; and the third letter was from L. S. Hutchinson, who had
visited Spillville in the summer of 1893. A letter was addressed to
L. B. Schmidt. Another document showed evidence from the session of the
Iowa State Senate, in May 29, 1945, and had to do with Dvořák. This connection seemed to me almost unbelievable. Which should I study first?

The essay by Mrs. Boston described the ceremony in Spillville on the
28th of September, 1925. The introduction, almost too saccharine in character,
contained a few useful facts. I learned who Mrs. Schmidt was, and what position she held in society. I also learned who Miss Lauraine Mead was. The
essay described the celebration in Spillville:

The spirit of Antonín Dvořák, noted Bohemian composer, seemed to hover over the never-to-be-forgotten scene which was enacted at Spillville, Iowa, September 28.

It was late afternoon and sun cast a pinkish glow over the surrounding hills as it sank lower and lower in the west. A few birds in nearby trees and the soft rippling of the Little Turkey River a few feet away were the only sounds to be heard. Seated on a platform which had been erected for the occasion, sat the Spillville brass band and a group of musicians, and speakers, including Mrs. Louis B. Schmidt of Ames, Miss Lauraine Mead of Cresco (whose music club held the first benefit for the cause), Rev. Father Dostal of Chelsea, Dr. R. Wistein of Cedar Rapids, Rev. Father George Bennett of Iowa City, George Kovarik of Vinton, and Mrs. Fred Swella of Spillville.

In front was a tense crowd of 3,000 persons who had gathered to watch the unveiling of the first memorial ever erected within the borders of our state in honor of a musician. One could almost hear a pin drop, so reverential was the hush which preceded the dedicatory address delivered by Mrs. Louis B. Schmidt, chairman of the Historic Spots Committee of the Iowa Conservation Association and a former president of the Iowa Federation of Music Clubs.

Mrs. Grace Boston then described the events concerning Dvořák, similar to those we already know from other sources, including the story about the composer's cuffs. She continued:

Mrs. Benda says also that although Madame Dvořák always held herself a little aloof from the village folk, Dr. Dvořák was quite the opposite. In passing down the village street of a morning, he would always stop for a little chat with her husband, Frank Benda, who was the official community shoemaker. What their line of conversation consisted of is still a mystery to this too-efficient laundress....

Many of the inhabitants of Spillville thought the head of the "family from Europe" was slightly demented as if by chance he was wandering through the woods along the Turkey River and caught a new note in the song of an Iowa bird, he forgot everything else in the world, including his dignity.... On one occasion he remarked to a friend: "I could sing from morning till night when I listen to birds and am walking alone in these wonderfully inspiring woods."

Dvořák's extreme sensitiveness to sound of any kind is still illustrated by the strange manner in which he acted when the hail beat on the tin roof which covered their rented apartment in Spillville. With his fingers in his ears, he would pace madly up and down, muttering to himself the while and could not seem to get hold of himself until the rattling had ceased.

According to Mrs. Benda and others whose work brought them in close contact with the Dvořák household, the Doctor would stop for his daily pail of beer at one of the numerous saloons (there were two breweries in Spillville at that time) and invariably fell into an argument with the bartender because the foam was on the top. He very much objected to this "Yankee" custom and always wound up the discussion with the remark that in Bohemia bartenders were more obliging and always put foam on the bottom and not on the top!

It was a matter of town gossip that the Dvořáks for all their means lived very simply and were not inclined to "put on airs."

The family was a large one, ten in all, including Mme. Dvořák's sister and the maid they had brought with them from the old country. But alas, no sooner were they comfortably located in their new quarters than they made the startling discovery that there was no community baking oven as in Bohemia—and the cook positively refused to learn how to bake bread. There were no public bakeries in the village, and it was up to the Kovariks and the Bilys to see to it that the family did not go hungry for want of the staff of life while in Spillville.

Mrs. Boston described what we knew from other sources: why Dvořák had come to Spillville; that he played organ in a church and liked the Indian songs.

She recollected that "he haunted the Kickapoo Medicine Show, which played in Spillville for several weeks that summer, and never seemed to weary of his new love, Indian folk lore." And, "He was a family man, in the strictest sense of the word, in spite of his many eccentricities which seem to be part of all geniuses. He simply worshiped his six children."

The author of the essay continued in a description of other Dvořák characteristics and habits. Most of all, she admired his piety, and recalled the spectacle when the family came into church Sunday mornings: "It was their habit to march down the long aisle in single file—ten of them, which was a procession in itself!"

Mrs. Charles Hauser, 1537 5th avenue, Cedar Rapids, was the
only woman Bohemian teacher in Spillville community in 1893,
and was privileged to meet the composer frequently as a guest
at the Kovarik home. Her father also invited him to dinner on
various occasions, one of which she recalls very distinctly. They
were just seated at the table and the roast goose was being
brought in, when Dvořák sprang from his chair and ordered the
horses hitched at once—"he must get home and at once!" The
spell of the muse was upon him and at such times, regardless
when or where, everything else was of no consequence—not
even a delicious goose dinner. This same performance occurred
at such frequent intervals while Dvořák was in Spillville that it
came to be taken as a matter of course, and the host was never
sure his guest would remain throughout the meal.

What became of his most beloved and much used piano
which he owned while in Iowa, has been a matter of interest to
the Iowa Conservation Association. After the family's return to
New York, it became the property of the public school and was
later lost track of. It now appears that when the piano was eventually dismantled, and burned with "other rubbish," the father
of C. A. Andera, assistant cashier of the Citizens Saving Bank,
Spillville, was the lucky person in whose hands fell the outer
covering, a handsome rosewood case. Being a carpenter, he
transformed it into a writing desk for his son, who today counts
it among his rarest possessions.

Mrs. Boston's essay is lengthy, indeed, but her information gives the
reader a lively and more intimate view of Dvořák's personality. In the conclusion of her essay, the author half admits that even if the score of the Symphony *From the New World* was completed, not written in its entirety in Iowa
as the findings of the Iowa Conservation Association show, nonetheless:

[I]n the Largo is unquestionably something of the loneliness of
far off prairie horizons, and the moaning of the wind through
the tall grasses....

In his last chapter of *The History of Iowa*, Honorable Cyre-
nus Cole of Cedar Rapids relates his reaction on hearing played
for the first time the New World Symphony by a Chicago
orchestra. His experience so nearly parallels that of other
Iowans, I quote it herewith:

"My mother rode into Iowa on the front seat of a covered
wagon. From my infancy she has tried to tell me how the winds

moaning through the prairie grasses had affected her in those early days, but I never fully understood what she told me about such feelings and impressions until many years afterward when for the first time I heard Dvořák's New World Symphony. As I listened to that beautiful music I recalled what she had tried to explain and the meaning of it was made plain to me. She had been homesick amid her new surroundings; she had longed for the old scenes. The composer of that music had lived on the same prairies and he had mingled their moanings with the same memories and longings of an alien soul...."

Other materials waited for me. I knew that Miss Mead from Cresco was also one of the enthusiasts. It was through her effort as well that the Dvořák memorial was built. She had arranged various musical activities and studied everything that was connected with Dvořák. Her correspondence with one of the composer's pupils, later a director of the music publishing house in Boston, William Arms Fisher, is not only interesting, but also important.

His letter written January 22, 1924, "sets forth in the first few lines the need of more publicity on Dvořák in Iowa as well as the preserving of those places associated with Dvořák's visit."

He wrote to her:

Dear Miss Mead,

In reply to your inquiry would say to begin with that I am glad to know that Spillville is really on the map. When I was in Davenport at the National Federation of Music clubs biennial about two and one-half years ago, I made a number of inquiries of Iowa people, and none of them heard of the town, my impression being that it is in Northwestern Iowa.

I was a pupil of Dvořák for two years, including the period when he wrote his New World Symphony. My impression is that he did not write the entire symphony in the summer he spent in Spillville, but that he finished it there and perhaps its orchestration.

One day after his return to New York, he invited me to go with him to Carnegie Hall in New York to hear the final private rehearsal of the Symphony. Outside of the orchestra and its famous leader, Anton Seidl, we were the only people in the hall. He told me then that he was hearing his Symphony played for the very first time (1883)....

I am including a copy of my partial arrangement of his

Largo as a song. As a musician, I am inclined to look with suspicion on any arrangement based on the work of the great composers. One day, in the summer of 1922, when somebody put in front of me the Largo in a piano arrangement, I played it only for old times' sake. However, as I played, I heard in my mind words coming unbidden: "Goin' home—I'm going home." I wrote them down and took my idea home. Obeying my inner impulse, I elaborated it accordingly.

You have written to me that you are going to organize a "Dvořák Center." Please, let me know what it is and where it would be located. Also, if there would be enough room in your "Center" for the autographed copy of my arrangement which I would send to you gladly. Reinald Werrenrath has sung it with extraordinary success everywhere.

I believe that my information could be useful to you,

cordially yours,

William Arms Fisher

"This letter must be significant," I thought out loud. Fisher's use of the Largo in the Symphony *From the New World* is known world-wide. Indeed, there were rumors that his arrangement existed prior to Dvořák's composition, and that the composer's second movement of the Symphony, the famous Largo, was based on Fisher's work.

Some time ago, I saw a television program from Berlin, which featured a Black singing "Going Home." Not one word had not said about the composition being only an arrangement of Dvořák's work. The song is, however, sometimes introduced as an original Negro spiritual. Thanks to Lauraine Mead, who had asked Fisher for his explanation, we have the authentic testimony by the composer himself, and we know what really happened.

I read a second letter from Fisher. It was written on letterhead paper of the music publishers, Oliver Ditson Company, Boston, Massachusetts. It was addressed to Miss Mead, and the date was February 9, 1924. The message was brief:

I thank you for your kind letter from the 4th of this month. I found in it an interesting remark about Dvořák's love of birds and nature in general. He was simple like a child, and completely unspoiled. You asked me to send copies of my manuscript "Goin' Home" to two historical societies; one in Iowa

City, another in Des Moines. I will do it gladly after I get the exact names and addresses from you.

The footnote said that a clipping from the *Boston Globe* was enclosed which he believed might be interesting to her. He added that his wife was also a native of Iowa, which fact supports his interest in the founding of a Dvořák Musical Center. Greetings. Signature.

The clipping was not in the file. Almost half a century later, it was probably lost. No copy of Fisher's arrangement "Goin' Home" was there, either.

"The second copy should be in Des Moines," Honza reminded me, but we did not find it there, either.

Another Fisher letter was in the file, written one-and-a-half years later. The text was long, and also important. The letterhead showed a slightly different design from the previous letters. The year 1834, when the firm was founded, was pushed back to "1783." It could improve the respectability of the publishing house, because the past in this country has the value of gold. The letter was from October 5, 1925, and William Fisher wrote:

> My dear Miss Mead,
>
> In answer to your letter from the 1st of October, which I just received, I would like to inform you that Reverend W. A. Dostal from Lawler, Iowa, wrote to me on March 23, 1924. He informed me that he heard from Prof. J. J. Kovarik of New Prague, Minn., who was the personal friend of Dvořák. Prof. Kovarik alleged that Dvořák had written his symphony prior to his visit in Spillville. I am including a copy of my answer to his letter from April 2, 1924.
>
> In addition to my letter to Father Dostal, I would like to inform you that on the 6th of May, I wrote to Dr. Schnoor, who has been working on Dvořák's biography for some time. I said that the score of the Symphony *From the New World,* which is the property of the Public Library in Boston, includes various published criticisms of this work. I am sending you a list of the statements to show how many contradictions are found:
>
> 1. "The Symphony was written last spring in New York, but was revised, and probably its instrumentation was finished during the composer's summer holiday in Spillville, Iowa." [The important parts of this statement were by A. Fisher.]

2. The *Independent,* 21st of December, 1893 talked about the Symphony: "with which the Bohemian composer was occupied for the best part of last summer."

3. The Boston press carried the news written by their correspondent from New York. His letter was dated December 21, 1893: "The manuscript was mostly written last winter and spring, and finished in summer."

4. On the programme of the Boston Symphony Orchestra, which has no date: "This symphony was written in the summer of 1893."

The first fragment without a date is from the review which was clipped from some New York article from December 1893; the writer's name was not given. I really would like to see the definite end of this controversy."

Fisher then apologized that he had no records from that period, and therefore could not know at what time Dvořák returned to his directorial job at the conservatory in the fall of 1893. His letter to Miss Mead continued:

He liked to speak about his visit to Spillville. On Sunday afternoon, a few weeks (or months?) after his return, he invited me to the conservatory to listen to the Kneisel Quartet playing his Quartet, Opus 96, and Quintet, Opus 97. As far as I can remember, a few more listeners were there; Mrs. Thurber (the chief of the conservatory), Mrs. MacDowell (mother of Edward MacDowell). Adela Margulies, and the critics, H. E. Krehbiel, now deceased. Richard Aldrich (still living in New York City, and (if I am not wrong) W. J. Henderson. These men created a group of the great critics associated with the most important papers in New York City.

The question of where Dvořák had written his Quartet and Quintet is also yet unsolved. [On the margin of the letter was somebody's note "solved."] As I had already stated in a letter to Father Dostal, Seidl must have started to rehearse the Symphony *From the New World* sometime in November. It is quite possible that the Philharmonic Orchestra began rehearsals in October. Because the copying of the individual orchestral parts of such a big symphony would usually take several weeks, we can deduce that the Symphony *From the New World* was actually finished after Dvořák's return to New York City from Spillville.

I am more anxious than anybody else to see this question

solved on an authoritative and truthful basis, and believe that this extended letter could help in some way. Cordially Yours,

Wm. Arms Fisher.

I put the letters with the important news back in the file, and quite tired, felt a need for coffee. Mrs. Hosek suggested a break in the library snack bar. However, I withstood the temptation for there was still a whole packet of materials we needed to search. Two more letters and a report from the Senate Session, which seemed to be most promising, awaited us.

The next letter was written in English, and the pages covered with dreadful handwriting were torn out of some school notebook.

Lilian took the first page and read it slowly. It was necessary to guess at the meaning of every sentence. The letters were erratic and it was not known to whom it was written.

There was just a salutation "Dear Miss Jayne," which told me nothing. On the top was somebody's note, "Answer 2. 4. 24, Mrs. Schmidt." The letter bore the date "Spillville, 28. 3. 1924":

Dear Miss Jayne,

I am writing to tell you that I have seen an article about Dr. Dvořák in the paper. We are Rozalie and Vaclav Bina from Spillville, the people who own the house in Spillville where Dvořák lived when he was here. The house stands apart from the road, and nothing in it is changed. Only electric lighting has been installed since then, and the new glass doors were put on hinges; that is all. The rest of the house stayed as it was in the time of Dr. Dvořák. I always say that it should be kept as a memorial. If I am right, please let us know, because we plan to trade this building. It is a big stone house with two floors and a brick front, standing in the middle of...[perhaps "pasture"; the word was fuzzy.] If someone from his family, and this you should note, would like to buy it, we would like to sell it to them. It would give them the opportunity to mark the place where Mr. Dr. Antonín Dvořák, the famous musical composer of Humoresque and Largo had [lived] then.

He lived upstairs, and the building is about 25 feet high. I remember fifteen years ago that I was told about him, but I have heard nothing about him since, except once, three years ago. Fifteen years ago they told me where he had lived and where he wrote his famous symphony; that he liked to walk along the river during the day and...[another hazy word] when he came home, he opened the window on the second floor and listened to the wind and the humming creek and the river; I always took it as a joke, when I heard about it the first time.

He had 2 daughters with him then, and at the same time, J. J. Kovarik was teaching in the school, and also teaching music. When he heard about the big works of Mr. Dvořák, he was not pleased because he wanted to be the leading music teacher in Winneshiek [County]. But the truth was that he never composed anything as Mr. Dvořák had, and I think that he tried to deny that Mr. Dvořák ever had done anything like that here. He had, however, because there are people who I have known who spoke about Mr. Dvořák. Some of them are already deceased ten years ago, and when they died, they were 72, so only they could know about him. About three years ago, 8 young boys, about 25 and 26 came here, and wanted to see the house where Mr. Dvořák lived. Unfortunately, I did not even ask them who they were and where they came from; so I am the only one able to help you.

If you would like to know more, you have to write me, and also inform Mrs. Schmidt, if it would be of any importance to her. Excuse please my terrible handwriting. I have arthritis in the hands and cannot write well. However, I hope that you can read it. In the firm hope that you will write to me when you receive my letter,

Cordially yours, Rozalie Bina.

I think that Mrs. Bina made a mess of what she said about Kovarik. The news came to Spillville that Kovarik denied that the Symphony *From the New World* was composed in Spillville, and the general rumor was that he envied Dvořák.

Meanwhile, Mrs. Marie made copies of the many documents we had already studied, and I tried to understand the letter written by Rozalie Bina. In 1924, the news about preparations for the erection of the monument in Spillville was traveling over the country, and this was a reason for some contemporaries to rush into print. Thanks to Mrs. Schmidt, I could use her material for further study. I could not understand Mrs. Bina's remark that "the house stands apart from the road," because we were in Spillville, too, and found the Bily Clocks Museum at the main road.

"Perhaps the road was moved," Honza speculated.

I shrugged my shoulders: "Hard to say. In a picture which Dvořák brought with him to Bohemia, the house was situated on the road."

But was it actually? I had a copy of that photograph with me. "Look!" It showed a dusty road, and on the back was Dvořák's handwritten note. He wrote it later probably and forgot the date of his visit in Spillville. It says:

"Spillville—where Dvořák spent his 1894 vacation, r e m e m b e r i n g h i s homeland."

But what if Rozalie Bina was wrong? She also wrote that Dvořák had two of his daughters with him, but we know for sure that his daughters Otilka, Anna, Magda, and the youngest Aloisie, all four of them, were there with him.

The last letter had no date, and the address on the letterhead was that of a dentist, L. S. Hutchinson from Elgin, Illinois, bearing also his office hours. It was typed, and the text had the character of a reminiscence and indicated that he was searching his memory for details:

> Mrs. L. B. Schmidt:
>
> I just read your article about Antonín Dvořák in the *Iowa Mag-azine*, and was surprised to learn about people who doubt the fact that Dvořák had written some of his music in Iowa. Perhaps you would be interested in the little knowledge I have about him.
>
> I was in Spillville one Sunday when Dvořák was living there. Our company of relatives and friends wished to spend a day in Spillville (we lived in Decorah, Iowa, 12 miles distant). Many of us never had been there before. It was then known that the settlement was almost like Europe, not only because of the climate, but because then, same as now, it was an isolated village where transportation for strangers was scarce. The village has been until now one of a kind.
>
> We came in by two light coaches, and arrived in Spillville at about 9:30 A.M. It was a holiday, and near the village we saw the women from surrounding farms walking to church. All of them were wearing the same kind of kerchief, a fashion which exists still to-day.
>
> Prof. Kovarik had his daily school on the opposite side from the church. This church had been built in the shape of a cross by the local people. Men and women from the village had built it with women hauling the stone, and men doing the mason's work.
>
> Behind Kovarik's school was a large pasture with a grove for our picnic dinner. In a nearby pasture were scattered several little shrines, with the same distance between each. That Sun-

day, the priest, followed by a long procession, carried the monstrance from one shrine to another, returning to their church. It is a Bohemian church, and they held that special service there every year.... At that time, the side-walks in Spillville were made of lime-stone slabs, which perhaps have survived until now. They looked very impressive, indeed; nice and well-laid as were also a few buildings with stores, built of the same stone. Some of them, with a rough texture, were plastered on the outside.

When I was about 14 years old, I remember buying candy in the local store. They had one kind only in a little glass bowl on the shelf, but that store was torn down later. When we had watched the procession returning to church, the bowling alleys and the bars were great attractions. Also, the bicycle was a hit then, and riders turning round the corner at the church, proudly rang the bells on the handlebars.

When I was standing with my friend in the pasture near Kovarik's house, Dvořák and another gentleman went out, and the composer, holding binoculars, allowed us to use them to observe distant hills; which I considered a kindly deed. From the local boys in the village, we learned that they regard the composer as a whimsical fellow, or better a "nut." They said that he was ready to compose every minute of the day; when he was talking, eating, or sleeping, and best of all when he was resting in bed. He could get up quickly, rub his eyes, and walk, moving his hands as if playing the piano. When he got an idea, he sat and wrote the melody down.

You have perhaps heard the story about his sudden departure. It must be true, and you could verify it with the old folks there. You better take a translator with you, one who knows the old people well and could get them to be more talkative.

I hope that this will be of some significance to you, and I assure you that I have no interest of being named in your publication, because there are still some others who know more about Dvořák than I was able to offer.

Mr. Hutchinson wrote in his conclusion:

Dvořák, sitting erect at the organ, played and swayed from side to side, never glancing at the keyboard.... I did not think too much of his performance in church. It seemed to lack harmony, and was noisy and somewhat jerky. He could compose gorgeous music for other musicians but it did not sound well when he played it himself. I will not correct my typing because I hope that you will excuse a few errors I made. My patients are waiting for me, and I want to send this to you now; otherwise I do not know how soon I will have time to mail it later. Please, let me know when you have received it.

Hutchinson's pages recalled the life in Spillville quite well. The settlement, which he called "one of a kind," was not touched yet by American customs. The women still wore their old-fashioned kerchiefs according to the custom of the Old Country, and everything that was typical and traditional there has survived the invasion of the modern world.

Because of the pasture extending beyond Kovarik's school, the houses were scattered, and every settler kept a reasonable distance from the next house, and the neighborhood had no definite plan. Also his mention of Dvořák's unconventional behavior could agree with other characteristics described in previous testimonies.

"More important is that he wrote nice music," Mrs. Hosek said, and showed me the important copies she had made for me. "Anything else I can do?"

There was one more document on the table for us to study. Four printed pages of quite impressive layout, especially the front page, showing a text:

State of Iowa

Senate Register

Tuesday, 29th of March, 1945

Printed daily by the State of Iowa during the official session of the general assembly. Subscription of the record from both rooms in session — $2 per session. Press Control by the State House, Des Moines, Iowa.

As I turned to another page, everybody in our group became curious of what had really happened in Iowa during the spring session of 1945. There was still a war in Europe, but its end was inevitable — and here? My eyes searched for the text, dated:

February 19, 1945.

Passed on File. By Vrba SENATE JOINT RESOLUTION

Joint resolution proposing the adoption of Largo by Antonín Dvořák as the official instrumental music of the State of Iowa.

WHEREAS, the State of Iowa will celebrate its one hundredth anniversary in 1946 and,

WHEREAS, it is the desire of this General Assembly to commemorate this centennial anniversary and,

WHEREAS, the Largo, a movement of the New World Symphony by the great Bohemian composer Antonín Dvořák, was written and composed in Spillville, Iowa, in July, 1893, while this outstanding musician was residing at Spillville, Iowa

Be It Resolved by the General Assembly of the State of Iowa:

Section 1. That the State of Iowa adopt as a centennial measure, the music of Largo from the New World Symphony by Antonín Dvořák as the State Official Instrumental Music, said music being composed at Spillville, Iowa in July, 1893, during the time Mr. Dvořák was residing at Spillville, Iowa.

THIRD READING OF BILLS

On motion of Senator Vrba, Senate Joint Resolution 6, a joint resolution proposing the adoption of "Largo" by Antonín Dvořák as the official instrumental music of the State of Iowa, was taken up and considered.

Senator Vrba moved that the resolution be read a third time now, which motion prevailed, and the resolution was read a third time.

On the question "Shall the resolution pass?" The vote was:

Ayes, 48 [The list of the names of the Senators followed.]

Nays, none.

Absent or not voting, 1;(Senator) Pine

The resolution having received a constitutional majority was desired to have passed the Senate and the title was agreed to.

Senator Vrba moved that the vote by which the resolution passed the Senate be reconsidered and that the motion to reconsider be laid on the table, which motion prevailed.

Being quite surprised by this document, we remained silent. I had read somewhere before that the official song of this state was a "Song of Iowa." The evidence, which we found in this official document, certified by the

Senate of the State of Iowa, has never been registered in any Dvořák literature before. In fact, it was not known.

Until then, Europe and Asia were under siege of war, and here, in the middle of the golden wheat and cornfields of Iowa, Senator Vrba (his name suggests a Bohemian lineage), proposed a motion that the "Largo," written by Antonín Dvořák—this sad beautiful melody, completed in these prairies and in the woods along the Turkey River, or in the cemetery with many Bohemians' names, around Saint Wenceslaus church—should be approved for the official instrumental music of the State of Iowa.

The victorious score: 48 : 0.

Return ⤳ A

THE DAYS PASSED UNEVENTFULLY at 327 East 17th Street in New York City, broken only by the famous premiere of the Symphony *From the New World*.

The American press outdid itself in complimenting the celebrated composer and his work, and the conservatory strove to match the enthusiasm of New York society. The institute honored their director with a special prize for his "original symphony."

Dvořák wrote to Simrock on the January 2, 1894: "You would be glad if my symphony were discussed in Europe as much as it is here, in America."

Emil Pauer, the conductor of the Boston Symphonic Orchestra, performed with Dvořák's approval the Symphony *From the New World,* on the 30th of December. Although this Boston production came after Seidl's performance in New York, Pauer's presentation affirmed once again that Dvořák was one of the most significant composers in the world.

The second concert, this time in Boston, was the other triumph for Dvořák's music. The premiere of his Spillville Quartet in F major was played by the famous Kneisel quartet on the 1st of January, and the performance was repeated twice more in Hartford and Washington. On the 11th of January, Anton Seidl's Philharmonic performed Dvořák's Symphony in Brooklyn (New York City then included Manhattan and the Bronx; and only in 1897, after Dvořák's return to Bohemia, was New York City united with Brooklyn, Queens and Richmond). The next day, the Kneisel Quartet played his Quar-

374

tet in F Major and the other work he wrote in Spillville, the Quintet in E-flat Major, for the first time in Carnegie Hall. The concert culminated with Dvořák's Sextet in A Major for strings.

The applause filled the music hall again, and the *New York Tribune* wrote this about it:

> For the first time ever, the auditorium was completely filled, and the galleries had to be opened during the chamber music performance. The audience responded in a very cordial spirit, its obvious wish to become familiar with this new music being greatly satisfied. After each movement of the Quartet, long, loud and enthusiastic applause filled the auditorium, and the excited composer, sitting in the audience, was obliged several times to express his thanks for the cordial manifestation given to his genius. Kneisel and his assembly enjoyed the greatest triumph they have ever achieved in New York.

The name "Dvořák" became famous, and the *New York Herald* led in promoting the composer's genius. Their friendly relationship with Mrs. Thurber also helped this paper, whose attention was focused on the newcomers from Middle Europe, to promote Dvořák.

On Monday, December 18, two days after the stunning success of the premiere of the Symphony *From the New World,* another significant article in *New York Herald* concerned Dvořák: "Prompt Aid Forthcoming." The impressive subheads proclaimed: "A Grand Popular Response to the *Herald's* Appeal for the City's Deserving Poor—ASSISTANCE FROM ALL SIDES," and so forth.

After a few more subheads, concerning this aid, came one which said: "Dr. Antonín Dvořák Will Give a Grand Concert in Aid of the Fund at Madison Square Garden."

In the fourth paragraph was a reference to Dvořák:

> DR. DVORAK'S PRINCELY CONTRIBUTION—The greatest musician of the day, Dr. Antonín Dvořák, whose glorious symphony, which is aptly described as marking a new epoch in American music, has created a profound sensation in the highest musical circles in the country, has made a princely donation to the Free Clothing Fund.
>
> In a letter addressed to the *Herald* yesterday, a facsimile of which is printed this morning, Dr. Dvořák refers in touching terms to the present period of unexampled suffering, and, as director of the National Conservatory of Music, announces that

he has engaged the Madison Square Garden for the evening of January 23, when he will conduct a public concert for the aid of the *Herald* Free Clothing Fund. The occasion will be one of the most memorable musical events of the season and will be the means of raising a magnificent sum to carry on the great charity.

Dr. Antonín Dvořák's autograph letter to the publisher of the *New York Herald* was printed in the middle of the same page. The composer used again the official paper of the conservatory with its letterhead on the left, the letter dated "December 17, 1893."

Dvořák wrote:

> To the Editor of the *Herald*.
>
> My Dear Sir:
>
> The *Herald*'s Free Clothing Fund is the best and most practical movement to relieve distress that has been organized since the beginning of this terrible period of suffering. It gives every man, woman and child in this City an opportunity to do something toward clothing the hopeless thousands pressing us on all sides for help. As Director of the National Conservatory of Music, I am authorized to arrange and conduct a public concert in aid of this great charity. Madison Square Concert Hall has already been secured for January 23rd and I will be most happy to do all in my power to make the concert a success.
>
> Yours very sincerely, Antonín Dvořák.

We might suspect that Mrs. Thurber was behind this action, but it could not change the fact that his deed was quite generous. Not only for the proceeds which aided the impoverished in New York, but for another reason, too.

The majority of the students from the National Conservatory of Music performing in the concert were Black! Only one young "talented pupil, Miss [Bertha] Visanska" (as Dvořák had remarked on his card to Seidl) was white. Otherwise—the singer, Sissieretta Jones (nicknamed Black Patti), baritone H. T. Burleigh, and the mixed choir—all were Black.

Dvořák conducted the orchestra of the conservatory, and besides several other compositions, the conservatory orchestra also played Dvořák's arrangement of Stephen Collins Foster's song "Old Folks at Home." Foster loved Negro spirituals which originated at the end of the eighteenth century during the plantation religious assemblies in the southern states. Foster was inspired by their spirit, and more than 150 of his songs gradually became folk songs.

Dvořák was familiar with a book of his songs, published in Boston in 1882, and arranged the best known of them for solos, choir, and orchestra. This work was premiered now, and the performance was glorious and successful. The entire production was actually a joint triumph of music and social politics, because in 1894 it was still quite difficult to organize any performance of Black students. It was not simple or easy, and such an action was against American conventions. Perhaps not many American aristocrats were pleased with such a benefit concert.

A discussion about the influence of Dvořák's Symphony *From the New World* on the beginning of a new era of American music had begun. It began to be understood that the situation was more complicated than it first looked. Still one year later, a review was published on this theme by W. S. B. Matthews in the monthly journal *Music*. The author tried to find new answers to the problem.

The questions were: "Did Dvořák, as it is claimed by his admirers, create a real 'American work'? Is his work indeed, great and beautiful?"

The author answered: "Let us start with the assertion that his symphony is very charming." He follows with a detailed analysis of the work, and finds his own ironical answer to the first question:

> The idea is questionable that a master who feels so strongly about his tribal identity [he meant Dvořák's Slavonic roots] and whose music shows so many typical features of his mature personality, could create the first "real American" music. It reminds me of a case of Mrs. Newrich, whose daughter lacked talent, and whose mother offered to buy it for her.

This was a cutting statement, and other answers were in the same character:

> For Dr. Dvořák his residence in America is an excellent deal; and also not bad for this country. The idea is to bring students from the New York area and apprentice them to one of the world's foremost composers....

but

> ...meanwhile, when every new work from his pen is welcomed with great joy and admiration, neither the American composers nor the American school would permit themselves to be exported to anywhere for $15,000 a year or for any price, because they know that they should grow here, in their native soil.

We can agree with that, but Dvořák never wanted to forget his homeland and his Bohemian identity, deeply rooted in his character, in exchange for something else, let's say for money. His loyalty to homeland cannot be removed from his music, for his homeland was always important to him. We can read about it in the recollection of F. Herites, the Bohemian writer, who met Dvořák in Chicago, and later several times in New York:

> The cafe was furnished in the European style, with magazines, journals and art reviews always in abundance. However, we did not talk much, and were deeply engrossed in reading. Dvořák was hungry to know what kind of news came from our country. He even studied the political articles which he usually ignored before.

Everyday life went on, however. His creative work was losing its tempo, and he now spent more energy in his teaching and with the directorship. Besides his somewhat complex Suite in A Major for piano (he rearranged it for an orchestra later) and the set of *Biblical Songs,* he had not started any larger work during the winter of 1894. Although we find several new ideas in a sketchbook from that time, he did not utilize them, because everything he had found that inspired him in New York (the scope of American life) he had already expressed in his Symphony *From the New World.* There was perhaps nothing left for him to add.

Also, his impressions of country life in Spillville were exhausted by the Quartet and Quintet that summer. We cannot be surprised when we realize how homesick he was again. Although his children were with him then, and his success surpassed all his musical ambitions, he started to count the weeks separating him from Bohemia. He looked forward to the moment when he would board the ship and wave good-bye to Battery Park and the Statue of Liberty on his way home.

Sometime earlier, Countess Kounic wrote a typical letter, her message a mixture of national feelings and other characteristic ideas:

> Although you are all together again, I feel sure that you still cherish some memories of your homeland, and that you remember us always, as we too, think of you. Therefore, you had better come home as soon as your pockets are full enough to leave. You know that home is the best place to be!

Dvořák was probably feeling the same way. As he previously wrote to Dr. Tragy in Prague, his American income was important for his family; his contract was renewed and signed on the 28th of April, 1894. Mrs. Thurber was unable to pay Dvořák his full salary, but the conservatory agreed to pay him $8,000 for his six months of work, from the 1st of November, 1894, to the 1st of May, 1895. For another possible eight-month extension, from 1895–1896, he would be paid $10,000. This contract persuaded Dvořák not to leave America for good but to visit his country for a short time and come back in the fall of 1894.

He left for Bohemia with his family and maid on the May 19, 1894, on the ship *Aller,* a steamer of average speed which transported the mail between New York and Bremerhaven (4,150 miles) in 10 to 12 days. The *Aller* made good time, and on the 30th of May, 1894, the twelfth day of their trip, Dvořák and his family were cordially welcomed at the railway station in Prague.

Everybody wanted to be there, musicians, composers, conductors of the National Theatre Orchestra, many opera singers, delegates of clubs, editors, friends—"everybody wanted to be the first to shake his hand and welcome him home. The famous Master was quite moved by their sincere praise. His friends embraced and kissed him." This was the description of the event carried by the Bohemian review *Dalibor.*

The *National Newsletter* wrote: "The crowds welcomed Master in Jezdecka Street, shouting 'Hurrah!' and their excitement quieted down only when the coach with the composer's family disappeared around the corner."

Dvořák stayed in Prague for a couple of days, and on June 2, he hurried to Vysoka, to see his garden, pigeons, hills, and meadows. The local people organized an evening procession for him, carrying paper lanterns, accompanying him to Fencel Inn where he told them how life was in America.

Vysoka was an oasis for Dvořák, the only place he wanted to stay. He refused to meet Simrock in Carlsbad; his strolls in the nearby forest were all he needed. He was working again; especially, on a revision of the opera *Dimitrij* (he started it in New York City), and wrote a few piano compositions, using the motives in his American sketchbook. This resulted in a set of eight Humoresques, of which no. 7 won world fame.

Of course, he did not forget to visit his church in Trebic, and in spite of his thrifty inclinations—as Otakar Sourek described his economic attitudes later—at the beginning of July, Dvořák purchased a new organ for his parish. It cost him 800 zlatys, and he explained the expense to his wife, with, "It is necessary to celebrate our happy return from America."

More weeks passed, the summer ended, and in September and October, Dvořák had several concerts of his work arranged for him in Bohemia. The most triumphant production was performed in the National Theatre in

Prague on the 13th of October. After the symbolic Overture *My Home,* the
concert culminated with the Prague premiere of his Symphony *From the New
World* (the composer had conducted it in Chicago the last time). The stormy
applause and the endless ovations of an enthusiastic audience marked this festive event.

On Tuesday, October 16, 1894, Dvořák went back to America. This time,
only his wife, their son Otakar (he was too temperamental to stay with
Grandma, who was taking care of the rest of the children now), and their
maid Barushka Klirova went with him.

On Wednesday, the Dvořáks visited J. B. Foerster, the Bohemian composer, in Hamburg, and on Thursday boarded the ship *Bismarck* for America.
Dvořák wrote about their trip to the Bohemian poet Heyduk in Pisek on the
29th of October: "It was an excellent ship and took us only six days, ten hours
and a few minutes to cross the ocean. On Thursday, October 25, at eight
o'clock in the evening, we saw New York City again."

On the same day, he wrote two more letters, to Antonin Rus and also to
Alois Gobl:

> On Thursday at 8 o'clock in the evening, we were already near-
> ing New York. However, our ship had to wait because no ship
> could enter the harbor after sunset. So we came into New York
> on Friday morning. We found everything here as we left it. New
> York is the same, and weather here is now similar to our sum-
> mer. I will start my job on the 1st of November. They are going
> to play my Symphony, the new one, called "American," again.
> So far as I know, it will be produced twice, by the Philharmonic
> Orchestra and by some other association, too. The Philhar-
> monic will perform also three of my Overtures in a single con-
> cert, which I will describe to you in my next letter.

Also another letter exists written by Dvořák during his overseas trip to
America. He used stationery of the "Shipping Company Hamburg-Amerika-
nische Gesellschaft, Am Bord des Schnelldampfer Fürst Bismarck":

> Dear children and Grandma!
>
> In the morning at sea,
> on the 25th, Thursday, 1894
>
> The weather is quite gloomy, and we must be only 200 miles
> from the American coast. [After his description of the overseas
> trip, he continues]: I would like to know what are you doing

now. Be good and obedient to Grandma. It will be good for everybody, and an especially great consolation to me, as you know well. Otilka, Aninka, and all the other children, you must know how painful and disturbing it would be for me if I heard something otherwise about you. Remember what I say, and go often to church. You know, Otilka, what I told you; especially on Sundays see that you go to church. Pray fervently, it is the one thing that can comfort you and us.

This tone—his concern for the children—was characteristic of all his letters. For example, on the November 31, 1894, he said:

I do not have to write you that we always think of you everywhere we are, and therefore I will be eager to hear from you soon, as to what the circumstances are there, what you are doing, and what is new. I have not started any new work yet, but I will be glad to start writing something soon, as I have had plenty of rest. I would like to write a concerto again, either for piano, violin, or violoncello, I don't know yet. I commend you to God's protection and kiss you a hundred times.

Your father Ant. Dvořák

Similarly he had written on the November 16, 1894:

The steamship *Aller* came today, and we went to Hoboken, but no letter came from you. You have to write more often, minimum twice a week. You can always send a few lines to us, to inform us of what and how are you doing.

In his letter from November 26 is a footnote: "When mother finished this letter, she read it to me—and cried."

Last year, in the same house, at 327 East 17th Street, there was a much more cheerful atmosphere. The six children of the Dvořáks could make a lot of noise; now, only Otakar was there. The maid's kingdom was in the kitchen, and Anna often used a handkerchief to dry her tears.

The good days were over. A great deal of apprehension and longing remained with them most of time. This atmosphere was not good for the composer's creative work. However, Dvořák attempted to write anyway; and what he only hinted at in his letter before—a concerto, either for piano, violin, or violoncello—he could now report as his finished work. He started to sketch it out on the 8th of November, and on the 18th, he began a score of the first movement.

He wrote to the children on the 11th of December:

> If I could, I would fly across the sea to see you. I have just
> finished the first movement of my new concerto for violoncello
> today. If you want to tell somebody about it, you can, but
> better don't—as you wish, Otilka. I commend you to God's
> keeping
>
> Your father, A. Dvořák

A kind of routine began to regulate his life: his Conservatory duties;
waiting for the letters; considerations of what the children are doing—if they
are not sick—all kinds of the most fatiguing worries were with him all the
time. In the evening, he sat at his desk and wrote to Prague, or added a page
or two to Anna's long letters to the children. Sometimes Otakar, too, wrote
home. In his memoirs, he recalled an interesting fact:

> For my father, it was a time of great tension. He smoked heavily
> and developed unusual anxieties and fears of various kinds.
> Fears of some impossible accident were agonizing and over-
> powering father's mind. The solemn peace of Spillville was
> exchanged for the nervous commotion of the metropolis, and
> this fact created a new obligation for me; I was to escort my
> father on his walks to the conservatory. He became scared that
> an electric wire above the tramway could fall on his head, or he
> could be knocked down by a vehicle at an intersection. Never
> before did he have so many questions to ask me as he had then.
> This state of mind brought him to make a definite decision that
> he would not sign another contract, and would live perma-
> nently where he was born.

This remembrance of Otakar was misplaced in his memoirs to the spring
of 1894, at which time all Dvořák's children were still in New York City, and
the fact that four of them were older than Otakar makes it unlikely that
Dvořák would choose little Otakar for his escort instead of an older child. It
could be an error in the date, and this situation had most probably developed
the next fall or winter, when Otakar was the only child who came to New
York City with his parents.

In Dvořák's letter to Bohemia, December 28, 1894, the composer continued to describe their sadness:

> It was a real joy! Almost indescribable! But only we can know
> how much we suffered during that Christmas celebration here,

beginning Christmas Eve!... It was, indeed, a very sad holiday for us. Mother was constantly saying that somebody must be sick. About our Christmas I can say that it was very sad without you and it is better not to talk about it. Oh yes, I got a nice gift from Kovarik, a lovely cigar-case, decorated with antlers; and a scarf from Otakar. Your mother did not want anything. The best present for her is when she gets your letters with good news that everybody is healthy and well, and obeying your Grandma.

I wish you good health and commend you to God's protection in this coming New Year!

Kisses from your father....

He made a similar confession in his letter to a music critic, Emanuel Chvala, dated January 14, 1895:

Since the time I came to America, nothing too much has changed here, and almost nothing new has happened that could be of interest to you. However, I must say that we are quite homesick here this time, and that I will thank God when I return to my friends and family. I cannot wait to sit again somewhere in a forest, for example in Vysoka. It would be wrong for me to say that I do not like it here, but we have had to leave our children in Prague, and miss them now terribly. We were used to having them around last year, and now we are worrying a lot. These conditions make us quite uneasy.

Dvořák then informed his friend about the opera *Dimitrij* which was recently produced in his revised version in Prague, and added:

Whatever happens, I will always go my own way, and take care that I don't get lost. I have just finished a concerto for violoncello and have begun to work on the instrumentation of its last movement. I hope that we will play it soon in Prague.

Although Dvořák had finished the sketch of the last movement of his Concerto for Violoncello in B Minor, Op. 104, he did not finish the score earlier than February 9, 1895. According to Kovarik, this work was initiated in the spring of 1894. Dvořák became captivated at that time by a performance of Victor Herbert's Second Violoncello Concerto, conducted by Anton Seidl in Brooklyn. But we also know that in November Dvořák was not sure yet what he should write.

Also in his letter to the critic and music composer, Josef Bolesek, written on January 15, 1895, Dvořák mentioned his new work again and of course, remembered also his homeland:

> Now, I am about to finish the finale of my violoncello concerto. If I could be less worried here, as I was in Vysoka, my work would be already finished. But things are different here. On Monday, I have lots to do at school—Tuesday is my day off— but I'm quite busy for the rest of week. In short, I don't have enough time for my composition now, and when I do, I am not in the mood for doing anything, etc. In fact, the best site for me would be in Vysoka. It is the best place for me to recover and rest, and be happy. Oh, if I could be there again!

His lamentations continued in every letter he wrote. Vysoka, violoncello concerto, children, Vysoka, concerto, children—it was his only interest and of the highest importance in his life.

It was Dvořák's custom to finish a new work with a note on the last page. At this time, beside the date of February 9, he wrote: "It is the birthday of our Otakar, Saturday morning at half-past eleven."

He could not know then that in a few weeks he would be in Bohemia working on his violoncello concerto again. He was inspired to extend it when he learned that his sister-in-law, Josefina, was dying. Josefina died on the 27th of May. She was his love when he was young; she was proud, direct, ambitious and intelligent, careful and good natured, even sometimes mocking. Dear Aunt Josefina. Now, she was dead, and Dvořák remembered her with profound sorrow.

Suddenly, he decided to dedicate the recently finished finale of his new violoncello concerto to Josefina. Instead of ten bars he had originally written at the end, he composed sixty more, and as usual, finished it with a new footnote: "The concerto was finished in New York City, but I made the entire change in the finale as it is here now, when I came back to Bohemia. Pisek, June 18, 1895."

He was still in New York City when he began to paraphrase for the second movement of his concerto a melody of the song which he wrote when he was young, "If Only My Spirit Alone," and which Josefina liked very much.

Now, after her death, his memories urged him to do more quoting of this sensitive song, and he used it almost directly in the extra sixty bars of the finale, in remembrance of Josefina.

However, let us return to the winter, when Dvořák wrote to Hodik on January 29:

> So, time is running on but too slow for us. We have already started counting the days which are still left on our calendar before we go. My wife is now staying at home all the time, making some useful things for the children; and I? If I'm not at school, I work at home, too.

In this dreadful situation, Jeanette Thurber finally gave Dvořák a long-desired libretto for a new opera, *Hiawatha*. She had purchased it some time ago in Vienna, and had it now translated to English.

The future of this work now depended on Dvořák only. A troublesome situation for him again, because the date of their departure was coming near. However, he started on sketches for it in the same book where he wrote his sketches for the violoncello concerto. Eleven pages were filled with the motives of *Hiawatha:* the wedding march, love songs, and other melodies without any specification.

Meanwhile, because the libretto was of a low quality, Dvořák's sketches were probably done only for the sake of Madam President of the Conservatory. His mind was with his children now, at home.

From now on, he was to refuse every offer which could prolong his residence in America. In his letter, dated "New York, February 5, 1895, Tuesday evening, after 7 o'clock," he expressed his restless feelings again:

> Dear Otilka
> Dear Grandma
> Dear Anda, Marenka, and Tony
> Dear Zinda,
>
> In the previous letter from Anna, you wrote that Zicku was sick again. It made us very afraid, and my mind is still not easy because I think of Zinda all the time. I can see her everywhere I go, and pray to God for her early recovery. I also mentioned to you that I will try to leave here as soon as possible. If it would be up to us, we would leave immediately. (Who knows? It might happen).
>
> Your mother and I have no pleasure in anything here any more, because you are not with us; and mother said that nothing in the world could bring her back here. As for me, I could not survive here without her and you, not even a week, you

know that. We do nothing more here but wait for the day when
we will be on the way home.

In the same mood he wrote to Otilka on January 18, saying: "Mother is
crying and lamenting almost all day long. In brief, she loves you very much
and longs for you all the time—afraid that something could happen to you."

All their apprehensions were enhanced by the distance and the time
before their departure. In this mood, Dvořák finished his score of the violoncello concerto. In addition to their worries, Jeanette Thurber was overdue
with her payment.

On Monday, February 25, 1895, Dvořák wrote to his children and
Grandma again: "We hardly can wait, and it might be that by the time you
get this letter, we could say—only six weeks, and with God's help, we will be
on the way."

In the same letter he also mentioned his violoncello concerto: "Thank
God, it is finished, only a few minor corrections here and there, but they are
unessential."

He wrote that he played it for the Kneisel Quartet, and the virtuoso
Holman from London was also present:

> Everybody liked my work and predicted for it an excellent
> future. So, in spite of all our anxieties and worries, and every-
> thing we went through here, with God's help, I have written a
> work again which gives me joy and consolation because I was
> able to overcome my moods and finished it.

His mind and heart were now focused on only a few matters which were
surrounding his life: the children, Vysoka, his concerto, and homeland. However, this circle was closing swiftly in to include only the children, his concerto, and homeland and finally, only his children and homeland.

On the 16th of April, Dvořák, famous and happy, accompanied by his
wife and son Otakar, left New York City on the *Saale,* the same steamship
which had brought them the first time, nearly three years earlier.

Mrs. Thurber tried to negotiate another contract with him for the next
two academic years, but he had no interest in being separated again from his
family and homeland, even for a short period of time.

On the 27th of April, he was back in Prague, with his children, in his
native Bohemia.

Return — B

B EFORE WE HEADED WEST, I had asked the New York City Public
Library on 43rd Street for photocopies of some articles about Dvořák
published by various New York City papers almost a century ago. When we
came back, the copies waited for us with our mail at the embassy.

Prior to our trip, I had hoped that this tour to Chicago and Spillville
would be successful, and we would find additional materials important for
our research. At that time, I had no idea what kind of person Mr. Roger
Dvořák of Chicago was, or how we could get to Spillville. Thanks to our
guides, Mrs. Lilian Picha, who offered to drive us there in her eight-cylinder
Ford, and Marie Hosek, our navigator, I was able to see the Mississippi River.
I could never have imagined the size of this majestic queen of all rivers in the
world. Now I know more about it, and well remember several people in
Spillville, among them the postmaster Balik, Mr. Kala, an openhearted man,
and Father Benda, who knows only two Czech sayings and hardly understands what they mean. I have copies of many documents found during our
trip, especially those which we discovered in the property of the late Mrs. L.
B. Schmidt from Ames. Perhaps she had left her collection for some future
researcher or writer—maybe for me.

I was sitting once again in Central Park, near a little zoo, thoroughly
enjoying the riotous colors of May. The sun was getting warm, and I lazily
opened my thick, worn-out calendar to check for work still to be done in
America.

Except for the approaching spring, nothing had changed here since we left. Life was busy as usual. The pulsating city with its immense skyscrapers was luring more and more people every day into its iron arms. I tried to recall everything about this strange atmosphere; the subway cars decorated with black, mysterious signs; the eccentric groups of adolescents in front of sex shops on 42nd Street; the statue of the Moor at the Metropolitan Opera; and everything that was so typical of New York City.

"Back home," I thought, "I'll stay in Prague for only two or three days, and then rush to our cottage in the Krivoklat Forest."

"To hang your chimes," laughed Honza.

"For sure, and to walk in the forest, too. And in the evening, I will listen again to the call of a screech owl across the river, my friendly company on the long, vigilant nights."

My mind was racing. Yesterday, only for a moment, I saw a part of Washington Heights (Dvořák used to watch the trains there), and saw a little red bird in Riverside Park. A woman called to it, "Cardinal! Cardinal!" She carried a bag full of birdseed, patiently inviting her winged friends from the nearby shrubs. And suddenly a red bird flew near, right here, in the middle of the city; a bird which I had tried in vain to see in Spillville. Not a tanager, but who knows what Dvořák saw and heard in the wild forest along the Turkey River back then? Nearby was also the tomb of President Grant. Because the blacks loved him, they painted the tomb walls and the nearby benches with their ornaments.

There were still a few things on my program in New York City. I wanted to see the Guggenheim Collection and visit the Museum of Modern Art with an exhibition of Giorgio de Chirico's paintings now on schedule. This painter also loved engines, and his father used to be a railway engineer. But most of all, I wanted to see the Statue of Liberty, and visit the Museum of Immigration, established on little Liberty Island in 1886.

Honza followed my plans with his usual skepticism, surprised that I hoped to find more facts relating to Dvořák, but he kept silent about his doubts.

Those were our last days in New York City. Soon, we were to leave for Bohemia. That last day, however, I still walked along Broadway, which spans almost twenty miles across Manhattan Island, passing numerous cinemas, cabarets, little theatres, and thousands of advertising signs, until I came to the former location of the Metropolitan Opera. This was the place where Antonín Dvořák came to hear Wagner, but left after the first act, not being able to stay till the end. I walked and walked, checking my long list of events situated in Dvořák's former neighborhood, and tried to find the buildings surviving since that time. The New York Stock Exchange has been there since 1792; Federal Hall, used by Congress for the first time in 1789, survived too; Lincoln Center was new; Trinity Church was founded in 1846, and nearby stood the oldest public building in Manhattan, the Chapel of St. Paul, built in 1766. Washington used to come there for services between 1789 and 1791, and one hundred years later, Antonín Dvořák appeared there regularly.

My trip throughout the city was actually my farewell to New York City. In the evening, when I sat at my desk at the Mission, all the papers, notes, maps, photocopies of the articles, with the pages typed and corrected by the composer K. B. Jirak—his study about Dvořák—everything was spread around me for reading and thinking about.

Amongst the documents, I examined a special study, published by the New York *Harper's New Monthly Magazine,* volume 90, no. 537, under the title "Music in America"—signed by Antonín Dvořák. He probably wrote it in March 1895, and the article concluded with a footnote: "The author acknowledges the cooperation of Mr. Edwin Emerson, Jr., in the preparation of this article."

Dvořák summarized his existing experiences, and admitted that his residence in America had been too short for him to form any precise opinions. ("I can only judge of it from what I have observed during my limited experience as a musician and teacher in America.") He said:

> The two American traits which most impress the foreign observer, I find, are the unbounded patriotism and capacity for enthusiasm of most Americans. Unlike the more diffident inhabitants of other countries, who do not "wear their hearts upon their sleeves," the citizens of America are always patriotic, and no occasion seems to be too serious or too slight for them to give expression to this feeling. Thus nothing better pleases the average American, especially the American youth, than to be able to say that this or that building, this or that new patent appliance, is the finest or greatest in the world. This of course, is due to that other trait—enthusiasm.
>
> The enthusiasm of most Americans for all things new is apparently without limit. It is the essence of what is called "push"—American push. Every day I meet with this quality in my pupils. They are unwilling to stop at anything. In the matters of their art they are inquisitive to a degree that they want to go to the bottom of all things at once. It is as if a boy wished to dive before he could swim.

At first, when my American pupils were new to me, this trait annoyed me, and I wished them to give more attention to one matter in hand rather than to everything at once. But now I like it; for I have to come to the conclusion that this youthful enthusiasm and eagerness to take up everything is the best promise for music in America.

Only when the people in general, however, begin to take as lively an interest in music and art as they now take in more material matters, will the arts come into their own. Let the enthusiasm of the people once be excited, and patriotic gifts and bequests must surely follow.

It is a matter of surprise to me that all this has not come long ago. When I see how much is done in every other field by public-spirited men in America—how schools, universities, libraries, museums, hospitals, and parks spring up out of the ground and are maintained by generous gifts—I can only marvel that so little has been done for music. After two hundred years of almost unbroken prosperity and expansion, the net results of music are a number of public concert halls of most recent growth, several musical societies with orchestras of noted excellence, such as the Philharmonic Society in New York, the orchestras of Mr. Thomas and Mr. Seidl, and the superb orchestra supported by a public-spirited citizen of Boston; one opera company, which only the upper classes can hear or understand; and a national conservatory which owes its existence to the generous forethought of one indefatigable woman.

It is truth that music is the youngest of the arts, and must therefore be expected to be treated as Cinderella, but is it not time that she were lifted from the ashes and given a seat among the equally youthful sister arts in this land of youth, until the coming of the fairy godmother and the prince of the crystal slipper?

Art, of course, must always go a-begging, but why should this country alone, which is so justly famed for the generosity and public spirit of its citizens, close its door to the poor beggar?

Dvořák continued to analyze the situation in Europe by pointing out what amounts the Europeans had spent to promote the arts—and continued:

The great American republic alone, in its national government as well as in the several governments of the States, suffers art and music to go without encouragement. Trades and commerce are protected, funds are voted away for the unemployed, schools and colleges are endowed but music must go unaided, and be content if she can get the support of a few private individuals like Mrs. Jeanette M. Thurber and Mr. H. L. Higginson.

Not long ago a young man came to me and showed me his compositions. His talent seemed so promising that I at once offered him a scholarship in our school; but he sorrowfully confessed that he could not afford to become my pupil because he had to earn his living by keeping books in Brooklyn. Even if he came on but two afternoons in the week, or on Saturday afternoon only, he said, he would lose his employment on which he and others had to depend. I urged him to arrange the matter with his employer, but he only received the answer: "If you want to play, you can't keep books. You will have to drop one or the other." He dropped his music.

In any other country, the state would have made some provision for such a deserving scholar, so that he could have pursued his natural calling without having to starve. With us in Bohemia, the Diet each year votes a special sum of money for just such purposes, and the imperial government in Vienna on occasion furnishes other funds for talented artists.

He remembered his beginnings:

Had it not been for such support I should not have been able to pursue my studies when I was a young man. Owing to the fact that upon the kind recommendation of such men as Brahms, Hanslick and Herbeck, the Minister of Public Education in Vienna on five successive years sent me sums ranging from four to six hundred florins, I was able to pursue my work and to get my compositions published, so that at the end of that time I was able to stand on my own feet. This has filled me with lasting gratitude towards my country.

Such an attitude of the state towards deserving artists is not only a kind but a wise one. For it cannot be emphasized too strongly that art, as such, does not "pay," to use an American expression—at least, not in the beginning—and that the art that has to pay its own way is apt to become vitiated and cheap.

It is one of the anomalies of this country that the principle of protection is upheld for all enterprises but art. By protection I do not mean the exclusion of foreign art. That, of course, is absurd. But just as the State here provides for its poor industrial scholars and university students, so should it help the would-be students of music and art. As it is now, a poor musician not only cannot get his necessary instruction in the first place, but if by any chance he has acquired it, he has small prospects of making his chosen calling support him in the end. Why is this? Simply because the orchestras in which first-class players could find a place in this country can be counted on one hand; while of opera companies where native singers can be heard, and where the English tongue is sung, there are none at all.

Another thing which discourages students of music is unwillingness of publishers to take anything but light and trashy music. European publishers are bad enough in that respect, but the American publishers are worse. Thus, when one of my pupils last year produced a very creditable work, and a thoroughly American composition at that, he could not get it published in America, but had to send it to Germany, where it was at once accepted. The same is true of my own compositions on American subjects, each of which hitherto has had to be published abroad.

Our musical conservatory in Prague was founded but three generations ago, when a few nobles and patrons of music sub-scribed five thousand florins, which was then the annual cost of maintaining the school. Yet that little school flourished and grew, so that now more than sixfold that amount is annually expended. Only lately a school for organ music has been added to the conservatory, so that the organists of our churches can learn to play their instruments at home, without having to go to other cities. Thus a school benefits the community in which it is. The citizens of Prague in return have shown their apprecia-tion of the fact by building the "Rudolphinum" as a magnificent home for all the arts. It is jointly occupied by the conservatory and the Academy of Arts, and besides that, contains large and small concert halls and rooms for picture-galleries. In the proper maintenance of this building the whole community takes an interest. It is supported, as it was founded, by the stock-holders of the Bohemian Bank of Deposit, and yearly gifts and bequests are made to the institution by private citizens.

If a school of art can grow so in a country of but six million inhabitants, what much brighter prospects should it not have in a land of seventy millions? The important thing is to make a beginning, and in this the State should set an example.

They tell me that this cannot be done. I ask, why can't it be done? If the old commonwealths of Greece and Italy, and the modern republics of France and Switzerland have been able to do this, why cannot America follow their example? The money certainly is not lacking. Constantly we see great sums money spent for the material pleasures of the few, which if devoted to the purposes of art, might give pleasures to thousands. If schools, art museums, and libraries can be maintained at the public expense, why should not musical conservatories and playhouses? The function of the drama, with or without music, is not only to amuse but to elevate and instruct while giving pleasure. Is it not in the interest of the State that this should be done in the most approved manner, so as to benefit all of its citizens? Let the owners of private playhouses give their performances for diversion only, let those who may, import singers who sing in foreign tongues, but let there be at least one intelligent power that will see to it that the people can hear and see what is best, and what can be understood by them, no matter how small the demand.

That such system of performing classic plays and operas pleases the people was shown by the attitude of the populace in Prague. There the people collected money and raised subscriptions for over fifty years to build a national playhouse. In 1880 they at last had a sufficient amount, and the "National Theatre" was accordingly built. It had scarcely been built when it was burned to the ground. But the people were not to be discouraged. Everybody helped, and before a fortnight was over more than a million had been collected, and the house was at once built up again, more magnificent than it was before.

In answer to such arguments I am told that there is no popular demand for good music in America. That is not so. Every concert in New York, Boston, Philadelphia, Chicago, or Washington, and most other cities, no doubt, disproves such a statement. American concert halls are as well-filled as those of Europe, and as a rule, the listeners—to judge them by their attentive conduct and subsequent expression of pleasure—are not a whit less appreciative.

Dvořák continued in his interesting and knowledgeable description of the situation in the fields of music and art, both in America and Europe, and gave his opinion about the future of American music:

I must give full expression to my firm conviction, and to the hope that just as this nation has already surpassed so many others in marvellous inventions and feats of engineering and commerce, and has made an honorable place for itself in literature in one short century, so it must assert itself in the other arts, and especially in the art of music. Already there are enough public-spirited lovers of music striving for the advancement of this chosen art to give rise to the hope that the United States of America will soon emulate the older countries in smoothing the thorny path of the artist and musician. When that beginning has been made, when no large city is without its public opera house and concert hall, and without its school of music and endowed orchestra, where native musicians can be heard and judged, then those who hitherto have had no opportunity to reveal their talent will come forth and compete with one another, till a real genius emerges from their number, who will be as thoroughly representative of his country as Wagner and Weber are of Germany, or Chopin of Poland.

To bring about this result we must trust to the ever-youthful enthusiasm and patriotism of this country. When it is accomplished, and when music has been established as one of the reigning arts of the land, another wreath of fame and glory will be added to the country which earned its name, the "Land of Freedom," by unshackling her slaves at the price of her own blood.

After this article, I proceeded to examine a study written by the composer K. B. Jirak approximately sixty years after Dvořák's analysis was published. The author tried to answer the basic question of whether Dvořák, indeed, was the founder of an American school of composition. He said:

When we talk [in Bohemia] about America, it is often forgotten that this is not a land of European proportions. This continent extends from the Atlantic Ocean to the Pacific, and from the subtropical area to the cold Arctic.... Bernstein was right when he suggested that centuries of development were needed for the creation of the national musical cultures of Europe. These started with primitive folk songs and dances, which became more refined with the gradual development of culture, until these simple melodies were finally moved into a higher sphere.

I had to admit that Bernstein was right, and continued reading his analysis:

At the time when a similar process could be initiated in America, the population here was entirely Indian. However, the population today is not Indian. Therefore, if the primitive, and also very poor Indian music, actually the music of a different race, would be used as the basis for contemporary creative work, it would only turn into music of an exotic character. The same thing could be said (mutatis mutandis) about the Negro music, especially if used by the white composer. This is my answer to the question of how the American musicians regarded the possibility that American national music could be created on the basis of Indian or Negro motives.

Actually, his opinion absolutely disproved Dvořák's theories, so much acclaimed in the *New York Herald*. Jirak also cited ideas about this problem by Roy Harris, a contemporary composer born in the 1890s:

> American music could never return to the romantic traditions of Dvořák's work.... [T]he modern American music...wants to express, similar to the tradition of other nations, its recent cultural and civil conditions. "There is only one musical element which could be influential for contemporary American music," Harris admitted along with Copland and Bernstein, "and that is jazz. Jazz in America is understood to be a wide complex of musical styles much developed from its original form, and containing at least as many white elements as black." This group of American musicians perceives the beginning of a new era in American music in the work of Gershwin.

I realized that I had thought about this before. Gershwin and Copland are considered to be pupils of Rubin Goldmark, the famous pupil of Antonín Dvořák. Regardless of how closely Dvořák's ideas were related to his era and its romantic understanding of music, his beliefs have indirectly influenced future generations of musicians. It was Gershwin, indeed, who used Dvořák's principles in his method of utilizing Negro folklore in his opera *Porgy and Bess*.

K. B. Jirak continued:

> Various opinions have been expressed by modern American composers about Dvořák's music written during his American residence. When we consider the question of whether Dvořák's music is truly American, and consider whether American music could be created on the basis of Negro motives, the fact remains that all musicians do respect and love Dvořák's music deeply. Bernstein expressed in the lecture I have already cited, that the

Symphony *From the New World* is a remarkable Bohemian, but
not American work.

However, Dvořák most probably would not have used many of these
special elements in his symphony in such quantity had he not lived in America. In the next paragraph Jirak wrote of Dvořák's residence in America, and
described the mastery achieved by the composer in this interval:

> On the one hand, his creativity was enhanced by the spiritual
> contentment arising from his successes which made him a
> center of interest here and abroad (a triumph probably never
> given to any composer before). On the other hand, Dvořák's
> residence in America gave his music a vibrant quality until then
> rare — his melancholy, enhanced by his homesickness. There-
> fore, I believe that Dvořák's American success was a result of a
> happy combination of the following: his world fame, his free-
> dom from financial problems, and favorable publicity. We
> should not forget his financial success which had set him free of
> all materialistic burdens. This is best seen in his letter to Sim-
> rock:

> "From now on, thanks to God, I can compose only for my own
> pleasure, because I am practically independent. I don't have to
> rush into publication!"

> His fame came when he was at the peak of his creative powers.
> Additional successes were made possible by clever publicity.
> Even if it was not always appropriate, the claim that his works
> initiated the beginning of "American music" was most beneficial
> to him. All of this influenced the music world market tremen-
> dously, and as a result, the works written during his American
> sojourn have overshadowed his previous and later composi-
> tions.

These American works, indeed, are really beautiful and absolutely
deserve their excellent worldwide popularity. However, it was late at night
and I had to finish and go to bed. Tomorrow, a trip to the Statue of Liberty
was planned.

Next morning, we boarded a boat for our last sight-seeing trip in New
York City. The little ferries to the colossal monument went from the very
southern tip of Manhattan, the Battery Park.

The distant statue emerged slowly above the horizon, dividing water and
sky less than two miles away. It looked like a mirage from here. The statue was

given to the American people by the Republic of France on the occasion of the hundredth anniversary of the founding of the USA. In every New York City guidebook are data for the information of visitors. For example: Frederic Auguste Bartholdi, the sculptor, was a little over fifty when he created it. The statue, 151 feet in height, was made of iron and copper; its granite base was purchased with money collected by American citizens. About 40 people can be placed in the statue's head, and from its headband can be seen the unforgettable Manhattan skyline.

It is almost obligatory for every European visitor to make the trip to the Statue. Today, you can take a lift to the very top, saving much stair climbing. This was not possible in Dvořák's time.

From the boat deck we observed Manhattan Island in the background, covered by a mass of imposing skyscrapers. The picture was almost surrealistic. In fifteen minutes, we passed an old pier, and sailed to a new port, situated on the opposite side of the statue. As we disembarked there was a long line of visitors waiting for our boat to take them back to Manhattan.

The huge base of the statue reminded one of a fortress built in my country by the Austrian empress, Maria Theresa, centuries ago. Nearby were the offices, playgrounds, a park with benches, a restaurant and gift shops, and the seagulls circling around, linking the land with the blue sea surrounding it.

There was a wide entrance, behind which was an extensive hall and the Museum of Immigration. The sign directed us to the lifts. From the tenth floor we had to climb the stairs. Honza was dragging all his photographic equipment again; the stairs were a narrow spiral, with an inside part for going up and outside for coming down. We counted 168 steps.

Suddenly, we were surrounded by the interior skeleton of the iron construction, the gray and massive project by Engineer Eiffel. Every step took us higher and higher, up to the headband of the statue. The little windows, spaced along a ramp, offered us a view of distant Manhattan. The colossal structure was a signal to immigrants from the whole world that this was to be their new home, for many, the beginning of freedom.

Most of them, indeed, had found what they wanted here, in spite of the price they paid. However, most of the time, the third or fourth generations lost their original national identity. How great really was the price they paid compared to the benefits gained?

We walked through a maze of corridors and came to the American Museum of Immigration. Both sides of the hall were lined with display cabinets which showed figurines, documents, materials, and objects belonging to the first pioneers. We saw an enormous wooden pestle, a sickle three times normal size, a six-shot revolver, a huge butcher's axe, a long rifle, and models of wagons covered with canvas for making the great journeys while giving the pioneers shelter and a place to eat and sleep. On display was the cross section of a ship which brought in its hold an untold number of immigrants. They suffered on their way, but carried hope and faith in the promised land across the ocean. After quarantine, they went to Ellis Island nearby, often to buy rail tickets to the West.

The immigrants came in the millions. We followed their path from the old cash register to a table with an ancient inkstand and strong clothes rack and came to another display, showing the figurines of the wealthy Frenchmen and the Hungarian immigrants wearing poor rags. The cabinets contained a great variety of materials and objects made by immigrants, and photographs of the famous amongst them. It was a roll call of great names: Enrico Caruso; Carl Milles, whose sculptures I had seen years ago in Stockholm; Alexander Graham Bell and the German inventor Studebaker; as well as the famous Irishman, Fitzgerald, whose name joined with the Kennedy family later. There were the Dutch immigrants, Vanderbilt and Roosevelt, Joseph Pulitzer from Hungary, and Albert Einstein from Germany. Some of the rooms were dedicated to certain nationalities, and four of the display cabinets contained embroideries from Bohemia and Slovak Easter eggs. There was no famous man honored in this sector—why?

"How many immigrants came from our country?" Honza asked.

I quickly opened my old diary and found there the notes which I had copied from the minutes of the Czech Preparation Committee of the World Exposition in Chicago in 1933. I found answers to Honza's question: 39,652 Bohemians and Moravians immigrated to America in 1870; ten years later, 85,361; and shortly before Dvořák's arrival in New York City—in 1890— 215,514. In 1900, the population of Bohemian and Moravian origin reached 356,830, and by the time these Czech Preparation Committee minutes were published, 1,382,079 Czechs and Slovaks were living in the United States.

These numbers were large; but how little was shown about those peoples in this display! I hoped that they had found happiness in America, at least.

Happiness does not depend on the amount of money you make each year. I began to understand that fact right here in this gigantic country, which gave unprecedented wealth, fame, and success to Dvořák but left him home-sick.

When I left my country, I had no idea about the existence of Camille W. Zeckwer, a composer and former pupil of Dvořák, whose testimony I found in an old dusty periodical. Although I have already quoted some of his recollections about the composer, I had to think again about his memoirs. As if by magic, his repetition of Dvořák's statement returned to me with a stronger message:

"You see, my dear Philadelphia, I'm now making fifteen thousand dollars a year. Fifteen years ago, when I was poor and hungry, I was happier."

In my restricted view from the Statue of Liberty headband, I saw the cliffs of the Manhattan skyscrapers, and somewhere in the sky above the Kennedy International Airport, I recalled another message learned from Dvořák: "If I could, I would immediately fly to you across the ocean."

My homeland, whose love I carried with me everywhere, was the answer to everything I asked. I was not sure if I had pronounced its name, "Bohemia," out loud—or had just whispered it or heard it in my heart.

Epilogue

I WAS HOME AGAIN.

My literary club owns a health spa in Carlsbad, and I was scheduled there for a treatment after my return from America.

During my stay, it was my custom to sit on a balcony with a nice view over the famous Bohemian spa and write about Dvořák's overseas trip. At noon, I would go to a hot spring to drink mineral water for my treatment, rushing back immediately to my typewriter. Day after day it was the same routine.

One day I had a meeting in the afternoon, important for my research about the Symphony *From the New World*. As I walked along the river up to the end of the valley, I saw a house marked with a small metal sign of oval shape and blue color. In the middle was a picture of a team of horses hitched to an old carriage. This commemorative tablet announced that this place was known as the "Post-Yard Cultural Memorial—an Empire Building from 1791, Originally the Carlsbad postmaster's estate with fresco ceiling paintings by Josef Cramolin."

A little poster announced a schedule for afternoon dances and concerts of the popular Melodic orchestra. It was good entertainment for the spa guests after the morning treatments. Above the entrance was another commemorative tablet, decorated with a picture of a lyre, a laurel wreath, and a few notes. The text said:

400

In this house, on the 20th of July, 1894,
was produced the European premiere
of Dvořák's Symphony *From the New World*
under the baton of August Labitzky
in the presence of the author

It was a two-story ochre building with a pretty gable and three half-rounded windows underneath. An orange mailbox at the entrance established the identity of the place. The cars on the nearby road contrasted with the coaches of Dvořák's time. Although I learned from the people there that the concert hall had been changed into a storage room, I ascended to the second floor and found the former Prussian Hall and the Labitzky salon, decorated with old frescoes. Everything needed a thorough restoration. There was a gallery in the Prussian Hall with a single row of seats for the musicians. This caught my attention. It seemed quite peculiar. Was the premiere really played here? The clerk who guided me upstairs, tried to dispel my doubts:

"There is a plaque about it downstairs."

It was true, but there was something not quite right about the whole set-up. The guide shrugged his shoulders and led me outside. In the Post-Yard garden, I sat at a small table and waited for my guest. He should have been here by now. The coffee was similar to what I used to drink in Central Park in New York City. Only the skyscrapers were missing from the site, and the valley was surrounded by hills covered with the dark lush forest.

My waiting was interrupted by the apology of my belated companion. He was a local historian, chronicler, collector, archivist, and scholar. I do not know which of these jobs he liked best.

"Have you been waiting long?" We shook hands.

"Just a while," I said, pleased to see him. "Meanwhile I went upstairs to see the interior of the Post-Yard."

"But that place has no relation to Dvořák's premiere at all," the historian assured me.

"And what about that plaque?" I asked.

"It is just a statement that the premiere of the Symphony was produced here, which is correct. But the concert began at four o'clock in the afternoon, which means that it was a performance of the Carlsbad Orchestra, and it was produced right here, where we are sitting."

My eyes searched the space in the front of the Post-Yard. It was covered with numerous yellow tables and chairs. At both sides of the platform were two large, nicely decorated pavilions, each with a dance floor inside.

"The orchestra was sitting under the roof, and part of the audience could be placed inside; but the rest had to sit under the sky," said the historian, continuing in his description. "It depended on the weather."

I listened to his explanation, and knew that he must be right. From 1890 to 1894, the Prague Conservatory of Music, too, gave most of its concerts in the afternoon. Only later was their schedule for concerts shifted to the evening. I had to admit that the doubts I had in the Prussian Hall with only one row of seats for the musicians, were well founded.

"It would have been impossible to put the whole orchestra up there, whatever size it was." I explained my skepticism. "The tablet mixed me up; better if it weren't there! The information was not correct anyway, because the European premiere was produced in London, England, on the 21st of June."

The waiter came to ask what we wanted, but I could think of nothing but Dvořák and his premiere. So the historian continued in his explanation:

"Dvořák's presence during the premiere is not accurately documented. As far as I know, there is no written evidence of it in the press. The German paper *Neue Freie Presse* wrote about the event after the premiere. They said that Dvořák's new work was accepted by the large international audience with ardent expressions of tremendous appreciation. Especially the Largo was most charming and had to be repeated. But this was all I have been able to find," he said and handed me a copy of another review in the *Carlsbad Magazine,* carried on the 22nd of July, 1894. Its author wrote:

> As its twelfth symphonic concert, the spa orchestra produced in the Post-Yard a new (fifth) Dvořák Symphony Opus 95 in E minor, which is an example of a new style in composition. The Slavonic Master, who has been working now as a teacher overseas, has reached with this work an imposing peak in his creative career.

The article also mentioned that "the title and every theme of the Symphony was elevated by Dvořák into the sphere of true art. His work showed an inexhaustible fullness of melodies and a rare softness of interpretation, reminding one of Grieg."

"It was a great success," added the historian. "Carlsbad was one of the most famous European spas in the last century, and the Symphony *From the New World* has spread from here all over the continent."

"I know. It is still one of the most played compositions in the world." I agreed eagerly, and we continued to discuss the Symphony from its different aspects; especially, its tremendous success everywhere. I felt that I was becoming possessed by some unusual mood.

"I have the same feeling now that I had once in Greenwich Village in New York City, during my research in the spring of 1982," I mused aloud; and my companion waited in silence for a further explanation.

We both settled into more comfortable positions at the yellow table with our afternoon drinks. I started to talk about my American experience:

"We were on our way back from seeing the Brooklyn Bridge, and had stopped to see Greenwich Village. The old houses and the quiet streets give no sign of the intensive activity only a short distance away. Instead of the domineering skyscrapers, only a few galleries, bookstores, theatres, and small hotels are scattered about.

"One can easily feel the atmosphere of the Parisian Montmartre, with its artistic charm and flavor. Famous American painters used to live there, too: George Innes; John Sloan; and Melville's illustrator, Rockwell Kent. Their recent successors climb ladders to paint their pictures on a large scale, or take charcoal and decorate the sidewalks or the asphalt of the paved road.

"My legs were hurting, so I looked for a bench. In the middle of the village there was a memorial park, and built in an antique style, the Washington Arch. The music being played there was mostly jazz of various styles. Hundreds of young people were dancing, singing, smoking, drinking, and kissing, giving the place an atmosphere of a great and wonderful fiesta. The memorial was finished in 1892, shortly before Dvořák's arrival in New York City. On the upper part, I noticed a saying of Washington: 'Let us raise a standard to which the wise and the honest can repair. The event is in the hand of God.'

"After all our sight-seeing, we were hungry and thirsty. So we looked for a place to eat and found a small restaurant, Eve, on West 8th Street. The building was overly green; green silhouettes of trees appeared on the white walls, dozens of containers with green foliage hung from the ceiling; even the waiters were wearing green T-shirts.

"On the green menu were all kinds of vegetables, olives, fish, and roast beef, but our attention was disturbed by the well-known melody filling the room.

"'What is that?' I almost jumped, turning to Honza, 'What do I hear?'

"'Some music,' he mumbled from the menu.

"A group of Japanese tourists sitting next to us had been quietly discussing something in French but suddenly everybody fell silent and listened to the melody dominating the room.

"'This is no ordinary music,' I said. 'Listen awhile! It must be the third movement from the New World Symphony! Probably from a tape.'

"We called a waiter, and asked to see the manager. The waiter, probably puzzled at what could be more important to us than a quick meal, nodded his head.

"He could not understand what had caused the sudden excitement shown by these funny foreigners.

"When the manager came we asked, 'Why do you play that music?'

"This only added to his uncertainty.

"'Gentlemen, I think it's very nice.' Apologetic, he tried to explain his reasons further.

"'And our guests like it quite well, too. However, if you don't want it, we can play something else.'

"At this moment, I was overwhelmed with that very unusual feeling of gratification which I have now; and in that special mood, I asked: 'Do you know the composer?'

"'The man was silent, as he tried to remember the name.

"'Somebody from Europe, in the last century; I don't know. But, Sir, it is beautiful music.'

"We took some time to explain our feelings and what we were doing in America. He straightened up and looked into my eyes with wonder, and probably realized we would agree with his choice of music, so he replied in a very quiet voice:

"'This is the most beautiful music I know.'"

Appendix
Antonín Dvořák's Family

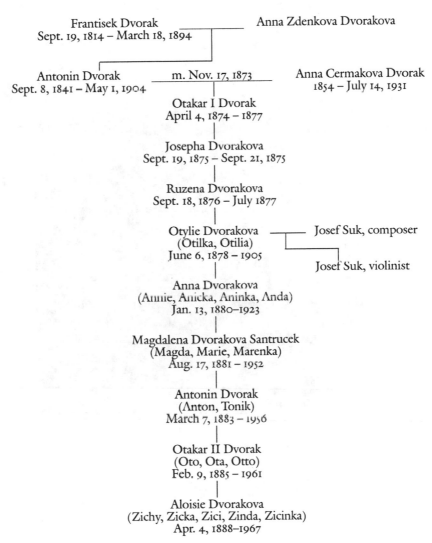

Frantisek Dvorak
Sept. 19, 1814 – March 18, 1894

Anna Zdenkova Dvorakova

Antonin Dvorak
Sept. 8, 1841 – May 1, 1904

m. Nov. 17, 1873

Anna Cermakova Dvorak
1854 – July 14, 1931

Otakar I Dvorak
April 4, 1874 – 1877

Josepha Dvorakova
Sept. 19, 1875 – Sept. 21, 1875

Ruzena Dvorakova
Sept. 18, 1876 – July 1877

Otylie Dvorakova
(Otilka, Otilia)
June 6, 1878 – 1905

Josef Suk, composer

Josef Suk, violinist

Anna Dvorakova
(Annie, Anicka, Aninka, Anda)
Jan. 13, 1880–1923

Magdalena Dvorakova Santrucek
(Magda, Marie, Marenka)
Aug. 17, 1881 – 1952

Antonin Dvorak
(Anton, Tonik)
March 7, 1883 – 1956

Otakar II Dvorak
(Oto, Ota, Otto)
Feb. 9, 1885 – 1961

Aloisie Dvorakova
(Zichy, Zicka, Zici, Zinda, Zicinka)
Apr. 4, 1888–1967

Miroslav Ivanov

About the Author

MIROSLAV IVANOV WAS BORN in Josefov, Czech Republic. His father was executed by fascists because of his involvement in the attempt on Reinhard Heydrich's life. After Miroslav was graduated from Charles University in Prague, he stayed to work as an assistant professor of the Philosophical Faculty, and he received the Doctor of Philosophy degree.

In 1960, Miroslav started work as an editor of *Hlas revoluce* (*Voice of Revolution*), a weekly paper of the Union of Antifascist Fighters. He was offered the appointment of Chief Editor under the condition that he join the Communist Party. After his refusal, he left his job to become a free-lance writer, in 1967.

He is the author of twenty-nine books, which were translated in nine different countries and languages. For example, his *Target Heydrich* reached the finals of the World Competition of Nonfiction Literature and was translated and published in France in 1972 and 1973, Italy (Mondadori) in 1972, Great Britain (McGibbon) in 1973, the United States (Macmillan) in 1974, Poland in 1978, Bulgaria in 1982, and the USSR in 1988. The total number of copies published in the Czech Republic to 1993 is 1,130,000.

Information about Miroslav Ivanov's work can be found in *Who is Who in the World*, *Contemporary Authors*, and other biographical sources. His works cover a wide range of cultural history and antifascism. In the Czech Republic, he is president of the Nonfiction Authors' Club, and is a leading representative of the nonfiction genre.

Sources

ARCHIVES AND LIBRARIES

Czech Republic
  Historical Museum. Slavkov at Brno
  Museum of Bohemian Music, Antonín Dvořák Foundation, Prague
Chicago
  Czechoslovak Society of America. Chicago
  Newberry Library
  University of Chicago
Iowa
  Bily Clock Museum
  Dvořák's Home. Spillville, Iowa
  Iowa State Historical Memorial and Art Building, Des Moines
  Iowa State University, Ames
New York City
  Columbia University. New York
  New York City Public Library
  Pierpont Morgan Library

PERIODICALS

American National, 1893–95. Chicago
Ames Daily Tribune, 1925. Iowa
Cedar Rapids Republican, 1925. Iowa

Dalibor, Bohemia 1892–95
Chicago Sun, 1893
Chicago Times, 1893.
The Des Moines Register, 1959. Iowa
The Etude, various volumes.
Harper's New Monthly Magazine, 1894
New York Herald, 1892–95
Domacnost [Household], 1892. Milwaukee
The Iowa Magazine, 1925
Iowa State Senate *Journal,* 1945
Labour Journal, 1893. New York City
Music Magazine, 1893–1894
Narodni listy (National Journal), Bohemia 1892–95
New York Evening Post, 1893
New York Journal, 1928
New York Times, 1892–95
Organ Brotherhood, 1893–95. Chicago
The Tribune Capital. Des Moines, Iowa
Sotek, 1894
Voice, 1933. New York

BOOKS AND ARTICLES

Burghauser, J., *Nejen pomniky.* Prague, 1966
——, *Komentar k IX. symfonii Ant. Dvořáka.* Prague, 1972
Burian, K. V. *Hudba domnova.* Prague 1979. *Czech Republic*
Centennial History of St. Wenceslaus Church. Spillville, Iowa, 1960
Clapham, J., *Antonín Dvořák.* London 1979
——, "Iroquois and Kickapoos," *Musical Review* 1956
——, "New Discoveries of Dvořák," *Musical Review* 1956
Ctrnacty, M., "Dvořák jako zakladatel hudby americke," *Dalibor* 1907
Destinova, E., "Dvořákova hudba v Americe. *Narodni listy (National Journal)* 1929
Dostal, W. A., "Dvořák's Visit to Spillville," *Iowa Catholic Historical Review* 1933
Dvořák, Antonín, *Pratelum doma.* Edited by O. Sourek. Prague 1940
— — —, "Music in America." *Harper's New Monthly Magazine* 1894
Dvořák, Otakar, *Antonín Dvořák ve vzpominkach synovych.* Manuscript, 1961
Emingerova, K. A., *Dvořák v Americe. Cesta* 1918
Foerster, J. B. A., " A. Dvořák v Hamburku," in *70 let Umel. besedy.* Prague, 1933
Herites, F., "Nekolik mych americkych vzpominek," *Maj* 1904
Huneker, J., *New Cosmopolis.* New York, 1915
——, *Painted Veils.* New York, 1920
——, *Variations.* New York, 1921

Jak v Praze pohrbivali Dr. Vaclava Kaunice. Prague, 1948

Jirak, K. B. *Antonín Dvořáka dnesni Amerika.* Manuscript. Chicago, 1950

Koptova, F., "Dvořák v Americe?" *Dalibor* 1891

Kounicova, J. *Moje vzpominky.* Manuscript (undated). Czech Republic

Kovarik, J. J., "Dvořák a Spillville," *Katolik.* Chicago, 1934

——, Dvořák as I Knew Him. Fiddlestrings 1926

——, "O Dvořákove kompozicni skole v N. Yorku," in *Podripsky Country* . Czech Republic, 1941

Kral J. J., Antonín Dvořák. *Music Magazine* 1893

Kuna, M. "Transkripcni problematika Dvořákovy korespondence. *Hudebni veda,* musicology, 1981

Kvet, J. M. Mladi Antonina Dvořáka. Prague 1943

——, "Z dopisu Frantiska Dvořáka" *Tempo,* 1933

Lowenbach, Jan, *Josef Jan Kovarik, Dvořákuv americky sekretar.* Prague, 1946

——, "Dvořák a Amerika." *Hudebni revue.* Dv. sbornik, 1911

Masarykova, A. *Hudba ve Spillville.* New York 1963

Nebuska, O. "Z dusevni dilny Dvořákovy za pobytu v Americe." *Hudebni revue.* Dv. sbornik, 1911

Pamatnik cs. vyboru Svetove vystavy v Chicagu. Chicago 1933

Pamatnik slavnosti odhaleni pametni desky dr. Vaclavu hrabeti z Kaunic. Slavkov, 1933

Pecinovski, G. G., *Protivin: A Czech Settlement.* Protivin, Iowa, 1978

Salaba-Vojan, J. E. *Ceska hudba v Americe. Tamtez.* New York, 1929

Schwab, A. T., *James Gibbons Huneker.* Los Angeles, 1963

Sip, E. *Iowske leto A. Dvořáka. Rude pravo.* Czech Republic, 1963

Skuderova-Klirova, B., *S Antoninem Dvořákem v Americe.* Zlonice, 1982

Sourek, O., ed., *A. Dvořák ve vzpomínkách a dopisech.* Prague, 1940

——, Zivot a dilo Antonina Dvořáka. Prague, 1956

——, "Americka pocta A. Dovrakovi," *Listy hudebni Matice.* Czech Republic, 1927

——, A. "Dvořák v Americe," *Radiojournal.* Czech Republic, 1933

——, "O americke hudbe A. Dovraka. *Listy hudebni Matice.* Czech Republic, 1923

Stefan, P., *Anton Dvořák.* New York, 1971

Stockl, K., and K. Doge. *Symphony No. 9, E minor.* Mainz, 1982

Sychra, A., *Estetika Dvořákovy symfonicke tvorby.* Prague, 1959

——, *Jeste jednou o Dvořákovi a indianske hudbe. Hudebni rozhledy.* Czech Republic, 1957

Valenta, E., *Noveho sveta.* Manuscript. Radio play. Prague, 1963

Weinberger, J. "Antonín Dvořák." *New York Review,* 1928

Index

411

Colophon

Design and typography by Timothy Rolands
Cover and title page by Teresa Wheeler, NMSU designer

Text is set in Galliard,
designed by Matthew Carter
and released in 1978 by Mergenthaler Linotype.
Display is set in Monotype Centaur,
the classic book type designed by Bruce Rogers in 1912–14.

Printed and bound by Edwards Brothers, Ann Arbor, Michigan
Distributed by University Publishing Associates